PUBLIC HEALTH IN INDIA

Thank you for choosing a SAGE product!
If you have any comment, observation or feedback,
I would like to personally hear from you.

Please write to me at **contactceo@sagepub.in**

Vivek Mehra, Managing Director and CEO, SAGE India.

Bulk Sales

SAGE India offers special discounts
for purchase of books in bulk.
We also make available special imprints
and excerpts from our books on demand.

For orders and enquiries, write to us at

Marketing Department
SAGE Publications India Pvt Ltd
B1/I-1, Mohan Cooperative Industrial Area
Mathura Road, Post Bag 7
New Delhi 110044, India

E-mail us at **marketing@sagepub.in**

Subscribe to our mailing list
Write to **marketing@sagepub.in**

This book is also available as an e-book.

PUBLIC HEALTH IN INDIA

Policy Shifts and Trends

Social Change in Contemporary India

Series Editor: Manoranjan Mohanty

Volume VI

Edited by

P. M. ARATHI

Los Angeles | London | New Delhi
Singapore | Washington DC | Melbourne

First published in 2022 by

SAGE Publications India Pvt Ltd
B1/I-1 Mohan Cooperative Industrial Area
Mathura Road, New Delhi 110 044, India
www.sagepub.in

SAGE Publications Inc
2455 Teller Road
Thousand Oaks, California 91320, USA

SAGE Publications Ltd
1 Oliver's Yard, 55 City Road
London EC1Y 1SP, United Kingdom

SAGE Publications Asia-Pacific Pte Ltd
18 Cross Street #10-10/11/12
China Square Central
Singapore 048423

Published by Vivek Mehra for SAGE Publications India Pvt. Ltd. Typeset in 10.5/13pt Bembo by Fidus Design Pvt. Ltd, Chandigarh.

Library of Congress Control Number: 2022931698

ISBN: 978-93-5479-370-7 (HB)

SAGE Team: Amrita Dutta, Syed Husain Naqvi and Rajinder Kaur

Contents

Section I: Political Economy of Health and Illness
Sectional Introduction

Section II: Questions of Women's Health and Reproductive Justice

Sectional Introduction

Section III: Nutrition: A Social Determinant of Health

Sectional Introduction

Section IV: Malthusian Spectre and Indian Public Health History

Sectional Introduction

List of Abbreviations

AD	Alzheimer's dementia
ANM	Auxiliary nurse midwife
BMI	Body mass index
CBR	Crude birth rate
CNA	Community needs assessment
CPHC	Comprehensive primary healthcare
CSD	Council for Social Development
DCAR	Demographic, Communication and Action Research
FP	Family planning
FPP	Family planning programme
GDP	Gross domestic product
HLEG	High Level Expert Group on Universal Health Coverage
HRT	Hormone replacement therapy
ICDS	Integrated Child Development Services
ICPD	International Conference on Population and Development
IMR	Infant mortality rate
IPC	Indian Penal Code
JSPE	Jefferson Scale of Physician Empathy
MCH	Maternal and child health
MDG	Millennium Development Goal
MTP	Medical Termination of Pregnancy
NFHS	National Family Health Survey
NHP	National Health Policy
NPP	National Population Policy
NSS	National Sample Survey
PDS	Public Distribution System
PPPs	Public–private partnerships
RCH	Reproductive and child health
SAP	Structural adjustment programme
SDG	Sustainable Development Goal

TFR	Total fertility rate
UHC	Universal healthcare
WHI	Women's Health Initiative
WHO	World Health Organization

About the Series

Social Change in Contemporary India is a series of thematic volumes carrying selected articles from the journal *Social Change* which is celebrating its Golden Jubilee. They are offered as important contributions capturing the momentous experience of people of India and their institutions since Independence.

Social change in independent India has gone through three distinct phases. The first two decades saw the impact of the freedom struggle in most arenas where policymakers and common people shared some perspectives to initiate concrete steps to reduce poverty, hunger and scarcity with the objective of making progress towards the goals enshrined in the Constitution of India. Planned development with a focus on industrialization, the Green Revolution in agriculture, building educational institutions of high quality and, above all, promoting democratic institutions and procedures to meet the aspirations of all sections of society characterized most of this era. The pluralistic character of Indian society, culture and polity was acknowledged, and some important policy initiatives emerged.

But by the late 1960s, the crisis of this model already surfaced. Food riots in 1966, the Naxalbari uprising in 1967 and the beginning of non-Congress governments in many states were all symptoms of the emerging environment. That heralded the start of the second phase, from 1970 to 1990, which witnessed the unfolding of most major contradictions in the Indian Republic. The assertion of rights by ethnic groups in different parts of the country was responded to by a certain centralization of power by the Union government, which was challenged by the emergence of strong regional parties and movements. Poverty eradication was prominent on the agenda, but progress was tardy. Education and health facilities were expanded, but not to the extent that was needed. Although an Indian middle class emerged, it became increasingly estranged from the masses. Challenges accumulated leading to mass movements and the Republic saw a declaration of Emergency, followed by rule of alternative forces and the return of the Congress to power. In the process, civil society organizations pursuing citizens' rights emerged, and the struggle for democratic rights continued to expand. Internal disturbances, communal riots and atrocities on Dalits, minorities and women occurred from time to time. However, the democratic structure continued to be consolidated, and people's consciousness to defend constitutional values continued to grow.

In 1991, neoliberal economic reforms were launched in the wake of a serious economic crisis. At that time, India was also experiencing a social upsurge over the rights of Dalits, backward classes, religious minorities and women. By this time, environmental issues had also acquired much attention. Thus began the third phase. The Indian elite, cutting across the dominant political parties, accepted the agenda of globalization, liberalization and privatization. Mobilization on caste and religious issues took a new turn with Hindu nationalist forces becoming stronger by the day. Initially, the Congress was able to halt this trend through its alliance of parties. For a decade, they handled contradictions through a strategy that promoted rapid economic growth, tried to provide rural employment and food security to the poor and addressed the grievances of minorities. But corruption and inefficiency made them unpopular, and a BJP-led government came to power. This third phase of neoliberal growth, steered by Hindu nationalism, is in full swing, though alternative forces continue to occupy a significant space.

This story of independent India is captured by scholars and commentators as it unfolded during the past 50 years as contributions to the Council for Social Development's social science quarterly, *Social Change*. They narrate the multidimensional dynamics of social change experienced by various sections of people at the local, regional and national levels as well as in the global context. We decided to share these contributions on specific themes in several volumes with a wider readership for good reasons.

First, *Social Change* is a unique, interdisciplinary journal that covers not only research papers in social sciences but also policy analysis and reports from the field in areas of social development. Right from the start, Durgabai Deshmukh, the founder of the Council of Social Development, wanted theory, policy and ground-level experience to be integrated, with each benefitting from the other. So each volume in this series has chapters by authors defining concepts, explaining theoretical frameworks, analysing policies and presenting survey results and other evidences from rural, urban and tribal areas.

Second, the journal includes contributions not only from senior scholars such as Nirmal Kumar Bose, B. N. Ganguly, T. N. Madan and B. K. Roy Burman, policymakers like C. D. Deshmukh, and social activists such as Devaki Jain but also from a large number of young academics from all over the country who used the forum to present their findings from their most important research projects. Some of them later became eminent academics and important policymakers. The contributions by these writers over a 50-year period can help us identify key points in the history of policymaking as well as discourses during the three major phases of contemporary India. Some contributions clearly impacted public discourses and the policymaking process. Thus, we are able to capture shifts in policy in the early 1970s, when the state took many active initiatives, as well as the big change in 1991, when the state took on a new role in the economy, giving a substantial role to the private sector. That trend continued in the first two decades of the 21st century. We may note the changing perspectives and the linkage with global processes not only in theoretical issues of social development but also in policy debates concerning questions such as the privatization of health, education, rural development, forest and environment. Their implications for people's welfare and human rights were also dealt with by many authors in recent years.

Third, an equally important consideration underlying these volumes is the fact that the Council for Social Development has a mission to serve the interests of marginalized groups: its research, publications, advocacy and indeed this journal reflect that commitment. Therefore, the volumes carry articles on selected themes such as health, education, poverty and agriculture, with a special focus on the marginalized groups including the Adivasis, Dalits, minorities, women, and urban and rural poor. Each of these volumes reflects on what has been done in respect of the specific marginalized groups and analyses the nature of the development experience from the vantage point of the marginalized.

Each volume is edited by an expert who has done considerable work on the subject. A major and substantive introduction by the editor of the volume not only puts the chapters in perspective but also identifies the strengths as well as gaps in the treatment of the subject. The editor's 'Introduction' also addresses current concerns in theory and policy, discourse and practice, and presents suggestions for further thinking and action. These volumes are designed as studies on a theme for ready reference and use by students, researchers and general readers. Besides the 'Introduction', presenting the current state of knowledge on the subject, the volume carries an extended bibliography, further adding to the volume's utility.

Manoranjan Mohanty
Series Editor

Foreword

This is an important and timely volume. The COVID-19 pandemic, which has caused havoc worldwide and had a devastating effect on the life and work of Indians in 2020 and 2021, should have put the health question at the centre of all development thought and action. But treating it as a matter of crisis management, politicians and policymakers remained busy with their usual preoccupation with economic growth and national mobilization for political power. This was exactly the dreadful anticipation that had moved Durgabai Deshmukh in the 1960s to launch the Council for Social Development (CSD) to warn leaders of nations that a country's progress must not be measured merely in terms of economic growth. Social development, especially health, education and livelihood for all, with a focus on the welfare of the marginalized, especially children, women, Dalits and Adivasis was the core of progress towards which economic policies and planning must be oriented. She had witnessed this problem as a member of India's first Planning Commission.

That contradiction between achieving economic growth by a fast pace of industrialization and allocating substantial amount of resources for health and education has persisted throughout in Indian policy discourses since Independence. After neoliberal reforms were launched in the early 1990s, even the lip service given to social development under some earlier five-year plans was given up, and achieving economic growth became the principal objective of all regimes. According to its political–ideological springboard, the Washington Consensus, the holy mantra was that after all resources must be created first through economic growth in order to use them for health, education and so on for people. It was of little concern that, in the process, gross inequities between the elites and the masses continued to grow in all spheres, including access to health, education and incomes. The pandemic brought out the vast gap even more glaringly than before.

For five decades, the journal *Social Change*, started by Durgabai Deshmukh and her colleagues, has consistently challenged the growth-centric model of development. This volume, the sixth in the series on *Social Change in Contemporary India*, contains a selection of contributions published in the journal over half a century and attempts to profile the history of the discourse on policies and practices of public health in India. The contributors, including many well-known names, range from policymakers, health experts and development thinkers to professional researchers, presenting an analysis of field studies in various parts of India. The 'Introduction' by community health scholar P. M. Arathi, who was on the faculty of CSD before moving to Mahatma Gandhi University, Kottayam, identifies the major contours of policy debates, paradigm shifts in policy in India and presents a perspective to assess them, taking insights from the Indian experience and the global discourse on health. Her sectional introductions further help in putting specific dimensions in theoretical and practical contexts.

As reflected in the chapters carried in this volume, public health debates have generally centred around three critical issues: first, whether to treat healthcare as a biomedical issue focused on disease or as a comprehensive wellness issue determined largely by socio-economic conditions; second, treating it as a set of public goods where public health facilities are freely available to all ensured by the state, rather than treating it as a set of private goods where people pay for health services directly to private and public providers or through insurance companies and, third, treating health as a demographic issue of population planning rather than a human right of all humans. No doubt, we see occasional debates on issues such as making choices regarding knowledge systems based on science guiding healthcare and accordingly viewing Western and non-Western systems of medicine, or the health consequences of climate change, or the degree of autonomy asserted by local institutions in the face of pressures of national and global commercial interests in handling health issues. In many ways, these issues often get subsumed under the above three broad questions. Interestingly enough, all these issues prominently emerged in public discussions worldwide during the pandemic with some clear lessons.

First of all, it should be pointed out that whenever any serious initiative was taken by important experts, such as the Bhore Committee, set up to assess the health condition of India, which gave its landmark report in 1945 or the international conference convened by the World Health Organization in 1978 in Alma-Ata, which famously adopted the monumental Declaration, 'Health for All', a broader perspective on health was stated as the key idea to pursue. They focused as much on preventive measures as on curative measures putting them in a wider social context and not just a biomedical question. The Alma-Ata Declaration in fact defined health as 'a state of complete physical, mental and social well-being and not merely the absence of disease or infirmity'. More importantly, they highlighted the relationship of nutrition and living conditions with health, which meant putting in the forefront the socio-economic determinants of health and nutrition. They uniformly saw the link between conditions of poverty, malnutrition and poor health. But as specialization of learning in medical sciences grew, it was accompanied by the commercialization of health products with the profit motives of big corporations driving advances in the field. Consequently, the socio-economic perspective steadily got relegated to the background and technology-with-profit emerged as the principal driver of most governments' health policy.

This story we find is enacted not only in India but almost everywhere in the world. During the pandemic, failure after failure was caused in most countries due to the narrow approach to treating the virus. The poor in cities and villages, migrant workers and workers in the low-paid unorganized sector suffered the most. Women as a whole went through multiple oppressions. This volume has many contributions that constantly dwelt upon the need to link health with socio-economic conditions. They help us to understand the background and dynamics of the contemporary health crisis and the search for alternative policies.

Second, the same story is seen in the history of increasing privatization of health services, replacing the initial commitment of the welfare state to providing universal primary healthcare. Paradoxically, the COVID-19 crisis compelled governments everywhere, including developed capitalist countries, to take the principal role in formulating, implementing and financing the entire process of testing, treatment and vaccination, besides the necessary economic support to the needy population, at least in the initial phase of the pandemic. Free testing, free treatment and free vaccination became the norm, even though due to the rulers' commitment to promote the market, even this process, especially the free vaccination policy by the government of India, was announced several months late. The rulers' neoliberal obsession with privatization got a jolt during the COVID-19 months, but still there was no sign that it would lead to a change in the perspective of the regime on the speed of privatization and a major reaffirmation of the government's primary duty to provide universal primary healthcare. The COVID-19 challenge exposed how poor the public health infrastructure at the grassroots level actually was in the villages and towns of India and how fast the private health industry had grown in recent decades. India spent only about 1 per cent of its GDP on healthcare for about 15 years, increasing to only 1.28 per cent in 2018 and 1.8 per cent in the pandemic year 2020–2021. The vision of having 6 per cent of the GDP devoted to healthcare seemed distant for an economy which was mainly steered towards achieving high economic growth. The vast population under the poverty line—officially about 21 per cent—and severe malnutrition affecting a vast population are among the reasons that make primary healthcare still inaccessible to the vast majority of the population (according to the fourth National Family Health Survey in 2015–2016, the prevalence of underweight, stunted and wasted children under the age of 5 was at 35.7, 38.4 and 21 per cent, respectively). It is often forgotten that better health and education produce a better-equipped workforce with greater earning capacity, which necessarily results in an even more positive impetus for the economy on all fronts. It is true that there have been some laudable initiatives, such as the Malaria Eradication Programme, the National Rural Health Mission and many immunization and child health programmes, but as contributions in this volume show, their effects were uneven, and vast areas and populations remained under poor health conditions due to poverty and social inequality besides sparse health facilities.

Third, another issue that has preoccupied policymakers on the health front is the issue of population control. No doubt, in a populous society like India, a rational and well-balanced perspective on planned parenthood is desirable not only for economic development but also for social development, especially for affirming the basic rights of women and for raising children with proper facilities. But the dominant

Western thinking on the subject locates the main cause of poverty and underdevelopment in developing countries in the phenomenon of a large population, thus creating a Malthusian spectre. That has often produced distorted policies. It has sometimes led to governments resorting to coercion, either directly compelling people to use contraceptives and limit the number of children, or indirectly through a system of incentives and deprivations in various government schemes and employment. Of course, the policy of the one-child family norm practised in China from 1980 to 2016, was not promoted in India. The Indian experience had varied degrees of successes in family planning and population control. In the southern states of India, especially in Kerala, population growth has reached below 1 per cent, whereas in the northern states, especially Bihar, Uttar Pradesh and Madhya Pradesh, it remained above 2 per cent. As the chapters in this volume, especially the section on women, show wherever education and health facilities were better, especially where women were more educated, the voluntary decision of the family has been to opt for one or at best two children. It was clear that the route to a balanced population policy is through education and health. The coercion route not only violates human rights but also results in an imbalanced age structure with a high proportion of old-aged people at a future point as is imminent in China. The health facilities therefore must be improved to provide nutrition support for pregnant and lactating women, immunization and nutritious food for children, and facilities for hospital deliveries besides improved medical support, accessible in all parts of rural and tribal India. In recent decades, much focus is visible in policy statements on all this but, without resource support, they remain scanty. This volume presents much insight on these issues.

Subsumed in these debates are many important issues critically relevant to the health question. For example, the environment crisis, now manifested in the tragedy of climate change, has placed in sharp relief the nature of the development path and the lifestyle accompanying it during contemporary times, which has caused many new diseases. Rising cases of cancer, pulmonary diseases, diabetes and heart ailments are some of the results of these development experience in the modern world. The use of chemicals in agriculture, fossil fuels in industrialization, deforestation and individual and mass transport systems have already reached a carbon emission level which causes unprecedented magnitude of deaths and diseases. The same development path that has produced massive inequalities and impoverishment has also produced climate change with long-term devastating consequences. Only in recent years has the world woken up to acknowledge the seriousness of climate change and is taking some initiatives. But these measures have serious limitations as they are pursued within the very neoliberal paradigm that has produced this phenomenon. They are advanced within a knowledge system upheld by European colonialism, which berated the knowledge systems of Asian, African and Latin American countries that have sustained nature-friendly lifestyles that saved energy, as well as health systems that emerged from that lifestyle with an integrated notion of mental, physical and social health. Along with this, it has also ensured mutual and collective care and empathy. It has operated production systems keeping those norms as the base and involving the community as a whole. Indeed, scientific knowledge must guide the understanding of diseases, design of treatment and production of medicines. Clearly, there are unhealthy practices in all traditions of all societies, which must be critiqued and rejected. But science must be applied fairly to all systems of medicine, social practices and production.

The cataclysmic experience during COVID-19 has highlighted the disastrous consequences of the present mode of living and demanded urgent reconsideration of the fundamental issues underlying the health crisis accruing from the development path and lifestyle in contemporary times.

This volume provides a picture of the crucial dimensions of health discourse, and it must prompt further debates. I complement the editor of this volume, P. M. Arathi, for her sustained efforts to produce this work that captures the history of the debates, identifying vantage points and critical issues on health policy in India so well. She has been part of the wonderful team of experts on the health question who were located in CSD during the past decade and more, including eminent scholar Imrana Qadeer and former Union Health Secretary K. B. Saxena. They have contributed consistently to public debates on health issues. Their researches have led to many valuable publications. In keeping with the foundational mission of CSD, this volume is presented as a Golden Jubilee offering of the *Social Change* journal to further the debate hopefully in a direction to build a healthy future for all.

The work on the publication of the six volumes of the series on *Social Change in Contemporary India* could not have materialized without the persistent efforts of two teams, one at CSD and one at SAGE for over three years.

At CSD, we owe a lot to the minute editorial support of *Social Change* Managing Editor, Mannika Chopra, who went through several drafts and helped the editors to finalize their introductions and selections. CSD Librarian, Gurmeet Kaur, was the key communicator who put all of the necessary papers and documents in order. The volume editors current and former members of the CSD faculty—Prasanta K. Trivedi, Jandhyala B. G. Tilak, Ghazala Jamil, K. B. Saxena and P. M. Arathi—stayed with the project despite many heavy odds, including multiple sufferings and losses during COVID-19. We deeply mourn the absence of Vinay Kumar Srivastava, the editor of the first volume, *Tribes of India: Unfolding Realities*, who was a victim of the pandemic in January 2021, a few months after the first volume was published. He had enthusiastically promoted the idea of the series and helped in conceptualizing the entire project.

The idea of the series struck the friends at SAGE as a worthwhile initiative, and they stood by the project despite much delay and many setbacks. Rajesh Dey checked with us on all aspects and helped us to move on. Amrita Dutta closely followed up on each and every detail. Syed Husain Naqvi took great care of the production. At a critical moment when the prospect of the progress of the project looked uncertain, Manisha Mathews, Associate Vice President, gave us concrete alternatives with deadlines and challenges. That actually put all the editors on high alert and pushed them to give priority to this work.

CSD President, Muchkund Dubey, not only extended his full support to the idea of the series but also helped us to tide over all of the crisis moments. Director, Nitya Nanda and, before him, Ashok Pankaj, helped us at every stage despite the unpredicted twists and turns. Administrative Officer Sheela Sabu always found out ways for us to steer out of difficult situations.

Thanks to SAGE CEO Vivek Mehra, the collaboration between CSD and SAGE has led to many excellent publications and celebrations, including this.

We record our grateful thanks to all of them and, of course, to the contributors to the volumes.

Manoranjan Mohanty
Council for Social Development
New Delhi

Introduction

P. M. Arathi

The global crisis of COVID-19 has forced governments to take drastic measures to reorder the everyday life of people, primarily by curtailing their mobility and routine activities. As a result of the pandemic, the previously ignored concerns of a people's health have taken centre stage in the public discourse. The experience of the disease and the fear of its spread have been internalized by both the state and the public which have begun to adhere to new habits by restraining their lives. Self-discipline and the state surveillance are the new order of the pandemic time. The pandemic has unfolded the sociopolitical context of the largest democracy in the world and revealed its failure to address the needs of a nation in crisis. The basic human rights questions of a people from vulnerable social sections have been ignored and that has created more fatalities than the actual pandemic itself. The political vision of the rulers and their impression of health and illness has once again become crucial in the public health history of humankind.

According to the World Health Organization (WHO) guidelines, each country has to assess the risks and rapidly implement necessary measures at an appropriate scale to reduce both COVID-19 transmission and its economic, social and public impact.[1] The past experiences of public health have reiterated the importance of addressing health needs of people beyond the domain of biomedicine and the question of health for all which is primarily a political commitment made by the state.

Evidences from the USA suggest that the country's Black population is more susceptible to the COVID-19 infection than others, since the community simply cannot afford to maintain physical or social distancing or even take on basic hygiene practices like the use of face masks (Garg et al., 2020). The kind of prerequisite that is required to avoid spreading the coronavirus demands a minimum level of social welfare to keep people away from crowding and adhere to minimal cleanliness. Adequate housing, a healthy work environment, nutrition, sanitation, food, employment pattern, wages—all the so-called good old social determinants of health become key players to ensure the self-disciplining required to follow the 'COVID-19 protocols' prescribed by the state (Kannan, 2020).

In a welfare state, developing a nationwide network of public health services was imagined to build an infrastructure to operate a people-centred basic healthcare. A fully state-sponsored service was to evolve as response to people's preventive and curative health needs, according to their specific social conditions, taking full advantage of available resources in India. However, the reality was that the neoliberal phase of the Indian economy destroyed public health monitoring and surveillance systems and weakened the public health service structure by introducing a rollback of resources, introducing casualization, opening it to markets and promoting public–private partnerships (PPPs) (Ghosh & Qadeer, 2020). The continuous struggles for the democratization of health services and accessibility, affordability of good quality health services reiterates its relevance more than ever during the current times. The present public health crisis invokes the primacy of revisiting public health debates in India to learn lessons from the past to address the present more democratically and plan the future more efficiently.

QUESTION OF HEALTH AND CONCERNS BEYOND BIOMEDICAL INTERVENTIONS

There is a long and rich history of progressive activism in medicine which demands 'health for all' irrespective any discrimination and the ability to pay. During the past two decades, we have seen the rapid expansion of the corporate agenda in the field of health and healthcare. Rather moving towards a system of universal access to healthcare and other welfare measures, which ensures people's health, the insertion of 'market rationality' has been counterproductive and has pushed us to a crisis situation in public health in India. This demands a fundamental rethinking of the social role of medicine, which is necessary to fight for a more democratic, less hierarchical model of healthcare and to achieve that illusive health-for-all goal.

Rudolf Virchow's work on typhus epidemic in 1848 discussed the term 'social medicine' first time in public health history. He took the debate beyond the boundaries of medicine and underlined the importance of social, economic, cultural factors and located the role of contradicting social forces as the primary reason for illness. Therefore, he suggested solutions beyond biomedical–clinal-based interventions but suggested a radical change for social reconstruction, such as universal education, full employment, higher wages and establishment of agricultural cooperatives. His ideas were radical enough to suggest disestablishment of the Catholic church. The Typhus Report, in the context of Medical Reform Movement, 1848, later on influenced the progress of the development of social medicine, which reiterated that the structural conditions of a society and inequalities generate morbidities and mortalities. For Virchow, the deprivations of working class life created a susceptibility to disease. When infectious organisms, climatic changes, famine or other causal factors were present, disease occurred in individuals and spread rapidly through the community. The present public health crisis due to pandemic, the experiences across the globe in the awake of spreading of the pandemic underscores the causal relationship between basic working and living conditions of people and incidence and fatality of the disease. When we discuss the question of the health of the population, one should not forget that other public health measures such as sanitation, hygiene, safe drinking water, good living conditions, nutrition, increased income through employment and land distribution enhanced the health status of people even before vaccines were introduced (Srinivasan & Aisola, 2019).

PUBLIC HEALTH IN INDIA

The much-acclaimed impressive growth of the Indian economy hides economic and social distress in large sections of the population (Selvaraj et al., 2014). But in the period when the economy has expanded fairly rapidly in past three decades, ironically, the health sector has performed particularly poorly. While the global historic experience has shown a positive correlation, the Indian experience shows an inverse relationship between economic growth and health outcomes (Sen, 2001). With the public health sector in a state of neglect, the private sector accounts for

80 per cent of outpatient and 60 per cent of in-patient care, making India one of the most privatized systems in the world (National Sample Survey Organisation, 2006). Publicly financed health insurance schemes have systematically handed over huge chunks of healthcare services to private hospitals and corporate hospital chains (Dasgupta et al., 2013).

The hallmark of public health services in India is poor access to services which are often of low quality and uneven geographical spreading with a huge urban–rural disparity (Ghodajkar, 2019). Different levels of inefficiency are built into the system. The lack of appropriate and skilled human resources plague health services, especially in rural and remote areas. The situation is a consequence of the significantly reduced government investment in public sector medical colleges and simultaneously the encouragement provided to private medical and nursing institutions (Sengupta, 2011).

An estimated 40 per cent of Indians still rely on the public sector for in-patient care (National Sample Survey Organisation, 2006), but in many regions it is poorly staffed with inadequate infrastructure and insufficient supplies of medicines and other consumables. The first wave of neoliberal reforms instituted in the 1990s saw the introduction of user fees and major cuts in public health expenditure, thus forcing public hospitals to recover some ground at the cost of services. For instance, public facilities as a result stopped supplying free medicines and diagnostics. Unfortunately, an erroneous understanding has been promoted that if people want quality care, they should go to a private facility.

The expansion of welfare not only became a way to increase production of services and goods, but it was also a means of creating employment. It is not surprising then that the notion of the state being the provider and regulator of services and economy, a centralized symbol of social responsibility and justice and a focal point of popular mobilization was neither unimaginable nor derided. This glorious phase of welfare capital all over the globe was however short-lived as it could not keep pace with the required speed of technological growth and production which required expanding markets for buyers (Qadeer & Arathi, 2016).

Over the past 40 years, conservative thinkers have spread the idea that 'individual liberty' can only be properly achieved through 'market freedom' (Hickel, 2014). This was translated into a programme of structural adjustment programme (SAP) which offered reforms in the health sector such as a rollback of investments, the entry of private capital in public institutions and opening up tertiary care to private providers, along with many other reforms such as the casualization of health personnel and introduction of user fees. All this negatively affected the public sector in health (Gangolli et al., 2005).

The WHO's significant concept of comprehensive primary healthcare (CPHC) was yet another victim of similar distortions as it moved away from its original mandate to selective primary healthcare, then primary level care and eventually now essential primary healthcare, becoming more and more narrow-minded in its journey (Qadeer, 2001, 2005). WHO itself participated in this mutation of ideas when it offered new public health (WHO, 1998). This new focus shifted responsibility to local bodies and communities through its talk of healthy cities and communities, non-governmental organizations partnerships and, in a sense, revealed that it's giving up on social measures to ensure health (Isaac and Sadanandan, 2020). Yet another idea currently in vogue is that of the stewardship of the state (Qadeer, 2013). Transformed into a regulatory body, the state has now vacated the field of provisioning allowing the markets to step in. This is closely linked to the state withdrawal from the welfare sector which, unlike the 1930s, now caters only to those who offer services through markets and hence to needs that are far from those of the majority of the people. Even the established notion of public goods as a product that one individual can consume without reducing its availability to another individual and from which no one is excluded, has been reinterpreted by redefining 'non-contestability' as an inability to enter the market rather than its character of non-rivalry between users. This then helps fragment services and extracts clinical services that can be marketed from the system (Qadeer, 2009). Interestingly, all these shifts in ideas help relieve the state of its responsibility towards production and provision, and give an impetus to non-state providers. They also tend to disintegrate complexities of public health, isolate single intervention points amenable to technological solutions and thus help move away from their contextual constraints. Health is no more the complexity arising out of living and working conditions of biological entities but a pure clinical challenge amenable to technological medical markets.

UNIVERSALIZING HEALTHCARE: EMERGING QUESTIONS

Universal healthcare (UHC) is like an elephant seen by blind people—very different things to different people. The dominant neoliberal argument for UHC equates 'coverage' with minimal, insurance-based packages. In contrast, public health logic requires that health systems be publicly provisioned and publicly financed, as well as comprehensive, integrated and accountable to the needs of the community. The enhancement of capacity in the public health system will require tackling deep-rooted corruption, engaging in systematic participatory accountability processes to ensure appropriate provision of services to communities and developing pro-people, rational technical norms, guidelines and protocols to operationalize any new regulation. The overall objective of such a regulatory system would be to move towards more equitable, accessible and quality healthcare under participatory governance.

Given the sheer size of the private sector, it is not possible to entirely ignore it while planning for equitable access to services. However, instead of financing the growth of the private sector (as is happening with the current insurance schemes), alternate ways of harnessing private resources for public health goals never be the point of intervention. Over the short term, this could involve in-sourcing some private providers to strengthen and complement the public health system, using them where and if necessary and under clear terms and conditions, all the while working to strengthen and expand the public system. Such in-sourcing should pursue public health goals and there should be no transfer of assets and resources into private hands. Importantly, kickback statutes should be put in place to ensure that there are no referrals with conflict of interests, especially where the same providers are working in both public and private facilities (Qadeer, 2017).

It is, at the same time, necessary to strictly regulate the private sector in terms of quality, cost of care and ethics. Mechanisms for harnessing private facilities and practitioners should be seen as supplementary and interim measures, and not as a substitute for very significant scaling up and strengthening of the public system both in terms of quality and accessibility.

Another corrective measure, ignored historically, is to close human resources gaps and build a public ethos by investing in medical, nursing and paramedical educational institutions that are primarily located in regions where needs are more pressing (Chakravarthi et al., 2017). It is also important to clearly identify skill requirements at different levels of care and to deploy health personnel based on these criteria. Effecting such a change requires alterations in existing curricula and calls for the creation of new professional categories. This has to be supplemented with a package of financial and non-financial incentives to work in the public sector and with sustained efforts to build a positive workforce environment that would retain the employees. For instance, it is not enough to berate doctors by saying that they are unwilling to serve in rural areas. Conditions of work need to be vastly improved to encourage them to work in underserved areas and to retain them in such areas. Minimum working conditions in terms of salaries, housing, rotational postings and secure conditions of employment are all necessary incentives.

The 'social logic' of public health services needs to be reclaimed if UHC is to make a real difference in health outcomes. Moving towards 'health for all' requires major transformations not only in the area of healthcare but also in a wide range of social determinants of health: food security and nutrition, water supply, sanitation, working conditions, housing, environment, education and other sectors. Working on all these fronts requires joining forces with like-minded campaigns, such as those on the right to food or water, to create a broad people's movement in the social sector that will challenge privatization and corporate-friendly PPPs.

The powerful political forces unleashed by the SAP and health sector reforms commodify illness (Saxena, 2019). The biomedical perspective of health promotes technology-centric strategies in the expansion of health markets and private sector rationality relies on profitability as the bottom line, ignoring equity and rationality: Madhavi (2013), Dhar, B., and Joseph, R. K. (2019) reiterates that the PPP push the line that all immunization is universal without providing an uncompromising scientific basis or committing itself to proven epidemiological needs of the population. She argues for a vaccine policy that has been designed to enhance the national public capacity for public immunization programmes as opposed to the current policy that justifies spending public money on privately produced vaccines in the name of protection from disease whose incidence figures and public health statistics are dubious and industry manufactured.

PRIVATIZATION OF HEALTH SERVICES AND RECLAIMING PUBLIC HEALTH IN INDIA

The public systems in developing countries face a serious challenge today. In these countries, a wide variety of public services was significantly expanded and generalized in the second half of the 20th century, as part of post-Independence promises of a 'welfare state'. In the decades following the overthrow of colonial rule, it was expected that the state, with the new optimism and energy borne out of the struggles for Independence, would reflect the wishes of a majority of people. Public services should have been significantly expanded and large public delivery systems should have been developed to provide certain basic services to people. However, the actual record of the post-Independence state and the public systems run by them was mixed; instead of being genuinely accountable and responsive to a majority of the people, public systems in areas such as healthcare have largely tended to be controlled by unaccountable bureaucracies. They operated under pressure from the powerful global elites located in an unequal international order. These public systems became increasingly distanced from the people they were supposed to serve and were in varying degrees, influenced by vested interests which frequently have used these systems as opportunities for expanding corruption and misusing public resources.

This is the background against which, during the last few decades, powerful international forces and their national allies have managed to push a neoliberal agenda, further weakening public systems in the name of 'austerity' and 'fiscal responsibility', along with promoting privatization and commercialization. Public services have been starved of funds and have often been partly privatized. This situation has led to a veritable crisis in systems like public health services in India (Saxena, 2019). With increasingly large sections of people being deprived of basic social services, the direction going forward now simply cannot be privatization. Different types of contracting of services and insurance schemes have contributed to commodification in healthcare services in India, making the situation more complex. The pattern of private sector investment in the public sector varies from state to state in India. To capture the nuances and complexities, we have to understand the patterns emerging globally (Chakravarti, 2019; Roy, 2019). It is important to understand the historical experience of private sector involvement in public sector health service provision and international comparisons may help to understand the Indian context better.

Urban metropolitan areas are endowed with corporate hospitals, all in the organized private sector. In rural areas, a large part of providers are individual practitioners in the unorganized sector. Corporate hospitals are only 1 per cent of the total establishments, have 5 per cent of beds and employ as much as 8 per cent of doctors. More than two-thirds of these corporate hospitals and almost half of the private hospitals were located in a few, 5 million-plus cities. The rapid transformation towards organized forms of healthcare delivery is taking place in the urban areas of the country: smaller providers and individual practitioners too are increasingly getting engaged into corporate networks. While ignoring key components of regulation such as patient rights, regulation of rates, standard treatment guidelines, multi-stakeholder bodies to oversee regulation, it proposed a watered-down accreditation, and a non-binding voluntary mechanism as a 'first step'. The concept of efficiency in public and private is different. What is meant by efficiency in private is all about making more profit. The logic is different from that of public where it is more service to more people. It is totally different and cannot be compared.

Public–Private Partnerships

To explain conceptually the model of PPPs is a complex process and, in practice, it is a clever move on the part of a neoliberal ideology to make private sector services flourish at the cost of public infrastructure. The areas identified for PPP appear to be a 'stand-alone' or the result of ad hoc steps rather than the outcome of well-planned components in a larger schemes or clear policy measures for involving private providers in health services. For instance, the procedural mechanism by which dialysis services, or other similar services, have been chosen are not available in the public domain. While the routine procedure for contracting with private parties, namely the process of requesting tender bids, have been followed for select private companies, and a memorandum of understanding been made on operational details, the rationale for selecting a dialysis system and other options for how it can be provided, or why this particular option has been chosen at all is information that is not available (Karpakam et al., 2013). The pattern that emerges regarding the functioning of the partnerships that were entered into did not take off: there were no takers, or the private partner had not abided by the contract and so ultimately services could not be provided. This should make the government undertake some serious analysis of the feasibility of relying on partnering with the private sector (Roy, 2019).

Citing the experience of the Aarogyasri Scheme in Andhra Pradesh, Reddy and Mary (2013) point out the kind of PPP which undermine the existence of larger public sector entities and their underutilization. They emphasize that the way forward for sustainable and comprehensive healthcare for people is to promote and strengthen the public sector. The PPP means to bring together a set of actors for the common goal of improving the health of a population based on the mutually agreed roles and principles (Karpakam et al., 2013). This experience of PPP has proved that it is promoting a system 'of the elites, for the elites, by the elites'. The private sector appears to be growing in a vacuum created by low public investment in health, a situation created by neoliberal economics. So a small section of society able to pay for these services has emerged. Being vocal, it is their voices that that have been demanding services, creating a dominant discourse in public health, further helping the private sector to intervene and grow.

A return to the largely unaccountable and unresponsive bureaucratic public system cannot be the answer. Instead, the way forward in the early 21st century must be based on a process of citizens collectively 'reclaiming public systems', forging new relationships between society and state where people occupy a central place as active protagonists and people from the grassroots play a significant role in public decision-making and the state is held accountable for all its actions (Shukla & Arathi, 2019). This inevitably implies the development of a new kind of work ethic and public spirit among public officials and providers, accompanied by a qualitatively different level of consciousness and action regarding public entitlements by organized people. In this context, public health scholar activists have raised some relevant questions: How have public institutions culturally changed? How truly public is the public today? How have institutions transformed in the context of changing structures? With the state and the market coexisting together, what has happened to values of democratic ethos? What is it that markets cannot buy? What is the nature and proportion of public investment in a commercialized healthcare?

HEALTH AS A DEVELOPMENTAL GOAL

By including several objectives related to public health in the Sustainable Development Goals (SDGs), different nation states and the international organizations are committed to a better health outcome. The Millennium Development Goals (MDGs) had their own limitations which have led to the political compulsions behind initiating SDGs. The MDGs fragmented health systems vertically while donor-driven programmes were segmented by age, with children and women being left out. The MDGs also bypassed non-communicable diseases and focused on mortality, ignoring a priority for morbidity. There was a focus on lower middle-income countries, while less attention was paid to middle-income countries. Liberal scholars have popularly argued that MDGs were skewed, whereas the SDGs had been improved, bridging areas of health, along with UHC as a platform to meet the various health needs of people. However, a deeper analysis of the political economy of the Indian public health system reveals that it was actually the different five-year plans and various committees on health in the past that were rooted in bettering the conditions of people and their lives. Many of these programmes, as familiar to us, offered free basic healthcare for all, but with the planning process becoming fragmented and different sections planning separately, an intersectional integration has been missed out.

The SDGs, including the SDG 3 target that aspires to the health and well-being for all, can be interpreted as political statements that define development more than economic growth rates and health more than universal health coverage. However, it is possible for technical support agencies, together with global health institutions, to amplify certain targets and attenuate or reinterpret others, a process that is well underway with respect to health targets. Technical considerations, both as a feasibility of measurement and achievement, are often used to rationalize such reinterpretations. Clearly, the achievement of SDG targets as stated currently is incompatible with the neoliberal understanding of growth and development that inform current national and international economic policies. These could either justify progressive academic and civil society sections distancing themselves from the entire project or be seen as an opportunity. Engaging with the discussion around its measurement, interpretation and implementation could provide the scope for questioning current economic policies and neoliberal understandings of health reform and posing alternatives to these.

The Alma-Ata declaration incorporated the principle of CPHC, integrating it with the developmental process, stating that a nation's health policy should be based on people's needs and epidemiological findings of society. However, the declaration was later reduced to 'essential primary healthcare' and then 'selective primary healthcare', meshing with the political shifts globally and adherence to neoliberal economic policies worsened the Indian scenario. In a neoliberal political context, policymakers are interpreting and defining 'universality' as a way to cut down on catastrophic healthcare needs, changing the focus on medical care, privatization of care and financing for insurance schemes. The priorities given to a cumulative growth rate, along with poor regulatory systems and pro-medical industry policies has made the crisis worse in India's public health scenario. A plan for the poor is different from a plan that is aimed at making profits. Then the obvious question that arises is can we wait for SDG and MDG to be implemented or should we intervene in an urgent basis in thinking and practising public health in India.

NATIONAL HEALTH POLICIES

A substantive policy document is one which clearly states the direction of an organization's future and its perspective. It is not required to elaborate on procedures as an advisory document, but it is incumbent on its authors to unambiguously state priorities and provide timelines for its objectives, outlining financial requirements. The review of the 2015 Draft National Health Policy (NHP) raised the primary concern that while the document accepted that only the health services provided by the public sector gave value for money, yet its emphasis remained on promoting the private sector. Qadeer and Arathi (2016) have argued that only a strengthened public sector can act as a regulator for CPHC if the national policy is serious about reaching out to the underserved. They have also pointed out that a policy needs to be located in a given epidemiological and socio-economic context. A careful reading of the NHP 2017 reveals that the generosity of its goals, the commitment to building public sector infrastructure, the principles of equity, affordability universality, professionalism, ethics and integrity, quality, accountability and so on are more in the nature of a window dressing for the continuation of its role as the steward of the private sector (Qadeer & Arathi, 2016).

The medical industry is mischievously labelled a 'healthcare industry', even though it is a part of the medical industrial complex that thrives on the tertiary medical care needs of the middle class and the elite, as indicated by the relatively higher rise in the out-of-pocket expenditure of richer population quintiles between 2004–2005 and 2011–2012 (Selvaraj et al., 2014). The NHP 2017 also considers medical industry 'robust' as the revenue it generates adds to the gross domestic product (GDP), but the shift of state subsidies and their negative impact on public sector infrastructure and distributive justice in healthcare is not considered as a contextual shift (Mukhopadhyay, 2019).

Rising catastrophic expenditure actually was the rationale behind accelerating the pace of private penetration of public institutions in the name of supporting and strengthening them and setting up PPPs (Puliyel, 2019). This link between the medical industry and rising expenditures is ignored even while recognizing that the latter pushes people living on the margins into poverty, impeding a faster pace of improvement in health indicators. The truth is that despite this rising expenditure, catastrophic or otherwise, the policy document continues to pursue 'inclusive partnerships' with the private sector as a 'public goal' when experience has clearly shown that this strategy is not only futile but also expensive, both for the state and the people. Yet another aspect of the contextual change postulated is the increased fiscal capability of the Indian state which now enables it to build its health sector infrastructure. The transformation of health services into a commodity and a means of capital accumulation in the process of building this fiscal capability are ignored (Qadeer & Arathi, 2017).

The unmentioned contextual shift of state subsidies towards the private sector and the restricted financing of the public sector are bound to further the bias against the marginalized and slow the pace of improvement in overall health indicators. This pragmatism has no doubt contributed to improved fiscal capability, but will that now transform into a vision that assures availability of free, CPHC services for all aspects of reproductive, maternal, child and adolescent health and for the most prevalent communicable, non-communicable and occupational diseases in the population?

There are guidelines that have waited in the queue for years such as making free drugs available at public hospitals, attention to occupational health, disease surveillance, male sterilization and regular services, in the place of camps and plurality of services. However, the closure of the National Nutrition Monitoring Bureau by the government, the past experiences in each of these areas, the paucity of finances and the present priorities infuse one with little confidence in their materialization. This is especially so as the policy, out of fear of legal implications, rejects making health services a justiciable right using the logic that health is a state subject or that given the multiple determinants of health, and types and levels of healthcare, the country is not ready for such a law. Behind this smokescreen, even emergency care is not seen as a fundamental right even though it is closely linked to Article 21 of the Indian Constitution that grants the right to life as a fundamental right. The document thus leaves us wondering about the nature of democracy in its largest abode.

Nutrition Policies in India

Human conditions, such as ecological settings, social organization of work, the nature of technology, political formation and power structures emanating from these (with varying degrees of equity), generate a range of lifestyles, human experience and knowledge at all points of time. This knowledge when extracted, coded and systemized with the help of technology into a disciplinary science, not accessible to the majority, may, instead of serving people, actually serve some narrow interests by deciding what is good or not good for them. The process of the evolution of sciences, deeply rooted in the notion of objectivity, at times, loses its ability of self-regulation (sensitivity to variability/uncertainty) to become instrumental in unintended goals (Council for Social Development, 2018).

The effort to create cheap balanced diets were this time combined with state policies of land reforms, price control and the public distribution system that went a long way in tackling malnutrition and severe forms of under-nutrition. However, instead of pursuing this effort to include larger numbers through balanced pulse cereal production and expanding the choice and variety of food for people, the late 1980s and 1990s saw drastic policy shifts in the structural adjustments, with market forces threatening food security. The trend of rising calorie intakes reversed in the late 1970s (Radhakrishna, 2005), but the initial success had diverted the nutritionists' attention to micronutrient deficiencies, fortification of cereals and later to obesity. Declining calorie intakes could not recapture their scientific curiosity and were left to be interpreted as a 'puzzle' or as an indicator of dietary variations (Qadeer et al., 2016). The recommended dietary allowances for calories in fact saw the downsizing of allowances by the last two committees of the Indian Council of Medical Research (ICMR, [1990] 2010).

Inequalities in the provisioning of social determinants of health and its impact on deterioration of wellness and health had become a question of economic concern, mostly during the industrialization era. The physical activity level, that is, the work-level and its relationship with economic productivity and economic growth, befall academic concerns in both economics and public health. Public health debates observed it as a vicious circle, where a reduction in work capacity or reduced productivity could translate into a reduced earning capacity which may lead to further poverty resulting in ill health. This relationship has been mediated and shaped historically through different apparatus of the state, especially through the legislative process and policymaking. This journey of law making witnessed several paradigm shifts in the developmental models of social welfarism to neoliberalism.

The State-Market Dualism and People's Health

The relationship and coexistence of the state and the market have played a toxic role in India's public health system, intensifying particularly in the past two decades. Let us discuss two solid examples of this: the commercialization of reproductive bodies (surrogacy debates) and gross negligence on the part of the state about poor women and their violation of human rights and reproductive rights (seen in sterilization camp deaths). Both extreme examples show how the nexus between market and the state has created an unregulated regime where exploitation has become an unquestionable practice.

Commercial Surrogacy

Commercial surrogates, often characterized by the medical market as 'womb providers', seem relatively both less inscribed and lowest in the production chain. Given capital's historic dependence on and production of geographic unevenness, this scenario was latent in the class, social market relations within which the technology of assisted reproduction unfolded. With neoliberal globalization, as the racialized, imperialist exploitation of women differing origins by a transnational market which normalizes the extraction of resources or cheaper services from less developed nations and enables the purchase of economically vulnerable women's procreative labour and custodial rights, became apparent. Commercial surrogacy was located, along with migrant domestic work and the global care chain, as another form of stratified reproduction in the multiple inequalities of the reproductive labour market (Qadeer, 2010).

Kumkum Sangari (2015) sketches the emergent practice of commercial surrogacy, its location in post-Fordist production, the symbiosis between assisted reproduction technologies and the post-Fordist organization of labour and wages within a specific class-determined domestic and transnational market configuration. Sangari perceives these in relation to the restructuring of both the state and social reproduction and to the instrumentality of waste, debt and poverty. Sangari places her argument against commercial surrogacy in the logic of the added sex selection of foetus (female foeticide), domestic labour markets and the present asymmetry of a surrogate pregnancy contract as opposite to the libertarian feminist arguments of free labour contract, reproductive autonomy and the intentional family.

Much of women's employment in India remains in the informal/unorganized sector that includes home-based works and piece rate contracts linked to both domestic and export-oriented production chains and low-paid service sector. The purchasing individual/couple is embedded in the political form of property as in the form of ownership of the child and family as the right to reproduce it, formed in the historical matrix of class, caste and colonial extraction, invigorated by the market, transnational circuit of capital, exchange and manufacture, and facilitated by the state. Legal laxity allows and consolidates the practice (Sangari, 2015). The pressures of a debt economy are producing subjects and agents of what Sangari calls self-directional violence. A surrogate, who in most cases belongs to a debt-controlled family, bears the health risks and the social costs. In most cases, surrogates only complain when they are less paid. This partially unpaid labour is transformed through the concerted market discourse of brokers and clients into gifts or donations, which again Sangari calls imputed altruism, saves and moralizes a market transaction as well as expels from the market transaction what the market has refused or failed to pay.

Sterilization Camp Deaths

The camp method for sterilizing women, where quality of care is deeply compromised and ethical and legal provisions violated, itself is a reflection of the systemic rupture of the public healthcare delivery system. Rather than addressing the question of how to improve public health systems to meet the requirements of the people, policy-level interventions through PPPs and insurance schemes, open the door for profit-making private providers and create lethal situations like the one at Bilaspur in 2014 (Arathi, 2019).

There is a shift in people's receptiveness and acceptability of fertility control measures over time. In the decisions of rural women to reduce their family size, one of the measures that needs to be addressed is their poverty. The 'unmet needs' for reducing family size is a major concern of family planning programme (FPP) in India; however, it does not really consider addressing the availability, accessibility, affordability and quality of health services. The reasonable expectation of the people from the state is to get quality services at an affordable price which is not being addressed adequately. Here, the lessons we learned are indicative that neither market rationality nor a non-responsive elite state approach is the solution.

The withdrawal of the state from being a provider of services to a facilitator of the market adversely impacts the quality of services in the public sector. The quality of service, defined as choice of method, dignity and comfort, privacy and confidentiality, safety procedure, follow-up and referral services, as well as space for feedback, ranges from low to very poor quality (Population Foundation of India et al., 2014). Chapter II of the draft National Health Bill describes the obligation of the government in relation to health. Section 3(a) mentions budgetary allocation that should be, 'Appropriate and adequate budgetary measures, as per globally accepted norms, to satisfy, the obligation and rights set out herein, throughout ensuring transparency and equity in the allocation, planning and rational allocation and distribution of resources for health and related issues and concerns' (Ministry of Health and Family Welfare, 2009, p. 13), but does not prescribe any minimum percentage of the GDP as a mandatory investment in the health sector allocation. Unless the 'appropriate and adequate' allocation of the budget is clearly defined in terms of proportion of the GDP, there will be no commitment to the objectives expressed. As a result, the obligation of the government towards health remains, but is barely met.

Just as the link between coercion and oppressive population policies is rooted in the denial of services to the poor, the felt need for birth control among rural poor women in India cannot be analysed within the reproductive choice framework of the WHO (2014). The choice framework emerged in the Western context where choice is a function of support systems for maternal and childcare, other social welfare measures and a better social environment for women to make their choices. However, in the given situation for the majority of women in India (both rural and urban), the 'choice' comes mostly out of necessity and desperation. Here, the affordable birth control measures mostly are permanent contraceptive methods, generally female sterilization and end up in mass sterilization camps without meeting any safety standards.

Regulatory Paradigms

The diminishing state investment in the social welfare sector, including public health and the introduction of market rationality in the social sector, has resulted in the inhumane treatment of poor, lower caste, rural women in the sterilization camps of Bilaspur. The accountability and legal regulation of the private sector is a mirage in a pro-market statehood. Hence, their partnership does not necessarily contribute to efficiency, but often damages more than it helps. Although the Parliament of India has passed the Clinical Establishments (Registration and Regulation) Act, 2010, which governs the regulation of all healthcare institutions including the private providers, it still remains on paper. The working draft of the National Health Bill (version, January 2009) states that the Union of India has the mandate to legislate on matters related to population stabilization and family planning (Ministry of Health and Family Welfare, 2009, p. 8). Struggles for health justice in developing countries historically relied on the judiciary through litigation, both in the form of public interest litigation and complaints filed by individuals based on their personal grievances. The history of public interest litigation in India marks an attempt to reframe health-related entitlements as legally enforceable claims. The individual or personal grievances were mostly around medical negligence or violation of consumer rights of patients seeking service (middle-class initiatives for entitlements). Judicialization (approaching the judiciary to get relief under a law or implementation of it) of medical negligence often interprets and visualizes these as pragmatic rights (recognized, but not acted upon) and not as justiciable in many legal fights. Structural and hierarchical discrimination also reflects in the healthcare delivery system, and many people who live in the periphery of the society are fatally affected. Here, it is important to establish linkages between the right to life and the right not to be discriminated against in health rights litigation. It demands an inclusive approach in the legal paradigm, which incorporates individual entitlements to healthcare, rewriting intellectual property rights rules, changes in policies related to social determinants of health, influence in the health priority setting forces and drive for more budgetary allocations (Yamin, 2014).

The judicialization of health rights cannot be seen or analysed in the abstract but has to be done in a specific sociopolitical and legal context. In India, this judicial process can be observed as the courts act on immediately enforceable minimum core content; judging the reasonableness of government actions; granting silent sanctions to corporate hospitals and pro-corporate government actions (Baxi, 1985, p. 132). The Indian legal system follows the British system of law due to the political and administrative experience of colonization. The criminal justice system still follows the colonial law of Indian Penal Code, 1860. The British system follows the notion of the tort of negligence when a patient has been injured due to a mistake made by the doctor or by the system of healthcare service delivery. To establish this principle of tort of negligence in classical notion of law, there should be three conditions: the patient must be owed by a 'duty of care' by the doctor; there should be a breach of duty by the doctor (doctor's conduct must be below the standard of care prescribed by law) and, finally, the breach of duty should cause harm to the patient (Arathi, 2019). Yamin (2014) argues that the blatant violation of human dignity in healthcare settings continue to occur across all development levels, despite well-established standards. Equity in health is a complex and multivalent topic, especially in a multi-layered stratified society. This makes questions on discrimination much more complex to negotiate litigation which alone cannot be the end or beginning, or the end of struggle for justice and rights in health.

IS INDIA'S UHC MODEL A SOLUTION?

UHC is considered as the magic potion for the healthcare needs of low- and middle-income countries. The ambiguities in the prevailing UHC model within the Indian context reflects the state's commitment to growth-oriented development and an intentional sabotage of health rights of the people. The West, which has nurtured the concept of UHC, began with the social solidarity acquired through welfare measures by the state. In that context, the UHC model emerged under the pressure of demand for medical care and pressures of the private providers for autonomy under the rising expectations of the populations which acquired a certain level of economic prosperity. These countries ultimately developed mixed models of medical care provided by public and private sectors. The former were strong partners ensuring basic care to all with market options for specialized care. The services were supported through state finances and well-regulated private sector (Qadeer, 2013).

Unlike in the West, in the context of India, the income disparities are too high, and there are various forms of discriminations based on caste, gender, religion and ethnicity with deep historical roots. The lives of people in the country have remained divided and are of poor quality for a significant proportion. The existence of rural and urban differences in terms of infrastructure development and access to healthcare services has made the situation much more intricate to imagine a healthcare delivery system. The need was for both welfare and medical care. However, UHC in India focuses on involving private sector for coverage, protection from financial catastrophe and basic medical care (without economic and social welfare). In India, PPPs, insurance, state health assurance schemes and medical market have become pivotal. This model transforms health into a commodity and a service that responds to demands. Given the vast majority that need, but are not able to demand services, their needs are to be met by the state through the state-led insurances/assurance in partnership with the private sector. This only adds to the conversion of the state not only into a steward but also into a client of the private sector. The shift of subsidies away from the health infrastructure leads to a paucity of infrastructure and absence of regular services (Qadeer & Ghosh, 2016).

The articulation and deliberations for a better world and the demands for health rights go beyond the demand for free medical services to ensure state accountability, to ensure justice to the hapless women of Bilaspur and similar situations. The accessibility of services that are non-discriminative will be inadequate without the assurance of a quality of service. The struggle for an equitable and just health system has to be part of the larger resistances for comprehensive rights and entitlements. The specific experiences of exclusion and discrimination during pandemic reiterates the importance of intensifying these struggles for just health system.

PANDEMIC AND CREATION OF THE 'MORBID OTHER'

The language of 'aggression', 'fight', 'war', 'elimination' and 'control' that dominates the political vocabulary has been transmitted to the scientific domain during the pandemic. This new normal has created new forms of discrimination and bias. Epidemics have conceptually become discursive in the context of what a disease is: how it originates and the ways in which it gets spread (Rosenberg, 1992). This has led to the marking of a certain category of people as the 'morbid other' (Cleetus, 2020), making them responsible for the origin and spread of the epidemic. Thus, the state and the dominant culture have relentlessly produced new and diverse forms of 'social distancing' to keep certain communities in the margins away from the mainstream and point to them as responsible for spreading the disease.

Every society, within its existing race/caste/communal prejudices, has reproduced its 'morbid other' during the outbreak. In the global context, the people of China, because COVID-19's origin is traced to a province there, are being marked as the 'morbid other'. In India, however, it is the Muslim community that is being targeted for spreading of the disease. Historical biases as well as popular prejudices, social inequalities and discrimination construct the 'morbid other' in times of a pandemic. In India, Muslims are not only harassed for being responsible for the origin and the spread of the disease, but they also bear an extra burden of the disease with a high relative risk. This extra burden of mortality and morbidity is due to the unequal treatment within and outside the healthcare delivery systems that tend to perpetuate historical and popular biases. Religious and cultural practices, combined with communitarian and social living, thus develop new medical topographies through identifying certain locales as the origin of the disease and certain people as its spreaders.

The Indian Muslim seems to have borne this extra burden of responsibility in spreading COVID-19 as also the disproportionate mortality and morbidity rates as compared to the rest of the population.

News reports from Western and northern India clearly indicate the reasons. Travel from the Gulf region; a significant share of community living; the habitats of a highly dense population; a lack of accessibility to healthcare services and poor living conditions are cited in many grassroots-level enquiries (Barngarwala, 2020). In the state of Maharashtra, 12 per cent of the population belongs to the Muslim community; however, in the COVID-19 mortality rate, the community represents 44 per cent in the early stage of spreading (till early May 2020).

The kind of trauma created among the community after the Tablighi Jamaat episode resulted in the non-reporting of cases or hiding of symptoms for fear of rampant social stigma. Adhering to the traditional and religious healing practices, many symptomatic patients tried to avoid the healthcare delivery system. Critical cases from low-income group of the Muslim community thus came late to the intensive care. Inherent biases within the health service system *towards* the community might also have resulted in the negative prioritizing of services and would have resulted in high mortality rates in the high-risk category. The popular way of understanding an epidemic has three methods: to identify it as a shift in the personal life of individuals; shifts in the economic activities of a community/population and categorize it as a matter of national security. All three methods basically impact the mobility of individuals, communities and people. The 'morbid othering' of the Muslim community is developed primarily through their mobility—both economic and social.

PUBLIC HEALTH IN INDIA: POLICY SHIFTS AND TRENDS

This edited volume on *Public Health in India: Policy Shifts and Trends* captures the transitions in the public health narrative in India through different lenses and from different vantage points within a broader frame of not dominant and popular understanding of what public health is. This helps to understand better the amnesia that seems to have pervaded not only the professional and the political class about the history of public health in our very diverse and dynamic country but also those who are being fed with the elitist biomedical perspective limited to hi-tech interventions at the cost of a balanced view on healthcare. This volume traces the history of public health debates in India over the past five decades.

The emphasis of this volume is to identify the paradigm shifts in the health needs of people in post-Independence India through government approaches with contradicting visions, approaches, strategies and policies. The transition of health policies and shifts in the commitment towards 'health for all', both measures and withdrawals, is part of the history of the debates in India. The most prominent among them was the scheme of providing comprehensive primary health services to the people. The Alma-Ata Declaration on Comprehensive Primary Health Care adopted in 1978 was embraced by India wholeheartedly and in totality which included ensuring the fulfilment of the socio-economic conditions conducive to CPHC. It regarded preventive and promotive measures of public health to be more important than the curative ones. It had built into its elements of inclusiveness and universality. The Government of India adopted a number of measures in the macro-economic domain as well as in social sectors, including health, in order to give an effect to these provisions. Further, a provision of such primary health services is related to the whole host of socio-economic factors such as the enhancement of income, its equitable distribution, ensuring livelihood security and providing related goods and services such as food, nutrition, water and housing. The selected chapters that appear in this volume examine the need of a coordinated, holistic and planned health strategy and argue that the state alone is in a position to design and implement them.

This edited volume marks the erosions reflected mainly in the policy changes relating to primary healthcare that have taken place at the national level. In India, the concept of comprehensive primary health services gave way to selective primary health services. In the next stage, it became confined to essential care. And in the past one decade, the concept that has come to dominate the field is UHC. This edited volume contains an in-depth analysis of these issues, mostly based on empirical studies and argues that health problems were not tackled in terms of basic health needs or epidemiological assessment, but on the basis of available technologies.

This volume indicates essentially that even when hunger and poor living conditions and lack of economic opportunities were recognized as being critical for health, policymakers did not discern the close links between the pattern and pace of India's future overall development and the implications for health and the growth of the health service infrastructure. Further, the chapters emphasize strongly that investing in the health of citizens engaged in the economy increases revenues through higher productivity of labour as well as taxation and by way of pooling resources to expand appropriate health services as well as employment. Thus, there is a two-way relationship between the health of a people and their economy.

This fast-transforming health sector is located in a larger context where the focus is on economic growth without much attention being paid to the redistribution or improving significantly the purchasing capacity of people. When health services become a commodity in such conditions and are brought into an unregulated market of sophisticated technologies, the majority of the working classes cannot access it until the state pays for them. The consequence of this is observed through the chapters in this volume. This volume locates the transformation in our understanding of the social determinants of public health and touches upon several aspects of women's health, fertility transitions and impact of coercive population policies, provisioning of health services, mental health problems, disease burdens, health problems of the elderly and so on.

The volume contains four sections: 'Political Economy of Health and Illness'; 'Questions of Women's Health and Reproductive Justice'; 'Nutrition: A Social Determinant of Health' and lastly 'Malthusian Spectre and Indian Public Health History'. These sections consist of 18 chapters that have appeared in the *Social Change* journal over the past five decades.

The first section, 'Political Economy of Health and Illness', emphasizes the formulation of academic debates in India beyond the notion of biomedical understanding. *Social Change* consistently took a position that the universalization of medical care alone, as it happened in Europe in the early 20th century through ensuring access to services, cannot be the answer to ensuring health in India. The country has neither achieved the required minimum standard of living for all nor has there been adequate infrastructure in the public sector to ensure basic health and welfare. Health, as is well known, is affected by levels of non-medical inputs such as food, drinking water, housing, sanitation, education and transportation. While the state does not assert itself to address their uneven distribution, these inequities are largely determined by an unequal social structure in which the powerful continue to be the beneficiaries of neoliberal policies. Chapters include social, cultural, economic, political and environmental factors such as national policies, social protection, living standards, working conditions, community social supports and physician–patient relationships. Social inequalities and social discriminations are key among these factors determining health status of the people.

The second section, 'Questions of Women's Health and Reproductive Justice', discusses the historical evolution of knowledge in medicine and society, and emphasizes the biological vulnerability/weakness of women in the initial stages, but when these weaknesses are found to be errors of scientific judgement, it slowly turns to biological specificity and then gives space to social constraints borne out of patriarchal structures and inherent gender roles. This transformation in our understanding of social determinants traces several aspects of women's health, provisioning of health services and women's access to health services. *Social Change* in its journey of five decades has covered several aspects of women's health comprehensively in its complexities.

The third section, 'Nutrition: A Social Determinant of Health', addresses the important interlinkages between nutrition and health outcomes. The complexity of this aspect of health is immense. It not only involves understanding the balance and synergy between nutrients, their requirements for different levels of growth and activity, processes of adaptation of the body to lower/higher states of nutrition and their manifestations, individual variations and age, sex differences but also intra-family distribution. Policymaking then is challenging as it requires simple, though not simplistic principles, for planning, critical knowledge of nutrition and its complexity and a political commitment to equity and inclusive development.

The last section, Section IV, 'Malthusian Spectre and Indian Public Health History', traces population policies in India. These policies have witnessed different trajectories, namely voluntary, coercive and targeted. In this section, we discuss these trajectories and see how women become 'targets' and continue to be the targets in recent policy statements. This section shows how the dominance of Malthusian ideology in conceptualizing, perceiving and drafting these policies persisted in India and stood as an iconic representation of anti-women and anti-poor strategies. FPP is one of the oldest components of healthcare systems in India and continues to be the focus of planning over the last five decades.

This volume provides a unique journey through public health debates showing not only the transformation in the public health discourse but also the transition in methods of academic writing and the patterns of social change we, as a society, went through. Narratives from the past will definitely ensure more clarity about the present as well as an appropriate vision about the future.

NOTE

1. https://www.who.int/news/item/29-06-2020-covidtimeline

REFERENCES

Arathi, P. M. (2019). Unaccountable deaths and damages: An analysis of socio-legal implications of sterilisation camp deaths in Bilaspur, Chhattisgarh. In I. Qadeer, K. B. Saxena & P. M. Arathi (Eds.), *Universalising healthcare in India from care to coverage* (pp. 211–227). Aakar.

Barngarwala, T. (2020). Minority surge in Covid deaths, Maharashtra plans messages in Urdu. *The Indian Express*.

Baxi, U. (1985). Taking suffering seriously: Social action litigation in the Supreme Court of India. *Third World Legal* Studies, 107–132.

Buse, K., & Walt, G. (Eds.). (2000). Global public–private partnerships: Part III. What are the health issues for global governance? *Bulletin of the World Health Organization, 78*(5), 6999–7709.

Chakravarthi, I. (2019). Universal healthcare and health assurance through healthcare industry and market mechanisms: Evidence verses ideology. In I. Qadeer, K. B. Saxena & P. M. Arathi (Eds.), *Universalising healthcare in India from care to coverage* (pp. 74–97). Aakar.

Chakravarthi, I., Roy, B., Mukhopadhyay, I., & Barria, S. (2017). Investing in Health. *Economic & Political Weekly, 52*(45), 51.

Cleetus, B. (2020). Tropics of disease: Epidemics in colonial India. *Economic & Political Weekly*. https://www.epw.in/engage/article/tropics-disease-epidemics-colonial-india

Council for Social Development. (2018). *Strategy for enhancing women's nutritional status via programmatic interventions* (Unpublished report). The author.

Dasgupta, R., Nandi, S., Kanungo, K., Nundy, M., Murugan, G., & Neog, R. (2013). What the good doctor said: A critical examination of design issues of the RSBY through provider perspective in Chhattisgarh, India. *Social Change*, 227–243.

Dhar, B., & Joseph, R. K. (2019). Developments in India's domestic pharmaceutical sector and implications for universal healthcare in India. In Imrana Qadeer, K. B. Saxena, & P. M. Arathi (Eds.), *Universalising healthcare in India from care to coverage* (pp. 271–286). Aakar.

Gangolli, L. V., Duggal, R., & Shukla, A. (2005). *Review of healthcare in India*. Centre for Enquiry into Health and Allied Themes (CEHAT).

Garg, S., Kim, L., Whitaker, M., O'Halloran, A., Cummings, C., Holstein, R., & Fry, A. (2020). Hospitalization rates and characteristics of patients hospitalized with laboratory-confirmed coronavirus disease 2019—COVID-NET, 14 states, March 1–30, 2020. *Morbidity and Mortality Weekly Report, 69*(15), 458.

Ghodajkar, P. (2019). Interrogating the proposed universal healthcare in India through a 'quality' lens. In I. Qadeer, K. B. Saxena, & P. M. Arathi (Eds.), *Universalising healthcare in India from care to coverage* (pp. 117–145). Aakar.

Ghosh, S. M., & Qadeer, I. (2020). Public good perspective of public health. *Economic & Political Weekly, 55*(36), 41.

Hickel, H. (2014). A short history of neo-liberalism (and how we can fix it). www.newleftproject.org/index.php/site/article_comments/a_short_history_of_neo-liberalism_and_how_we_can_fix_it accessed 20–02–2020

ICMR. ([1990] 2010). *Nutrient requirements and recommended dietary allowances for Indians* (A report of the expert group of the Indian Council of Medical Research, New Delhi). The author.

Isaac, T. M. T., & Sadanandan, R. (2020). COVID-19, public health system and local governance in Kerala. In M. Jomon & V. Jinis (Eds.), *COVID-19: Unmasking the post-pandemic realities* (pp. 13–31). DC Books.

Kannan, K. P. (2020). COVID-19 lockdown: Protecting the poor means keeping the Indian economy afloat. In M. Jomon & V. Jinis (Eds.), *COVID-19 unmasking the post-pandemic realities* (pp. 32–40). DC Books.

Karpakam, S., Roy, B., Seethappa, K. V. & Qadeer, I. (2013). Evidence-based planning—A myth or reality: Use of evidence by the planning commission on public-private partnership (PPP). *Social Change*, 213–226.

Madhavi, Y. (2013). Vaccines and vaccine policy for universal healthcare. *Social Change*, 263–291.

Ministry of Health and Family Welfare. (2009). *GoI working draft version 2009, the national health bill 2009*. http://www.prsindia.org/uploads/media/Draft_National_Bill.pdf.

Mukhopadhyay, I. (2019). National health policy 2015: Growth fundamentalism driving universal health coverage agenda? In I. Qadeer, K. B. Saxena, & P. M. Arathi (Eds.), *Universalising healthcare in India from care to coverage* (pp. 98–116). Aakar.

National Sample Survey Organization (2006). India - Service Sector in India 2006-07, NSS 63rd round http://microdata.gov.in/nada43/index.php/catalog/115/study-description accessed on 20th March 2020.

Population Foundation of India, Parivar Seva Sansthan, Family Planning Association of India and Common Health. (2014). *Robbed of choice and dignity: Indian women dead after mass sterilisation* (Report of Situational Assessment of Sterilisation Camps in Bilaspur District, Chhattisgarh). The authors.

Puliyel, J. (2019). Vaccine policy of Government of India: Driven and controlled by vested interests? In I. Qadeer, K. B. Saxena, & P. M. Arathi (Eds.), *Universalising healthcare in India from care to coverage* (pp. 287–310). Aakar.

Qadeer, I. (2001). Impact of structural adjustment on concepts in public health. In I. Qadeer, K. Sen, & K. R. Nayar (Eds.), *Public health and the poverty of reforms: The South Asian predicament* (pp. 117–156). SAGE.

Qadeer, I. (2005). Continuities and discontinuities in public health: The Indian experience. In A. K. Bagchi & K. Soman (Eds.), *Maladies preventives and curatives: Debates in public health in India* (117–156). Springer.

Qadeer, I. (2010). New reproductive technologies and health care in neo-liberal India: Essays. *Monograph*, 1–73. Centre for Women's Development Studies.

Qadeer, I. (2013). Universal healthcare: The trojan horse of neoliberal policies. *Social Change*, 43(2), 149–164.

Qadeer, I. (2017). The national family health survey: An early warning. *Social Change*, 47(3), 421–425.

Qadeer, I., & Arathi, P. M. (2016). Words, ideas and ideology in the shifting sand of markets. *Indian Journal of Gender Studies*, 23(1), 105–132.

Qadeer, I., & Ghosh, S. M. (2016). Public health's in the infirmary. *The Hindu Business Line*. http://www.thehindubusinessline.com/opinion/public-healths-in-the-infirmary/article8486437.ece

Qadeer, I., Ghosh, M. S., & P. M. Arathi. (2016). India's declining calorie intake: Development or distress? *Social Change*, 46(1), 1–26.

Radhakrishna, R. (2005). Food and nutrition security of the poor: Emerging perspectives and policy issues. *Economic & Political Weekly*, 40(18), 1817–1821.

Reddy, S., & Mary, I. (2013). Aarogyasri scheme in Andhra Pradesh, India: Some critical reflections. *Social Change*, 43(2), 245–261.

Rosenberg, C. (1992). *Explaining epidemics and other studies in the history of medicine.* Cambridge University Press.

Roy B. (2019). Role of Public Private Partnerships in Ensuring Universal Healthcare for India. In Qadeer, I., Saxena, K. N., & Arathi, P. M. (Eds.), *Universalising healthcare in India: From care to coverage.* Delhi, Aakar Books.

Sangari, K. (2015). *Solid: Liquid a (trans) national reproductive formation.* Tulika Books.

Saxena, K. B. (2019). The elusive development: Poverty, inequality and vulnerability. In I. Qadeer, K. B. Saxena, & P. M. Arathi (Eds), *Universalising healthcare in India: From care to coverage* (pp. 377–403). Aakar.

Selvaraj, S., Karan, A. K., & Mukhopadhyay, I. (Eds.). (2014). Publicly-financed health insurance schemes in India: How effective are they in providing financial risk protection? In I. Qadeer (Ed.), *Social development report.* Council for Social Development and OUP.

Sen, K. (2001). Health reforms and developing countries—A critique. In I. Qadeer, K. Sen, & K. R. Nayar (Eds.), *Public health and the poverty of reforms* (pp. 137–153). SAGE.

Sengupta, A. (2011). Health care and medical education in India, situationalising corruption: The MCI story. *India Current Affairs*. http://indiacurrentaffairs. org/health-care-and-medical-education-in-india-stitutionalising-corruption-the-mci-story-amit-sen-gupta/

Shukla, A., & Arathi, P. M. (2019). Challenges of reclaiming the public health system: Experiences of community-based monitoring and planning in Maharashtra. In I. Qadeer, K. B. Saxena, & P. M. Arathi (Eds.), *Universalising healthcare in India from care to coverage* (pp. 422–439). Aakar.

Srinivasan, S., & Aisola, M. (2019). Availability and access to medicines: Some issues in pricing. In I. Qadeer, K. B. Saxena, & P. M. Arathi (Eds.), *Universalising healthcare in India from care to coverage* (pp. 311–333). Aakar.

WHO. (1998). *Health promotion glossary*. https://www.who.int/healthpromotion/about/HPR%20Glossary%201998.pdf

WHO. (2014). *Ensuring human rights in the provision of contraceptive information and services*. http://www.who.int/reproductivehealth/publications/family_planning/human-rights-contraception/en/.

Yamin, A. E. (2014). Promoting equity in health: What role for courts? *Health and Human Rights, 16*(2), 1–9.

Section I

Political Economy of Health and Illness

Sectional Introduction

P. M. Arathi

'Medicine is a social science, and politics is nothing but medicine at a larger scale'; the famous epidemiologist and founder of the concept of social medicine Rudolf Virchow's voice still rings true. There is a long and rich history of progressive activism in medicine, which demands 'health for all'. The question is what have we learned from the past to deal the present to achieve this goal of health for all? Over the past three decades, we have witnessed rapid expansion of the corporate agenda in the field of health and healthcare. Rather than moving towards a system of universal access to healthcare and improvement in other welfare measures, which ensures people's health, there has been an insertion of 'market rationality' which has been counterproductive and pushed us to into a public health crisis in developing countries, especially in India. Present-day debates in reclaiming public health in India reiterate the requirement for a fundamental rethinking of the social and political role of medicine, necessary to fight for a more democratic, less hierarchical models of healthcare and improved social determinants of health to achieve the goal of 'health for all'.

To understand the dynamics of a political economy perspective and the relevance of social medicine in public health which enabled to address the health issues beyond biomedical regime entails the systemic study of relationships among society, disease and medicine. The political economy perspective argues that if the disease is socially derived due to poverty and unequal social relationships, then ill health is an indictment of the political system. Scholars holding this perspective through their academic writings attempt to link macro-social phenomena to more local experiences, meanings and health outcomes. Crucial to all this perspective in public health is a commitment to rigorous empirical research such as ethnographic engagement, historical analysis, sociological and social epidemiological analyses and contextual ethics.

Rudolf Virchow argued that defects of society formed a necessary condition for the emergence of epidemics. He classified certain disease entities as 'crowd diseases' or 'artificial diseases' such as typhus, scurvy, tuberculosis, leprosy, cholera, relapsing fever and some mental disorders. According to this analysis, inadequate social conditions increased the population's susceptibility to changes in climate, infectious agents and other specific causal factors—none of which alone are sufficient to produce an epidemic. For the prevention and eradication of epidemics, social change was as important as medical intervention. The experience of China after the Cultural Revolution showed how the improvement of medicine would eventually prolong human life, but improvement of social conditions could achieve this result even more rapidly and successfully. The contemporary experiences of fighting COVID-19 pandemic by different nation states reiterate the same.

The Russian philosopher Georgi Plekhanov's (1947) concept of the 'laws of digestion' can be considered as an early version of political economy of health. He articulated:

> Once the stomach has been supplied with a certain quantity of food, it sets about its work in accordance with the general laws of stomachic digestion. But can one, with the help of these laws, reply to the question of why savoury and nourishing food descends every day into your stomach, while in mine it is a rare visitor? Do these laws explain why some eat too much, while others starve? It would seem that the explanation must be sought in some other sphere, in the working of some other kind of laws.[1]

The links between social structure and disease become even more urgent, as economic instability, unreliable food supplies, depletion of petroleum, nuclear and toxic chemical wastes, global warming and related problems threaten humanity's very survival.

Another distinction between a political economy perspective and biomedically dominant public health concerns the static versus dynamic, nature of health versus illness, as well as the effect of social context. Political economy framework conceptualizes 'health–illness' as a dialectic process rather than a dichotomous category. As in Fredrich Engels' earlier and Richard Levins' and Richard Lewontin's (1985) more recent interpretations of the dialectic processes in biology, critical epidemiologists have studied disease processes in a contextualized model, considering the changing effects of social conditions over time. The epidemiologic profile of a society or group within a society requires a multilevel analysis of how social conditions such as economic production, reproduction, culture, marginalization and political participation affect the dynamic process of health–illness.

According to the latest Socio Economic and Caste Census (2011) of the Government of India, 73 per cent of the nation's households live in rural areas; of these, 74 per cent earn less than ₹5,000 per month, 56 per cent are landless and 51 per cent work as casual manual labourers. Only 30 per cent are cultivators. Agriculture is declining; farmer's suicides have acquired serious dimensions,[2] job opportunities are scarce[3] and industrial growth, if any, is in its informal sector with unhealthy working conditions. Natural resources are being handed over to the corporate sector[4] and welfare services have been declining with massive cuts in subsidies in food security and the National Mahatma Gandhi Rural Employment Guarantee Scheme that offered partial income security to the poor during lean periods.

Most of the writings in *Social Change* in the past five decades have used political economy perspective as methodological framework for analysis. Among the 183 published articles in the area of public health, 73 of them analyse different health issues such as chronic diseases, malnutrition, the health of elderly, mental health issues and women's health through the lens of the relationship of health issue with the larger political economy of the country. While it is hard to cite all of them, some important articles need to be mentioned here. The political economy of ageing is illustrated by narrating the financial and social security of the elderly (Rajan, 1999); gender bias in ageing issues by Bambawale (1999) and Balakrishnan (1999) brings the notion of development to the issue of the aged. The work on the urban poor of Delhi slums by K. Basu and S. Basu (2000) shows the relationship between coping with poverty and illness. Later works of critiquing the privatization process as part of health sector reforms by Qadeer (2013), Chakrabarthi's (2013) analysis of healthcare industry and market mechanism, Mukhopadhyay's (2013) critical engagement with the National Health Policy as growth fundamentalism and Ghodjekar's interrogation of quality of care (2013) show the role of political economy as a deciding factor in people's health in this country. The strong criticism developed by scholars of public health on the commodification of health service sector through the implementation of the public–private partnership by narrating empirical evidences (Dasgupta et al. 2013; Karpakam et al. 2013; Reddy & Mary, 2013). The scholarly works by Madhavi (2013) and Bhargava (2013) exposed the corporate nexus of the nation state and pharmaceutical companies.

The broad theoretical framework of political economy can help us in a better understanding of the economic, political and socio-historical forces which shape contemporary health problems and our approaches to these problems. Political economy framework's attention to the dynamics of caste, class and gender, and the intersectionalities of these categories of lives of individuals and social groups, makes a political economy approach an important supplement and complement to other macro- and micro-level theories as primary in public health debates in India. Existing socio-economic inequalities and everyday experiences of historic discriminations based on these inequalities reflect the mental well-being of people of India, where complex and multiple webs of stratification exist. To address these issues, a collective thinking beyond a clinical approach of a biomedical framework is essential.

This section consists of six chapters: the first one is by Sharma (1984) who establishes the correlation between social stratification and mortality patterns. This chapter discusses the determinant of mortality transition and inequality in developed and developing countries; an enquiry towards socio-economic epidemiology of mortality. 'Unless a conscious attempt is made to reduce general social inequality, medical inventions and government sponsored health programmes will be of limited use in this regard' (Sharma, 1984, p. 41). This chapter affirms that mortality levels are determined both by the development and availability of medical technology and the social context. The author concludes the importance of a conscious attempt to reduce general social inequality for better use of medical invention and health programmes of government in Indian context where multiple inequalities coexist.

The improvement of the overall health status of people is linked with the socio-economic development of the country. The chapter by Som, Pal and Bharati examines the relationship between the socio-economic development and general improvement of health through a comparison among Indian states and argues that causality works both ways. The chapter shows this relationship between socio-economic development and health status by analysing regional variation of analysing state-level data of the National Family Health Survey and National Sample Survey data. The result shows that the southern states indicate an inverse relationship between an increase in socio-economic development and decrease in morbidities.

Saxena in the third chapter elaborates how the commercialization of the health service sector from service to commodity adversely affects the people's health of this country. This chapter locates the paradigm shift in health service as a tradable commodity after the neoliberal transformation of the global economy with the WTO as its powerful regulator. The author argues that this transition has made a shift in the role of the state in the provisioning of health services with very adverse consequences for the access of healthcare services by the poor and for the quality of the public health system. Saxena strongly argues that India should therefore oppose further liberalization of the health sector in any future negotiations in the WTO and demands that research should be publicly funded and strengthened by intellectual independence and social commitment.

Shenoi's chapter specifically focuses on the legal and ethical aspects of biomedical research in India. By discussing the scope of regulating biomedical research in industry in India, the author identifies legal clinics for students as a possibility of the intersectional relationship between law and ethics. By using case studies of recent advocacy initiatives against unethical clinical trials on marginalized sections, the author shows the complexity of legal and ethical issues, questions and controversies involved in biomedical research today.

Borkar in the fifth chapter writes a thematic review of empathy in a physician–patient relationship and argues that it is a critical input that helps to enhance the effectiveness of a therapeutic process and improves the well-being of the relationship. The author discusses the question of what empathy is, and the relationship between empathy and a patient–physician relationship and its role and a patient-centred approach in empathy. Borkar examines the feasibility of the idea in India's healthcare and discusses the macro-collective dimension of empathy and sectoral changes for that such as universal access to healthcare, fair distribution of financial costs burden for treatments, training the providers with empathy and accountability, quality of care and effectiveness and finally special attention to vulnerable groups such as children, women, the disabled and the aged. This chapter critically examines the role of private sector and the notion of empathy and cites exceptional examples from India.

In Chapter 6, Pal, Diwedi and Kumari analyse changes in the employment pattern and narrate the causal linkages between long working hours and the risk of chronic disease. The authors by using data from a World Health Organization's (2007) study argue that the number of hours has an impact of disease prevalence in people by looking at their post-work histories on morbidities such as diabetes, hypertension, stroke, angina and depression in India. The study reports that the non-manual, urban elderly are considered a high-risk category in almost all diseases selected for the study except depression. The authors suggest an initiative from the government for specific policy measures which will help employees cope with a harmful work schedule.

NOTES

1. https://www.marxists.org/archive/plekhanov/1895/monist/ch05c.htm
2. http://www.ncbi.nlm.nih.gov/pmc/articles/PMC4230648/. Kennedy and King show the links with increasing indebtedness, marginalization of farmers and shift to cash crops.

3. http://isidev.nic.in/pdf/ICSSR_TSP_PPS.pdf. Papola and Sahu present evidence of near stagnation in employment in rural and urban areas.
4. http://www.networkideas.org/ideasact/dec11/pdf/Smita_Gupta.pdf

REFERENCES

Balakrishnan, R. (1999). A note on aging and the elderly in the less developed world. *Social Change*, 29(1&2), 207–210.

Bambawale, U. (1999). Ageing issues and challenges: Gender bias in the care of elderly. *Social Change*, 29(1&2), 126–137.

Basu, K., & Basu, S. (2000). Urban poor women: Coping with poverty and ill-health in slums of Delhi. *Social Change*, 179–191.

Bhargava, M. P. (2013). Drugs and vaccines in healthcare: Problems and possibilities. *Social Change*, 303–309.

Chakrabarthi, I. (2013). The emerging health care 'industry' in India: A public health perspective. *Social Change*, 43, 165–176.

Dasgupta, R., Nandi, S.,, Kanungo K., Nundy M., Murugan G., & Neog, R. (2013). What the good doctor said: A critical examination of design issues of the RSBY through provider perspective in Chhattisgarh, India. *Social Change*, 43, 227–243.

Karpakam, S., Roy, B., Seethappa K. V., & Qadeer, I. (2013). Evidence based planning—A myth or reality: Use of evidence by the planning commission on public–private partnership (PPP). *Social Change*, 43, 213–226.

Madhavi, Y. (2013). Vaccines and vaccine policy for universal health care. *Social Change*, 43, 263–291.

Mukhopadhyay, I. (2013). Universal health coverage: The new phase of neoliberalism. *Social Change*, 43, 177–190.

Plekhanov, G. (1947). *The development of the monist view of history*. International Publishers.

Ghodjekar, ParachinKumar. (2013). Locating 'quality' in health care and universal health care Mosaic. *Social Change*, 43, 191–212.

Qadeer, I. (2013). Universal health care: A trojan horse of neoliberal policies. *Social Change*, 43, 149–164.

Rajan, S. I. (1999). Financial and social security in old age in India. *Social Change*, 29(1&2), 90–125.

Reddy, S., & Mary, I. (2013). Aarogyasri scheme in Andhra Pradesh, India: Some critical reflections. *Social Change*, 43, 245–261.

Sharma, A. K. (1984). Stratification and morality. *Social Change*, 14(3), 41–49.

Chapter 1

Stratification and Mortality*

A. K. Sharma

Due to obvious humanitarian considerations reducing mortality level and improving health and longevity are the commonly accepted goals formulated by the state planning bodies in all parts of the world. It is also recognized that the decline in death rate and the associated decline in morbidity contribute to economic development also through raising the health status and therefore the human productivity. As a result, mortality has declined in all countries and now the WHO has set a goal of 'health for all by 2001'. But at the same time, there are very wide differences both in longevity and health between and within the nations. There is a more than 35 years range of expectation of life at birth at the international level. The developed industrialized and technologically advanced nations are the nations where chance of dying is less, and a greater proportion of people can expect to live longer. On the other hand, in less developed countries, mortality and particularly infant and child mortality rates are high. The fall in death rate in advanced countries has largely affected the age distribution and led to the contemporary problem of ageing. This has also changed significantly the cause of death structure in favour of causes related to old age, accidents and violence. So the world is sharply divided not by the longevity only but also by the causes of deaths. Today the people of the developed countries die from higher levels of cancer, cardiovascular diseases, accidents, violence and diseases related to overconsumption and survive longer and in the poor countries where

* *Social Change* 14, no. 3 (September 1984): 41–49.

people die from malnutrition, diarrhoeal diseases and respiratory infections, expectation of life at birth is low. In this chapter, we are concentrating on the link between stratification and mortality. Health and mortality are functions of the material conditions in which human beings live and act, and the wide international as well as the intra-national differences in mortality ensue from the same factor—inequality of the socio-economic statuses.

Despite the non-availability of sufficient and reliable data on mortality differentials, particularly in the less developed countries, it has been established directly and indirectly that there are great socio-economic differences in the levels and structures of mortality in all the countries and more in the poor countries where over all levels of mortality are relatively higher. These differences have usually been observed in terms of urban rural residence occupational, ethnic, educational income, geographical and racial characteristics, vis-a-vis the demographic traits, for example, age, sex, marital status and family size. It has also been marked that the less developed countries are also characterized by a more rigid stratification system. The point which has already been made in international context stands for the sub-national differentials also: there is a higher expectation of life among the social elite and the longevity of the underprivileged, backward and poor people is low. Since the variables defining dimensions of stratification are oblique and not orthogonal, the high or low mortality sections can be identified only by a proper combination of these dimensions. For example, in a study in Matlab thana area of Comilla District Bangladesh, an inverse relationship between mortality in all the age groups and socio-economic status was observed for each indicator of status years of education of the head of household or mother, occupation, size of dwelling, ownership of cows and use of fixed latrine. But the various indicators of socio-economic status were not highly correlated.[1] In other words, various dimensions of inequality exert independent influence on mortality—the relative contribution of each of these dimensions needs to be established separately for theoretical and policy purposes. Nonetheless, as it has been shown in this chapter, there is some key social inequality in a society on which other forms of inequality are contingent.

DETERMINANT OF MORTALITY TRANSITION AND INEQUALITY DEVELOPED COUNTRIES

Mortality rates were usually high and fluctuating in all parts of the world up to the beginning of the 19th century. At present, though knowledge of mortality trends even for developed countries in distant past is not complete, it is commonly believed that due to wars, famines, floods and epidemics as plague and smallpox, death rates were irregular and high. But due to differences in conditions of living, expectation of life at birth was more in Europe than in the other continents. In many countries of Europe during the 18th century, expectation of life at birth ranged from 35 years to 40 years. On the other hand, during the same period, expectancy of life at birth in many countries of Asia, Africa and Latin America fluctuated around 20 years. In the first phase of mortality decline, death rates started declining in late 19th and early 20th centuries in the economically most advanced countries of Northwest Europe, Central Europe, USA, Canada, Australia and New Zealand. Mortality transition in this part of the world was followed by similar decline in East-South Europe in the beginning of the 20th century. Explanations of the mortality transition in both these phases are similar. The major reduction in death rates in these regions was due to innovation in public health and sanitation as much as or more than increase in per capita income.[2] According to McKeown and Record, the reasons for the decline of mortality in England and Wales during the 19th century are as follows: improved hygienic standards, better diet, variation in the virulence of infections agent and effect of therapy that was restricted mainly to smallpox and produced trivial changes in total death rates.[3] All factors in mortality decline in developed countries, as suggested by the UN,[4] are as follows:

1. Economic development and rising income levels
2. Sanitary reforms and public health measure
3. Social reform
4. Advances in medicine
5. Natural factors (changes in virulence of disease-causing organism or in the resistance of human host, or both)

It is believed that though a general decline in death rates occurred with industrialization starting after middle of the 19th century, the agricultural development had already lowered the peaks of mortality during catastrophes. The agricultural revolution, had increased the productivity and that not only reduced mortality due to reasons related to chronic food shortages, malnutrition and crop failures but that also provided surplus for rapidly growing population. As a matter of fact, industrialization in the West was in many ways result of the agricultural development and secular rise in wages as a consequence of economic development, reduced mortality through better diet. Industrialization increased the efficiency of transportation system that made it easier to exchange agricultural commodities in need, and it also led to general improvement in housing, medical research, clothing and sanitation. At the same time, the concept of community health was developed and due to the efforts of individuals and governments concern for purification of water, removal of dust, personal and community cleanliness started. Woollen undergarments were gradually substituted by cotton which were easier to wash. And in the beginning of this century, the filtration of water was replaced by chlorination which is a more effective method of purifying. A number of social reform measures were also taken in different countries of the West in much of the 19th century to improve the living and working conditions of the people, for example, raising minimum age of employment, shortening working hours, providing for social security and improving housing conditions by imposing occupancy standards, which all contributed to gradual improvement in expectancy of life.

It is difficult to separate out the contributions of economic development, sanitary reforms, social reforms and medical therapy to the fall in death rates in the West during mortality transition. They all worked together. No systematic studies of this kind were conducted in that period. This is a problem that cannot be solved in the absence of data, but nobody can deny that improved medical practices played a very significant role in the reduction of mortality, especially the discoveries of anaesthesia, smallpox vaccine, antiseptic precautions, chemotherapy and use of pharmaceuticals. However, most of them became available only in the present century, and a fall in mortality in 18th–19th centuries was due to factors unrelated to medical advances.

Some writers believe that in addition to the above-mentioned reasons, decline in the virulence of disease-causing organism or increase in the resistance of the human host or both also contributed to mortality decline from smallpox, scarlet fever, diphtheria, plague and possibly some other diseases. However, we do not know much about such natural factors.

It is also maintained

whatever the broad categories used for analysis, it is clear that underlying the multitude of individual factors responsible for the reductions in mortality have been the more or less continuous economic advances resulting from the so called agricultural and industrial revolutions; this progress made possible the development and applications in technology, public health, sanitation and medicine which were crucial for substantial mortality decline.[5]

In many low-mortality and developed countries, life expectancy at birth is around 7 years for males and 75 years for females. Any significant extension of longevity in these countries is now generally not foreseen, though it is in principle possible to eliminate or reduce some causes of deaths with further technological advancements.

In the early 1950s, it was thought that social class inequality in mortality is a feature of early stages of industrialization and with the economic and technological developments, not only the overall death rate but also the inequality with respect to death will be reduced. People felt that the death rate is a simple function of medicine and the development of medical system and the easy availability of health services to people are sufficient for reducing chance of dying in various sections of the society. But the social differences in death rate do still exist in the low-mortality and developed countries and cannot be explained simply in terms of the differential availability of medical treatment.

Inequality in respect of death is only one dimension of social inequality. It was an illusion to imagine that one could be eliminated without the other. Today that illusion has been destroyed. That does not mean that the present situation must be accepted. Inequality in respect of death is still one of the most disgraceful consequences of social inequality. Its disappearance must remain our aim. Obviously, however, this aim cannot be achieved by the health service alone.[6]

There are problems in measuring differential mortality and status. But the available tools and techniques have often documented noticeable differences in mortality rates by age, sex, marital status, social class, occupation urban–rural residence, nature of employment, income and education. A number of causes of deaths, for example, alcoholism, accidents, suicides, cancer and cardiovascular diseases in developed countries are related to social class. The inequality of longevity arises from social class differences in true morbidity, felt morbidity, medical consumption and behavioural factors associated with change in social status. Now it is felt that death is a complex function of healthcare, genetic heritage, behaviour, environment and geographical factors. Simple medical care approach to inequality in longevity is therefore inadequate.

LESS DEVELOPED COUNTRIES

In the less developed countries of the triad of Asia, Africa and Latin America, mortality decline started only in the post-war period in this century. Expectancy of life at birth in the first decade of the century in these continents was below that in the West up to 1850 and also below contemporary East-South Europe. This has also been observed that mortality decline in less developed countries that began in the 1940s was neutral with respect to economic growth and its trends matched or even exceeded the maximum decline ever found in the industrialized and low mortality countries of the world. The basic factors of mortality decline in less developed countries were (a) availability of public health and disease control that are today more cost-effective, easily importable, and unhindered by social and structural obstacles and (b) the interest taken by respective governments and their public health agencies and international technical assistance, independent of the fiscal systems of the countries.[7] Although the strategy of control of infectious diseases worked, it was expected that expectancy of life at birth can easily be raised to 40 years, but it is harder to increase the expectancy of life from 50 years to 60 years than from 30 years to 40 years and it will be harder still to go from 60 years towards 70 years, at least at the present stage of medical technology. In other words, above 50–55 years, further extension in longevity will be slower.

However, due to implicit assumptions of 'irreversibility', 'continuity' and 'similarity of mortality patterns', it was expected that expectancy of life at birth will continue to increase even though at diminishing rates, and similar to the experience of North, there will be disproportionately mere gains in probability of survival at early ages.[8]

Contrary to above expectations in many less developed countries, the levels of mortality started showing signs of stagnation, retardation in the pace of decline or even reversal of the trend in 1970s, with lower levels of expectancy of life at birth and chances of survival during infancy and childhood than expected. Commenting on Asian situation, Ruzicka and Hansluwka maintain that (a) in a number of countries in South and East Asia such as Sri Lanka, Western Malaysia, India, Indonesia, the Philippines and Thailand, there was no progress in infant and childhood mortality in the 1970s; (b) differentials between subgroups did not decline and rather increased as the disadvantaged groups in general could not benefit equally from the mortality and morbidity control programmes and (c) slowing in gains in life expectancy and economic growth started simultaneously. In this period, according to them, the growth of income slowed mainly due to some uncontrollable factors as increasing bills of energy imports, worldwide inflation, unemployment and decreasing foreign aid. At the same time, a number of these countries experienced rapid population growth that affected healthcare, education, environmental sanitation, housing and transportation badly.[9] They have suggested a list of the following causes which are responsible for the present-day trends in mortality in these countries:

1. Changes in population structure
2. Emphasis on curative rather than preventive strategies of healthcare
3. Unfavourable supply and distribution of food

Death rate at the national level is a function of composition of population and mortality rates specific for the relevant criterion of the composition. And the composition may be defined in demographic, social or economic terms, for example, age, sex, social class, occupation, income, etc. Therefore, the trend in national death rate is determined by both true changes in mortality risks and changes in stratification.

It is possible, say Ruzicka and Hansluwka, that in many developing countries the growth-oriented national economic policies adopted in the recent past have failed to reduce the gap between rich and poor; rather, in some countries, increase in gross domestic product has led to increase in income inequality also; the rich have become richer and poor have become poorer.[10] Since mortality in the less advantaged sections of many South and East Asian countries exceeds the national average by a factor of two or three and sometimes by an even greater margin,[11] increase in the size of poor population will push the rational death rate upwards. In the recent past, in these countries, increasing economic gap may, therefore, have offset the influence of improvement in general health conditions on the national death rate. The problem of poverty has become more acute because the modern economic policies are working at a time when in the poor countries the traditional fealty or kinship systems are being replaced by modern contractual relations at an unprecedented rate. Palloni has similarly argued, though in a different context, that trends in infant mortality do not represent genuine change over time because infant mortality is strongly related to mother's age and the relation is U-shaped or sometimes J-shaped (if mothers aged 15–19 years and 20–24 years are excluded from the analysis).[12]

This observation necessitates that to explain stagnation in mortality levels in the less developed countries, a detailed investigation of changes in dimensions and quantum of inequality should be undertaken. The significance of inequality is increased further because in a rigidly divided society with emphasis on curative rather than preventive strategies of healthcare, the distribution of availability of medical resources is in itself unequal. And if the emphasis is shifted to preventive strategics and community health, the disadvantaged groups will be benefitted in greater proportion. Sri Lanka is one country with low per capita income of South Asian standard but with the expectation of life at birth of East Asian standard. Mortality in Sri Lanka after 1947 declined in a continuous manner due largely to tremendous extension of education, development of public health conscience and free milk and mid-day meal for schoolchildren. The basic health hazards in the poor countries are inadequate food, malnutrition, absence of sanitation, superstitions and non-availability of potable water—in general, unmet minimum needs. The Western model of healthcare is unlikely to effectively deal with the mortality and morbidity problems of these countries. It should now be realized that the good experience of other countries cannot be borrowed mechanically, and health prospects cannot be isolated from changes in sociocultural milieu.[13]

After analysing data on mortality trends in Latin American countries in 1970, Palloni has concluded:

> The influence of socio-economic factors on mortality at various ages is paramount in any prognosis for further reductions. Social and economic factors related to the rate of adult literacy appear to be by far the most relevant; they are surely among those to be manipulated if any further improvements are to be realised.[14]

On the basis of secondary and fragmentary data, Gaisie has also argued that 'poor health conditions are self-perpetuating not only because of sluggish economic growth but also because of institutions and development policies that inhibit the spread of health and medical facilities to a large proportion of tropical Africans.'[15]

We have noted that during the period from 1945 to 1960 when rapid improvement in mortality was noticed in a large number of less developing countries, it was largely due to relatively cheap and effective technologies of the control of disease vectors, immunization and effective treatment of diseases. The health programmes which concentrated on the control of infectious diseases were commonly assisted by international agencies or the developed countries. They did not have the problems of logistics and did not face the institutional constraints on a large scale. Consequently, with increased scientific communication, international cooperation and availability of insecticides like DDT, antibiotics like penicillin and vaccines like BCG, epidemics became rare and less dangerous and together with the disappearance of large-scale famines contributed to the extension of longevity. Diseases such as malaria, smallpox, yellow fever, cholera, tuberculosis and measles were under control. But soon it became clear that without socio-economic development, the reduction in mortality can only be limited. Further, if a disease control programme depends largely on the foreign aid, its success and survival become highly susceptible to the laws of political economy and international order.

The failure of malaria eradication programme in India is partly due to such reason. As the diseases have strong relations with nutrition, environment and attitudes, the public health programmes cannot succeed without progress in education, road connectivity, basic administrative infrastructure necessary for public health measures and economic development. It has been learnt from the Cuban experience that modern chemotherapeutic agents, sulphonamides, antibiotics and other insecticides cannot work for a long time without development and effective government.[16] And changes in economic conditions are followed by changes in mortality levels. In this light, it deserves our attention that it is only smallpox that is eradicated completely, and endemic plague, cholera, tuberculosis, bacterial pneumonia, poliomyelitis, diphtheria, tetanus, measles, gastrointestinal, respiratory diseases and malaria are still prevalent in many poor countries and increasing in a number of cases. The following list of causes of constraints to malaria control presented by the WHO[17] clearly shows the importance of socio-economic factors in declining mortality.

1. Increased costs of material and equipments and global inflation
2. Inadequacy of administrative and general services to support anti-malaria activities
3. Shortage of trained manpower
4. Rudimentary health infrastructure in developing countries and limited involvement of rural health services
5. Ecological and ethological factors that increase man–vector contact
6. Difficulty to access malaria-infected areas for natural or security reason
7. Uncontrolled development of irrigation, deforestation and human settlement in malaria-infected areas and increased breeding of 'anopheles' vectors subsequent to construction
8. Inadequate knowledge of the cost-effectiveness of the various control measures under different local conditions
9. Resistance of many vectors to insecticides that could be safely used in human dwellings
10. Vector behaviour leading to avoidance of contact with the indoor insecticide deposit on walls

11. Development of resistance in malaria parasites, particularly *Plasmodium Falciparum* to certain anti-malarial drugs, etc.

12. Inadequate research support

In brief, the medical approach to reduction in mortality in isolation is inadequate both in developed and developing countries. For the maximum gains, it should be supplemented by environmental development and socio-economic epidemiology.

SOCIO-ECONOMIC EPIDEMIOLOGY OF MORTALITY

The issues of socio-economic epidemiology of mortality were raised and debated greatly for the first time in the UN/WHO meeting on socio-economic determinants and consequences of mortality held at Mexico in June 1979. Epidemiology has been defined as the study of events in population/field to suggest ways for their explanations and control. It enjoys the use of varieties of techniques drawn from statistics, demography and social and clinical sciences. An attempt is made to relate the events to groups in population and time. According to the concept of socio-economic epidemiology of mortality, health and mortality levels can also be changed by altering the class structure and not only by medical action: the changes in death rates at the macro level depend significantly on the development of the poor backward, malnourished and disadvantaged groups.[18] Figure 1.1 shows the systematic relation between changes in class structures and level of mortality.

There are some direct and indirect links between changes in social class structure and changes in level of mortality. The direct link is simple. Even if the social class-specific mortality rates remain constant over time, changes in class structure will produce changes in the overall health and mortality status. In other words, if the proportion of subgroups, defined in terms of age, sex or social class, in which mortality is high, increases, mortality at the national level will also increase. It is established that age pattern of mortality is U-shaped in developing countries and J-shaped in developed countries; the expectation of life at birth is generally higher for females than males except in the countries of South Asia, and mortality and social status

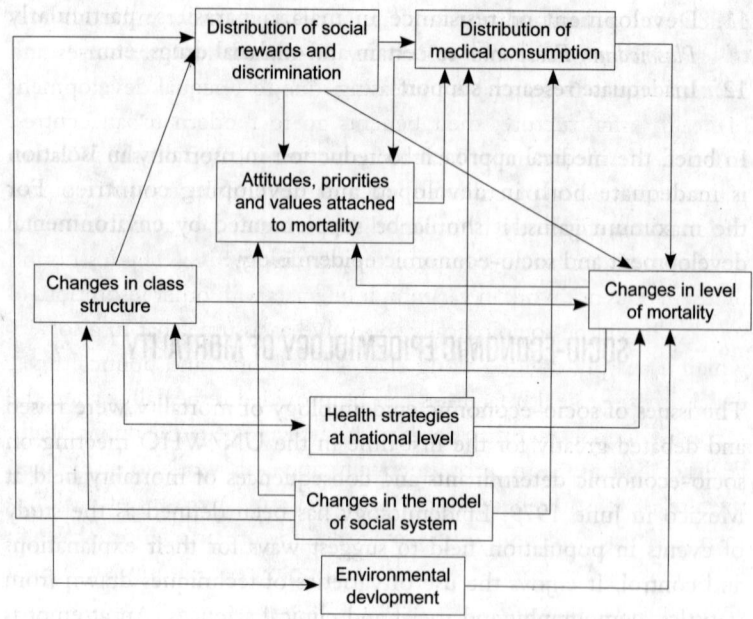

Figure 1.1 *Region between Changes in Class Structure and Level of Mortality*

Source: Social Change 14, no. 3 (September 1984): 41–49.

are negatively associated. Therefore, the level of mortality is sensitive to dependency ratio, sex ratio and proportion of people below poverty line. For example, in the countries in which urban mortality is less than rural mortality, the process of urbanization and transfer of population from rural to urban areas will in itself lead to reduction in mortality if both urban and rural mortality rates remain constant. Such changes in age, sex and social class compositions of populations are largely independent of the growth and effectiveness of medical system and exercise their influence on mortality. At the same time, changes in class structure influence mortality through affecting nutritional level, medical consumption, environmental development, health strategies at the national level, and model of social system. In a large number of developing countries, due to their colonial past, there is an emphasis on curative and hospital-based side rather than preventive side of health policies and a disproportionate share of the investment in health goes to cities. Even where the availability of trained doctors, nurses and health facilities in general is increasing, due to unequal development of health infrastructure, their benefits go to modern urban centres. Since the development of health manpower is based on the Western pattern, the medical practitioners and their methodologies and resources which work efficiently in urban elite are either not available to the disadvantaged and rural groups or they are ineffective. The institution of health does not work in vacuum. It interacts with other institutions of society. It will be sociologically too naive to assume that in a society which is sharply divided along class, caste, ethnic and political lines, equal access to health facilities can be provided, especially when the supply is much shorter than demand. In such a society, the public health facilities will be distributed unequally and will work to strengthen the already existing inequalities. In Mao's terms, ministry of health in such a society will be ministry of health for urban overlords. When legal, religious, cultural, economic and political institutions are used and manipulated by the elite, health institutions too are vulnerable to be exploited by the elite to maintain their supremacy. One important way to change the distribution of health facilities is to change the class structure through changing the model of society.

The distribution of medical consumption is unequal not simply because the development of health infrastructures reflects class inequalities but more because the different classes inherit the different cultural systems with differences in attitudes, priorities and values with regard to morbidity and mortality. People in less developed countries are divided by their attitudes towards scientific and traditional medical systems. Scientific and all traditional medical systems exist in a cultural context and serve important social functions. The majority of people belonging to rural areas and poor sections rely more on traditional systems even in cases of serious diseases and even when they have access to modern medical system.[19] Majority of women in rural areas of UP in India preferring to avail the services of traditional *dais* at the time of childbirth rather than trained midwife is one such example.[20] Traditional medicines have been more successful than modern medicines in certain areas and are claimed to cause least side effects. In many areas, such as hypertension, cold, common stomach disorders and stone formation in kidneys, even urban educated people in India are increasingly depending on homoeopathy, traditional systems and yoga, and many people, even in urban areas, have some doubt in the efficacy of scientific medicine.

Cost-effectiveness of the various health strategies is an important moral as well as scientific problem.

> We must all die sooner or later. The crucial question is not the prolongation of life or the avoidance of death but rather unnecessary death. The fact of socioeconomic differentials in mortality means that success has been achieved in one segment of the community which is not available to other segments. Though the concentration has been on mortality, this must set in the context not only of when one dies but of how one lives.[21]

> In the last analysis, from the point of view of those in health services, the issue is a moral one. They can choose to go on, as they have done in large measures, disregarding the issue, in the calm consciousness that they are doing their best for the individual patient. They can oppose or acquiesce to pressures from without to change. Or they can actively take part in seeking to transform the health services so that they do not continue to live in a society where the ratio of infant mortality in the highest social class to that in the lowest social class is 100:233.[22]

There are a number of questions related to the formation of strategies to reduce mortality and their cost effectiveness. Sometimes they involve moral considerations and justification. What should be the priority structure of research and services for different diseases and causes of mortality? Can the techniques of operations research help in budget allocation for cancer and children's tetanus? The two affect the different sections of the people, the two will have large differences in input–output ratios, and they require different social organizational approaches. Should we save an old man from cancer for a few years and allow thousands of children (mainly rural) to die from ordinary diarrhoeal diseases and tetanus? How can we justify building most modern medical service and research centres with most modern capital using technology if under the present system they practically serve only the elite and exclude the majority of population which is malnourished, without access to simple medical system, education and suitable employment? On the other hand, as the expectancy of life increases, the causes of mortality also change and the proportion of cancer, neoplasm and cardiovascular diseases increases, as has recently happened in Hong Kong, Singapore, Japan and Sri Lanka. The treatment of these causes is more complex and costlier than of many infectious diseases.

Sickness or health conditions also in turn affect the standards of living and class situation of individuals. Repeated sickness causes undernourishment and makes the individuals further susceptible to infection in a disease-hidden environment.[23] In brief, such is the nature of mortality–inequality relation.

The importance of the role of the model of social system in health development cannot be overemphasized. India and China, liberated at nearly same time (India in 1947 and China in 1949) started with similar economic, demographic and structural conditions: heavy population pressure on limited arable land, subsistence farming with semi-feudal land tenure relationships, continuous subdivision and fragmentation of smallholdings, widespread rural underemployment and unemployment, inadequate transportation and marketing facilities and a high rate of illiteracy. But China had achieved a much lower level of death rate, including infant mortality rate in the 1970s than India. The average Chinese death rate in this decade was only 7 per 1,000: the present life span is above 68 years. In India, in the same period, death rate was around 15 per 1,000: the present life span is about 52 years. The present differences in demographic conditions of the two countries should be due to the difference in the methods adopted for rural modernization and health planning. However, the main explanatory factors for relative success in China is not strategic but historical. The ideology of modernization in China has developed out of the daily activities of the workers which in true dialectic spirit, in turn, changed their world.

Peasants who overthrow their landlords not only change the class structure and institutions of their society. In the revolutionary process they also change their own conceptions of the world—including their values, needs, abilities and aspirations. The economic policies flow out of the interaction between human and material development which is a revolutionary process with deep historical roots. It appears that the Chinese peasants have not only achieved control over their own lives, but also an understanding of the causes of their poverty. This revolutionary process has unfolded in China in complex ways, while, it has been developing more slowly and in different forms in India.[24]

It has been shown that employment issue in rural China is much less serious than in India. The meaning of decreasing urban rural differences is also different in Chinese context where it has been recognized that not the absolute difference in income but access to tools of modernization, industrialization and mechanization of agriculture will in the long run promote urban–rural equality.[25] The major approach to provide employment in China is to develop more labour-intensive trades such as light industry, commerce and service trades, which need less investment but can have quick returns. A more diversified rural economy has been developed and enterprises run by communes or production brigades have been expanded. In the recent past, enterprises of collective ownership and individually run trades have also been promoted to some extent.[26] At the same time, people's health conditions have been improved with the popularization of free medical treatment among the workers and functionaries and cooperative medical services among the peasants.[27] Hsu's thesis is as follows: 'The health care system of a country tends to be consistent with, and supported by, the political structure of the country, and that one cannot thoroughly understand a country's health care system without understanding its interaction with the political structure which supports it.'[28]

There are three components of China's healthcare system: a state healthcare sector, a military healthcare sector and a rural healthcare sector. The state sector is responsible for the provincial-, city- and country-level hospitals and delivers free medical health services to workers of state-run enterprises, government functionaries and schoolteachers. The military sector is responsible for the army and also provides substantial technical assistance to the rural healthcare sectors. The rural healthcare sector of China is unique in the world and reflects the uniqueness of China's rural political economy. It is a cooperative medical system and relies largely on the barefoot doctors. It is organized at the level of production brigades. Although it is assisted by the state and military sectors, it is basically run by contributions from individual brigade members and collective welfare funds of the communes and brigades. Therefore, it is highly integrated into conditions of the brigades in the context of the decentralized nature of rural economy. The barefoot doctors are the local members of brigades with minor educational level, and they are given a short training in the treatment of common diseases. They participate both in health and farm work—and in their medical work they have a high degree of professional autonomy but, at the same time, they are subject to double administrative controls from government and party. In addition to their other commitments, they are also supposed to involve in political and ideological works. Their work on farms is expected to maintain their enthusiasm to serve the fellow workers and raise their political consciousness. It has been argued that

> The barefoot doctors are valuable precisely because they are 'barefoot'. Because they are 'barefoot' with dust on their feet and medicine chest on their shoulders, they have the poor lower-middle peasants and other commune masses in their hearts. Just imagine once they wear 'leather shoes' how can they serve those commune masses who work primarily in the fields?—The recalcitrant element in the party taking the capitalist road advocates that the barefoot doctors wear shoes. Their real intention is to make them deviate from chairman Mao's revolutionary line, to make them wear the shoes of revisionism and walk on the road of capitalism.[29]

It is not our aim to critically analyse the Indian rural health sector at this juncture, but it should be mentioned that the health system in rural India is mainly sponsored by government. It is a system developed from outside and city experience. It is unreliable, inadequate and biased. If at all it provides basic services mainly to rural elite. Colonial history and Westernization have affected badly the indigenous medical systems. The masses have very limited access to health facilities, and they largely depend on quacks, charlatans and witchcrafts that we have discussed elsewhere.[30]

CONCLUSION

Mortality levels are determined both by the development and the availability of medical technology and the social context. Due to former coupled with some improvement in economic and social conditions, mortality levels have declined by varying ratios in different parts of the less developed countries. But the stagnation of the 1970s has indicated the limits of medical approach to mortality and health. Further improvement in expectancy of life at birth in these countries will depend mainly on the changes in the aspects of social class structure. Unless a conscious attempt is made to reduce general social inequality, medical inventions and government-sponsored health programmes will be of limited use in this regard.

NOTES

1. Stan D' Souza and Abbas Bhuiya, 'Mortality Differentials in Rural Bangladesh', *Population and Development Review* 8, no. 4 (1982): 753–770.
2. G. J. Stolnitz, 'Recent Mortality Trends in Latin America, Asia and Africa', *Population Studies* 19, no. 2 (1965): 117–138.
3. Thomas McKeown and R. G. Record, 'Reasons for the Decline of Mortality in England and Wales during the Nineteenth Century', *Population Studies* 16, no. 2 (1962): 94–122.
4. United Nations, *The Determinants and Consequences of Population Trends* (Vol. 1; New York, NY: United Nations, 1973), 146–153.
5. Ibid., 146.
6. Viilfai Jacques, 'Socio-Economic Determinants of Mortality in Industrialized Countries', *Population Bulletin of the United Nations* 13 (1980): 26–34; and Bourgeois Pichat and Jean (Eds.), *Socio-Economic Differential in Mortality in Industrialized Societies* (C1CRED; Paris: UN, 1981).
7. Stolnitz, 'Recent Mortality Trends in Latin America', 117–138.
8. Alberto Palloni, 'Mortality in Latin America: Emerging Patterns', *Population and Development Review* 7, no. 4 (1981).
9. L. T. Ruzicka and Harald Hansluwka, 'Mortality Transition in South and East Asia: Technology Confronts Poverty', *Population and Development Review* 8, no. 3 (1982): 567–588.
10. Ibid., 569–570.
11. L. T. Ruzicka and Harald Hansluwka, 'Mortality in Selected Countries of South and East Asia', in *Mortality in South East Asia*, WHO (Manila: WHO, 1982).
12. Alberto Palloni, 'A Review of Infant Mortality Trends in Selected Underdeveloped Countries', *Population Studies* 35, no. 1 (1981): 118.
13. WHO, *Health Trends and Prospects in Relation to Population and Development* (Bucharest: WHO, 1974), 19–30.
14. Palloni, 'A Review of Infant Mortality Trends in Selected Underdeveloped Countries', 645.

15. S. K. Gaisie, 'Some Aspect of Socio Economic Determinants of Mentality in Tropical Africa', *Population Bulletin of the United Nation 13* (1980): 16–25.

16. S. Diaz-Briquets, 'Determinants of Mortality Transition in Developing Countries Before and After the Second World War: Some Evidence for Cuba', *Population Studies* 36, no. 3 (1981): 399–412.

17. WHO, *Expert Committee on Malaria: Technical Report Series* 640 (1979): 10–11.

18. WHO, 'The Inequality of Death', *WHO Chronicle* 34, no. 1 (1980): 9–15.

19. Gaisie, 'Some Aspect of Socio Economic Determinants of Mentality in Tropical Africa', 22–26.

20. A. K. Sharma, *A Longitudinal Study of Fertility and Family Planning in Rural Areas* (PhD thesis [Unpublished]); Mumbai: IIT Bombay, 1980).

21. Aaron Antonovsky, 'Implications of Socio-economic Differentials in Mortality for the Health System', *Population Bulletin of the United Nations* 13 (1980): 50.

22. Ibid., 52.

23. L. T. Ruzicka, 'Implications of Mortality Trends and Differentials in the ESCAP Region', *Third Asian and Pacific Population Conference* (Colombo, 1982).

24. Jon Sigurdson, 'Development of Rural Areas in India and China', *Amblo* 5, no. 3 (1978): 99–107.

25. Jon Sigurdson, 'Rural Industrialization: A Comparison of Development Planning in China and India', *World Development* 6 (1978): 667–680.

26. Jim Hua, Wei Mini, Zhou Jin, and Zhou Zheng, 'Population and Other Problems', *China Today, Beijing Review* (1981): 61–66.

27. Zhao Zhipei, 'China Population Policy', Paper presented in Regional Seminar on Strategies for Meeting Basic Socio-economic Needs and for Increasing Women's Participation Development to Achieve Population Goals, ESCAP (Pattaya, 1982), 15.

28. R. C. Hsu, 'The Political Economy of Rural Health Care in China', *The Review of Radical Political Economics* 9, no. 1 (1977): 134–140.

29. *Hung-Chi* 4 (1976): 9.

30. A. K. Sharma, *A Longitudinal Study of Fertility and Family Planning in Rural Areas*.

Chapter 2

Do Socio-economic Development and Improvement of Health Go Together?*

A Comparison among Indian States

Suparna Som, Manoranjan Pal and
Premananda Bharati

INTRODUCTION

The improvement of overall health status of the people in a country is very much linked with the socio-economic development in the country. Improvement of health is one of the primary goals of development. Health is thus only one aspect of development. The human development index (HDI) proposed by the United Nations has three components. One component is the life expectancy at birth. It may be a difficult task to see the link between the socio-economic development and the improvement of health in a vast country like India, where there is much regional diversity almost in all aspects of life besides being overpopulated. It cannot be denied that there has been economic growth over the last few decades. There has been improvement in the overall standard of living. The level of poverty has declined. So has been the improvement of health situation. The life expectancy at birth has increased by 17 years in the last five decades

---

* *Social Change* 40, no. 4 (December 2010): 525–543.

and reached 64 years in 2001. But there are considerable differences in the levels of attainments of people on various aspects of well-being. Not only there are state-wise differences but also there are differences between rural and urban areas. In fact, most indicators show a dismal situation for people residing in rural areas.

Poverty and inequality have a negative impact on the health of population. Past studies have documented a strong association between income inequality and excess mortality (Ben-Sholmo et al., 1996; Kaplan et al., 1996). The most important societal factor related to health appears to be the degree of poverty (Haines & Smith, 1997; Reutter, 1995; Warden, 1998). British scientists have identified the social gradient, stress, early life, social exclusion, work, unemployment, social support, etc., as key determinants of health. Economic inequality plays an important role in both increasing the extent of poverty and weakening the social structures that support the health (Raphael, 2001). Work of Purohit (2004) depicts the prevalence of inequity favouring high-income group of states in terms of healthcare resources.

Slow and unequal social mobilization in various parts of India led to an uneven economic growth. Caste and social polarization, literacy and educational levels, natural resources, levels of corruption, role of political leadership, etc., are the factors responsible for creating differences among the states in India (Ahluwalia, 2000). This basic inequality was magnified by the rapid but unequal economic growth that India has witnessed in the last two decades. Amid the rising standards of living lie pockets of terrible poverty and deprivation.

Human development, in this chapter, means raising the level of well-being. It is reflected through a range of indicators. Some of these indicators signify development (e.g., literacy rates and per capita income), while others just mean the opposite (e.g., the degrees of inequality and poverty). The different health indicators also have similar contrasts. Since the status of health is viewed differently for different groups of persons such as children, women and old persons, the indicators are also taken differently. There are, of course, some indicators that can be applied to all persons. The health situation of a child can be addressed by weight-for-height, weight-for-age, height-for-age, infant mortality, occurrence of diarrhoea, etc. Women's health situation in a region can be measured by maternal mortality, body mass index (BMI), presence of anaemia, etc., and the overall health situation can be measured by life expectancy at birth.

The limitation of the study is that as the data set is secondary and the periods do not match, there is a limited scope for multiple comparisons.

The main objective of this chapter is to find out the status of human development among the major states in India and relate it to the status of health of the corresponding states. The main points are a s follows:

1. To see whether the health and development indicators vary over different states
2. To see whether there are urban-rural differences of key development determinants and women-child health for the major states of India
3. To see whether the development and the improvement of health is complementary to each other

MATERIALS AND METHODS

The health data primarily have been taken from state-level National Family Health Surveys (NFHS-2 and NFHS-3). In addition, data from alternative sources include National Sample Survey Organization (NSSO). To maintain the uniformity, we have taken data only from the major states. The states are Andhra Pradesh (AP), Assam (As), Bihar (Bi), Gujarat (Gu), Karnataka (Ka), Kerala (Ke), Madhya Pradesh (MP), Maharashtra (Ma), Orissa (Or), Punjab (Pu), Rajasthan (Ra), Tamil Nadu (TN), Uttar Pradesh (UP) and West Bengal (WB). The NFHS and NSS data are known to be the most authentic sources for the national- as well as state-level information. NSS data are available for a long period of time, whereas NFHS data are on child and women health and are available for three periods. The present study uses the NFHS-2 and NFHS-3 data corresponding to the years 1998-1999 and 2005-2006 and 55th round NSS data corresponding to 1999-2000, which is contemporary to NFHS-2 data. The comparisons have been done mainly between NFHS-2 and NSS-55 data. However, some results from NFHS-3 data, especially the health parameters, have also been discussed in this chapter. Indicators are chosen both for development and health-related attainment of the society. Four items indicating overall development have been chosen. The first two are the head count ratio (HCR) and the real mean consumption (RMC) indicating economic development and the other two are the literacy rate and the sex ratio (adult) showing the other two dimensions of development.

HCR is defined as the percentage of people below poverty line. The data of HCR are taken from NSS 55th round, that is, for the year 1999-2000. The other aspect of development taken here is RMC. RMC measures the economic status of the people in the region. The RMC value for different states in India is taken from the 53rd round (1997) data of NSS. The time period of 53rd round of NSS is very close to that of NFHS-2 round. The adult sex ratio used in this chapter is taken from NSS record of 55th round. Sex ratio, that is, female-male ratio (FMR) is defined by the ratio of number of females to number of males. It is also sometimes expressed as number of females per thousand males. In an ideal situation, FMR should have some value greater than 1 but very close to 1, because for the same situation age-specific mortality rate is less for women. The FMR value is regarded as an indicator of development. The states with higher value of FMR are regarded as more developed. The data on literacy level were taken from NFHS-2. Sex-wise literacy level is not considered here.

There are reasons why we might expect to find urban-rural difference in these development parameters. In India, more than 70 per cent people live in rural areas. Strong differences in environment and individual opportunities exist between urban and rural areas. So rural-urban differences have pronounced impact in the development and health status in different states of India. Greater the gap, lower is supposed to be the overall improvement of that state.

Among the health outcomes, infant mortality and some health-related morbidity indicators are taken to measure the health status. For child health, acute respiratory infection (ARI), diarrhoea, child anaemia and nutritional status of children are taken. The weight-for-height index examines body mass in relation to body length. Two standard deviations below the median of the reference population in terms of weight–for–height are taken as the cut–off point. Children whose weight–for–height are below this cut–off point are too thin and are considered to be malnourished or wasted. The percentage in this category indicates the prevalence of acute undernutrition. Acute respiratory infection, primarily pneumonia, continues to be a leading cause of mortality in infants and children. Diarrhoea is also one of the most common killers of children under the age of 5.

Source of drinking water is one of the leading causes of diarrhoea. The children of the household with open drinking source are more susceptible to diarrhoea. Nutritional status plays a vital role in deciding the health status, particularly in children. A child's nutritional status also depends on the economic status of the household to which the child belongs. Access to food is a necessary condition for food security. Nutritional deficiencies give rise to various morbidities, which in turn may lead to mortality. It should be mentioned that the children whose nutritional status is measured are coming from the age group of 3 years or less. The International Conference on Primary Health Care held in Alma–Ata in 1978 was the first global forum to consider how child mortality could be reduced by systematic development of a primary health care system. Women whose age belongs to the age group of 15 to 49 years, that is, women of reproductive age group, are considered here.

Anaemia and low BMI are considered to be vital for women's status of health. The BMI is defined as the weight in kg divided by the square of height measured in metres (kg/m^2). The value of BMI less than $18.5 \ kg/m^2$ is considered as chronic energy deficiency (CED). These indices excluded women who were pregnant at the time of survey or women who gave birth during the two months preceding the survey. Since the CED is mainly because of the prolonged low level of food and nutrition intake, higher proportion of women with a BMI below $18.5 \ kg/m^2$ is thought to be the result of lower economic position of the state. Anaemia is characterized by the low level of haemoglobin in the blood. It may have detrimental effect on the health of women and children, and may be an underlying cause of maternal mortality. Moreover, anaemia results in an increased risk of premature delivery and low birth weight (Seshadri, 1997).

We have three distinct types of state-wise data presented in this chapter. These are (a) the morbidity patterns of children, (b) the morbidity patterns of women and (c) the development parameters. One can find if there is a relation between these variables: pair-wise and also between groups. In other words, we would like to know whether the states with indications of high development have also the low morbidity patterns, and also whether the morbidity patterns of children and women go together when compared state wise (Table 2.6). The correlation coefficients between the variables throw some lights on these relations. However, to find out the relations between groups of variables, one has to find out canonical correlations. Here, we first find linear combinations of variables within each group and then find the correlation coefficient between the two linear combinations. Linear combinations are taken in such a way that it gives the maximum correlation. Thus, the value of the canonical correlation must be greater than or equal to the maximum of the correlations between all the pairs of variables such that one variable is taken from each of the two groups. The problem with the canonical correlation is that it always gives the non-negative value as in the case of multiple correlation coefficient. Second, much degree of freedom is lost due to taking linear combinations. Observe that we have only 14 states, whereas the number of variables in the groups are 10, 8 and 4 for children morbidity, development and women morbidity, respectively. This is because rural and urban sectors are considered separately for each variable. Thus, it is not possible to find canonical correlation between the groups of children morbidity and development. If we further subdivide states by separating out the rural and urban sectors, then it is possible to find out the canonical correlation between any two groups. To overcome these problems of canonical correlations, we have resorted to another method by ranking the states according to morbidity and development parameters in both the sectors. Each item of child health outcomes is then ranked separately according to their values. Ranking is done in such a manner that the same highest rank (i.e., rank = 1) is given for the value that is most favourable to development. In cases where low proportion represents favourable condition for development, for example, low percentage of ARI or diarrhoea, the lowest value has been given rank 1, and where the highest proportion represents for betterment like that of literacy level, then the highest value has been given the rank 1. When the ranks of each item are put for each group, the ranks for all items are added. Now this variable is again ranked to get a representative rank value of the group. In this way, we get a representative rank of each group. It is given in Table 2.12. The Spearman's rank correlations were then computed using SPSS package for rural and urban sectors separately and also jointly. The SPSS package also gives the significance of the rank correlations. Since the direction of the ranks is taken care of while taking the ranks, the rank correlation will obviously give positive values for most cases.

RESULTS

Child Morbidity Parameters

State-wise percentage distribution of child health parameters in India is given in Table 2.1. Child health is seen to be better in the urban areas for most states. It is quite surprising that in some states such as Madhya Pradesh, Maharashtra, Punjab, Orissa, Andhra Pradesh and even in Kerala, the proportion of children affected with diarrhoea is higher in urban area than in rural area. In fact, there are many states in which children of urban areas suffer more from acute respiratory disease and diarrhoea than the children of rural areas. The results of NFHS-3 also confirm the same (Table 2.4). For a better understanding, we have computed the difference between urban percentage and rural percentage for each state along with their ranks (Tables 2.2 and 2.5).

In case of Kerala, rural sector is in a better position than urban sector for most parameters. The difference between rural and urban sectors is quite noticeable in case of Gujarat, Assam, Maharashtra, West Bengal and Karnataka. The children of the rural sector of these states compared to the urban sector seem to be more neglected than other states. The infant mortality for urban areas is less than rural areas in all the states except for Kerala, though the difference is low in Kerala. Previous studies pointed out that education has a direct influence on infant mortality rate. Kerala is having highest literacy

Table 2.1 State-wise Percentage Distribution of Child Health in India; 1998–1999)

State	*Acute Respiratory Infection		Diarrhoea		Anaemia		Malnutrition through Weight-for-Height		Estimated Infant Mortality Rate, 1999**	
	Rural	Urban	Rural	Urban	Rural	Urban	Rural	Urban	Rural	Urban
AP	20.0	16.5	14.7	16.1	73.3	69.5	9.5	7.6	75	37
As	18.3	10.0	8.4	4.1	63.8	52.3	13.4	10.4	79	36
Bi	21.7	21.5	17.9	15.6	81.3	80.7	21.4	17.1	64	55
Gu	11.4	10.4	21.4	17.0	78.5	67.9	19.2	11.3	70	45
Ka	7.1	9.6	14.6	12.4	72.7	66.3	21.8	16.2	69	24
Ke	22.8	23.0	11.0	12.7	43.2	46.8	11.2	10.9	14	16
MP	30.9	23.4	22.4	26.6	75.4	73.7	20.6	17.3	96	55
Ma	15.6	10.3	22.9	29.1	78.0	72.8	24.8	15.7	58	31
Or	22.4	23.3	28.0	29.2	72.7	68.3	24.4	23.6	100	65
Pu	14.0	15.9	9.4	11.0	80.9	77.2	7.0	7.4	57	39
Ra	21.3	24.5	19.9	19.2	82.6	81.3	12.5	8.6	85	59
TN	10.0	10.7	14.0	15.0	70.5	66.2	19.5	20.6	58	39
UP	21.5	18.9	24.1	19.4	73.9	74.1	11.4	9.5	88	66
WB	25.6	21.2	8.6	6.9	81.5	64.1	14.2	11.1	55	40

Source: SRS Bulletin, Sample Registration System, Register General, India, Vol. 36, No. 2, October 2002.
Note: *ARI = Cough accompanied by fast breathing in 1998–1999.

Table 2.2 Urban–Rural Difference of State-wise Percentages of Child Health Parameters in India (1998–1999)

State	Acute Respiratory Infection		Diarrhoea		Anaemia		Malnutrition through Weight-for-Height		Infant Mortality		Overall Rank of Differences
	Diff.	Rank	Diff.	Rank	Diff.	Rank	Diff.	Rank	Diff.	Rank	
AP	-3.5	5	1.4	10	-3.8	8	-1.9	9	-38	4	7
As	-8.3	1	-4.3	3	-11.5	2	-3.0	8	-43	2	1
Bi	-0.2	8	-2.3	4	-0.6	12	-4.3	4	-9	13	9
Gu	-1.0	7	-4.4	2	-10.6	3	-7.9	2	-25	8	2
Ka	2.5	13	-2.2	5	-6.4	4	-5.6	3	-45	1	3
Ke	0.2	9	1.7	12	3.6	14	-0.3	12	2	14	14
MP	-7.5	2	4.2	13	-1.7	10	-3.3	6	-41	3	6
Ma	-5.3	3	6.2	14	-5.2	5	-9.1	1	-27	6	4
Or	0.9	11	1.2	9	-4.4	6	-0.8	11	-35	5	10
Pu	1.9	12	1.6	11	-3.7	9	0.4	13	-18	11	13
Ra	3.2	14	-0.7	7	-1.3	11	-3.9	5	-26	7	11
TN	0.7	10	1.0	8	-4.3	7	1.1	14	-19	10	12
UP	-2.6	6	-4.7	1	0.2	13	-1.9	10	-22	9	8
WB	-4.4	4	-1.7	6	-17.4	1	-3.1	7	-15	12	5

Diff. = difference.

Table 2.3 *Product Moment Correlations among the State-wise Percentages of Child Health Parameters in India*

	ARIR	DiaR	AneR	WAHR	InfMR	ARIU	DiaU	AneU	WAHU	InfMU
ARIR	1.00	0.18	-0.05	-0.13	0.21	0.83**	0.23	0.04	-0.04	0.42
DiaR		1.00	0.29	0.56*	0.60*	0.23	0.91**	0.48	0.46	0.66*
AneR			1.00	0.19	0.53	-0.02	0.21	0.85**	0.00	0.54*
WAHR				1.00	0.25	-0.18	0.57*	0.14	0.86**	0.13
InfMR					1.00	0.11	0.44	0.50	0.23	0.78**
ARIU						1.00	0.26	0.21	0.00	0.48
DiaU							1.00	0.45	0.50	0.46
AneU								1.00	0.04	0.64*
WAHU									1.00	0.19
InfMU										1.00

ARI: Acute respiratory infection, Dia: Diarrhoea, Ane: Anaemia; WAH: Malnutrition through weight-for-height, InfM: Infant mortality.

**Correlation is significant at the 0.01 per cent level (2-tailed).

*Correlation is significant at the 0.05 per cent level (2-tailed).

Table 2.4 State-wise Percentage Distribution of Child Health in India (2005–2006)

State	Acute Respiratory Infection		Diarrhoea		Anaemia		Malnutrition through Weight-for-Height		Estimated Infant Mortality Rate, 2005**	
	Rural	Urban	Rural	Urban	Rural	Urban	Rural	Urban	Rural	Urban
AP	2.7	1.5	4.8	5.4	72.8	61.3	10.4	8.8	63	39
As	4.9	6.0	8.2	7.8	70.3	60.4	10.6	12.1	71	39
Bi	7.4	5.3	10.5	12.0	79.1	68.4	22.7	23.7	62	47
Gu	4.0	6.6	13.0	13.1	74.7	62.4	16.6	14.1	63	37
Ka	2.2	2.0	8.5	9.0	72.7	66.8	16.9	15.2	54	39
Ke	4.6	6.4	6.5	7.5	44.7	44.5	16.9	9.2	15	12
MP	4.2	2.1	11.1	14.2	75.7	62.0	30.4	27.5	80	54
Ma	4.0	4.6	8.8	7.6	67.2	59.2	14.3	12.8	41	27
Or	5.9	8.0	12.0	9.9	67.0	54.8	15.7	12.5	78	55
Pu	6.8	5.5	8.0	7.4	66.4	65.9	8.3	6.5	49	37
Ra	5.6	7.7	9.1	14.9	72.4	63.9	16.7	19.1	75	43
TN	4.3	2.8	6.5	4.6	62.6	65.8	19.2	18.1	39	34
UP	6.1	7.0	8.1	10.6	74.6	69.7	10.6	8.5	77	54
WB	11.9	8.5	6.8	5.1	64.0	52.1	16.2	12.7	40	31

Source: SRS Bulletin, Sample Registration System, Register General, India, Vol. 41, No. 1, October 2006.
*ARI = Cough with fever accompanied by fast breathing.

Table 2.5 *Urban–Rural Difference of State-wise Percentages of Child Health Parameters in India (2005–2006)*

State	Acute Respiratory Infection		Diarrhoea		Anaemia		Malnutrition through Weight-for-Height		Infant Mortality		Total of Ranks	Overall Rank of Differences
	Diff.	Rank	Diff.	Rank	Diff.	Rank	Diff.	Rank	Diff.	Rank		
AP	-1.2	6	0.6	9	-11.5	5	-1.6	9	-24	5	34	6
As	1.1	10	-0.4	6	-9.9	7	1.5	13	-32	1.5	37.5	7
Bi	-2.1	2.5	1.5	11	-10.7	6	1.0	12	-15	8.5	40	8.5
Gu	2.6	14	0.1	7	-12.3	2	-2.5	5	-26	3.5	31.5	4.5
Ka	-0.2	7	0.5	8	-5.9	10	-1.7	8	-15	8.5	31.5	4.5
Ke	1.8	11	1.0	10	-0.2	13	-7.7	1	-3	14	49	12
MP	-2.1	2.5	3.1	13	-13.7	1	-2.9	4	-26	3.5	25	2.5
Ma	0.6	8	-1.2	4	-8.0	9	-1.5	10	-14	10	41	10
Or	2.1	12.5	-2.1	1	-12.2	3	-3.2	3	-23	6.5	25	2.5
Pu	-1.3	5	-0.6	5	-0.5	12	-1.8	7	-12	11	40	8.5

(Continued)

(Continued)

State	Acute Respiratory Infection		Diarrhoea		Anaemia		Malnutrition through Weight-for-Height		Infant Mortality		Total of Ranks	Overall Rank of Differences
	Diff.	Rank	Diff.	Rank	Diff.	Rank	Diff.	Rank	Diff.	Rank		
Ra	2.1	12.5	5.8	14	−8.5	8	2.4	14	−32	1.5	50	13
TN	−1.5	4	−1.9	2	3.2	14	−1.1	11	−5	13	44	11
UP	0.9	9	2.5	12	−4.9	11	−2.1	6	−23	6.5	54.5	14
WB	−3.4	1	−1.7	3	−11.9	4	−3.5	2	−9	12	22	1
Total		105		105		105		105		105		525

Diff. = difference.

Table 2.6 Product Moment Correlations among the State-wise Percentages of Child Health Parameters in India (2005–2006)

	ARIR	DiaR	AneR	WAHR	InfMR	ARIU	DiaU	AneU	WAHU	InfMU
ARIR	1.00	-.03	-.09	-.03	-.10	.68**	-.12	-.21	-.04	.03
DiaR		1.00	.45	.43	.51	.27	.76**	.17	.45	.50
AneR			1.00	.15	.80**	-.21	.52	.78**	.43	.78**
WAHR				1.00	.10	-.26	.48	-.01	.91**	.21
InfMR					1.00	.03	.63*	.52	.32	.92**
ARIU						1.00	.18	-.35	-.27	-.02
DiaU							1.00	.30	.57*	.53
AneU								1.00	.27	.59*
WAHU									1.00	.38
InfMU										1.00

ARI: Acute respiratory infection, Dia: Diarrhoea, Ane: Anaemia; WAH: Malnutrition through weight-for-height, InfM: Infant mortality.
**Correlation is significant at the 0.01 per cent level (2-tailed).
*Correlation is significant at the 0.05 per cent level (2-tailed).

with least infant mortality. Punjab, Maharashtra and West Bengal are ahead of others so far as literacy is concerned. There is no strong similarity of rural-urban differences among the different child morbidity parameters as the pair-wise rank correlations of these differences were found to be small. If the result is compared with NFHS-3 data, it is found that, apart from Gujarat and West Bengal, rural-urban difference is very high in Orissa, Andhra Pradesh, Madhya Pradesh and Karnataka also.

We have also found the pair-wise correlations of the morbidity parameters of the children to see whether the different parameters are similar (Table 2.3). Only the correlations between rural and the corresponding urban percentages are seen to be quite high. Most of the other correlations are not so large. The only exceptions are between diarrhoea and infant mortality and between infant mortality and anaemia of urban India. It means that the states with high infant mortality are also the states with high occurrence of diarrhoea. But the other correlation seems to be spurious.

Development Indicators

Table 2.7 shows the state-wise percentage distribution of four development indicators such as HCR, RMC, literacy and sex ratio (adult).

In case of development parameters, a wide gap has been noticed in Table 2.7. Proportion of rural poor is far more than that of urban poor except for the states of Kerala and Punjab. Kerala and Punjab are regarded as the top two most developed states in India, and the gap between rural and urban poor in those two states is also very low. The figures confirm our popular idea that less developed states such as Bihar, MP and UP have low values of adult female-male ratio regardless whether rural or urban sector is considered. It is found from Table 2.7 that Punjab and Kerala started with low values of HCR compared to other states. Punjab maintained the top rank in both rural and urban sectors. The states that have very good positions in the urban sector are Gujarat followed by Kerala, Tamil Nadu, Andhra Pradesh and Assam. The situation was bad in states such as Bihar and Orissa in both sectors.

Table 2.7 *State-wise Percentage Distribution of Development Parameters in India*

State	Head Count Ratio (HCR)		Real Mean Consumption (RMC)		Literacy (Lit.)		Sex Ratio (Adult) (FMR)	
	Rural	Urban	Rural	Urban	Rural	Urban	Rural	Urban
AP	27.9	11.3	93.1	105.4	49.6	76.1	1.007	0.976
As	35.7	12.1	52.3	117.4	65.1	87.3	0.913	0.846
Bi	39.3	23.5	48.5	90.2	46.0	73.9	0.946	0.824
Gu	20.4	6.6	67.6	98.2	55.6	79.0	0.935	0.946
Ka	30.3	11.5	63.4	112.4	56.1	81.2	0.961	0.964
Ke	11.6	10.5	70.3	112.4	87.7	92.3	1.198	1.124
MP	31.2	14.1	59.4	81.2	51.9	77.8	0.905	0.882
Ma	30.8	13.0	61.2	92.1	64.5	82.7	0.995	0.902
Or	41.3	15.6	59.5	86.5	62.0	78.0	0.995	0.900
Pu	2.8	4.0	88.0	130.1	64.4	88.0	0.986	0.915
Ra	16.2	10.6	58.2	88.1	48.3	74.4	0.973	0.922
TN	25.6	11.1	68.2	93.2	62.0	82.3	1.034	1.019
UP	20.8	16.5	64.3	87.9	52.9	74.9	0.960	0.848
WB	22.7	11.4	71.2	98.4	61.2	83.3	0.943	0.910

HCR = head count ratio, RMC = real mean consumption, Lit. = literacy,
FMR = female-male ratio.

Real mean consumption shows the economic status of a state directly because it takes actual consumption. Punjab, Andhra Pradesh and Kerala maintained the top places. Assam shows some peculiarities. It has very high real mean consumption in the urban sector but very low consumption in the rural sector. The fact that Assam is not a very developed state is clear from the rural-urban gap. Other states that show better position are Karnataka, Gujarat and West Bengal.

Kerala has the highest literacy level among the states. Even the percentage of literacy in rural Kerala (87.7%) is above than those in the urban sector of many states. The states such as Punjab, Assam, Karnataka, Maharashtra, Tamil Nadu and West Bengal are in good position in comparison to other states. The sex ratio is thought to be one of the development indicators. Once again, Kerala is at the highest position. The ratio is slightly higher in rural areas than in urban areas.

The rural-urban difference of all these development parameters is also an important indicator of development (see Table 2.8). It is found from the table that Tamil Nadu, Gujarat, UP and West Bengal have low differences. Developed states are expected to have small gap than the comparatively less developed states. This difference is high in Bihar, Assam, Karnataka, etc.

The pair-wise correlations of the development parameters (Table 2.9) show that there is a negative relation between poverty and other development parameters, especially with mean consumption level. This is expected, since poverty is inversely related with development, whereas other variables are directly related with development. Rural development is found strongly related with the corresponding urban development.

Women Health

We now focus our attention to the health issues of women. State-wise women health position is shown in Table 2.10. It is found from the table that the women of urban sectors are in a better condition than in rural sectors. Here also it is found that Kerala and Punjab are in good positions. The worst affected states are Assam, Bihar, Orissa and West Bengal in case of anaemia in NFHS-2. However, many of the states have improved their positions in 2005-2006 in absolute term. The urban-rural difference is not so marked except for the states of Gujarat, West Bengal, Karnataka and Orissa (Table 2.11).

Table 2.12 presents the correlations of the health parameters of women. Only the correlations between rural and the corresponding urban percentages are seen to be quite high. Other correlations are not so prominent (Table 2.13).

Table 2.8 *Urban-Rural Difference of State-wise Percentage of Development Parameters in India*

State	Head Count Ratio (HCR)		Real Mean Consumption (RMC)		Literacy (Lit.)		Adult Sex Ratio (FMR)		Overall Rank of Differences
	Difference	Rank	Difference	Rank	Difference	Rank	Difference	Rank	
AP	−16.6	6	12.3	14	26.5	2	−0.031	10	8
As	−23.6	2	65.1	1	22.2	8	−0.067	7	2
Bi	−15.8	7	41.7	5	27.9	1	−0.122	1	1
Gu	−13.8	9	30.6	7	23.4	7	0.011	14	12
Ka	−18.8	3	49.0	2	25.1	5	0.003	13	3
Ke	−1.1	13	42.1	3	4.6	14	−0.074	5	10
MP	−17.1	5	21.8	13	25.9	4	−0.023	11	9
Ma	−17.8	4	30.9	6	18.2	12	−0.093	4	4
Or	−25.7	1	27.0	10	16.0	13	−0.095	3	5
Pu	1.2	14	42.1	4	23.6	6	−0.071	6	6
Ra	−5.6	11	29.9	8	26.1	3	−0.051	8	7
TN	−14.5	8	25.0	11	20.3	11	−0.015	12	14
UP	−4.3	12	23.6	12	22.0	10	−0.112	2	11
WB	−11.3	10	27.2	9	22.1	9	−0.033	9	13

Table 2.9 *Correlation among the Development Parameters in India*

	HCRR	RMCR	LITR	FMRR	HCRU	RMCU	LITU	FMRU
HCRR	1.00	−.586*	−.344	−.397	.717**	−.472	−.417	−.449
RMCR		1.00	−.148	.318	−.630*	.492	.241	.456
LITR			1.00	.738*	−.362	.469	.904**	.631*
FMRR				1.00	−.175	.241	.511	.845**
HCRU					1.00	−.595*	−.533*	−.475
RMCU						1.00	???	.295
LITU							1.00	.509
FMRU								1.00

HCRR = head count ratio (rural), RMCR = mean consumption (rural),
LITR = literacy (rural), FMRR = sex ratio (rural), HCRU = head count ratio (urban),
RMCU = mean consumption (urban), LITU = literacy (urban),
FMRU = sex ratio (urban).
*significant at 5 per cent level.
**significant at 1 per cent level.

Table 2.10 *State-wise Percentage Distribution of Women Health in India*

	Women Anaemia				Percentage of Women with BMI < 18.5			
	1998–1999		2005–2006		1998–1999		2005–2006	
State	Rural	Urban	Rural	Urban	Rural	Urban	Rural	Urban
AP	50.6	47.4	64.6	55.0	43.2	19.7	38.7	21.0
As	69.9	67.2	70.2	66.0	27.9	18.8	38.2	26.2
Bi	63.9	59.6	67.5	66.7	40.3	31.1	45.3	31.5
Gu	51.3	39.5	58.6	50.9	47.7	22.8	44.2	24.2
Ka	46.0	35.7	53.5	48.3	47.0	23.8	40.4	25.6
Ke	23.4	20.4	32.1	34.1	19.9	14.7	19.1	14.9
MP	57.0	46.2	59.6	43.4	41.8	28.2	43.7	29.3
Ma	51.2	44.8	50.5	47.9	49.3	26.2	44.4	27.5
Or	64.1	54.8	62.2	56.0	49.9	32.9	43.3	27.8
Pu	42.5	39.0	37.4	39.2	20.5	9.2	19.4	16.9
Ra	49.1	46.7	55.3	48.0	38.7	28.5	38.0	30.8
TN	59.1	51.6	54.3	51.5	35.2	17.5	33.0	19.3
UP	49.4	46.0	50.3	46.3	39.1	23.3	37.2	23.2
WB	64.2	57.8	64.7	56.4	49.8	24.5	45.3	19.5

Table 2.11 Urban-Rural Difference of State-wise Percentage of Women Health Parameters in India

State	Women Anaemia (1998–1999)		Women low BMI (<18.5) (1998–1999)		Overall Rank of Differences (1998–1999)	Women Anaemia (2005–2006)		Women Low BMI (<18.5) (2005–2006)		Overall Rank of Differences (2005–2006)
	Diff.	Rank	Diff.	Rank		Diff.	Rank	Diff.	Rank	
AP	-3.2	11	-23.5	3	8	-9.6	2	-17.7	3	2
As	-2.7	13	-9.1	13	13	-4.2	8	-12.0	11	10
Bi	-4.3	8	-9.2	12	11	-0.8	12	-13.8	9	12
Gu	-11.8	1	-24.9	2	1	-7.7	4	-20.0	2	3
Ka	-10.3	3	-23.2	4	2	-5.2	7	-14.8	6	6
Ke	-3.0	12	-5.2	14	14	2.0	14	-4.2	13	13.5
MP	-10.8	2	-13.6	9	6	-16.2	1	-14.4	7	4
Ma	-6.4	6.5	-23.1	5	7	-2.6	11	-16.9	4	7
Or	-9.3	4	-17.0	7	4	-6.2	6	-15.5	5	5
Pu	-3.5	9	-11.3	10	10	1.8	13	-2.5	14	13.5
Ra	-2.4	14	-10.2	11	12	-7.3	5	-7.2	12	8.5
TN	-7.5	5	-17.7	6	5	-2.8	10	-13.7	10	11
UP	-3.4	10	-15.8	8	9	-4.0	9	-14.0	8	8.5
WB	-6.4	6.5	-25.3	1	3	-8.3	3	-25.8	1	1

Table 2.12 *Correlations among the Women Health Parameters in India (1998–1999)*

	WomanaR	WolowBMIR	WomanaU	WolowBMIU
WomanaR	1.00	.462	.959**	.500
WolowBMIR		1.00	.297	.756**
WomanaU			1.00	.404
WolowBMIU				1.00

**significant at 1 per cent level.

Table 2.13 *Correlations among the Women Health Parameters in India (2005–2006)*

	WomanaR	WolowBMIR	WomanaU	WolowBMIU
WomanaR	1.00	.812**	.900**	.588*
WolowBMIR		1.00	.639*	.728**
WomanaU			1.00	.485
WolowBMIU				1.00

WomanaR = women anaemia (rural), WomanaU = women anaemia (urban), WolowBMIR = women with low BMI (rural), WolowBMIU = women with low BMI (urban).
*significant at 5 per cent level.
** significant at 1 per cent level.

State-wise Comparison of Groups of Variables

Since relations between two groups of variables are best described by canonical correlations, we have computed the same in Tables 2.14 and 2.15. It can be seen from the canonical correlation tables that all the values are quite high. The groups are closely related. Thus, the development of a state goes side by side with child and women health. However, it has already been pointed out that it is not possible to compute the values of the canonical correlations when there are large numbers of variables and also it fails to capture the direction of relations. To overcome these problems of canonical

Table 2.14 *Cannonical Correlations between Child Health, Women Health and Development Indicators (Rural versus Rural and Urban versus Urban)*

Rural vs. Rural / Urban vs. Urban	Child	Development	Women
Child	1.000	0.970	0.846
Development	0.967	1.000	0.904
Women	0.794	0.893	1.000

Table 2.15 *Cannonical Correlations between Child Health, Women Health and Development Indicators (Rural versus Urban)*

Urban / Rural	Child	Development	Women
Child	0.988	0.978	0.911
Development	0.940	0.975	0.908
Women	0.736	0.743	0.973

correlations, we have resorted to rank correlation method as described before.

On the basis of the ranks of the states for each group of variables (Table 2.16), it was seen that Kerala and Punjab are at the top places. But if we consider only the child health, Assam takes the top position. Bihar, Orissa and Madhya Pradesh come at the end of the list (Table 2.16).

The Spearman's rank correlations of groups of variables are given in Tables 2.17 and 2.18. Most significant correlations have been found for urban versus urban pairs. It may be because the links among urban sectors are more than among rural sectors. In case of urban sectors, development is found correlated with both child health and women health, whereas the correlation between child health and women health is not much. For the same group, rural versus urban correlation is found to be more than correlation between groups. Thus, the rural sectors of each state move along with the urban sector.

Table 2.16 *Average Ranks of Child Health,Women Health and Development Indicators*

State	Average Child Health Rank		Average Women Health Rank		Average Development Rank		Overall	
	Rural	Urban	Rural	Urban	Rural	Urban	Rural	Urban
AP	6	7	7	7	9	10	7	8
As	1	1	8	10	12	6	5	6
Bi	12	11	11	14	14	14	13	14
Gu	8	8	10	4	6	4	9	5
Ka	5	5	5	3	8	7	4	4
Ke	2	2	1	1	1	1	1	1
MP	14	13	9	9	13	12	12	12
Ma	9	9	12	8	5	8	11	9
Or	13	14	13	13	11	11	14	13
Pu	4	4	2	2	2	2	2	2
Ra	11	12	3	11	10	9	10	11
TN	3	6	6	5	4	3	3	3
UP	10	10	4	6	7	13	6	10
WB	7	3	14	12	3	5	8	7

Table 2.17 *Rank Correlations among the Three Groups of Variables (Rural versus Rural and Urban versus Urban)*

Rural vs. Rural Urban vs. Urban	Child Health	Development	Women Health
Child health	1	−0.319	0.446
Development	0.758**	1	0.248
Women health	0.490	.846**	1

**significant at 1 per cent level.

Table 2.18 *Rank Correlations among the Three Groups of Variables (Rural versus Urban)*

Rural \ Urban	Child Health	Development	Women Health
Child health	0.934**	0.789**	0.544*
Development	0.519	0.792**	0.670**
Women health	0.285	0.397	0.846**

*significant at 5 per cent level.
**significant at 1 per cent level.

DISCUSSION

India has recently been showing keen interest in regards to human development. The 8th Five-Year Plan (1992-1997) identified 'human development' as its main focus with health as one of the objectives. In our chapter, we have tried to find out how close the states are in their positions with respect to development and morbidity patterns. It also shows how the rural sectors differ from the corresponding urban sectors. This is an attempt to see whether the health situation in the states move along with the level of development.

The variables considered in the chapter have been found to move together at the expected directions. There are some variables that are rightly found to be positively linked with the development measured through RMC, literacy and female-male ratio. There are also some variables that are negatively linked with the development. These are the child and women morbidity parameters and HCR. These two types of variables may be termed as 'positively linked' and 'negatively linked' variables. There is a clear association among these variables. The variables within each of these groups are found to be positively related through product moment correlation coefficients and the 'positively linked' variables have been found to be negatively correlated with the 'negatively linked' variables. There are some minor exceptions.

So far as individual states are concerned, Kerala and Punjab top the list of developed states. But there are some differences between these two states. Kerala is developed in all aspects, but Punjab is more developed in economic aspects only. Bihar and Orissa are at the bottom of the list. Katakam (2002) in an article of *Frontline* reports that widespread inequalities in the distribution of resources have led to glaring regional disparities, acute poverty and a high level of unemployment. Assam, though poor in development aspects, has been moving towards the attainment of the 'health for all'.

A number of studies regarding different aspects of health show that urban areas are in a better position. The urban areas offer more choices: greater availability of electricity, water and sanitation services, health services and so on (Smith et al., 2005). We have in our study found similar results. Moreover, the rural–urban difference is found to be more in less developed states, but the correlations between rural and urban sectors of the same states are very high. It means that development of sectors goes together, but the gaps between the sectors widen for less developed states.

To compare the groups of variables, the help of canonical correlation analysis is taken. The results are similar. Rural–urban correlations of the same group of variables are found to be more. Since there are degrees of freedom problem in this analysis, we have resorted to the rank correlation methods. Urban sectors have been found to be more linked with urban sectors.

Assam is not regarded as a developed state. But surprisingly this state comes in the forefront when child health is considered. One has to probe it further to see the reasons behind it.

REFERENCES

Ahluwalia, M. S. (2000). Economic performance of states in post-reforms period. *Economic & Political Weekly, 35*(19), 1637-1648.

Ben-Sholmo, Y, White, I. R., & Marmot, M. (1996). Does the variation of socio-economic characteristics of an area affect mortality? *British Medical Journal, 312*(7037), 1013-1014.

Haines, A. and Smith, R. (1997). Working together to reduce poverty's damage. *British Medical Journal, 314*(7080), 529-530.

National Family Health Survey (NFHS-2), Andhra Pradesh, Assam, Bihar, Gujarat, Karnataka, Kerala, Madhya Pradesh, Maharashtra, Orissa, Punjab, Rajasthan, Tamil Nadu, Uttar Pradesh, West Bengal (1998-99) IIPS, Mumbai, India. The authors.

Kaplan, G., Pamuk, E. R., Lynch, J. W., Cohen, R. D., & Balfour, J. L. (1996). Inequality in income and mortality in the United States: Analysis of mortality and potential pathways. *British Medical Journal, 312*(7037), 999–1003.

Katakam, A. (2002). Maharashtra HDR: A state of disparity. *Frontline, 19*(13), http://www. hinduonnet.com/fline/fl1913/19130810.htm

Purohit, B. C. (2004). Inter-state disparities in health care and financial burden on the poor in India. *Journal of Health & Social Policy, 18*(3), 37-60.

Raphael, D. (2001). From increasing poverty to societal disintegration: How economic inequality on the health of individuals and communities. In H. Armstrong, P. Armstrong and D. Coburn (Eds.), *Unhealthy times: The political economy of health care in Canada.* (pp. 223-246). Oxford University Press.

Reutter, L. (1995). Poverty and health: Implications for public health. *Canadian Journal of Public Health, 86*(3), 149-151.

Seshadri, S. (1997). Nutritional anemia in South Asia. In S. Gillespie (Ed.), *Malnutrition in South Asia: A regional profile.* (pp. 75-124). Regional Office for South Asia, UNICEF.

Smith, C. L., Ruel, T. M., & Ndiaye, A. (2005). Why is child malnutrition lower in urban than in rural areas? Evidence from 36 developing countries. *World Development, 33*(8), 1285-1205.

Warden, J. (1998). Britain's new health policy recognizes poverty as major cause of Illness. *British Medical Journal, 316*(7130), 495.

Chapter 3

Trade in Health Services Implications for People's Health*

K. B. Saxena

THRUST OF GLOBALIZATION

Globalization has virtually emerged as the ideology of our times. Its impact on the economy, society and polity can hardly be missed. Triggered by global economic forces of investment capital, finance and trade, the revolutionary changes in information and communication technology have shaped a new development paradigm with market as its pivot. This development model has aggressively displaced the welfare state consensus accepted since the Second World War. The transformation is being steered by three global governance institutions, namely the International Monetary Fund (IMF), the World Bank and the World Trade Organization (WTO), the first through macroeconomic management, the second through provision of development finance and investment, and the third through trade. The normative framework of 'welfare state' was built on a delicately crafted balance between the imperatives of economic growth and the demands of social development. Good health being necessary as much for personal well-being and social progress as for economic development, the provision of healthcare to the people constituted an important

---

* *Social Change* 41, no. 2 (June 2011): 183–213.

Note: This is a revised and updated version of a paper written for the International Seminar on Coping with Globalisation in New Delhi organized by the Institute of Applied Manpower Research (IAMR) in 2004.

component of social development. This balance has been aggressively replaced by a tilt towards economic growth with deleterious effects on the human and social development. Health subsector, therefore, cannot remain untouched by this change.

Health outcomes in a society are influenced by activities in the economy, social practices and cultural values. Three factors contribute towards them. The first relates to living conditions which prevent occurrence of ill health. The access to food security, balanced nutritional diet, safe drinking water, sanitation arrangement, etc., is necessary for it. The second is availability of health services which include preventive and curative medicine and hospital care. The developments resulting from consumption of products, use of services and social intercourse also produce profound consequences for health. This constitutes the third factor. Market-driven changes represented by globalization have affected all the three factors. The living conditions for a large section of people have deteriorated as the role of state has shrunk in the subsidized provisioning of various social services resulting from the IMF mandated restructuring of the economy. The access to health services and quality of care for those who cannot afford to pay have worsened under the impact of reforms introduced by the World Bank. The international trade regime is not only commodifying healthcare but is also introducing new threats to health, some of which are beyond the capacity of the state to prevent or control. The structure and processes of the WTO are even reducing state's capacity to design health policy and regulations autonomously. It is difficult to apportion precisely the influence of the three institutions on each of the three factors affecting people's health as their activities overlap considerably and are also strongly integrated in terms of the ideological thrust towards neoliberalism.

The healthcare system in India after Independence took shape broadly on the lines recommended by the Bhore Committee. This has been getting slowly dismantled since the economic and health sector reforms were introduced beginning with the 1990s, though some change in thinking could be noticed even earlier. A great deal has been written on the impact of these reforms (Qadeer et al., 2001). International trade, however, has received little attention in this discourse. One reason could be that the movement for reforms in health system started earlier while the new international trade regime came into existence later. The other reason perhaps is that the threats to health from trade unravel slowly while those emerging from economic and development policies create more pronounced and immediate impact. Also, perhaps, the predominantly public funded health system was not perceived to carry much potential for trade and, therefore, liberalization of economy to facilitate trade posed less of a threat. The added difficulty is that tradable health goods and services are spread over diverse sectors and an integrated picture is not easy to figure out. But, in view of its wide-ranging ramifications, international trade would produce far more damaging consequences on health of the people than what the market-driven changes in health services have inflicted so far. This is due to the paradigmatic change that has occurred in the new global trade regime from that of the previous General Agreement on Tariffs and Trade (GATT) 1947, in terms of reach, intensity, powers and the directional thrust.

NEW TRADE REGIME

The following features of new trade regime distinguish it from its predecessor:

- The scope of trade has been widened from exchange of products to incorporate services, intellectual property and life forms. Health sector activities constitute one of the services and have, therefore, become tradable for the first time.
- The discourse on trade and its operations has shifted attention from tariff concessions and transgressed into the arena of domestic policy and regulations, resulting in reduced role of nation state in governance (O'Brien et al., 2000).
- The framework of negotiations has moved from terms of exchange relating to products to creating conditions for facilitating competition.
- The WTO is more institutional and powerful than its predecessor in view of the punitive instruments available to it for seeking compliance of its decisions.

- The processes of trade negotiations and decisions pursue an expansionary agenda through 'deeper integration' and 'policy harmonization' in respect of subsidies, investment and services (Shukla, 2002).
- The trade regime has empowered itself to take decisions on matters having a bearing on fields other than trade for which it has no expertise.
- The mode of decision-making in the existing trade body reflects democratic deficit as the decisions can be enforced on unwilling members (Helleiner, 2002).

In view of the above architecture of the trade regime and the enormous power appropriated by it, some understanding of its structure, operational processes and the evolving credo is necessary to assess the impact of its activities on health currently and in future.

INSTITUTIONAL ARRANGEMENTS

The new institutional trade arrangements emerged after the conclusion of Uruguay Rounds in 1994. Their ambit is defined by various multilateral agreements which consist of 29 individual legal texts covering a wide range of subjects from agriculture to intellectual property. This is supplemented by more than 25 ministerial declarations, decisions and understandings. General Agreement on Trade in Services (GATS) is one of these wide-ranging multilateral agreements. Health sector is one of the 12 sectors listed in GATS. Of the wide-range of multilateral agreements which WTO administers, GATS deals with exchange of services. It is considered to be the single most important development in multilateral trading system since GATT (1947). It makes no distinction between public services or those provided for profit. Only, the service which state provides entirely free and without any competitor is out of its ambit (Bertrand & Kalafatides, 2001; Sexton, 2003). Services include 160 items and health is one of them. Healthcare dimensions are involved in some other agreements as well. Among the agreements more directly affecting health are the Agreement on Application of Sanitary and Phytosanitary Measures (SPS), Agreement on Trade Related Aspects of Intellectual Property

Rights (TRIPS), Agreement on Agriculture (AOA), Agreement on Technical Barriers to Trade (TBT) and GATT. Health outcomes may also emerge from operation of trading activities in other sectors through pattern of investment, production, consumption and exchange of products, use of technology, and human and cultural intercourse. But GATS has wider ramifications and implications for the health sector compared to the other agreements. This chapter will, therefore, deal with GATS in relation to health services.

GATS identifies four ways ('or more') in which services can be traded. These are as follows: Mode 1: Cross-border supply services applied from one country to another. Mode 2: Consumption abroad-consumers/organizations making use of a service in another country. Mode 3: Commercial Presence—A foreign country establishing a unit to provide services in another country. Mode 4: Movement of natural persons–individuals going over from one country to another to supply services. Each country has to incorporate in its declaration of obligations and restrictions relating to market access and national treatment in respect of each subsector. Market access implies treating all countries alike and national treatment requires treating foreign and domestic suppliers on equal footing. Where no restriction is indicated, the commitment is BOUND; where restriction/limitation is indicated, the entry in UNBOUND.

The unique feature of the current trade system is that a distinct entity has been created to regulate international trade which had not existed earlier. This is called the WTO. The overarching consideration for the WTO is that there should be no restriction in trade between nations. National policies, regulations and governing structures should conform to this objective. The trade principles it enforces for this purpose are market access (treating all countries alike) and national treatment (considering foreign and domestic suppliers on equal footing). WTO is also unique in that it makes its own rules which evolve through its operations. It pursues an evidence-based system within the structure of a rule-based organization (Obrinski, 2001). Of the rules which define its working, the most overriding is the primacy of trade over other considerations. Exemptions contained in any agreement which permit trade to be restricted on grounds of public health, environment, social protection, etc., are narrowly interpreted by it so as to favour the cause of trade (Hong, 2000). The other is that when a country raises any issue against unrestricted trade, such as risk to public health or damage to environment, WTO rules seek convincing scientific basis for such contentions (Wallach, 2001). As a result, it has disallowed 'precautionary principles' as the basis for restricting trade where the scientific evidence does not exist or is weak in the short run even though potentially serious risk may emerge later. WTO also takes the position that there should be no distinction between similar products irrespective of how they are produced (Hong, 2000). All such products should be treated in a similar manner so that the national governments are discouraged from restricting or avoiding import of certain products on the ground of risk to public health from a process of production.

WTO AND HEALTH

Even in a short period of its existence, WTO has taken far-reaching decisions which have wide-ranging implications outside the trade sector. Health and environment are among the affected sectors. Although some agreements permit a member country to restrict trade in the interest of public health, WTO rulings have upheld the interest of trade and disregarded/undervalued objections relating to health as, for example, in the hormone-treated beef case between European Union (EU) and the USA (Retallack, 2001; Wallach, 2001). The insistence in this case on production of conclusive scientific evidence concerning risk to public health by the state rather than transferring the burden of proof on the industry to deny the existence of such risk clearly displayed tilt against public health.

The adverse decisions of this sort have weakened the ability of countries to respond to health threatening situations. The prospects of a possible challenge of decisions in the WTO are forcing them to change or remove their health safety regulation standards to avoid punitive consequences (Wallach, 2001). The South Korean action in shortening production inspection turnaround time to permit marketing of food products before carrying out the microbial tests, Thailand's decision to disband its consumer pricing board for medicine and Guetamala's capitulation in exempting imported baby food products from the purview of its breastfeeding promotion law provide evidence of this behaviour (Bertrand & Kalafatides, 2001; Wallach, 2001).

WTO rulings are also undermining national priorities in health-related matters as, for example, evidenced by the USA being forced to change its clean air regulations governing petrol cleanliness against challenge by Venezuela and Brazil (Wallach, 2001). Its actions are virtually determining standards of public health regulations for which it does not have the necessary expertise. Its decisions rely on bodies which are driven by commercial interests (Codex Alimenterius in food products) rather than on the advice of international expert bodies such as the Food and Agriculture Organization (FAO) and World Health Organization (WHO) (Hong, 2000). As more such decisions are delivered, WTO takes on the mantle of domestic policymaking and dictates the agenda which a country should adopt, thereby encroaching on the domain of the sovereign legislature in terms of the existing national laws (Shukla, 2002). India's decision to enact amendments to the Patents Act (1999) to provide for exclusive marketing rights and arrangements to receive product patent applications in the interim period was an instance of compliance of WTO direction, though the government considered it unnecessary in view of the executive action it had already undertaken in the matter.

GATS laid down general framework of trade in services and mandated further negotiations to liberalize services within a period of five years. The first phase of these negotiations incorporated the following three safeguards. Each country is empowered to regulate supply of services in accordance with its national policies. It can restrict entry of foreign suppliers to specified services under stipulated conditions. The developing and least developed countries would be allowed flexibility in implementation of decisions. The 2001 Doha Ministerial Declarations incorporated these aspects in the Doha Development Agenda. Further progress in the matter has not been registered due to acute difference of opinion between developed and developing countries. The overall position is that of all the services, health sector has attracted the least number of commitments and achieved the least level of liberalization in the initial offers from member countries and Doha declaration has made no advances. It has virtually been a 'non-event' with only 11 out of 95 members making improved commitments. This has led critics to declare that GATS is not a liberalizing force (Adlung, 2009). The commitments are 2.3 times more restrictive than the current policies and do not reflect the liberalization that has already taken place (Gootiiz & Mattoo, 2009).

INDIA'S POSITION ON COMMITMENTS UNDER GATS

India submitted its conditional initial offer during the process of negotiations on GATS-94 under Article 19 and in pursuance of para 15 of Doha Ministerial Declaration. This offer has been made subject to the following:

- Other members making substantive and satisfactory offers in sectors and modes of supply where India had indicated its interest.
- India would have a right to withdraw, modify or reduce any part of its offer and any subsequent conditional offer that may follow, in whole or in part, at any time and/or prior to the conclusion of the negotiations.
- India also reserves the right to make any technical amendment or correction, initially or subsequent conditional offer.
- The outcome of negotiations in progress on development of discipline of domestic regulation.

There are four categories of services which together constitute health services: (a) medical and dental services, (b) services of nurses, midwives, etc., (c) hospital services and (d) other human health services. In the revised proposal, India offered to undertake extensive commitments under Modes 1 and 4. In addition, India substantially improved access in critical service sectors. Which, in the context of health care, are (a) medical and dental services, (b) services provided by midwives, nurses, physiotherapists and paramedical personnel, (c) health services and (d) tourism services while making commitments under different modes, it has recorded commitments and limitations in respect of market access and national treatment covering all four categories of health services. The limitations, wherever recorded, largely relate to provision of services on provider-to-provider basis under Mode 1, foreign equity ceiling and its conditionalities, Foreign Investment

Promotion Board (FIPB) approval in case of foreign collaboration under Mode 3, access to scheduled and tribal areas and the period of stay of foreign professionals under Mode 4 in market access and differentially priced services to foreigners and public funded services only to Indian citizens, subsidies, where granted, only to domestic service suppliers, preference for service suppliers who offer best terms for transfer of technology, special treatment to Scheduled Castes (SCs)/Scheduled Tribes (STs) and weaker sections in national treatment.

In terms of the offer made, India has opened up the service sector substantially. This will have its impact on the health sector as some interconnectivity is embedded in GATS. Sequencing of commitments may lead to opening up of other sectors earlier. The domestic economy may react to such changes in market demand structure which may affect health sector (Sahni & Kala, 2004). But even with regard to the health sector itself, India has opened up under all four modes of supply taking into account its perception about the competitive advantage and the existing pattern of health services export. Under Mode 1, it is telemedicine. Medical tourism has weighed in making commitments under Mode 2. Clinical trials for drugs may have been in view as business process outsourcing under Mode 1. India has opened up Mode 3 both for attracting investment internally and exporting services which include, besides hospitals, medical education and research services. Mode 4 has been high on the agenda of negotiations as it involves export of service providers which meets stiff resistance from developed countries in the shape of various restrictions. The overall position of commitments made by other countries points towards 'unevenness' in market access, particularly in Mode 4 where India is most interested. Even limited commitments made by various countries have been further narrowed down by Horizontal limitations, such as economic and market needs tests, licensing and recognition requirements, immigration regulations. GATS, like all other WTO agreements, is not neutral to the capacity and competitive ability. The opening up of its market would, therefore, benefit foreign suppliers enormously due to their control over capital and technology. It would also be conditioned by unequal power relations in global negotiations, which would determine who is able to extract what concessions. Developed countries are seeking limitation-free access and broad liberalization in the form of horizontal commitments across all four modes

(Abrol, 2003). The apprehension is that India may be forced to make more liberal commitments which may have adverse equity implications. It may also be vulnerable to negotiation deals struck across sectors whose implications for health would be difficult to predict. This apprehension is reinforced by the statement of the Union Commerce Minister (Business Standard, 2005) that India was willing to consider flexibilities in Modes 1 and 3 of services as a probable bargaining point to seeking flexibility in Modes 1 and 4 where India had 'extensive interest' in liberalizing export of services. The prospects of enlarged commitments and shrinking of limitations are therefore on the cards whenever a final agreement is reached and health sector may also be a part of this deal. The economic growth obviously takes precedence in India's overall position under GATS and equity dimensions in healthcare take a back seat. This is likely to be the trend of future negotiations as well.

COMMITMENT TO INTEGRATE WITH GLOBAL ECONOMY: LIBERALIZATION IN HEALTH SECTOR

Apart from the specific commitments made under GATS which may have implications for the health sector, government has repeatedly expressed its commitment to integrate the country with the global economy and, accordingly, liberalized its policies to facilitate this process. This includes the health sector. Health sector also cannot be insulated from impact of activities in other sectors. In the current regime of international trade, multinational companies (MNCs) backed by their home (developed) countries are looking for even a little opening in developing countries to ensure that the existing protective mechanisms are dismantled as trade barriers. This opening has already been created by liberalizing the healthcare services for entry of the private sector not merely as a parallel provider but also as a partner in public funded health services. As a result of the latter, the state-funded health segment is no longer 'a supply in exercise of government authority' to claim exemption from the operations of GATS.

Trade Liberalization in Health Sector

While some trading activity has taken place in certain segments of health sector such as pharmaceuticals, medical manpower even prior to the onset of globalization, a major thrust in this direction has come after the establishment of WTO. Health sector covers a wide gamut of products and services under GATS. For the government, however, attracting medical tourists and clinical trial business and export of drugs and manpower is on the top of the agenda.

MEDICAL TOURISM

a) Medical tourism:

Government has been actively promoting medical tourism to its medical facilities which provide services at much cheaper rates than those charged in developed countries but are of comparable quality. It anticipates huge foreign exchange earnings from this trade. This objective is enshrined in the National Health Policy, 2002, and the Tenth Five-Year Plan. The corporate/private health sector and the tour and travel operators have undertaken various promotional measures to attract foreign tourists (Reddy & Qadeer, 2010). Some state governments such as Karnataka, Kerala, and Maharashtra have also done likewise to publicize healthcare facilities in their jurisdiction for this purpose.

b) Development and fiscal policies:

The opening up of insurance sector, 100 per cent foreign direct investment (FDI) in healthcare and automatic approvals of their investments proposals, setting up of a venture capital fund to promote drugs discovery and infrastructure in the pharma sector, amended Patents Act are some of the measures introduced to give a push to trade in the health sector. Some corporate/private hospitals have already benefited from supply of land at concessional rates, infrastructure development and tax exemption/reduction for import of medical equipments. The pharma and healthcare industry has been active to cash on this opportunity and have tied up with MNCs for this purpose. The pharmaceutical companies have also upgraded their infrastructure facilities, rationalized their product portfolio and increased their research and development (R&D) budget besides scouting for acquisition of companies for increasing their reach. The industry perceives trade as a knowledge transfer mechanism.

c) Clinical trials:

Both industry and government are promoting outsourcing of clinical trials. The steps taken to facilitate it include removal of service tax on clinical trials, incentivizing government-funded research and medical institutions to take up such trials in public hospitals, expeditious clearance of clinical trials projects, timebound issue of license to import supplies, training of human power in dedicated institutions, improving standards of data collection and analysis and removal of 'phase lag' in permitting clinical trials by amending the Drug and Cosmetic Rules, 2005 (Srinivasan, 2009).

d) Manpower export:

Government wishes to aggressively push removal of entry restrictions relating to economic need test, immigration policies, certification arrangements, professional qualifications and issue of visa in respect of foreign professionals imposed by developed countries during negotiations show us to benefit from remittances and upgradation of knowledge and experience.

IMPLICATIONS OF TRADE LIBERALIZATION

State and Healthcare: Paradigm Shift in the Role

Implicit in the health sector reforms carried out/under way is gradual dismantling of the public health system from its erstwhile status as a predominantly publicly funded arrangement accessible to all free of cost and without discrimination. It is now giving way to multiple channels of healthcare responding to the socioeconomic capacity of different classes of healthcare seekers. This transformation has gone through a four-stage evolution:

• The first stage recognized the need for private sector developing as a parallel system of healthcare to tap resources outside the government for meeting the needs of the people. The National Health Policy 1982 and the Sixth Five-Year Plan document registered this catalytic step. This phase also suggested introduction of user charges and pay clinics/cabins in tertiary care units of government hospitals.

- The second stage brought in the concept of differential healthcare catering to different segments of population according to their paying capacity. Simultaneously, the ambit of services provided free of cost by the public health system was curtailed. Varying patterns of privatization were also brought into the public health system through extension of paying arrangements, contracting out certain clinical and non-clinical services, shared responsibility with private sector labelled as public-private partnerships and diversification of financing sources for provisioning of healthcare. The central and state healthcare projects financed by the World Bank operationalized some of these changes.

- In the third stage, the government went a step further towards privatization with its policy to purchase healthcare services from private sector for reducing its responsibility in its provisioning. This can be seen in the arrangements evolved in externally funded projects, conceptual design of the National Rural Health Mission, the provision of reimbursement of expenditure on healthcare incurred in private hospital units under the Central Government Health Scheme (CGHS) and the push towards insurance-driven healthcare for different social groups including the very poor.

- The fourth stage emerges when healthcare services are promoted as an instrument of growth to be globally traded. This is reflected in the liberalization of foreign direct investment in health and insurance, deregulation of pharmaceutical industry, active support to medical tourism, encouragement of outsourced clinical trials, aggressive export of manpower, etc.

Thus, India's willingness to open up health sector for international trade under GATS is not a sudden decision but a culmination of progressive movement towards emulation of the healthcare system in the industrialized countries, particularly the USA. These processes unmistakably point towards a paradigm shift in the role of state in the provisioning of health services. This shift can be conceptualized in terms of the changes occurring in following dimensions of healthcare: approach to healthcare, provision of healthcare, financing of healthcare, access to healthcare and maintenance of public health.

There is a paradigm shift in the approach to healthcare from being a 'service' which every citizen is entitled to without discrimination and state had the responsibility to provide in the pre-reform period, it has now become a marketable commodity sold, purchased and traded at a cost. With regard to the provision of healthcare, the altered policy has diluted both the entitlements of citizens to get free healthcare without discrimination and the duty of the state to provide it. The provision of free medical care to all has been restricted to essential primary care, emergency life-saving services, treatment under disease central programmes and facilities under family welfare programme. The rest has to be purchased. The universality and equality of healthcare has been disregarded. The state has also shed its exclusive responsibility to finance healthcare by diversifying financing sources of curative healthcare. It has promoted private sector in health and encouraged non-governmental organizations (NGOs), community and charitable institutions to provide healthcare with a view to sharing its burden. This has drastically affected access to healthcare. The earlier policy of universal and equality of access has given way to differentiated access defined by affordability and payment capacity. The equality in access is eroded as multi-tiered healthcare facilities get promoted. The poor are at the bottom of the ladder whose access gets restricted to unqualified medical practitioners in private sector and poor quality of services in public sector due to their inability to afford paying arrangements. The maintenance of public health system deteriorates due to the dwindling role of state in provision of social services, effective preventive healthcare and comprehensive primary healthcare. The introduction of privatization has shrunk access of the poor to social services. The reduced expenditure on public health has impacted the effective reach of preventive care, while the primary healthcare has been restricted to immunization, emergency services, Reproductive Child Health (RCH) and specific communicable diseases. This adversely affects conditions for attaining good health outcomes. The pre-existing inequalities in distribution of healthcare characterized by uneven spread of infrastructure and rural-urban differentials in the quality of services have widened across states, between regions and within communities (Baru et al., 2010) after the onset of economic reforms. This is sought to be neutralized by stress on health insurance. But insurance coverage, both public and private, is very low and even a targeted social insurance for Below Poverty Line (BPL) families does not reduce catastrophic expenditure due to its restricted application to hospitalization episodes of serious nature (Mitchell et al., 2011). The diversification of financing healthcare far from addressing inequities would widen them. The iniquitous access has already produced adverse health outcomes as observed in the stagnation/deterioration levels in the poorer sections (Peters et al., 2002). Unregulated private health sector and escalating cost of care has affected the access to healthcare of the lower middle classes as well and would have on their health attainments.

DISTORTIONS IN HEALTHCARE

Trade in health services is an extension of the comodification of healthcare with buyers and sellers cutting across national borders. It will not remove or reduce the existing inequities. Rather, it would aggravate them as the foreign suppliers join the local private sector in further skewing the distributional arrangements. The foreign direct investment in healthcare and the tie-up between business groups and health providers has produced a multi-tiered system in which the cost of healthcare, particularly in the private tertiary healthcare, has shot up. The categorization, standardization and accreditation of healthcare facilities would institutionalize these divisions. The promotion of medical tourism would weaken the efforts to reduce cost of public healthcare as well (Sexton, 2003). The liberalization in the insurance sector would replicate the 'managed care' health system of the USA which is loaded against the poor, chronically ill and the elderly besides being plagued by financial and performance problems (Krugman, 2005). The export of professional manpower would intensify the brain drain (Koivusalo, 2003) and distort the public health content of medical education and training already oriented towards specialization and urban areas (Bajaj, 1998). This will also undermine the knowledge production system in the country to prepare the kind of medical professionals we need particularly for rural and underserved areas (Khadria, 2003). The outsourced clinical trials, given our dismal record in enforcing medical ethics, would increasingly suck in the poor, uninformed and gullible patients into becoming helpless subjects for market-oriented medical research, a danger to which *The Economist* caustically termed as one of 'the odder ways in which India is making mark in services than it has ever done in manufacturing' (*The Economist*, 2000). The organ donation in the evolving scenario may cater to the foreign patients as it is now doing the affluent Indian patients.

AFFORDABILITY OF DRUGS

With the coming in of TRIPS-compliant patent regime, the patented drugs have become increasingly unaffordable for a large number of people, particularly the poor. This would be significantly more in the case of newly discovered drugs. Their distribution in public health services may also become difficult due to constraints of allocations. This welfare loss was anticipated by experts even before the amendment of the Patent Act. The recourse to 'compulsory production' and 'parallel imports' by other countries for obtaining cheap drugs under TRIPS is likely to be subverted by the developed countries given the recent experience with Human Immunodeficiency Virus (HIV)/Acquired Immune Deficiency Syndrome (AIDS) drugs (Hong, 2000). Besides, the solution would be decidedly worse for countries which have no or insufficient manufacturing capacity for taking advantage of compulsory licensing to meet their domestic health needs. They would face the most acute problem in catering to it. Pharma MNCs are also trying to bring unpatented drugs much in public demand within the ambit of 'patents' through some changes in the products. Certain medicines which are in low demand may go out of production altogether (Hong, 2000; Orbinski, 2001). The MNCs have even acquired patents in respect of homemade remedies from local produce such as *haldi* and neem, and herbs used by the Indian people for healing. As there is no meticulous record of traditional knowledge in public domain (some effort has been made in recent years), it will be difficult as well as expensive for the government to contest such patents in international courts and get them cancelled notwithstanding an odd success achieved here and there. At the same time, it will take many years and huge resources for the country to convert the rich treasure of traditional knowledge in medicines into patents by national government, companies and social organizations. There is also no evidence that with the onset of the new patent regime, the focus of multinational pharmaceutical companies is shifting from the diseases of the affluent countries to those of the developing countries because higher profits can be made from the former where the patients have higher paying capacity and drug penetration is high (Kulkarni, 2004). Contrary to the expectation, these companies are not locating their R&D research units in developing countries. In fact, a number of MNEs have closed down their R&D facilities in India (Lalitha, 2002). Thus, the much-touted transfer of technology from developed to developing countries and setting up production facilities for drugs in them also does not materialize as the pharmaceutical firms are merely interested in the distribution of their products. The aggressive takeovers and mergers in the industry would enable them to take control of the national enterprises and their production and distribution processes as well. This development has the potential of destabilizing even the national companies from primarily catering to the needs of the local people. It is also becoming evident that even the national pharmaceutical companies, like their foreign counterparts, are looking for profitable markets in the developed countries for their growth and development (Mishra et al., 2003). There is a shift away from bulk drugs towards high valued formulations (Jha, 2007). They are making investments in those countries, forging tie-ups with foreign companies and focusing on discovery of drugs which can capture their market (The Associated Chambers of Commerce and Industry of India, 2005). WTO regime, in any case, would make it difficult for small manufacturers to survive due to low volume, high cost and inadequate capital. India also faces the prospect of dumping of large volumes of many intermediate and bulk drugs at a much lower cost from China which would throw such producers out of market. This has already happened in Gujarat, A.P. and Karnataka (Lalitha, 2002). Besides, the changes in the patent regime have also led to decline in exports and increase in imports (Joseph, 2009). They impact both the patients and the manufacturers (Jha, 2007).

DAMAGED TO PUBLIC HEALTH

The trade liberalization in health services will capture the most profitable components of public health services and would increasingly tap public funds for expansion and sustenance of their business. It will create markets in public health services where none existed earlier, thereby reorienting their character. More serious, under the pressure of the WTO, the existing national or local health regulations may be dismantled so as not to restrict free flow of trade. It would also fail to protect public health against factors injurious to health such as environmental degradation, bio-piracy, export of hazardous wastes, contaminated food, import of alien organisms, exports of diseased products, aggressive advertisements for consumption of potentially harmful commodities (tobacco, alcohol, soft drinks), distribution of banned and bannable drugs and equally risky combinations, promotion of health-threatening food habits and cultural items impacting lifestyle, values and social practices, etc. (Hong, 2000; People's Health Assembly, 2000). That some of it is already happening, as reported in the media from time to time, would suffice to convince that these apprehensions are not misplaced. There is thus an enormous potential for international trade to cause damage to public health, deepen and widen iniquities. Given the unequal power structure at the global level, the developing countries would have little leverage in protecting national interests not to speak of the interests of the poor in any international agreement on the subject which some experts suggest as a way out.

PRIMACY OF PUBLIC INTEREST

Prior to the onset of economic reforms and integration with the global economy, the polity in India had been premised on the conception of a state which represented 'public interest' and was differentiated from 'private interest' of individuals, institutions or groups. The private enterprise did enjoy the constitutional freedom to operate in the economy but subject to the state policy which was committed to uphold public interest. This constituted the philosophical rationale for state to provide essential social and economic services to the people and regulate the private sector activities. Public health facilities from primary care to tertiary level were established by the government with public funds because it was in public interest to do so. Similar considerations weighed with the government in regulating the private pharmaceutical manufacturers and setting up public enterprises to produce essential drugs for making them available at reasonable prices (Sengupta, 1999). This, however, changed when the government started dismantling regulatory structures and shedding responsibilities in many areas of social provisioning. In the health sector, it first created space for the private sector to establish facilities and later even provided incentives for its growth. It also restricted access of people to subsidized public healthcare to facilitate expansion of private healthcare. The public–private partnership was the next step in the evolution of the policy. With trade liberalization, this process has taken a quantum leap and extended to include deregulation of licensing and control, attracting foreign direct investment, curtailing existing public funded services, creating markets in public health system for purchase of healthcare from private suppliers, promoting diverse financing arrangements and other facilitating instruments.

These measures would unmistakably show that state has taken a complete about-turn from its earlier stance of a tilt in favour of public interest and, at the least, neutrality between public and private interests in matters of growth. It is now actively moving to promote commercial interests. It no longer sees any contradiction between supporting private interest of health industry and serving a public purpose of providing healthcare to its people. Rather, it believes that the former ensures the latter. In the free trade regime with focus on export as an engine of economic growth, the state policy would increasingly uphold commercial interests, more so when it has virtually emerged as the dominant player. The creation of markets where none existed and prising open public funding for private services in health sector constitute the distinct evidence of this trend. Much greater penetration of private sector will take place as new agreements on services are concluded in the WTO. The MNCs engaged in trade in health products and services are lobbying hard backed by their national governments to remove barriers to trade in developing countries so as to create competitive environment for their entry as suppliers. They find the publicly funded health sector as a large and lucrative business opportunity easy to tap by virtue of their strength, financial and technological (Sexton, 2003). They are adopting various tactics from subterfuge to pressure and threat to get an opening so as to break the resistance of developing countries (Hong, 2000; Sexton, 2003).

The public health services cannot escape increasing intrusion of foreign suppliers unless they are 100 per cent funded from public funds and without diverse providers. (Sexton, 2003). The opening of public health services to national private suppliers, even partially, would create enough ground for foreign providers to seek entry as competitors. It would no longer be possible to ward off this contingency or even limit the competition to national suppliers.

In the new ambience of a transformed state, private sector in India has already started determining the discourse on health sector and laying down the policy on the design of health services. It is now emboldened to suggest that the government's role in promotion of health services should remain confined to primary healthcare, epidemics, public health and sanitation and the rest can be catered to by the private sector (*Business Standard*, 2004). That this has already been accepted broadly as the policy frame shows the influence which the private industry exercises in the public policy process. The private sector now uses its clout to get decisions which serve its commercial interests. It is already lobbying for measures which can spur growth such as direct tax concessions, relaxations in the norms for setting up medical colleges and reduction exemption in indirect taxes on purchase of equipment, medicines, medical consumables and devices, etc. The health industry is actively pursuing the demand for getting the 'infrastructural status' with benefits such as tax holiday, concessional utilities and preferential land allotments and easier terms of finance in order to create an enabling environment. But the private sector is not prepared to abide by its responsibility for free treatment to a specified percentage of poor patients in return for concessions availed of which has led the courts to take action of against them (*The Hindu*, 2005). A more revealing fact is that even the government is now unwilling to enforce the contractual arrangement (*The Indian Express*, 2004). This is the clearest indication yet of how health policies are and, in future, would be guided by commercial considerations. In yet another instance, striking discordance in perspective and content between the National Health Policy, 2002 (Ministry of Health Family Welfare, 2002), and the Pharmaceutical Policy, 2002, both issued in the same year, emerges from the way the latter has been entirely focused on pharmaceutical industry to the neglect of people's interest, while the former, at least, highlights the huge challenges faced in public health from communicable and non-communicable diseases and lack of access to affordable essential drugs by a large majority of people (Bhargava, 2004). The least that was expected from the Government of India, the source of both the policies, was that pharmaceutical policy would harmonize with the needs articulated in the National Health Policy in making essential drugs easily available and affordable to the people. Drug prices show enormous variation in retail prices indicating huge trade margins and translate into unaffordable treatment costs. It should have put essential drugs under price control, come down heavily on continued circulation of spurious drugs, banned and irrational drugs and hazardous formulations, etc. (Bhargava, 2004). While it has not taken the desired steps, the list of drugs under Drug Price Control order has been drastically reduced from 347 in 1979 to 74 in 1995 to serve the interests of the industry. This will make off patent but essential drugs also costlier. When this order was challenged in the Karnataka High Court and stay order was granted against the operation of Drug Price Control Order (DPCO), the Government of India filed SLP (C) 3668/2003 for impugnment of the High Court's order (LOCOST, 2004). Several public interest bodies filed affidavits in the Supreme Court (WP [Civil] 423/2003) against the criteria for DPCO as it would increase the price of medicines and, therefore, affect the health of the people and sought the Courts' extensive directions to the Government of India to protect people's interest (LOCOST, 2004). Government of India's response to this petition could be deduced from the position taken by the National Pharmaceutical authority that there was no case for expanding the control list (*Economic & Political Weekly*, 2004).

Supreme Court vide its interim order dated 10 March 2003 suspended the Pharmaceutical Policy, 2002, and stayed the order of the Karnataka High Court besides giving directions about formulating an appropriate criteria for keeping the essential and life-saving drugs not falling out of price control and review of list of essential and life-saving drugs. In response to this order, Government of India brought out an updated National List of Essential Medicines, 2003, consisting of 354 drugs. The reports of two committees set up by it (Sandhu Committee 2004 and Pronab Sen Task Force 2005) to look into the pricing issue along with the report of commission on macro-economics and Health, 2004, endorsed the price control of drugs. The Draft Pharmaceutical Policy, 2006, was also prepared after the suspension of Pharmaceutical Policy, 2002, by the Court which has proposed that all 354 drugs in the National List of Essential Medicines, 2003, would be brought under Price Control in addition to the existing list of 74 drugs and would apply to formulations and not bulk drugs. It has also proposed exemption of several drugs from price control along with some structural changes in the drug pricing mechanism. Due to strong objections of industry and stiff lobbying by it, however, the drug pricing issue was entrusted to another committee (Reddy, 2006) which suggested that the method proposed by industry could also be one of the criteria for ensuring that essential drugs do not fall out of price control besides the cost-based price control proposed by other committees. The matter was referred to the Group of Ministers for reconciling the viewpoints of 'stakeholders' which could not come to a decision due to divergent opinions, resulting obviously from intense pressure exerted by industry. Meanwhile, the Parliamentary Standing Committee on Health and Family Welfare in its Forty-fifth Report, tabled on 4 August 2010 in Lok Sabha, recommended a blanket cap on profit margins of all medicines across the board. Government has so far conveyed no decision to the Supreme Court after the latter's order of March 2003. The case has not yet come up for further hearing.

Similarly, on the patent law, government's bias towards the industry was evident. The ordinance issued prior to the new enactment had reflected its anxiety to promote the interests of pharmaceutical companies rather than the concern for easy access of people to cheaper drugs—a truth which even an editorial in a premier American Newspaper was constrained to highlight (New York Times, 2005). The pressure of Left parties, at least, forced the government to insert some amendments taking into account several issues raised by public interest groups. Still, the law that has emerged fails to 'protect the public from the aggressive monopolies that Patents confer on right holders'. The law has not incorporated flexibilities that are available within TRIPS to safeguard public interest (Gopakumar & Amin, 2005). But even this law is not considered sufficiently friendly to the pharmaceutical industry. There are pressures from the USA to further tighten the patent law to suit their MNCs. It is evident that the government is reluctant to expand the list of drugs in DPCO or regulate prices despite reports of the two committees set up by it, recommendations of the Parliamentary Standing Committee on Health and Family Welfare and approve the Draft Pharmaceutical Policy, 2006, due to the pressure of the pharmaceutical lobby, ignoring the stark reality of 500-600 million people in the country lacking regular access to essential medicines and cost of medicines forming up to 50 per cent of medical expenditure of which 80-90 per cent is out of pocket (*Economic & Political Weekly*, 2006), Even the unnecessary, unscientific and therapeutically useless drugs have not been weeded out for the same reason (Srinivasan & Bhargava, 2006). Meanwhile, the situation of overpricing of drugs continues unabated and has aggravated in many ways. The petitioners have moved the Court for issue of directions for regulation and control of medicines, vaccines, sera and biological products.

Medical education is yet another area where public interest will be ignored. With its declared commitment to push export of manpower under GATS, the government would have to remodel curricula of medical education and training to suit the needs of the foreign market. The pressure would also come from the health personnel intending to migrate. Government is already lobbying for relaxation of entry restrictions and norms of qualifications imposed by developed countries. It is seeking acceptance for formulation of international standards which would be acceptable across countries. This obviously implies that the syllabi of medical teaching in future would be determined by foreign markets rather than the needs of our own health system, epidemiological profile and socio-economic conditions besides commercialization of medical education has already pushed up the cost of entry which has barred access to large segment of population besides affecting its quality adversely (Bhargava, 2010).

Government is already faced with increasing demand to purchase more health services from the private suppliers in its public health system which has already enjoyed huge subsidies in its growth. The liberalization of insurance sector would facilitate this trend. That the government may be moving in this direction is indicated from a reported proposal (not a decision yet) to explore the possibility of converting CGHS into an insurance policy. A national health insurance scheme (Rashtriya Swasthya Bima Yojana [RSBY]) for the rural poor has already been put in place. National Rural Health Mission has also outlined District Missions' Strategy to move towards paying hospitals for services by way of reimbursement. All this indicates that government is increasingly changing over to a purchaser rather than a supplier of health services.

The promotion of medical tourism as a policy would inevitably and increasingly lead to decisions about healthcare facilities suited to commercial interests.

The industry is keen to utilize its facilities which remain underutilized due to a small number of high-end income users. One of its demands was to categorize hospitals according to costs, quality and range of services. Government has recently enacted the clinical establishments (Regulation) Act, 2010, which would presumably work out such a classification institutionalizing multi-tiered healthcare infrastructure. The easy import of latest equipment and consumables to suit foreign patients has been permitted at the behest of the industry. Government is also planning to develop tourism infrastructure so as to synchronise it with medicare. These technology-centric islands of excellence would push up the cost of healthcare. This may serve the interests of industry but would enormously hurt public interest with resultant distortion in the demand structure (Godwin, 2004). Public sector health services would be faced with growing pressure to emulate these standards with neither the need nor resources to match them. This would have negative effect on the quality of care. It may also lead to unethical organ transplantation and medical research (Godwin, 2004). Even from the viewpoint of financial gains, the enthusiasm of policymakers about medical tourism is overstated due to over-competition involving 35 countries serving a little more than million medical tourists annually, low returns on investment and incommensurate gains compared to resources spent. On the other hand, diversion of scarce resources from addressing the health needs of people would be incompatible with the social objectives of universal access, quality of services and seriously constrain realization of Millennium Development Goals (Cattaneo, 2009). But there is also considerable scepticism about the potential of medical tourism to attract quality-conscious Western patients merely on cost grounds (Marcelo, 2003).

Clinical trials carry few benefits but enormous risks to health and safety of the subject population. India has fallen into the trap set by industry and Western research institutions in this regard. The drug industry sponsoring clinical trials is not interested in meeting prevailing health challenges such as infectious diseases which are a major killer each year in India but in diseases and patients that assure highest financial returns. This orients the focus towards diseases in the developed countries where nationals have paying capacity and drug penetration is very high. Most of the recent drugs are merely an improved version over the existing therapies aimed at extending the patient life without offering significant benefits but are more expensive than the older drugs. Besides, there is little possibility that the drugs tested here would be introduced in the country at prices which people can afford. Government also has not extracted such a commitment from the concerned companies before consenting to their clinical trials. This is unethical since the risks are borne by the people, while the benefits are derived by others. The increasing linkages of academic/research institutions with drug/pharmaceutical industry has led to a shift in the focus of research and raised other ethical problems such as recruitment practices in clinical trials and impact on the publication of clinical data. Also, this has resulted in public resources (infrastructure and scientists) being used to further the commercial interests of industry rather than to address the health priorities of society. The regulatory guidelines of Indian Council of Medical Research (ICMR) and provisions of the Drugs and Cosmetics Act are ineffective in protecting the interests of subject participants. Some of the clinical trials are camouflaged as research and demonstration projects and there is lack of clarity about the objectives, and serious concerns about the process of approval, nature of selection of the area subjects, lack of full and complete information, monitoring, the manner of obtaining consent and follow-up of those who have been administered drugs/vaccines have emerged from studies even in trials carried out by government agencies with the knowledge and collaboration of ICMR (Bagla, 2007; Srinivasan, 2009). The situation where such trials are carried out by private agencies would be worse (Sarojini et al., 2010). Even premier medical institutions of the country are not free from lack of observance of the guidelines issued by ICMR which, pending enactment of a law, require ethical review and monitoring of trials by the Ethical Committee. But the compliance of these requirements is very poor. The regulatory authority, that is, Drug Controller General of India carries out no site inspections or data audit in respect of these trials leaving the entire responsibility to contract research organizations (CROs) or sponsors. It is not difficult to imagine the resultant hazards to the subjects. Lack of adequate funding by the government for medical research even in its own reputed institutions is driving them to accept projects which compromise public interest. The research budget of All India Institute of Medical Sciences (AIIMS) from internal resources is a mere 0.1-0.2 per cent of the total budget (Saraya, 2010). Clinical trials also undermine the integrity of investigators through financial inducements, disregard risks to participants and at the same time do not produce a scientific innovation to justify it. There is little technology transfer since the industry has complete control over trial design, access to raw data and its interpretation. The outsourcing of clinical trials to CROs and site management organizations and competition for obtaining projects have further undermined the scientific rigour of the work and selection of participants.

Even in respect of preventive health, the decisions to pursue aggressively (even obsessively) the goal of eradication of polio, continue with Vitamin A food supplements, addition of Hep. B as also pressure for inclusion of expensive vaccines of little utility like pentavalent in the ambit of universal immunization involving huge public resources are influenced by commercial interests, national and international and not determined by priorities based on our epidemiological situation and needs of the society (Mittal, 2005). Government may simply shrug off its responsibility having issued ethical guidelines through its apex medical research agency. But such guidelines would have dismal prospects of effective enforcement, given the TRIPS complaint provisions regarding restrictions on disclosure of information, the absence of statutory safeguards and implementation machinery and the incapacity of the affected subjects to seek accountability against violations. The prospects of economic growth and pressure of the industry outweigh known hazards to the lives and health of the clients.

REGULATION OF PRIVATE SECTOR

Health sector reforms have helped private health sector emerge as a dominant player. The rationale for health sector reforms is based on the supposed efficiency and quality of the private healthcare as against the public health services. This assumption has, however, been disproved by studies which have exposed the poor quality of care, unnecessary investigation and surgery, substandard health facilities, unsatisfactory working conditions, untrained healthcare providers, violation of laws and high cost of care in the private sector (Nandraj, 1994). Obviously, the market has failed to regulate these problems. The consumer pressure does not emerge due to the vulnerability of patients and the supplier dominance. Effective regulations are, therefore, needed to protect consumer interests against malpractices due to assumtry of information between service providers and patients (Cattaneo, 2009). But the health sector in India is very weak in this regard even compared to the more market-friendly countries (Jessani, 2002). There is virtually no regulation of the private sector healthcare. Even the few regulations that exist in the country are poorly enforced (Mishra et al., 2003). The trade liberalization would increase the need for regulation more and better rather than less to adopt higher standards of service supply by hospitals and clinics. Trade promotion, even its protagonist's caution, is not to denigrate public health system which is crucial to meet the health needs of people and conduct of medical education. It should 'not only be seen as a source of income in balance of payments but primarily a means to remady shortages and improve domestic health system' (Cattaneo, 2009, p. 4).

The efforts at regulating private health sector, however, present a dismal picture. Three arrangements exist to regulate private sector at present. One is the regulatory bodies, such as medial councils at the central and state levels whose mandate is to discipline medical practitioners and set standards. The other consists of the laws, namely the Drug and Pharmaceutical Act, the Consumer Protection Act and laws relating to organ transplants, sex determination diagnostic tests, food adulteration, environmental pollution, etc., besides state laws regarding health establishments. The third is the recourse to judicial action by consumers. But all these instruments have failed to deliver.

There is a rare case where punitive action is awarded by a state or Central Medical Council even when formal complaints are registered (Bhatt, 1996). The Councils are termed 'useless' even by professionals besides being plagued by corruption. There is strong resistance from professional groups towards self regulation (Iyer & Jessani, 2004). Most states, in any case, do not have laws for regulation of private hospitals, nursing homes, diagnostic centres and pathological laboratories. Those which have such laws have not updated them to remove loopholes (Bhatt, 1996). Only nine states have such laws (A.P, Maharashtra, Delhi, Madhya Pradesh, Manipur, Nepal and Odisha, Punjab and West Bengal). Of them, only A.P. law is relatively recent. In Maharashtra, the Bombay Nursing Homes Regulation Act was enacted in 1949, but the rules were not prepared for 55 years and the draft rules prepared after this huge delay are pending for approval for four years (Phadke, 2010). The central laws relating to drugs and pharmaceuticals, organ donation, female foeticide, food adulteration and pollution, have failed to create any deterrence, considering the number of prosecutions launched and convictions achieved. The situation has led to Supreme Court's interventions in some Public Interest Litigation (PIL) cases for strengthening the regulatory regime and its enforcement. The recourse to judicial action by consumers is time taking, costly and visited by retaliation in varied forms such as inappropriate care and defensive medicine. This then highlights the enormity of the tasks involved in regulating healthcare.

But the state's capacity to put in place a comprehension and effective regulatory regime has dwindled in the new political order resulting from a globalized economy; MNCs have emerged as dominant players which are not easily amenable to the discipline of national regulations for several reasons. Their headquarters/primary facilities are located outside the country. A large part of their business transactions takes place within the organization. They threaten to retaliate with shifting production base, capital flight and withdrawal of products/facilities if action is taken against them. The pressure exerted by them through their home governments is well known (Clarke, 2001). More serious, they use the threat of raising a dispute in the WTO forum against regulatory provisions not suited to them as trade barrier. The important rulings of WTO involving health and environmental issues sufficiently underline the difficulties of any developing country to regulate the MNCs. The private sector players, national as well as international, have also resisted attempt at regulation of the prices of essential drugs or determination of optimum profit margin on them. The enforcement of ethical guidelines in the case of clinical trials and research is considerably hindered by state's inability to access crucial information from the industry—a problem made even more difficult by TRIPS complaint Patent Law. As the international suppliers proliferate and products from foreign lands flood the market, government's ability to protect the health of citizens has been found wanting. The export of contaminated blood products from the UK to India which has remained undetected illustrates the complexity of the problem. Thus, compared to the expanding ambit of regulations required, the authority and will of the Indian state to undertake them is shrinking. Unlike the pre-reform phase, the freedom of state to act against the industry to protect public interest has whittled down and space to assert its authority narrowed substantially. This is because, at the national level, it is on the industry's piggyback that the export potential and the high rate of growth have to be realized while, at the global level, the threat of an adverse ruling by WTO would always loom large.

Under great pressure from civil society and the direction of the Court, however, the central government has recently enacted the clinical Establishment (Registration and Regulation) Act, 2010. But the Act is not applicable to states unless consent is conveyed to adopt it through a resolution of their legislature. Besides, a lot of rule making is required before the Act gets enforced which can take enormous time. With only modest financial penalties for violation of its provisions, the Act is unlikely to create any deterrence against negligence, substandard services and unethical practices. It is also not clear whether the Act would regulate cost of care. Most likely, it would not as the industry would oppose it. The lobby of medical professionals (Indian Medical Association [IMA]) has already made loud and 'irrational' protests even against such a minimal regulatory measure (Phadke, 2010). There is also a proposal to amend the Drugs and Cosmetics Act for regulating quality of blood products, conduct of clinical trials, etc. The Medical Devices Regulation Bill has also been introduced in the Parliament (Baru et al., 2010). Given the experience with other regulatory health instruments, it is to be seen whether there would be effective enforcement of these regulations when they are notified as the states lack the will and capacity for strong action.

AUTONOMY TO DESIGN HEALTH POLICY

In making health policy, state in India has traditionally been influenced by considerations of equity and democratic pressures. In the pre-reform period, it has acted, by and large, to protect the interests of the people, particularly the poor and vulnerable sections, in provizion of healthservices, the needs of the national producers and suppliers in the economy and the interest of patients against the drug industry in the market. When not under pressure of external interests, it has sought to prioritize its healthcare interventions taking into account the epidemiological situation and the constraints of resources and infrastructure. But the reforms carried out in health services have already eroded the structure of equity considerably by undermining state's autonomy to design, distribute and manage healthcare arrangements. This is the experience of developing countries across the globe. Although rhetoric of equity may continue to be voiced and some ad hoc measures may also be taken to protect the interests of the poor, such as the National Rural Health Mission, RSBY for BPL households for meeting hospitalization cost or increased allocation for public health services to silence critics, the market-driven approaches to healthcare would continue to guide its action. Trade liberalization would increasingly interfere with domestic governance to ensure free trade and, therefore, reduce state's power to provide equitable healthcare since non-market devices for this purpose such as risk pooling, cross-subsidization, block contracts, etc., may be declared as trade barriers. In the case of a challenge in the WTO in respect of such measures, an adverse decision would most likely emerge and public funded services could be opened up to private sector suppliers much against the will of the government. Transparency provisions in the GATS (Article III) may expose the fragility of national regulatory mechanisms in the trade body, thereby forcing the government to dilute or change them (Sahni & Kala, 2004). The country may, therefore, not be free to design health policy as per the felt needs of its people or even to determine national priorities in healthcare provisioning and financing arrangements. Integration with global economy would shrink the space of manoeuvre ability since major interventions in disease control are being initiated by global players and international donors (Mittal, 2005). This has already been happening for sometime. The attention and resources bestowed on HIV-AIDS, Tuberculosis (TB) and Polio, and technology choices for curative intervention have all been externally determined.

IMPROVEMENT OF PUBLIC HEALTH SERVICES

Prior to reforms, state sought to correct these deficiencies through expansion of health services, additional resource allocation and manpower, improving infrastructure and intensified supervision. But the health sector reforms have instead focused on the promotion of private healthcare, purchasing healthcare from private suppliers, contracting out public services to private suppliers and curtailing the level of public health services rather than expanding, strengthening and improving them. The efficiency is sought to be provided by introducing private sector management in public funded primary, secondary and tertiary services, public- private partnerships and decentralization of funding arrangements and management structures. The thrust of new strategy is on pricing open the public funded health system to private sector providers, creating internal markets and offloading the residual responsibility to lower level agencies. The fundamental issues of quality improvement are, therefore, bypassed and inspiration is sought from coopting the private health sector. The state has thus not only abandoned the responsibility to strengthen public health sector but has also virtually demonstrated a loss of faith in its capability to improve it. It looks upon private health sector as a model of efficiency and quality, and is keener on emerging as a purchaser of healthcare rather than its dominant provider. This paradigm shift in attitude is the most debilitating threat to public funded services and equitable healthcare arrangement. Trade liberalization will intensify if this denigration of public health sector as the techno-centric and high-cost standards of healthcare set by the private sector would be difficult for it to follow.

THE SUGGESTED ACTION

What should be done to stem this onslaught of iniquitous changes and protect people's basic right to healthcare?

Health of the people is far too important a matter to be sacrificed for faster economic growth. A health policy focused on equitable healthcare should be beyond compromise in any society but more so in a democracy. Trade policies may involve some give and take. But the government should be firm that it would never agree to any proposal during negotiations in international fora which dilutes or curtails state's responsibility to provide equitable and need-based healthcare to its people without being linked to the capacity of the seeker to pay (Koivusalo, 2003). This imperative must have national endorsement by the Parliament cutting across party lines. Market-driven health sector reforms have already moved away from this objective. Opening up of health sector to international trade would only push this process irreversibly. A lot of damage has already been done to the health of the people by trade agreements concluded so far. With regard to GATS, no fresh agreement has yet emerged. Only negotiations have been carried out. Therefore, India can still say 'no' to further negotiations on trade liberalization in the health sector. Once, however, an agreement is reached even on a limited agenda, increasing inroads would be made into the health sector by global competitors. This would set in irreversible changes which would be unstoppable. The structures of international trade, compulsions of the negotiation process, unequal global power relations and diverse pressures brought to bear on the developing countries would leave no room to scuttle the adverse effects of international agreements. If the government is genuine about its commitment to equitable healthcare of its people, there should be a firm 'no' to any negotiation on the opening up of the health sector under GATS. Unlike TRIPS, it is still possible to take this position. But this opportunity may be lost if the government goes ahead and concludes an agreement.

India should also strive for a composite stand of the developing countries as a group to keep health out of negotiations on services and to oppose primacy being given to trade against health by the WTO. But India, sadly, appears to be distancing itself from such a stand with the intention of extracting additional concessions in sectors considered more important by it. This is precisely what the developed countries and their trade interests would be looking for to divide the developing world and get through with their agenda of increasing trade liberalization in health and other service subsectors. It is evident that the country's leadership considers economic growth as an overriding priority and feels that health-related adverse externalities, if any, can be managed or at least compensated by gains elsewhere. This position seriously jeopardizes prospects of sustaining an equitable healthcare system and protecting interests of the poorer sections in this arrangement.

While GATS incorporates all services within its ambit, it excludes those supplied in 'the exercise of government authority'. This has been interpreted narrowly to imply any service which is supplied neither on a commercial basis nor in competition with one or other service suppliers. This conservative interpretation need not apply to health services as per the view taken by the WTO council for trade. Nonetheless, the danger persists that dispute may be raised and an adverse ruling may ensue. The dilution of public health services carried out by introducing elements of privatization such as user charges, pay cabins, contracting out services and purchasing of services from private suppliers creates the prospects of entry of foreign suppliers through a WTO decision. With a view to keeping the health services out of the trade negotiations, government should reverse the private sector intrusion into public health services in order that the latter remain a facility entirely funded and provided by the government. Private sector in healthcare can exist for those who wish to avail of its services on its terms. But it should not get any concessions, incentives, subsidies for its growth or a share of market in the public health system. Rather, public health system should be strengthened in terms of resources, manpower, training, management, accountability mechanisms and quality enforcement norms. It should also revert to its comprehensive character. The secondary and tertiary care should not be delinked from it. The introduction of irritants like user charges should be withdrawn as the resources generated by it are negligible but deprivation resulting from it is extensive. Similarly, paying wards/cabins should be merged with the general wards so that limited hospitalization services can be optimally utilized for the neediest patients. Thus, opposition to trade liberalization in health services should accompany movement for restoration of the original Alma Ata paradigm of healthcare and citizen entitlement backed by statutory guarantee. It is this goal which should define the brief of the national negotiators in the international trade fora and on which no compromise should be accepted.

It is also important that health sector is not conceived as an instrument of economic growth. Such a view strikes at the root of the healthcare as a service for the welfare of people. Rather, healthy people are a condition for economic progress of the nation. Health services should overwhelmingly operate without an element of profit. The promotion of medical tourism, encouragement of outsourced clinical trials, vigorous export of health manpower and commercialization of healthcare would introduce unalterable changes in health care system which would jeopardize people's health. Some exchange of health services would take place, in any case, because India is a large economy and has more advanced health facilities compared to many underdeveloped countries. But it should not be promoted as a tradable commodity to generate wealth. The social cost of doing so is much too high compared to the small economic gains it may entail. This principle should be firmly embedded in the state policy and approach to international negotiations.

Trade discussions in the WTO in other sectors of services as also on other agreements involve issues supposedly outside the health sector, such as policy on procurement, competition, subsidies, investment, intellectual property rights, etc., but have many adverse implications for healthcare system some of which may not be comprehensible to the participants immediately. This is what has been called 'trade creep' (Koivusalo, 2000). The decisions in regard to them may affect access to and quality of health services and curtail state's power to protect people's health. The commitment/agreement on these issues may irreversibly bind the government to serve the interest of the private sector—national and international—from which it may be difficult to extricate later (Koivusalo, 2000). This underlines the urgency of building up expertise to examine the health implications of each agenda for discussion by a group of competent experts and social activists in order that caution is exercised at the time of negotiations. It would also be advisable to associate some of these experts during the negotiation itself so that the new proposals coming up in the course of discussions are comprehensively analysed for the national negotiators.

A large measure of liberalization has already taken place in the service sector and outside and more continues apace. Very little is known about its impact on the health outcomes in general and those of the poorer sections, the women, the children, the socially disadvantaged in particular. Scientifically collected information on this subject is necessary to assist negotiators in resisting further push towards trade liberalization in global negotiations. To be equipped with adequate information on this aspect, an effective mechanism is required to be in place to provide the government with necessary feedback on this social reality. At present, a Trade and Health cell exists in the Ministry of Health and Family Welfare to assess the impact of WTO and other trade agreements on public health in India and suggest ways to formulate effective legislation and policy initiatives to deal with them. It is intended to provide technical assistance to the Ministry in areas of international trade-related agreements. The cell is engaged to evolve policy coherence between trade policy and health policy with special focus on institutional mechanisms. The cell has been carrying out quantitative and qualitative research and analysis of international trade issues for which some studies were commissioned and completed. It has also taken preliminary steps to implement WHO Resolution 61.21 on Global Strategy and Plan of Action on Public Health (Ministry of Health and Family Welfare, 2009). Government should associate, besides competent professionals, social activists and public advocacy organizations committed to equity concerns and place research outputs and other feedbacks in public domain for a wide public discussion. It should also have periodical consultations with civil society on the issue. This material should be effectively used to resist trade liberalization in the health sector during negotiations.

As it is, even outside GATS, the disturbing effects of international trade on health outcomes are becoming increasingly evident. The deterioration in diets, aggressively induced consumption of products injurious to health, contaminated food products, etc., have already posed serious threats to health. Dumping of harmful technologies and products create health hazards difficult even to isolate let alone neutralize. The environmental degradation has deteriorated the quality of life, livelihood opportunities and food security of a large section of the people (Koivusalo, 2003). The adverse impact of cultural products is destabilizing the social support and value systems which increase manifold the incidence of mental disorders. The microbial traffic through increased human contact is manifesting in new diseases and aggravation of existing ones beyond the capacity of health system to control (Hong, 2000). This underlines the need for social science research, of a continuing nature, on the health outcomes, particularly of the vulnerable population so that government's position is strengthened during negotiations when it resists liberalization. Needless to say that research should be publicly funded and carried out by organizations known for their intellectual independence and social commitment.

The suggested course of action can only be carried out by a strong state determined to assert its autonomy on domestic policy in the international fora, resist pressures from commercial and elite interests in the country and evolve its stand on the health sector issues through democratic consensus. Sadly, the governance in India has displayed absence of this capacity. The democratic bodies including political parties too have failed to move the government in this direction. It is time that the intense pressure is exerted by civil society through mass mobilization to force the government to take note of people's concerns and comprehensively accommodate them in its health policy paradigm, operational processes and negotiation strategy in the international fora. This task needs to be pursued on top priority by social and political groups cutting across their organizational boundaries and ideological lines.

REFERENCES

Abrol, D. (2003). *Higher education under WTO: An Indian perspective, in GATS and education*. Lady Irwin College and Transform India Group.

Adlung, R. (2009). *Trade in healthcare and health insurance services: The GATS as a supporting actor (2)* (Staff Working Paper). WTO; Economic Research and Statistics Division.

Bagla, P. (2007). Despite note that AIDS vaccine had failed, India changed rules and continued trials. *The Indian Express*.

Bajaj, J. S. (1998). *Medical education and healthcare: A Pluridimensional paradigm*. IIAS.

Baru, R., Acharya, A., Acharya, S., Shiva Kumar, A. K., and Nagaraj, K. (2010). Inequities in access to health services in India: Caste, class and region. *Economic & Political Weekly*, *45*(38), 49–59.

Bertrand, A., & Kalafatides, L. (2001). World Trade Organization and the liberalization of trade in healthcare and services. In J. Mander & E. Goldsmith (Eds.), *The case against the global economy, and for a turn towards localization* (pp. 189–201). Earthscan Publications.

Bhargava, A. (2004). Pharmaceutical policy (PP) (2002) and national health policy (NHP) 2002, discordance in perspectives and content (LOCOST/JSS2004). All India Drug Action Network (AIDAN).

Bhargava, P. M. (2010). Whither medical and healthcare: The government has deliberately allowed its hospitals to go to seed so that private hospitals can flourish. *The Tribune*.

Bhatt, R. (1996). Regulation of the private health sector in India. *International Journal of Health Planning and Management*, *11*(3), 253–274.

Business Standard. (2004). Stay off healthcare, govt. told.

Business Standard. (2005). India may cede ground on services.

Cattaneo, O. (2009). *Trade in health services: What's in it for developing countries?* (World Bank Policy Research Working Paper). World Bank.

Clarke, T. (2000). Mechanism of corporate rule in gold smith. In J. Mander & E. Goldsmith (Eds.), *The case against the global economy, and for a turn towards localization*. Earthscan Publications.

Economic & Political Weekly. (2004). Editorial: prescription and practice. *39*(34), 3763–3764.

Economic & Political Weekly. (2006). Corporate irresponsibility in drug pricing. *41*(48), 4927–4928.

Godwin, S. K. (2004). Medical tourism. *Economic & Political Weekly*, *39*(36), 3981–3983.

Gootiiz, B., & Mattoo, A. (2009). *Services in Doha: What's on the table?* (Policy Research Working Paper). World Bank, Developing Research Group Trade Team.

Gopakumar, K. M., & Amin, T. (2005). Patents (amendment) bill 2005: A critique. *Economic & Political Weekly*, *40*(15), 1503–1505.

Helleiner, G. K. (2002). *Developing countries in global economic governance and negotiation processes, in governing globalization: Issues and institutions* (edited by Deepak Nayyar). Oxford University Press.

Hong, E. (2000). *Globalization and the impact on health; a third world view*. Third World Network.

Iyer, A., & Jessani, A. (2004). *Medical ethics*. Voluntary Health Association of India.

Jessani, A. (2002). Social objectives of healthcare services; regulating the private sector. In S. K. Prabhu & R. Sudarshan (Eds.), *Reforming India's social sector: Poverty, nutrition, health and gender* (pp. 205–220). Orient Black Swan.

Jha, R. (2007). Options for Indian pharmaceutical industry in the changing environment. *Economic & Political Weekly, 42*(39), 3958–3967.

Joseph, R. K. (2009). Estimating India's trade in drugs and pharmaceuticals. *Economic & Political Weekly, 44*(2), 18–23.

Khadria, B. (2003). *Paradoxes and pitfalls in globalization of education under the WTO regime of trade in education services in GATS and education.* Lady Irwin College and Transform India Group.

Koivusalo, M. (2000). Presentation on behalf of European Health Management Association before European Commission Consultation on Trade and Health, GASPP (Globalism and Social Policy Programme).

Koivusalo, M. (2003). *Impact of WTO agreements on health and development policies* (GASPP Policy Brief). GASPP.

Krugman, P. (2005). Passing the buck. *The Hindu.*

Kulkarni, M. (2004). Drug makers, providers and users. *Economic & Political Weekly, 39*(50), 5291–5293.

Lalitha, N. (2002). Indian pharmaceutical industry in WTO regime, a SWOT analysis. *Economic & Political Weekly, 37*(34), 3542–3555.

LOCOST. (2004). *Impoverishing the poor, pharmaceutical and drug pricing in India.* All India Drug Action Network (AIDAN).

Marcelo, R. (2003). India fosters growing 'medical tourism sector'. *The Financial Times.*

Ministry of Health and Family Welfare. (2009). *Annual report 2009–2010.* Government of India.

Mishra, R, Chatterjee, R., & Rao, S. (2003). *India health report.* Oxford University Press.

Mitchell, A., Mahal, A., & Bossert, T. (2011). Healthcare utilization in Andhra Pradesh. *Economic & Political Weekly, XLVI*(5), 15–19.

Mittal, O. (2005). International health governance in the era of imperialist globalization. *Revolutionary Democracy, II*(1).

Nandraj, S. (1994). Beyond the law and lord, quality of private healthcare. *Economic & Political Weekly, 29*(27), 1680–1685.

New York Times. (2005). India's choice dated, reproduced in *The Indian Express.*

O'Brien, R., Goetz, A. M., Scholte, J. A., & Williams, M. (2000). *Contesting global governance: Multilateral economic institutions and global social movements.* Cambridge University Press.

Obrinski, J. (2001). Health, equity and trade: A failure in global governance. In G. P. Sampson (Ed.), *The role of the World Trade Organization in global governance* (pp. 230–231). United Nations University Press.

People's Health Assembly. (2000). *Health in the era of globalization* (Paper by PGA Drafting Group, PHA Secretariat, G. K. Savar).

Peters, D. H., Yazbeck, A. S., Sharma, R. R., Ramana, G. N. V., & Pritchett, L. H. (2002). *Better health systems for India's poor: Findings, analysis and options.* World Bank and Hindustan Publishing Corporation.

Phadke, A. (2010). The Indian Medical Association and the Clinical Establishment Act, 2010: Irrational opposition to regulation. *Indian Journal of Medical Ethics*, *VII*(4), 229–231.

Qadeer, I., Sen, K., & Nayar, K. R. (2001). *Public health and the poverty of reforms: The South Asian predicament*. SAGE.

Reddy, S. (2006). Report of the Joint Committee on the Draft Pharmaceutical Policy headed by Secretary, Department of Chemicals and Petrochemicals Ministry of Chemicals and Fertilizers.

Reddy, S., & Qadeer, I. (2010). Medical tourism in India: Progress or predicament? *Economic & Political Weekly*, *45*(20), 69–75.

Retallack, S. (2001). The environmental cost of economic globalization. In J. Mander & E. Goldsmith (Eds.), *The case against the global economy, and for a turn towards localization* (pp. 189–201). Earthscan Publications.

Sahni, R., & Kala, S. (2004). GATS and higher education: Some reflections. *Economic & Political Weekly*, *39*(21), 2159–2164.

Saraya, A. (2010). *Industry sponsored clinical research: A boon or a curse* (Unpublished). All India Institute of Medical Sciences.

Sarojini, N., Anjali, S., & Ashalata, S. (2010). *Findings from a visit to Bhadrachallam: HPV vaccine demonstration project sale in Andhra Pradesh, New Delhi*.

Sengupta, A. (1999). Infrastructure development in healthcare and the pharmaceutical industry: Implications of the world development report. In M. Rao (Ed.), *Disinvesting in health: The World Bank's prescriptions for health*. SAGE.

Sexton, S. (2003). *Trading healthcare away: the WTO's general agreement on trade in services (GATS) in restructuring health services: Changing contexts and comparative perspectives*. Zed Books.

Shukla, S. P. (2002). From the GATT to the WTO and beyond. In D. Nayyar (Ed.), *Governing globalization: Issues and institutions* (pp. 254–286). Oxford University Press.

Srinivasan, S. (2009). The clinical trials scenario in India. *Economic & Political Weekly*, *44*(35).

Srinivasan, S., & Bhargava, A. (2006). Medicines: Why is Paswan's price reduction a let-down? *Economic & Political Weekly*, *41*(50), 5101–5105.

The Economist. (2000). Clinical trials in India, patient capital.

The Hindu. (2005). Govt. fails to take action against erring hospitals.

The Indian Express. (2004). Statement of principal secretary of India, Delhi govt.

Wallach, L. (2001). The World Trade Organizations' five year record. In J. Mander & E. Goldsmith (Eds.), *The case against the global economy, and for a turn towards localization* (pp. 175–188). Earthscan Publications.

Chapter 4

Biomedical Research in India*
Law and Ethics at Crossroads

Anjali Shenoi

INTRODUCTION

Medical research is shaped by a variety of social, political and economic interests. These interests affect, among other things, the type of research that gets done, who does it and whether the results are made public. As the world of medical research becomes increasingly globalized, several pharmaceutical companies have started outsourcing drug trials to contract research organizations (CROs) in developing countries which now make up a 'specialized global industry' in the recruitment of and research on human participants (Petryna, 2005, p. 183). In India, trials are increasingly being conducted on foreseeably vulnerable populations, with profits as the bottom line. Exploiting opportunities rather than public health priorities appear to drive this industry. Drug companies' apparent easy access to such populations raises serious questions about the unequal social contexts in which research is being performed and about how conditions of inequality are at present facilitating a global proliferation of drug trials. These developments reflect high levels of corporate involvement in research and have not only ethical implications for both medical research and practice but also raise relatively newer questions around the conduct of such biomedical research in marginalized or vulnerable populations, particularly in the context of international and national laws on human rights.

* *Social Change* 42, no. 4 (December 2012): 527–538.

It is this disillusionment in the existing system, given the failure of medical councils and other professional bodies to ensure ethical behaviour, that gave birth to the bioethics movement in the country. The movement, though still at a nascent stage in India, has been attempting to expand the traditional boundaries set by the physician–patient relationship and the practice of high-tech medicine in the developed world towards establishing an ethic that is more responsive to the vagaries of the research industry in the country as well as towards the many public health crises it seeks to address. In this endeavour, multi dimensional efforts are also on to amalgamate this philosophy into education curricula and to set up formal training courses and workshops for young researchers and scientists in collaboration with institutions such as the Indian Council of Medical Research (ICMR), now offering post graduate diplomas in bioethics. A special case can also be made for legal clinics for students seeking to explore the intersectionality between law and ethics in the field of biomedical research in India. This is particularly important given the dynamic pace and scope of the industry that creates complex legal and ethical issues, questions and controversies which often seem to fall between the cracks. This chapter tries to lay out these inter sectional linkages through the means of recent advocacy initiatives against the unethical conduct of trials on marginalized communities along with the broader scope of regulation of the biomedical research industry in India. As is further illustrated through the course of this chapter, there is an urgent need to set out parameters and define a certain direction which regulation of medical research in the country should take, given the existing scenarios of increasing globalization in the field, albeit with little harmonization of international guidelines.

TAKING ON INDUSTRIAL PROPORTIONS—DRUG TRIALS IN INDIA

India, with its huge 'treatment naïve' patient base, low-cost advantage, completion of clinical trials on time, improving infrastructure and strong support from the state, is witnessing an unprecedented growth in its drug trial markets (see Figure 4.1). Many major pharmaceuticals and CRO[1] have started conducting their clinical trials in India. With state patronization, 'improving' infrastructure, industry-friendly regulation and trained workforce, the growth is projected to increase by leaps

---

India ranks as the second most attractive destinations after China, for clinical trials for the following reasons

- Large patient pool, a diverse gene pool
- Considerable low per-patient trial cost
- Drug-naive and treatment-naive patients suffering from every conceivable disease
- Well-trained and enthusiastic investigators and premiere medical institutes available in the country, as compared to developed countries
- Good patient compliance/retention
- An 'increasingly accommodating regulatory environment'

Figure 4.1 *Why India?*

Source: Rajan (2007).

and bounds (RNCOS, 2007). According to a report by the Associated Chambers of Commerce and Industry, India was set to grab clinical trials business valued at approximately US$ 1 billion by 2010, up from US$ 200 million in 2007 (Chatterjee, 2008). Most pharmaceutical companies conduct trials through CROs. Its market in India has grown from ₹4,230 million in 2005 to ₹16,110 million in 2010, while it is expected to cross ₹27,210 million by 2012 (Paliwal, 2011). An industry report predicts that India by 2011 will be conducting more than 15 per cent of the total global clinical trials (RNCOS, 2007). In October 2008, the Drugs Controller General India (DCGI) stated that there were 582 (registered) clinical trials being conducted in India, of which 72 per cent were carried out by the pharmaceutical industry (Srinivasan, 2009).

MAJOR STAKEHOLDERS

At the core of the industry are the pharmaceutical companies, whose products are tested through these clinical trials. Particularly striking in this regard are the interests of the Indian pharmaceutical companies that are in the process of retooling their business models in the wake of India signing on to the patent regime imposed by the World Trade Organization (WTO).

A close second are members of the CRO industry, estimated by the Chemical Pharmaceutical Generic Association to be worth between $100 and $120 million in 2005, while growing at 20 to 25 per cent per year (Greene, 2007, p. 12). These are the most immediate beneficiaries of trials coming to India and are therefore keen to create conditions for these trials to grow in a sustained and streamlined fashion. Another sub set in this category would be the physicians who actually conduct the trials though, in the Indian context, they have a relatively marginal presence compared to the CROs in setting the infrastructural and regulatory agenda for research.

A third set of actors consists of the regulatory agents of the state. The DCGI and the Ministry of Science and Technology are actively involved through its Department of Biotechnology which looks at clinical research as part of a wider initiative to make India a global biotechnology power.

Thus, while there are convincing market rationales for taking trials to India and an already strong flow of trials through the multinational CRO industry, much of the efforts towards the capacity-building of the industry are still targeted with a profit motive and to encourage further outsourcing of such trials in the future. In this effort, ethics legally enshrined and contractually enforced are integral to the capacity-building efforts around clinical research in India. Not surprisingly, members of the CRO industry are the most active drivers in building ethical regulatory infrastructure. However, the form this ethic takes in no way takes into consideration the structural violence and human rights violations that occur during trials (see Figure 4.2).

EXISTING REGULATORY MECHANISMS IN INDIA

Over the last two decades, along with the drive for liberalization, several debates have emerged over the conduct of clinical trials by CROs, research institutions, pharmaceutical industries, international health NGOs and the state. The office of the DCGI and the Central Drugs Standard Control Organisation (CDSCO) under the Ministry of Health and Family Welfare (MoHFW) are responsible for the regulation of clinical trials in the country. Clinical trials and their regulation, unlike health however, come under the concurrent list.

Although the country has more than half a million practising doctors, fewer than 200 investigators have been trained in good clinical practice, with even fewer with any sort of background in bioethics.

- Among some 14,000 general hospitals, no more than 150 have the adequate infrastructure to conduct trials
- There are fewer than a dozen pathology laboratories that meet the criteria for compliance with good laboratory practice.
- Only about half of the large hospitals have institutional review boards, and even these boards have not yet formulated standard operating procedures, and they, too, often lack the expertise with which to evaluate protocols. Information about conflicts of interest is neither sought nor voluntarily provided by investigators

Figure 4.2 *What the Figures Show*

Source: Bhaumik et al. (2010, p. 15).

Schedule Y of the Drugs and Cosmetics Act, 1945

A first in this regard was the incorporation of the Schedule Y in the Drugs and Cosmetics Act, 1945. The enforcement that came into existence in 1988 was, at that time, essentially for the provision of support specifically designed in such a way so as to further promote the upscaling of indigenous generic pharmaceutical companies through basic guidelines on research. However, with the entry of large pharmaceutical companies along with the several multinationals in field of biomedical research, the existing provision underwent a second amendment in 1995, leading to a revised document in line with the ICH-GCP (International Council or Harmonisation Guidelines for Good Clinical Practice).[2] However, the most recent amendment to the Schedule Y, made in 2005, has only served to further the interests of the markets and to protect a growing industry that is clearly driven by profits rather than the well-being of the trial participants or public health priorities. This gives rise to what may be seen as an ambiguous and practically ineffective latent regulatory tool (see Figure 4.3).

Some important features of the Schedule Y amended in 2005

- Arbitrary powers to the DCGI to waive off the need of earlier phases of trials
- Does away with the earlier prescribed phase lag for drugs discovered in other countries
- A special waiver clause was introduced, wherein Phase I trials of foreign drugs were not permitted, except for drugs of special relevance to India.
  This clause enabled, for example, Phase I trials of HIV vaccines in India.
- The earlier minimum requirement of number of subjects for Phase III trials to be conducted for drugs approved in other countries was removed and made discretionary
- There are no specific listed requirements for sites where clinical trials can take place, such as availability of expertise and infrastructure to deal with unexpected adverse drug reactions and ICUs.

Figure 4.3 *Important 2005 Amendments of the Schedule Y*

Source: Bhaumik et al. (2010).

Ethical Guidelines for Biomedical Research on Human Participants

The Ethical Guidelines for Biomedical Research on Human Participants first drafted in 1980, formulated by the ICMR,[3] loosely based on the Declaration of Helsinki,[4] was the first document of its kind, published in 2000, to be devoted solely to the prescription of different notions of regulation in this regard. These guidelines, further modified in 2006 along with the guidelines on Good Clinical Practice, have been considered the hallmark in the endeavour to regulate biomedical research in the country. However, the lack of legislative powers has been a major drawback in the proper implementation of these guidelines. A draft bill to make the guidelines legally binding is pending with the MoH. The law is meant to provide for the setting up of a 'Biomedical Research Authority' to oversee research in the country and also to evaluate the functioning of ethics committees.

Registration of Clinical Trials

In an attempt to further the transparency and accountability of clinical research, internal validity of clinical trials and to facilitate the oversight of ethical conduct of trials, the ICMR has initiated a process to provide an online facility for the registration of any form of interventional trial. The Clinical Trial Registry of India (CTRI) is this online registry. The registry that began as a voluntary provision has since then been made mandatory by the DCGI for all trials since 15 June 2009. Any researcher who plans to conduct a trial involving human participants of any intervention such as drugs, surgical procedures, preventive measures, lifestyle modifications, devices, educational or behavioural treatment, rehabilitation strategies as well as trials being conducted in the purview of the Department of AYUSH has to register the trial in the CTRI before the enrolment of the first participant (CTRI, 2010). However, several other research studies continue to go unregistered as 'observation studies', 'operations research', 'demonstration projects' and so on, including several others conducted at private sites by CROs.

ISSUES OF GOVERNANCE: WHERE LAWS ARE TREATED AS GUIDELINES, AND GUIDELINES ARE NOT LAWS

There are many examples of clinical trials that have taken place without proper protocols of consent. Currently, without any independent institutions for monitoring and auditing of drug trials, the infrastructure for regulation, ethics review and monitoring is insufficient. There have been many instances where ethics committees are controlled by the research organizations and cannot act independently. An ICMR survey found that only 40 of 179 institutional ethical committees follow the prescribed legal provisions and function according to various ethical guidelines (Mudur, 2005). Moreover, as a study by Srinivasan (2009, p. 7) shows

> there is no central register of EC decisions, and if a protocol is rejected by one local EC it may be submitted elsewhere. The sponsor is not obliged to inform an EC—or the DCGI—if the protocol being submitted to it has been rejected elsewhere.

Similarly, the lack of coordination between the various ethics committees in a multi-centric trial raises serious concerns of an absence of rigorous approval processes.

In the absence of such a mechanism, it is difficult to ensure that scientific standards are upheld and that good research practices and required trial protocols are fulfilled. Moreover, claims that clinical trial protocols and data are protected pose a serious threat to the tenets of transparency and hence accountability in clinical trials in India. Similarly, lack of any form of regulatory control over the mushrooming CRO industry too has raised several pertinent concerns. Further, several concerns have been raised regarding the lack of human resources at DCGI which are consequently not equipped to monitor existing clinical trials in India. The DCGI's office currently has a staff of four or five professionally qualified people and at present does not inspect clinical trial sites, though the government has announced that it is recruiting new staff for this purpose. Audits of clinical trial data are at present only conducted by CROs and sponsors. The United States Food and Drug Administration (USFDA) have recently started auditing trial sites (Srinivasan, 2009).

RECENT EXPERIENCES OF UNETHICAL CONDUCT OF CLINICAL TRIALS

HPV Vaccine Trials—'Minor' Deficiencies, Lessons for the Future

The recent clinical trials of the Human Papilloma virus (HPV) vaccine in India illustrate how shifts in the very science of drug development have influenced the nature of participant recruitment in the country. These trials also exemplify how far removed India's research priorities are with respect to the community's needs and interests and the country's public health priority.

In mid-2009, the Indian unit of the US-based Programme for Appropriate Technology in Health (PATH) began a two-year HPV vaccination drive in India, ambiguously termed as 'demonstration project'. In collaboration with the ICMR, two state governments and with support from the Bill and Melinda Gates Foundation, over 23,000 girls were given the vaccines Gardasil (by Merck Sharpe and

Dohme) and Cervarix (by GlaxoSmithKline) in the southern state of Andhra Pradesh and the western state of Gujarat, respectively (Sarojini et al., 2011).

Public health groups, health networks, women's groups and human rights groups in the country voiced their concerns regarding the unethical promotion of the vaccines in the private and public sectors; the public health implications of their administration; the lack of transparency surrounding the trials; ambiguity in nomenclature and the need to account for reported deaths and adverse events post vaccination. Subsequently, a fact-finding visit to Bhadrachalam in Khammam district, one of the trial sites in Andhra Pradesh, reported serious breaches in medical ethics of the study. Young girls selected for participation here were from poor and disadvantaged social groups— Scheduled Tribes, Scheduled Castes, Muslims and Other Backward Communities. The majority were ethnically tribal and children of agricultural labourers. It became evident that for a population that was particularly vulnerable, adequate information was not provided, appropriate consent or assent was not gathered and no provisions for follow-up care were established (Sarojini et al., 2010).

On 7 April 2010, the government called a halt to all HPV vaccine trials in the country, after a strong campaign by civil society groups and opposition by a Member of Parliament (Dhar, 2010). However, a report from the committee set up by the MoHFW to investigate into the 'alleged irregularities' of the project while identifying and verifying reports of several deficiencies in the planning and implementation of the project consequently failed to impose any liability on any individual or organization responsible. Instead, a case was made by the committee that these 'minor' deficiencies serve as lessons for strengthening clinical research in the future (Sarojini et al., 2011). Moreover, issues of transparency continue to shroud these trials with the attempt to keep the committee's report and its damning observations away from the public domain.

Unethical Trials at the Bhopal Memorial Hospital and Research Centre (BMHRC)

BMHRC, started in 2000, following a directive from the Supreme Court of India, to provide 'advanced tertiary level super-speciality care to the victims of the Bhopal gas tragedy' in 1984, has instead become a hotspot for pharma-sponsored clinical trials recruiting a foreseeably vulnerable population of survivors of the disaster as participants (Pandeya, 2010). The drugs tested in these trials included new chemical entities (NCEs) or investigational new drugs not approved for human use anywhere and spanning across a large canvas of disorders (MIMS, 2010). From 2004 to 2008, the BMHRC was engaged in 10 different drug trials involving several international pharmaceutical companies. Trials were conducted on 279 patients, of which 215 were 'gas patients'. In response to an RTI enquiry, the hospital stated that 80 per cent of the trial participants were 'free patients', that is, those entitled to free services at the hospital, in other words, gas victims (Sama, 2011).

These trials included studies on the effects of the antibiotic televancin, tigecycline, which minimizes antibiotic resistance, prasugrel, a drug for cardio vascular disorders, fondaparinux, which prevents blood clots and a combination of the antibiotic cefoperazone and sulbactum, a chemical salt (MIMS, 2010). Cefoperazone, for instance, is no longer marketed anywhere, while the fixed dose combination was denied approval in the USA. Similarly, the telavancin trial was testing the drug for hospital-acquired pneumonia (HAP), an indication for which it had not received approval elsewhere. In fact, in the USA, the drug is approved for use only in indicating skin infections, while the approval for use in HAP is still pending. In a period of four years (2004–2008), clinical trials were conducted on 151 patents in four departments—cardiology, gastroenterology, pulmonary medicine and anaesthesia (Pandeya, 2010).

Apart for the apparent illegality of the conduct of these trials on a population with reduced autonomy and with unapproved drugs, several questions have been raised regarding the nature of consent taken during the studies, post-trial access and compensation for those suffering from side effects and for families of the deceased. Moreover, as with the HPV trials, here too the lack of transparency was glaring and the lack of accountability only too visible. Despite repeated requests, the hospital has failed to produce copies of prior approvals from the DCGI that are mandatory for all trials involving human beings and which legally should be in the public domain. Although these trials have since been suspended and an investigation is in process, neither the centre, medical professionals nor the pharmaceutical companies in question have been held accountable.

Without adequate and necessary regulatory jurisdiction or systematic review, the reliability and validity of medical research is jeopardized. Considerations of transparency and protection of participant rights have to be made a priority for policy that truly engages and respects the public. This is particularly critical in the context of drug and vaccine trials, placebo-controlled trials and genetic studies that are often in violation of both the Declaration of Helsinki, as well as the guiding principles laid down in the ICMR's ethical guidelines for biomedical research. India requires more substantial regulation and effective implementation that can institutionalize the highest standards of independent enquiry, good clinical practice, protocols, monitoring and follow-up so that a strong and science-friendly policy framework can be put in place to enable and empower medical research.

INTERVENTION STRATEGIES—LESSONS AND CHALLENGES: A CASE FOR LEGAL CLINICS ON HEALTH, ETHICS AND HUMAN RIGHTS

In the Indian context, clinical trials have become a burgeoning industry with globalization. But without adequate legislation and accompanying implementation, the opportunity to connect science with exemplary research practice and meaningful public engagement stands to be lost. In its capacity as a public enterprise, science makes an invaluable contribution to the lives of the people. This contribution is also an obligation. Within the given context, there is an earnest need for a multi dimensional engagement to ensure that the rights of participants of research are upheld at all times, particularly in the case of marginalized populations and not only of the burgeoning industry and its players. A formal training on bioethics as a part of medical as well as legal education curricula is an extremely important step in this regard. Health, bioethics and the women's movement have been working on this front through multi faceted intervention strategies and advocacy initiatives.

It is these very strategies that also make a strong case for legal clinics in regulation and ethics, for not just law students but also medical professionals and those interested in research on human participants.

Use of Legal Instruments—Right to Information Act, 2005

India's fledgling Right to Information Act, drafted to provide a platform for citizens to access information under the control of various public authorities and to promote transparency and accountability in the public bodies, also plays an important role in the field of research, particularly with regard to the approval procedures, funding and acquiescence to the law with regard to the actual conduct of the trial. The Act casts an important obligation on public authorities to facilitate citizens in accessing information held under their control.

Ground Realities—Fact Findings and Community-based Research and Dissemination

Maintaining a constant touch with the ground realities and the communities involved is of prime importance to the success of any advocacy initiative. In the case of large-scale violations, it is vital to get first-hand information and an accurate report of the situation at hand. For instance, in the case of the HPV vaccine trials, members from the advocacy groups themselves travelled to Bhadrachalam block, one of the research sites in Khammam district in Andhra Pradesh. While there, the team spoke to teachers, girls who had received the vaccine, parents of the girls who had died post vaccination and local activist organizations, to examine the extent of violations. Documentation of these visits also played a critical role in monitoring and highlighting the accountability of the state and other institutions.

Engagement with Policy makers and Parliamentarians

While building a collective consciousness around issues such as these, it is extremely important to engage with policy makers and parliamentarians to share the concerns and lobby for political and legislative changes. This kind of initiative can be of a varied nature and take on different forms, ranging from presenting petitions and memorandums; organizing for public meetings; meetings with the individuals/institutions on the issue; making the most of available spaces and opportunities to push for greater change, for example, giving recommendations on regulation of clinical trials to the working group on drugs appointed by the Planning Commission for the 12th Five-Year Plan processes. Similarly, processes should also be undertaken to sensitize state officials and parliamentarians on such issues.

THE ROLE OF LEGAL CLINICS

Civil society organisations, people's health movements, women's movement and students have contributed significantly to bring about social change. Given the present context, such collaborative actions are presenting themselves as essential tools to combat larger global forces and safeguard the interests of vulnerable groups and communities. Students can play a critical role as they bring in new ideas, enthusiasm and energy to the movements and it is in this way that legal clinics with organizations working on issues of social justice and rights can create a two-way learning process. The initiatives taken by students in their own contexts or as part of larger movements have immense potential to carry ongoing advocacy initiatives forward. It is towards this goal that legal clinics play an extremely important role in creating awareness and empowering students. These clinics could include interning with organizations working on issues of ethics and regulations. Further, students could also partake in the organization and participate in the National Bio ethics Conference that is held once every two years to familiarize themselves with ongoing debates and discussions in the area as well as to develop a sense of the direction in which ethical discourse is headed in the country.

ACKNOWLEDGEMENT

The author would like to acknowledge Sarojini, N. for her critical inputs and support.

NOTES

1. A CRO, (clinical research organization) is a company or an organization contracted by a pharmaceutical, medical device or biotechnology company (called a clinical trial sponsor) to assume various aspects of the clinical research

process (i.e., to conduct clinical research trials on behalf of the sponsor). There is an urgent need to further explore the legal void that CROs function in currently. It is important to consider the legal recourses one can seek in the case of non-compliance. It has to be legally established, who bears the liability; whether the indemnity clause applies to CROs or to the sponsors. Moreover, with a change in Schedule Y in 2005, an opportunity was created for the West to use the developing world to enhance their knowledge base by exploiting the human resources to generate knowledge.

2. International Conference on Harmonisation drafted in 1996. It facilitates mutual acceptance of clinical trial data by the regulatory authorities of Japan, EU and the USA—the three major drug manufacturers.

3. The ICMR is the premier research institution of the country responsible for the formulation, coordination and promotion of research in the country.

4. The Declaration of Helsinki was developed by the World Medical Association (WMA) as a set of ethical principles for the medical community regarding human experimentation and is widely regarded as the cornerstone document of human research ethic.

REFERENCES

Bhaumik, D., Chandira, M., & Chiranjib, B. (2010). Emerging trends of scope and opportunities clinical trials in India. *International Journal of Pharmacy and Pharmaceutical Sciences*, 2(1), 7–20.

Chatterjee, P. (2008). Clinical trials in India: Ethical concerns. *Bulletin of the World Health Organization*, 86(8). http://www.who.int/bulletin/volumes/86/8/08-010808/en/index.html

Clinical Trial Registry of India. (2010). Home page. http://ctri.nic.in/Clinicaltrials/login.php

Dhar, A. (2010). Centre halts HPV vaccine project. *The Hindu*. http://beta.thehindu.com/news/national/arti- cle391024.ece

Greene, W. (2007). *The emergence of India's pharmaceutical industry and implications for the US generic drug market* (Office of Economics Working Paper). US International Trade Commission.

MIMS. (2010). Bhopal gas victims used as guinea pigs. *Monthly Index of Medical Specialities* (Editorial).

Mudur, G. (2005). India plans to audit clinical trials. *BMJ*, 331(7524), 1044.

Paliwal, A. (2011). Ethics on trial. *Down to earth*. http://www.downtoearth.org.in/content/ethics-trial

Pandeya, R. (2010). Drug regulator seeks inquiry into Bhopal clinical trials. *Live Mint*. http://www.livemint.com/2010/08/04215714/Drug-regulator-seeksinquiry-i.html?atype=tp

Petryna, A. (2005). Ethical variability: Drug development and globalizing clinical trials. *American Ethnologist*, 32(2), 183–197.

Rajan, S. K. (2007). Biocapital: Indian clinical trials and surplus health. *New Left Review*.

RNCOS. (2007). *Booming clinical trials market in India*. http://www.rncos.com/Report/IM564.htm

Sama. (2011). *National consultation on regulation of drug trials: A report*. Sama Resource Group for Women and Health.

Sarojini, N., Shenoi, A., Srinivasan, S., & Jesani, A. (2011). Undeniable violations and unidentifiable violators. *Economic & Political Weekly*, *46*(24), 17–19.

Sarojini, N., Srinivasan, S., Madhavi, Y., Srinivasan, S., & Shenoi, A. (2010). The HPV Vaccine: Science, ethics and regulation. *Economic & Political Weekly*, *40*(48), 27–34.

Srinivasan, S. (2009). *Ethical concerns in clinical trials in India: An investigation*. Centre for Studies in Ethics and Rights.

Chapter 5

Empathy in Physician–Patient Relationship*
The Construct and Its Applicability to India's Healthcare

Sharmila Borkar

WHAT IS EMPATHY?

The word 'empathy' is said to have its origins in the German word *einfulung* which literally means 'feeling within'. Tichener coined the term 'empathy' from two Greek roots, *em* and *pathos* (feeling into). Empathy is a quality, an ability to enter into the life of another person, to be able to accurately perceive their current feelings and their meanings. According to theorists of psychological therapy, empathy is vital in any interpersonal process. In medical care, empathy when communicated helps to evolve an effective relationship between a physician[1] and a patient.

Empathy is complex to understand, has umpteen dimensions and the theory of empathy is deeply rooted in philosophy and spans many disciplines like sociology and psychology. It is not easy at all for human beings to fully express the essence of their inner being to another, but in empathy, such an attempt is made. Macarov summarizes the varied uses of the word empathy to make three compact divisions:

1. Taking the role of the other, viewing the world as they see it, experiencing their feelings

* *Social Change* 44, no. 3 (September 2014): 423–438.

2. Being capable of reading non-verbal communication, interpreting the feelings underlying this communication
3. Giving off a feeling of caring, or sincerely trying to understand in a non-judgemental and helping way (Macarov, 1978)

We can view empathy as an aspect of human personality, or as a behaviour, or as an experienced emotion. A component definition of empathy given by Morse (Mercer & Reynolds, 2002) features four important attributes: emotive, moral, cognitive and behavioural. In the emotive component, the physician should be able to subjectively experience and share in patient's inner feelings and their psychological state. The moral component involves the physician's internal altruistic force that motivates the practice of empathy. In the cognitive component we see the physician's intellectual ability to identify and understand patient's feelings very objectively. And finally, behavioural component involves a communicative response of the physician to convey understanding of patient's perspective.

EMPATHY AND THE PHYSICIAN–PATIENT RELATIONSHIP
Developing Empathy

An empathetic process has to be understood in terms of its critical features. Empathy involves trying to understand immediate, current feelings of the patient. So, for instance, it would be improper on the part of the physician to base their behaviour towards their patient solely on their past experiences as such past experiences can interfere with the current interactive process. The empathy factor attains preciousness at the very moment of encounter between the patient and the physician, or else if timely help is not given, it would be no help. An empathetic understanding requires the physician to go beyond what the patient says, and see and find meaning in what the patient 'is'.

In empathy, the physician will borrow the patient's feelings, but they are always a separate self and throughout know that the feelings of the patient are not their own feelings. In sympathizing lies a fear that a physician may identify so much with the patient that they may actually find themself in the place of their patient (Kalisch, 1973). Such a behaviour may obscure attempts to truly know a patient and their feelings. In empathy, a better process prevails as physician concentrates more on the patient and their viewpoint. This may be no easy feat: How can a physician borrow a patient's feelings and yet remain a separate self?

Pemberton's (1972) elaborate interpretations on different types of physician–patient relationships can be insightful in developing a context for empathy. Her first view defines the doctor–patient relationship as an 'I–It' relationship. Here, the doctor is active and independent and the patient is passive and dependent. The doctor needs to be objective in their encounter and the patient fully depends on them to get a proper diagnosis. But in reality, we know that the patient is not an 'It' and is a 'Thou'. As much as the physician's objectivity is important, the person-hood of the patient is also important. So the first view is rejected. The second view considers both these factors and tries to include the 'I–It' component and the 'I–Thou' component. The 'I–It' relationship is the impersonal and objective component of the relation and the 'I–Thou' component is the personal, subjective component. This sort of view entails dual feature. In one, the physician alternates between treating the patient as an 'It' (objective) and as a 'Thou' (subjective). The other type results in an arbitrary separation of the patient into soul (subject) and body (object). But even here, there is a fear that in these dual states, the 'I–It' relationship can predominate and prevail over the 'I–Thou' relationship, thus giving a small insignificant place to the latter. Therefore, the third refined and inclusive view describes the doctor–patient relationship as fundamentally an 'I–Thou' relationship (the personal and subjective component), but the only constant challenge here is to maintain the physician's objectivity. This problem is solved by understanding the 'I' both as a person who relates to their fellow-man and as a person who is the soul of their body. Here, 'I' has a comprehensive interpretation which allows for the objective stance of the doctor to be a part of the I–Thou relationship, without treating the patient as an 'It'. Pemberton feels that any doctor–patient relationship is truly to be seen as a 'person-to-person encounter' in which both doctor and patient remain 'I's'.

The Role of Empathy in Physician–Patient Relationship

Till the 20th century, for a physician, compassion in thinking was considered an essential input for understanding human nature and through compassion, a physician would be expected to get motivated enough to take care of patient and become a good effective healer. Osler (Pembroke, 2007) later argued that such a practice may interfere with objective judgement and suggested 'detached concern' or what we call 'equanimity' to understand patient's physical and emotional needs. Detached concern is also a form of empathy, but here physician's or patient's emotions do not interfere with the objective judgement of the physician.

Empathy plays a crucial supplementary role along with the other process of objective judgement, and the use of technology in medical care. How can empathy help the process of objective judgement? Empathy actually can help the physician not to overlook certain critical features of the patient which might never get deciphered if we use detached concern. In the words of Halpern (2001), 'the pursuit of a correct diagnosis requires a full, as well as accurate understanding of patient's problems. Empathy involves discerning aspects of a patient's emotional experiences that might otherwise go unrecognised…'.

Another very important use of empathy according to Halpern is to help a patient regain 'psychological autonomy'. Empathy gives a patient the needed support to process difficult information. For instance, if empathy is provided, a patient can better cope up with the news that they suffer from, say a severe illness, and they can be more enabled to participate in the process of their recovery.

When we conceptualize empathy as a detached concern, we view it mainly as a cognitive understanding of the subjective experience of the patient. But empathy involves both cognitive and affective elements. Pembroke opines that genuine empathy involves not just feeling and recognizing what the suffering of the patient feels like, but genuinely reaching out to the other. Succinctly put, 'It is an imaginative projection into their inner world of experience'. In the Western religious traditions, 'going out of the self' has been referred to as 'Ekstasis'[2] (Pembroke, 2007). So the goal of empathy is to imaginatively understand 'what it feels like to be in the patient's actual, individual life, feeling what the patient is feeling', rather than what one would feel in their situation, and this requires the physician to distinguish between oneself and the patient.

Does empathy interfere with an objective and scientific assessment of a physician? On this Halpern strongly puts it that in understanding a patient, partly cognitive and partly emotional aspects are involved, and the physicians must have or rather develop the proper skills to effectively use their emotional responses in any good medical therapy or care. Every illness episode is an experience for a patient; it has a meaning for the patient. So the physician needs to have 'emotional resonance' to connect to the patient and provide holistic healing care.

As medical technology expands and new advances take place in diagnostic procedures and the treatments, 'dehumanization of medical encounter' takes place and the relationship between the doctor and the patient becomes less and less humane and impersonal. Technologies such as CT scan, MRI and X-rays increase the wedge between the physician and the patient, as the physician at times need not even have a personal encounter with the patient, as they have access to these tools to get a feel of the patient's illness. Pembroke feels that such diagnostic procedures reduce a human being to an X-ray film or any image and 'abstract a disease from its living context' (Pembroke, 2007). In this sense, we could view empathy as playing a gap-filling role to reduce this newly created wedge between technology and the person.

Arguments for empathy are often seen as a counter to views of the current biomedical approach. Whereas the biomedical approach is based on disease-centred care, the empathetic understanding underscores the relevance of a patient-centred approach. It revolves around the issue of whether disease and pathogens are more important in care, or whether along with these, the patient's illness experience should be also taken into consideration. But in reality, can one ever deny the ever expanding role that technology plays in current diagnostics/modern medical care? It emerges then that what we actually need is a synthesizing approach which embraces empathy and patient-centred care, along with an acceptable role which technology plays and deserves to play in a patient's life.

In the meantime, new theoretical formulations and reformulations in the application of clinical empathy in physician–patient relation evolve. The recent focus of thinking is a kind of patient-centred approach in which the physician makes a collaborative sort of effort with their patient to be empathic. Current theories base empathy on an imagined experience of patient's illness, and they stress on the need for a collaborative experience of illness. Garden (2007) warns that such approaches must not get influenced by power relations. For instance, in a collaborative effort, a physician should not let their superior power position (they are more knowledgeable than the patient) obstruct their empathetic understanding and they should still keep in mind that no matter how powerful they are as a 'knowledgeable person', a patient is still an authority in their illness experience.

Empathy, Patient-centred Approach and Health Outcomes

The patient-centred approach draws from a thinking which includes the inter-personal and social aspects of patients' lives along with biological processes. Studies on empathy are primarily meant to understand its effects on health outcomes and often they explore physician–patient communication and understand in what way empathy either singularly or together with other positive attributes helps not just to evolve a better therapeutic relation but also to improve patient and physician well-being.

A lot of research has gone into evolving various measures of empathy. Defining empathy as a predominantly cognitive attribute that involves an understanding of experiences, concerns and perspectives of another person combined with a capacity to communicate this understanding, Hojat (2009) believes that clinical empathy can lead to positive patient outcomes, greater patient satisfaction, lower costs of medical care and lower rate of medical errors and even helps to improve well-being of the physician. Hojat advocates the use of empathy education to train all kinds of healthcare providers and has prescribed 10 approaches for enhancing empathy in the healthcare environment, some of which include improving interpersonal skills, exposure to role models, role playing, studying literature and the arts, improving narrative skills, among others.

Hojat and his research team at Jefferson Medical College developed the Jefferson Scale of Physician Empathy (JSPE),[3] an instrument to measure empathy in medical care, which specifically targets medical students, physicians and other health professionals. In a significant study which tries to validate this scale on two cohorts of medical students, scores on JSPE declined during the medical school, the decline in empathy was observed to be highest for the later years of medical schooling. In every year, women scored significantly higher over men in the measure of empathy. Hojat's team conducted two more cross sectional studies, one on Italian physicians and the other on Japanese medical students to confirm the psychometrics of the JPSE scale, and to see if there are differences between empathy scores of men and women. Women scored higher over men for both these studies, resulting in an observation that there could be differences among gender in displaying an attribute like empathy (Crandall & Marion, 2009).

In a clinical encounter, the word 'enablement' describes the effect of a clinical encounter on a patient's ability to cope with and understand their illnesses. Mercer et al. (2001) collected 200 valid questionnaires from 230 consecutive outpatients attending the Glasgow Homoeopathic Hospital, an NHS facility that integrates complementary and orthodox approaches. Measures included three aspects, a patient enablement instrument, perception of the doctor's empathy and knowing the doctor well.

Enablement was not directly related to the length of consultation, but correlated with the patient's perception of the doctor's empathy. When this was done, empathy emerged as a critical input in enablement. No patient reported a high enablement score with low empathy score.[4] A recent study on empathy by Michigan State University demonstrated that trust and empathy shown in a physician–patient relationship is good not just to make patients comfortable, but helps the patients to relieve stress and even increase pain tolerance. Patients were randomly assigned to one of two types of interviews with a physician before they underwent an MRI scan. In the patient-centred approach, doctors addressed all types of concerns about their patients and also listened to them about their personal, social life and their illness. The other set of patients were asked limited questions about their medical history and drugs. Post-interview questionnaires revealed that the former patients reported better confidence and greater satisfaction levels. Even when the patients were later exposed to an MRI scanner, the former patients showed greater pain tolerance,[5] indicating that an empathetic encounter was much more fruitful.

IS EMPATHY POSSIBLE IN INDIA'S HEALTHCARE?

Having accepted the importance of ideological construct of empathy in practice of healthcare, one needs to see if empathy can be best utilized to get better health outcomes and bring about systemic transformation in our society. Though no one-shot solution to empathetic provision exists, in real world of healthcare, examples of empathetic behaviour do exist, and so do challenges to its application. We examine these by considering the following notions of empathy, as applied to India's healthcare scenario.

Individual versus Collective Dimension of Empathy

The Micro (Individual) Dimension of Empathy

To better understand empathy and the challenge in its application to India's healthcare, one needs to separate the micro dimension of empathy which pertains to the relationship between a physician and a patient from the macro dimension of empathy which pertains to the larger context of provision of overall empathetic healthcare. At individual level, empathy can be viewed at best as a cognitive attribute of a person (physician) that benefits both the physician and the patient towards a better health outcome. In the larger macro context, it matters whether the collective conscious of Indian health system, with its vast levels of organizational networks and providers can deliver truly empathetic care in a society. The micro dimension is the sole individual responsibility of the physician, whereas the efforts at macro level can lead to a systemic transformation in society, a task which faces challenges.

Francis Weld Peabody (1927) once stated,

> The treatment of a disease may be entirely impersonal; the care of a patient must be completely personal. The significance of the intimate relationship between the physician and the patient cannot be too strongly emphasized,

for in extraordinarily large number of cases, both diagnosis and treatment are dependent on it, and the failure of the young physician to establish this relationship accounts for much of his ineffectiveness in the care of his patients.

Healthcare is essentially a market like any other. There is a provider (physician, the seller) and there is a receiver (patient, the buyer). But healthcare is a market like no other—it has peculiar characteristics, one such being the informational asymmetry between the seller and the buyer. The physician knows information about the patient which the patient knows little about or does not know at all (diagnosis of illness, treatment). In such a circumstance, when a physician in a specialist position has scope to bid up their price or reduce the time given to a patient, how would they be motivated to go out of their way to provide empathy? Keeping their moral dilemma aside, there is every reason for them to fear that a market can hardly offer them a material compensation for the provision of empathetic care, or offer them additional monetary incentives for the additional time they need to spend for empathetic encounter. A major hindrance is the length of consultation to provide for 'empathetic' clinical encounter which may make it just impossible for the lone physician to take care of all kinds of patients, each with their own individual expectation, behaviour traits and needs (Toop, 1998). Again, how does the physician strike a right balance between the personal goals of self-actualization, prestige and monetary returns, on the one hand, and service towards their patient or patient's emotional needs, on the other? A physician can often refuse the notion of empathy, on grounds that they are not adequately trained to provide it or they may feel it is their prime duty to focus only on acute medical problem of their patient, or they may feel too exhausted to provide empathy.

The Macro (Collective) Dimension of Empathy

At the macro level, in true economic sense, empathy in healthcare creates positive externalities and happier patients and physicians together add up to the society's welfare, besides leading to a culturally caring and enriched state with better citizens. Often, our real world of medical care with overcrowded wards, clinics and hospitals presents a big disconnect to the world of debates, writing and research on empathy and its useful application, and this prompts a question: Is empathy-based delivery of healing holistic care a mere idealistic notion? In rural India, where the physician–population ratio is low, how do the physicians cope up with the workload and to what extent can they survive and strike a balance between their own private lives, on the one hand, and delivery of empathetic care to the patients, on the other? Based on their own survey findings on resident surgeons in India's four medical colleges, Agarwal et al. (2011) point out to the lack of effective communication and very little conversation time spent by surgeons with the patients to highlight the need for effective physician–patient communication. They see patient contact with a physician as a step towards 'reconnection' as an ill patient disconnects from society, and a need for a physician to provide for listening and healing comfort. Pointing out that empathy and effective doctor–patient communication forms a part of training curricula in medical and nursing colleges in many parts of the world, they urge for a need to imbibe this practice in Indian medical schools to foster a better therapeutic relationship. 'Empathy is sincere and successful when a patient acknowledges that he or she has been seen, heard, and accepted as a person' (Agarwal et al., 2011). The larger macro application of empathy necessitates that empathy is formally accepted as a value in medical education and that learners of medicine practice the value while they serve care.

The Sectoral Challenges to Empathy

Srinivasan (2000) suggested the following four criteria in his vision for healthcare:

1. Universal access and access to an adequate level, and access without excessive burden.
2. Fair distribution of financial costs for access and fair distribution of burden in rationing care and capacity, and a constant search for improvement to a more just system.
3. Training providers for competence, empathy and accountability; pursuit of quality care and cost-effective use of the results of relevant research.

4. Special attention to vulnerable groups such as children, women, disabled and the aged.

For the first time, the third criterion stated above on training concretely formulated empathy as a factor in the provision of quality healthcare. But how this was to be achieved has been far kept aside in agendas on healthcare.

India's health sector is fast advancing with modern technology, public–private partnerships, different delivery models, increasing infusion of internal and external capital, while at the same time the sector is marked by unevenness in access and utilization of healthcare, inadequacy of health spending and major personnel and workforce issues that grip India's health delivery systems. Health systems with a proper mix of quality and distribution of medical personnel that include physicians, nurses, paramedics and public health workers are the need of the hour. The application of empathy is desirable at the level of health personnel, both in public and private sectors.

Baru et al. (2010) have highlighted three forms of inequities that characterize India's health sector. Historical inequities that have their roots in the policies and practices of British colonial India, many of which continue till date; socio-economic inequities which manifest in caste, class and gender differentials; and inequities in the availability, utilization and affordability of health services. Of these, quite critical they feel is the need to address inequities in provisioning of health services and assurance of quality care. And empathy is a key input in quality healthcare.

The Public Sector: India's healthcare has two broad components. One component 'public health' focuses on prevention to control the risk factors associated with disease; the other component 'healthcare (medical care)' focuses on curative aspects aimed at restoring health when people are sick. Following from the British tradition of the biomedical approach, our focus remained essentially on the healthcare (medical care) component. The expansive public health network belonging to India's healthcare organization has been seldom put to use to play a formidable role in disease prevention. Promotive and preventive aspects of health have been neglected and a larger financial allocation and thought have gone into few major vertical disease control programmes. The public health centre (PHC) approach in India deviated from its major concerns which were preventive and public health action. The PHCs have been criticized for not effectively performing their role as local epidemiological information centres, and have not been disseminating community-focused public information to the extent required.

India's focus on biomedical model has been responsible for a healthcare delivery system that prioritizes curative healthcare, at times even at the expense of preventive care. Curative care by its very nature has an element of emergency, is urgent and rushed care. Indian health sector is besotted by unlimited patients in queues and for the states and as a whole, India has low doctor–population ratio. In public sector, the preventive health network is largely crowded. A high premium is placed on the time factor. Holistic care and empathy are very much at the periphery.

The epidemiological transition that India currently witnesses is marked by increasing presence of non-communicable and lifestyle-related diseases, which do not just require medical cure but also prevention and management. Such diseases do not necessarily lead to mortality but do increase morbidity levels, thereby increasing inpatient and outpatient care. Along with medical care, they necessitate the services of primary providers who help to prevent and manage the disease. This requires a patient-centred approach with high levels of listening to the patient and many empathetic encounters. The 'cure-oriented' public sector has not been able to adapt itself to this role necessitated by our epidemiological transition.

Verma (2013) critically points out that though the High Level Expert Group on Universal Health Coverage (HLEG 2010) recognized the role of patient-centred care, merely increasing the inputs in terms of nurses and doctors, as well as greater financial allocations devoted to healthcare as suggested by HLEG may not help as much as giving a thrust to patient-oriented care and a personalized approach to medical care. Verma suggests the need to 'reposition the role of a general practitioner' in the context of primary healthcare in India. He recommends that primary physicians be provided with market incentives, as they alone are better suited to offer 'patient-oriented holistic care', and that a transformative change in primary health delivery can happen if the primary physician is restored in their role, as a first consultant to the patient.

The Private Sector/Corporate Sector

The structural adjustment programmes of the 1990s led to many changes in the health sector. Along with the cuts in budgetary spending, there began an entry of private sector in medical care, opening up of public health institutions to private investments and introduction of all sorts of user fees. Imrana Qadeer (2007) observes that the quality of a clinical service not only depends on diagnostics and curative potentials of a service but also depends on patient satisfaction, social skills of physicians, individual practitioner support and teamwork at the hospital level. If each has to perform well, it needs the right mix of manpower and proper referral facility. The majority of private practitioners operate quite independently of each other, while the public sector has provisions for referral. Many a time, Qadeer laments that the patients face expensive informal linkages in the private sector and this finally makes them turn to the public sector. She observes that the private sector can provide facilities, but may not provide referrals and universal coverage to patients. The private sector is disaggregated, scattered and highly unregulated. There is no direct way by which the government can regulate private practitioners and their practices. The private entities such as nursing homes run by doctors are unregulated in standards of quality, accountability and medical records. The need to make more money in less time can lead to deterioration of standards, and empathy may be overlooked as a standard for healing holistic care by individual private practitioners.

Corporatization of healthcare in India increased hospital care which was being largely facilitated by provisions of concessional land and tax breaks but there are no proper procedures to ensure that the poor get free beds in these hospitals. In the absence of transparency and poor grievance redressal systems for patients, the goals of empathy can be far beyond reach. The secondary and the tertiary levels of India's healthcare have gone through phases of corporatization. The presence of competitive element in health services provision leads to innovative search for newer and better ways of selling care, and this is achieved by two ways: one by cost cutting and the other, by giving innovative, faster, efficient and better care. At the level of the corporate sector, the word empathy is often a seller's way of enticing the buyer better healthcare. Huge corporates, often with the mediation of health providers like insurance authorities, can use 'empathy' as a selling proposition to attract patients who can afford to pay more better healthcare. Corporates have doctors themselves as their major stakeholders, who in their drive for greater profits may be forced to compromise on ethical care by indulging in practices like over investigations and supply of excessive care to patients.

So the notion of empathy with a wider holistic and deeper meaning often runs a danger of getting narrowed down to a small supply-side saleable idea, meant to generate higher demand from the patients. The moot question is: How far will a corporate with a business objective be motivated to push the ideological construct of empathy in imparting actual healthcare to its people? In a market economy, healthcare is said to have three links: the link between state and citizens' entitlement for health, the link between the consumer and provider of health services and the link between the physician and patient. The link between the physician and the patient in corporate healthcare is more based on the idea of profit, and here, the 'disease' rather than the 'experience of illness' attains importance. And empathy becomes a business idea rather than a tool to forge better health outcomes. Sadly, no such studies exist in India which could enhance our understanding of the exclusive role of empathy in healthcare. In essence, it becomes difficult to measure levels of empathy in macro health scenario of India.

Is Empathy beyond Sectors?

However, empathetic care need not confine itself to the realm of a specific sector at all times. At the macro level, a systemic transformation can take place and goals such as equity and access to healthcare can be achieved by service providers, as these become the closest approximation of holistic healthcare with an empathetic understanding. Umpteen examples exist where healthcare has been characterized by empathetic provisions, at the level of NGOs, or hospitals, or individual service providers in India. Health schemes have tried to incorporate the notion of empathy, like in the case of Yeshaswini Micro Health

Insurance Scheme in Karnataka which has a huge coverage and which provides world-class healthcare facilities to poor farmers with country's lowest premiums in health insurance (Nagaraj, 2010). Several attempts have been made by NGOs in the health sector to bring healthcare to the millions of poor in India like in the case of tribal healthcare provided by practitioners such as Dr Abhay Bhang and Dr Rani Bhang, whose collective efforts to provide health and well-being to the tribals in Gadchiroli speak volumes about empathy and holistic care. Dr Devi Shetty and his pioneering efforts in the field of healthcare are an exemplary evidence of real-life approximation of empathetic healthcare in India. The business model of healthcare of Narayana Hridayalaya of Dr Shetty is largely based on numbers but aims to provide low-cost, affordable, holistic and accessible care to people, many times, the poor, and thus combines the goals of equity and efficiency in healthcare.

A recent piece of news on India's medical care shows how empathy and care may well be a part of healing culture in nursing for patients. A dozen students of Linfield Nursing College visited healthcare network in many parts of India and observed that despite the most basic issues in health that India grappled with (such as clean drinking water and basic infrastructure), there was 'healing care'.[6]

> Remarked a nursing student on India's healthcare, 'Buildings are sometimes open to the weather, nurses sleep onsite on metal bunks and clinics have older equipment than the US facilities. But the care of the staff is still there, the dedication nurses have to their patients is inspiring, and many clinics provide primary care to rural populations at little to no cost'.

All this could not have been envisaged without an innate construct of empathy in the mind of the health service provider. Thus, the Indian healthcare experiences empathy not through a formulated organized network but through the altruistic efforts of such scattered dedicated providers of healthcare, especially for the poor.

The Importance of 'Criticality of Illness' in Empathy

To a considerable extent, the application of empathy in healthcare has to do with the type of illness, and a patient-centred approach becomes all the more crucial when certain critical illnesses threaten to increase morbidity and mortality levels for patients. Critical illnesses, some of which are also associated with stigma such as cancer and AIDS, need greater levels of empathy. Arora's (2009) narrative as a cancer survivor for 14 years spells out the need for an approach which blends high-quality technical care with patient-centred care, which alone can reduce suffering for a patient and enhance their well-being. Patient-centred measures focus on high interpersonal quality, view a patient as a whole and provide care that would include the medical and the psychosocial needs of the patient. In sum, both the 'medical' and the 'care' aspects of 'medical care' are a must. The same is true for mental illnesses. Based on his personal experiences and study reviews, Swaminath (2007) urges for a critical need for effective doctor–patient communication in general medicine and in the field of psychotherapy. Highlighting that an empathic relationship is primary, he remarks that without a sense of connection and mutual understanding, physician–patient relation becomes 'an exchange of medical information divorced from the context and complexities of the patient's life'. The above studies are a pointer towards understanding the challenge of giving healing care with intense flow of empathy to diseases which are particularly threatening or disturbing to individuals and which create their own scars and scares in patients.

What follows is that different disease types would require different levels of empathetic understanding. States a WHO (2008) report,

> People want to know that their health worker understands them, their suffering and the constraints they face. Unfortunately, many providers neglect this aspect of the therapeutic relation, particularly when they are dealing with disadvantaged groups. In many health services, responsiveness and person centredness are treated as luxury goods to be handed out only to a selected few.

The report goes on to state that in many countries including the developing ones, efforts are on to 'put people first' in the health agenda for HIV and many other disease control programmes.

India's epidemiological transition over the last few decades shows a disease profile with predominance of non-communicable diseases and lifestyle diseases such as cancers, mental illnesses, accidents and trauma. Though there is no formula for empathy provision, there surely exists a need to imbibe the culture of empathy to India's growing health problems. Slowly, India's healthcare is adapting to these challenges. For instance, in the new Mental Health Care Bill[7] (2013) which seeks to replace the Mental health Act of 1987, the government for the first time has come up with a rights-based approach in the mental health law which now seeks to decriminalize suicide and make access to affordable mental healthcare a right for all. The Bill clarifies that the act of suicide and the mental health of the person committing the act are inseparably linked and have to be seen together and not in isolation. It seeks not only to provide for mental healthcare for persons with mental illnesses and to protect, promote and fulfil the rights of such persons during the delivery of mental healthcare and services but also guarantees several rights to the mentally ill—from the right to privacy in mental health establishments to the right to dignity. It bars inhuman practices such as electro-convulsive therapy without anaesthesia, sterilization as a treatment for illness and chaining in any form of the mentally ill and has strict punishment for offences done in this manner. This is a welcome step in healing care which incorporates empathy. But such efforts are few and far in between and more needs to be done to make empathy truly felt in India's healthcare.

CONCLUDING REMARKS

Empathy, when communicated, helps to evolve an effective therapeutic relation and enhances positive health outcomes. The emergence of theoretical construct on empathy points out to a patient-centred approach wherein both the physician and the patient make a collaborative effort to have an empathic encounter. Studies on empathy too tend to emphasize effective physician–patient communication and patient-centred care. Often, due to its very nature, empathy cannot be isolated as the single most critical factor to positively affect health outcomes and this remains a limitation of some of the studies on empathy. Which is why, perhaps, despite attempts to understand empathy, it does remain only partly explained, only partly understood. India's excessive dependence on the biomedical model and curative approach to healthcare often poses challenges to application of empathy in healthcare. But efforts at the level of individual health practitioners, business models which incorporate empathy, as well as innovative government steps like the Mental Health Bill are a testimony to a hope that even with challenges, India's healthcare can look up to higher levels of empathy.

NOTES

1. Though the word physician here refers to a physician (interchangeably a doctor) in a clinical set-up, we must appreciate that in reality, empathy has a useful role to play in nursing and for any provider of healthcare.

2. Pembroke brings in the Christian theological concept of Ekstasis and observes that when empathy has both cognitive and affective elements, it has the 'power to bring about a deep level of connectedness between the physician and the patient'.

3. JSPE has been translated into 25 languages and is being used by researchers in the USA and abroad. This is a constructed 20-item scale with three meaningful factors: perspective taking, compassionate care and standing in the patient's shoes. JSPE was originally developed to measure the orientation of medical students towards physician's empathy (Student or 'S' Version). The researchers later developed a revised version of the scale to assess empathy in physicians and other health professionals ('HP' Version). The 'HP' Version as a modified version includes the caregivers' behaviours. (Many measures of empathy have been developed. JSPE is one recent example.)

4. Price et al. (2006) attempted to measure acupuncture patients' perceptions of practitioner's empathy at the initial consultation and its relationship with the patient enablement—15 acupuncturists asked consecutive new patients to complete a questionnaire within two days of the first consultation. The questionnaire included the Consultation and Relational Empathy (CARE) measure (a consultation process measure), the Patient Enablement Instrument (PEI, a consultation outcome measure) and the Measure Yourself Medical Outcome Profile (MYMOP), a patient-centred measure. The findings of the study pinpoint to an association between patients' 'perceptions of practitioner empathy' and 'patient enablement' at initial consultation.

5. 'Empathy Raises Patients' Pain Tolerance', a report dated 8 December 2012, in *India Medical Times* by Michigan State University research team.

6. 'India Gives Health Care Students a Lesson in Empathy', news from Linfield College of Nursing, published on 22 February 2011.

7. The Mental Health Care Bill, 2013 (as introduced in the Rajya Sabha).

ACKNOWLEDGEMENT

I wish to convey my sincere gratitude to anonymous referee of this chapter for helpful comments and suggestions.

REFERENCES

Agarwal, A., Agarwal, A., Nag, K., Chakraborty, S., & Ali, K. (2011). Doctor patient communication: A vital yet neglected entity in Indian medical educational system. *Indian Journal of Surgery, 73*(3), 184–186.

Arora, N. (2009). Importance of patient-centred care in enhancing patient wellbeing: A cancer survivor's perspective. *Quality of Life Research, 18*(1), 1–4. http://www.jstor.org/stable/40302447

Baru, R., Acharya, A., Acharya, S., Shiva Kumar, A. K., & Nagaraj, K. (2010). Inequities in access to health services in India: Caste, class and region. *Economic & Political Weekly, 45*(38), 49–57.

Crandall, S. J., & Marion, G. S. (2009). Commentary: Identifying attitudes towards empathy: An essential feature of professionalism. *Academic Medicine, 84*(9), 1174–1176.

Garden, R. (2007). The problem of empathy: Medicine and the humanities. *New Literary History, 38*(3), 551–567. http://www.jstor.org/stable/20058022

Halpern, J. (2001). The concept of clinical empathy, in *Detached concern to empathy: Humanizing medical practice* (pp. 67–94). Oxford University Press. http://site.ebrary.com/id/10375062

Hojat, M. (2009). Ten approaches for enhancing empathy in health and human service cultures. *Journal of Health and Human Services Administration, 31*(4), 412–450. http://www.jstor.org/stable/25790741

Kalisch, B. (1973). What is empathy? *The American Journal of Nursing, 73*(9), 1548–1552. http://www.jstor.org/stable/3422614

Macarov, D. (1978). Empathy: The charismatic chimera. *Journal of Education for Social Work, 14*(3), 86–92. http://www.jstor.org/stable/23038835

Mercer, S. W., & Reynolds, W. J. (2002). Empathy and quality of care. *British Journal of General Practice*, Quality Supplement, 52, S9–S13.

Mercer, S. W., Graham, C. M., & Reilly, D. (2001). Empathy is important for enablement. *British Medical Journal, 322*(7290), 865. http://www.jstor.org/stable/25466696

Nagaraj, N. (2010, 3 March). Managing power with surgical precision. *Times News Network.*

Peabody, F. (1927). The care of the patient. *JAMA, 88*(12), 877–882.

Pemberton, B. L. (1972). A comprehensive understanding of the doctor–patient relationship. *Journal of Religion and Health, 11*(3), 252–261. http://www.jstor.org/stable/27505131

Pembroke, N. F. (2007). Empathy, emotion, and ekstasis in the patient: Physician relationship. *Journal of Religion and Health, 46*(2), 287–298. http://www.jstor.org/stable/27513009

Price, S., Mercer, S. W., & MacPherson, H. (2006). Practitioner empathy, patient enablement and health outcomes: A prospective study of acupuncture patients. *Patient Education and Counseling, 63*(1–2), 239–245.

Qadeer, I. (2007). The status of health services in India. Report on status of health and education in India: Critical questions in nation's development.

Srinivasan, R. (2000). Healthcare in India: Vision 2020. In *Indian vision 2020*. Planning Commission, Government of India.

Swaminath, G. (2007). Doctor patient communication: Patient perception. *Indian Journal of Psychiatry, 49*(3), 150–153.

WHO. (2008). *Primary health care: Now more than ever.* Author.

Toop, L. (1998). Primary care: Core values: Patient-centred primary care. *British Medical Journal, 316*(7148), 1882–1883. http://www.jstor.org/stable/25179580

Verma, S. (2013). Repositioning the general practitioner. *Economic & Political Weekly, 48*(26–27), 18–19.

Chapter 6

Long Working Hours and the Risk of Chronic Disease*

Anita Pal, Laxmi Kant Dwivedi and Dolly Kumari

INTRODUCTION

A discernible change in trends and the nature of occupation and working hours over time has changed the prevalence of disease among people. One's work environment, especially work stress and characteristics of the job, play an important role in the development of a multitude of chronic conditions. It is a serious threat to the health and longevity of people, especially those living in developing countries. Earlier, people were mostly affected by communicable diseases, but recently, non-communicable diseases have rapidly increased among all age groups. This may be due to a change in the nature of work as there has been a gradual increase in the tertiary sector, which is made up of a number of jobs that are sedentary in nature. The physical as well as the mental health of people is affected by a change in occupation and the nature of work. According to an International Labour Organization (ILO, 2012) report, globally, around 2 million workers die annually due to occupational diseases and injuries.

Several studies have identified long working hours as a potential work-related risk factor behind ill health, and this has raised some questions about the role of working hours in the health of people. Lower occupational positions are related to poor health and a variety of diseases, such as depression, diabetes, ischaemic heart disease, muscle pain and neck and back pain (Volkers et al., 2007).

★ *Social Change* 48, no. 1 (2018): 72–84.

For instance, among South Koreans, compared to other occupational groups (manual and non-manual) and the total population, farmers have a higher prevalence of arthritis and intervertebral disorders in both men and women while other chronic diseases such as hypertension, diabetes, chronic lung diseases, asthma, cancer, and cataracts are low (Cha et al., 2009). Less job security among people also tends to increase musculoskeletal disorders and liver disease (Kim et al., 2008). There is a considerable array of empirical evidence that shows job stress negatively affects both physical and mental health: for example, excessive stress has been related to back pain, colorectal cancer, several infectious disease and cardiovascular problems, and it can double the risk of heart attack (Chandola et al., 2007; Health Canada, 2000; Rosengren et al., 2004). Another study found that after adjusting for age, occupation, shift work, smoking status, frequency of alcohol consumption and cohabiting status/marital status, there was a positive association between working hours and metabolic syndrome which was identified in 110 Japanese men workers (Kobayashi et al., 2012). Literature suggests that depression is independently associated with part-time work, a shorter job tenure and long working hours (Burke & Cooper, 2008; Dembe et al., 2006; Jaeyoung, 2013). Exposure to psychosocial risk factors has a greater detrimental effect on the health of people in the middle age and early old age groups compared to the 'oldest old' (House et al., 2005).

Some literature suggests that the risk factors for any chronic disease are the same. Some other literature has also investigated that each chronic disease is co-morbidities of another one. People whose deaths were caused by non-communicable diseases had at least one form of cardiovascular condition recorded, with coronary heart disease being the most common, followed by hypertension, heart failure and chronic kidney disease (Tong & Stevenson, 2007; Zygmuntowicz et al., 2012).

Westernization and industrialization have caused a drastic change in the global work pattern, thereby increasing the chances of several health complications. The purpose of this study is to assess the contribution of work history, such as the job of respondents, types of occupation, working time and days in developing chronic conditions. An attempt has been made to comprehend the existence of co-morbidities correlated with various chronic conditions.

MATERIALS AND METHODS

Data

This study is based on data from the Study on Global AGEing and Adult Health (SAGE), 2007–2008, in India. The SAGE study was a follow-up of households covered across six states in the World Health Survey, India, 2003, conducted by the International Institute for Population Sciences. SAGE was a global study implemented in six countries: China, India, Ghana, Mexico, Russia and South Africa. In India, SAGE was conducted in six states: Assam, Karnataka, Maharashtra, Rajasthan, Uttar Pradesh and West Bengal. These six populous states, spread across India, account for around 37 per cent of India's population as per the 2011 census. The purpose of the SAGE survey programme was to collect data on a broad range of self-reported assessments of health and well-being.

A multi-stage, stratified, clustered sampling design was used. In India, 19 states were selected on the basis of their geographical location and level of development. These 19 states were grouped into six regions: north, central, east, north-east, west and south. A composite index was used to categorize states in to different levels of development. The states were selected randomly so that one state was selected from each region as well as from each level of development category. The nationally representative sample was stratified by state and locality (urban or rural), resulting in 12 strata. A two-stage and three-stage sampling was adopted in rural and urban areas, respectively (SAGE, 2012). It involved face-to-face interviews with 12,198 individuals in the age group of 18 years and above. It collected information about self-reported morbidities and health conditions based on interviews and health measurements, anthropometric measurements and blood tests.

The study population was restricted to actively working men and women who had at least worked 10–15 years in their lifetime. As the aim of this study was to find the effect of work history on the prevalence of chronic conditions, the population taken for this purpose was aged 45 years and above. A total of 5,158 men and women who were employed and had been diagnosed with any of the selected chronic conditions were analysed.

Variables Description

Dependent Variables

In this study, hypertension, diabetes, stroke, angina and depression were used as dependent variables. These were assessed through a self-reported mechanism and elicited by questions that were dichotomous in nature, coded as '0' for 'no' and '1' for 'yes' as follows:

1. Have you ever been diagnosed with high blood pressure (hypertension)? (Yes/No)
2. Have you ever been diagnosed with diabetes (high blood sugar)? (Yes/No)
3. Have you ever been diagnosed with angina or angina pectoris (a heart disease)? (Yes/No)
4. Have you ever been told by a health professional that you have had a stroke? (Yes/No)
5. Have you ever been diagnosed with depression? (Yes/No)

Independent Variables

The SAGE data collected information on the respondent's socio-economic and demographic characteristics and details of their work histories. Demographic and socioeconomic characteristics, such as residence, sex, age, marital status, caste, religion, level of education, wealth quintile and body mass index (BMI), were used. For analysis, the characteristics of work, such as working hours, the primary job which was undertaken by the respondents, the type of occupation and the number of working days in a week, were used. The main focus of this study was on working hours and types of occupation. In SAGE, occupation was categorized by the International Standard Classification of Occupation 2008 (ISC0-08). But to fulfil the purpose of this study, occupations were classified into two categories: nonmanual and manual. Non-manual occupations included managers, professionals, technicians and clerks, while manual occupations encompassed service and sales workers, agricultural and fishery workers, craft- and trade-related workers, plant and machine operators, assemblers and elementary occupations. According to the Factories Act, 1948, and Labour Act, 2003, the working hours were also classified as less than equal to eight hours and more than eight hours, respectively. Working days were categorized as less than equal to five days and more than five days.

Statistical Methods

The Z-test was used to examine differences in the prevalence of diseases by two categories of independent variables. Binary logistics regression was used to examine the effect of independent variables on dependent variables. The correlation matrix held correlation coefficients stating the amount of correlation between chronic diseases. Data analysis was performed using Microsoft Excel and STATA version 12.0 software.

RESULTS

Table 1 showed that 26 per cent of the study samples belonged to urban areas and the rest were from rural areas. The proportions of male and female respondents were approximately the same. Most people belonged to the 55–64 years age group. More than half the respondents were illiterate and 40 per cent belonged to the poorest and poorer households. Approximately seven out of eight respondents were engaged in manual work, and 53 per cent were working for more than eight hours.

Table 6.1 *Correlation between Selected Chronic Conditions India, 2007–2008*

	Hyper-tension	Diabetes	Stroke	Angina	Depression
Hypertension	1				
Diabetes	0.21*	1			
Stroke	0.13*	0.04*	1		
Angina	0.17*	0.11*	0.08*	1	
Depression	0.05*	0.04*	0.0037	0.08*	1

Source: Computed by authors.
Note: * indicates values at the 10 per cent level of significance.

Correlation between Selected Chronic Diseases

Table 2 showed the positive association among all the selected chronic conditions except between depression and stroke. The relationship between the prevalence of hypertension and diabetes was found to be highly significant.

Table 6.2 *Percentage Distribution of the Study Sample by Selected Background Characteristics India, 2007–2008*

Distribution of Sample	Percentage (%)	Frequency	Sample Size
Place of Residence			
Urban	25.93	2,033	7,841
Rural	74.07	5,808	
Sex			
Female	50.90	3,991	7,841
Male	49.10	3,850	
Age			
45–54	30.00	2,352	7,841
55–64	36.19	2,838	
65–74	24.38	1,912	
75+	9.42	739	
Level of Education			
No education	55.02	4,314	7,841
Up to primary	23.53	1,845	
Secondary	9.17	719	
Higher secondary and Above	12.28	963	
Wealth Quintile			
Poorest	20.00	1,568	7,841
Poorer	20.00	1,568	
Middle	20.01	1,569	
Richer	20.00	1,568	

(Continued)

(Continued)

Distribution of Sample	Percentage (%)	Frequency	Sample Size
Richest	20.00	1,568	
Type of Occupation			
Manual	86.92	4,474	5,147
Non-manual	13.08	673	
Working Hours			
Less than equal to 8 hrs	47.09	2,424	5,147
More than 8 hrs	52.91	2,723	
Total	100	7,841	

Source: Computed by authors.

Socio-economic and Demographic Characteristics

In Table 3, as expected, it was seen that most people who were ever diagnosed with chronic diseases belonged to urban areas, which were proportionately significant at 5 and 10 per cent levels of significance. All chronic conditions were more prevalent among males except hypertension. These diseases increase proportionately and significantly with increasing age. Hypertension (33.14 per cent), diabetes (15.6 per cent), angina (7.07 per cent) and depression (9.53 per cent) were higher among overweight people. Excluding depression, the prevalence of all these chronic conditions was found to be higher in the richest quintile.

Effect of Work History on the Prevalence of Chronic Disease

The prevalence of hypertension, diabetes and stroke was found to be higher among people who worked more than five days a week, while the prevalence of angina and depression was lower among them when compared to their counterparts, those who worked less than five days a week.

Table 6.3 Prevalence (per 100 population) of Selected Chronic Conditions by Selected Socio-economic and Demographic Characteristics India, 2007–2008

Socio-economic and Demographic Characteristics	Hypertension	Diabetes	Stroke	Angina	Depression
Place of Residence					
Rural®	10.21	4.49	1.49	3.45	3.95
Urban	21.37*	9.45*	1.48**	6.70*	5.38**
Sex					
Female®	17.94	4.12	0.88	4.3	3.48
Male	11.19*	6.43**	1.72*	4.28**	4.65*
Age					
45–54®	10.31	4.34	1.03	1.75	4.72
55–64	13.96**	6.91*	1.51	6.3	3.63**
65–74	19.03*	7.58*	2.35*	7.51*	4.71
75+	17.27*	8.10*	2.99*	8.29**	3.06
Level of Education					
No education®	10.64	3.56	1.15	3.27	4.86
Up to primary	9.14*	3.81*	2.13**	5.66*	4.39
Secondary	16.16*	7.41*	1.51**	5.04*	3.3

(Continued)

(Continued)

Socio-economic and Demographic Characterisitics	Hypertension	Diabetes	Stroke	Angina	Depression
Higher secondary and Above	22.16*	12.45*	1.34**	4.28*	3.62**
Wealth Quintile Index					
Poorest®	6.28	1.24	0.86	3.28	2.28
Poorer	8.16*	3.21	1.33**	3.06	2.47**
Middle	11.83*	6.39*	1.25	4.61	6.73*
Richer	16.55*	7.33*	0.76	4.20*	7.51*
Richest	24.32*	11.62*	3.38*	6.68*	2.97
BMI					
Normal®	12.75	6.75	1.82	3.39	3.82
Underweight	7.85*	1.75*	1.11	4.46	3.35
Overweight	33.14*	15.6*	0.93	7.07*	9.53
Obese	31.55*	11.57*	1.71	2.34	2.39
Total	100	100	100	100	100

Source: Computed by authors.

Note: ® denotes the reference category. * and ** indicate that prevalence between different categories and reference category is statistically significant at 5 per cent and 10 per cent levels of significance, respectively.

A significantly greater proportion of non-manual workers were diagnosed with chronic diseases than manual workers. Considering the type of job, employers who worked in the private or informal sector or were self-employed had a significantly lower proportion of being diagnosed with hypertension, diabetes, stroke and angina, at a level of 5 per cent significance. People who worked more than eight hours a day had a higher prevalence of diabetes, angina and depression, which was proportionately significant at a level of 5 and 10 per cent significance when compared to their reference category, which was people who worked less than eight hours a day (Table 4).

According to Table 5, people who worked more than five days a week had 53 per cent less chance to suffer from depression than those who worked less than or equal to five days a week after adjusting important background characteristics. Non-manual workers were at a higher risk of chronic diseases. The odds of having hypertension were 1.31 times, diabetes 1.80 times, angina 1.54 times, stroke 1.89 times and depression 1.14 times higher among non-manual workers compared to their counterparts. The odds of having diabetes were significantly higher among those who were engaged in the private and informal sector as compared to the people who were engaged in the public sector. The prevalence of diabetes was 1.37 times and stroke was 1.20 times higher among people who worked more than eight hours a day, and that was found to be statistically significant, too.

DISCUSSION

Most of the world's population is suffering from negative health repercussions as a result of industrialization and mechanization. Changing work patterns is one of the problems that have contributed to increasing levels of developing non-communicable diseases. In recent years, the burden of non-communicable diseases and the increase in the number of older populations has emerged as an important public health concern in developing countries. In this study, we examined the association between long working hours and the risk of chronic diseases as well as the correlation of selected chronic diseases in India by using SAGE 2007–2008 data. The study found that the prevalence

Table 6.4 Prevalence (per 100 population) of Selected Chronic Conditions by Selected Working Characteristics, India 2007–2008

Working Characteristics	Hypertension	Diabetes	Stroke	Angina	Depression
No. of Days in a Week					
Less than equal to 5 days®	11.30	4.21	0.99	5.09	6.66
More than 5 days	13.34	6.17*	1.60	4.09	3.80*
Type of Occupation					
Manual®	11.37	4.57	1.46	3.91	4.55
Non-manual	25.06*	14.08*	1.66*	6.90*	2.84
Job Sector					
Public®	20.93	13.37	1.93	7.50	2.81
Private	19.13*	8.46*	1.75**	4.12*	2.92
Self-employed	12.59*	5.14*	1.57	3.93	3.04
Informal employment	9.51*	3.47*	1.13	3.85*	7.26*
No. of Hours Per Day					
Less than equals to 8 hours®	13.32	4.28	0.98	4.39	5.66
More than 8 hours	12.92	7.02*	1.91*	4.20**	3.20*
Total	100	100	100	100	100

Source: Computed by authors.

Notes: ® denotes the reference category. * and ** indicate that prevalence between different categories and reference category is statistically significant at 5 per cent and 10 per cent levels of significance, respectively.

of all selected diseases was higher among urbanites and a literate older population with an increase in income and BMI. This result was similar to the earlier studies conducted in India (Mahmood et al., 2011; Patel et al., 2011). Obesity stands as a major covariate in developing chronic diseases. All these diseases are mostly found among males, but in this study, while comparing, we found that the prevalence of hypertension was higher among female respondents. This may be because females over the age of 40 might have been subjected to family stress and gained more weight over time or age (Caruso et al., 2004; Ramin et al., 2015).

All selected diseases were found to be higher among non-manual workers and a reduction in work time positively affected an individual's health behaviour (Berniell, 2012). In this study, people who worked more than 8 hours were found to have a higher prevalence of chronic diseases as this type of schedule had a stressful influence on employees. Professional and white-collar workers were shown to walk less (as measured by a pedometer) and have a lower volume of occupational physical activity than blue-collar workers (Steele & Mummery, 2003). Professional and associate professional women provided evidence that better lifestyles could lower the risk of obesity and overweight gain (Allman-Farinelli el at., 2010).

A lack of control over work has a powerful effect on health. It was damaging to health and could lead to premature death (Marmot et al., 1997). A longitudinal study based in the Netherlands found that the influence of health problems between 1991 and 1995 was negligible. In a working population, for manual workers as compared to non-manual workers, the odds ratio for less than perceived good general health was underestimated by 34 per cent in 1995 (Van de Mheen et al., 1999). Occupational factors such as higher levels of responsibility and irregular shifts were associated with the development of coronary diseases (WHO, 2001). All selected chronic diseases, except for depression, were found more common among the working age group. Mean annual working hours have declined, and bankruptcy, unemployment and suicide have increased as a result of the economic recession, which has induced job stress (Uchiyama et al., 2005).

Table 6.5 Odds Ratio and its 95 per cent Confidence Level Obtained from Logistic Regression Analysis for Selected Chronic Conditions by Selected Working Characteristics India, 2007–2008

Working Characteristics	Hypertension	Diabetes	Stroke	Angina	Depression
No. of days in a week					
Less than equal to 5 days®					
More than 5 days	0.8(0.7, 1.1)	0.9(0.6, 1.2)	1.03(0.6, 1.8)	0.9(0.6, 1.2)	0.47*(0.3, 0.6)
Type of Occupation					
Manual®					
Non-manual	1.3*(1.02, 1.7)	1.8*(1.3, 2.5)	1.9*(1.03, 3.4)	1.5*(1.01, 2.3)	0.9(0.5, 1.7)
Job Sector					
Public®					
Private	1.1(0.8, 1.5)	1.5**(0.99, 2.3)	1.4(0.7, 3.1)	1.3(0.8, 2.2)	1.5(0.7, 3.4)
Self-employed	0.8(0.6, 1.1)	1.3(0.9, 1.9)	1.1(0.5, 2.1)	0.8(0.5, 1.3)	1.1(0.6, 2.3)
Informal employment	1.02(0.7, 1.4)	1.8*(1.2, 2.8)	1.2(0.5, 2.5)	1.5(0.9, 2.5)	2.8(1.4, 5.8)
No. of hours per day					
Less than equal to 8 hours®					
More than 8 hours	0.9(0.7, 1.1)	1.3*(1.01, 1.7)	1.2*(1.0, 1.8)	1.1(0.8, 1.5)	0.5*(0.4, 0.7)

Source: Computed by authors.

Notes: *$P \leq 0.05$. **$P \leq P. 10$, ® denotes reference, category, place of residence, age, sex, education, BMI, wealth quintile, marital status, caste and religion were controlled in the analysis.

This study also showed a positive correlation between various chronic diseases. Literature also suggests a complex inter-relationship between depressive disorders and chronic diseases (Chapman et al., 2005). According to a study of Australian National Seniors, respondents suffering from any chronic disease had an average of 2.4 comorbid diseases, as shown by the correlation of chronic diseases in the age group of 50 years and above (Islam et al., 2014). A study done in North America and Europe found that hypertension was a common comorbidity among people diagnosed with any chronic condition (Arauz-Pacheco et al., 2004).

This study found the working respondents, aged 45 years and above, were positively associated with chronic conditions and were found to suffer from two or more chronic conditions, indicating that there was some correlation between these selected chronic conditions.

CONCLUSIONS AND RECOMMENDATIONS

The young population in India is on the rise. Long working hours and inadequate breaks affect a worker's health. The government has recognized that the safety and health of workers not only affected workers' productivity but also had a great impact on economic and social development. Based on the critical findings of the study, some recommendations for policy inputs for improving the health of those aged 45 and above are listed as:

Although there are very few employees in the organized sector, the government needs to pass legislation related to workers' welfare for both the government and the private sector.
Both the government and employers should promote a healthy working environment through some small interventions like breaks between long working hours.

The government should also undertake some specific policy steps that would help in coping with harmful work schedules and by designing workplace environments that lead to the least disruption to the mental, physical and social well-being of employees. India needs to improve its healthcare facilities in accordance with demographic and epidemiological shifts from communicable to non-communicable diseases. Currently, a limited overtime-working-hours scheme is employed to maintain the efficiency of workers; however, the government should modify rules according to a worker's age.

REFERENCES

Allman-Farinelli, M. A., Chey, T., Merom, D., & Bauman, A. E. (2010). Occupational risk of overweight and obesity: An analysis of the Australian Health Survey. *Journal of Occupational Medicine and Toxicology, 5*(1), 14.

Arauz-Pacheco, C., Parrott, M. P., Raskin, P., & American Diabetes Association. (2004). Hypertension management in adults with diabetes. *Diabetes Care, 27*(1), S65–S67.

Berniell, M. I. (2012). *The effects of working hours on health status and health behaviors.* Centro de Estudios Monetarios Y Financieros. https://conference.iza.org/conference_files/SUMS2012/berniell_m7629.pdf

Burke, J. R., & Cooper, C. L. (2008). *The long work hours culture: Causes, consequences and choices.* Emerald Group Publishing.

Caruso, C. C., Hitchcock, E. M., Dick, R. B., Russo, J. M., & Schmit, J. M. (2004). *Overtime and extended work shifts: Recent findings on illness, injuries, and health behaviors* (DHHS (NIOSH) Publication No. 2004-143), b13. https://www.cdc.gov/niosh/docs/2004-143/pdfs/2004-143.pdf

Cha, E. S., Kong, K. A., Moon, E. K., & Lee, W. J. (2009). Prevalence and changes in chronic diseases among South Korean farmers: 1998 to 2005. *BMC Public Health, 9*(1), 268.

Chandola, T., Britton, A., Brunner, E., Hemingway, H., Malik, M., Kumari, M., Badrick, E., Kivimaki, M., & Marmot, M. (2007). Work stress and coronary heart disease: What are the mechanisms? *European Heart Journal, 29*(1), 640-648.

Chapman, D. P., Perry, G. S., & Strine, T. W. (2005). Vital link between chronic disease and depressive disorders. *Preventive Chronic Disease, 2*(1), A14.

Dembe, A. E., Erickson, J. B., Delbos, R. G., & Banks, S. M. (2006). The impact of overtime and long work hours on occupational injuries and illnesses: New evidence from the United States. *Occupational and Environmental Medicine, 62*(1), 588-597.

Health Canada. (2000). *Best advice on stress risk management in the workplace.* Health Canada.

House, J. S., Lantz, P. M., & Herd, P. (2005). Continuity and change in the social stratification of aging and health over the life course: Evidence from a nationally representative longitudinal study from 1986 to 2001/2002 (Americans' Changing Lives Study). *Journals of Gerontology. Series A: Biological Sciences and Medical Sciences, 60*(2), 15-26.

ILO. (2012). International Standard Classification of Occupations: ISCO-08. https://www.ilo.org/wcmsp5/groups/public/---dgreports/---dcomm/---publ/documents/publication/wcms_172572.pdf

Islam, M. M., Valderas, Yen, L., Dawda, P., Jowsey, T., & McRae, I. S. (2014). Multimorbidity and comorbidity of chronic diseases among the senior Australians: Prevalence and patterns. *PLoS One, 9*(1), e83783.

Jaeyoung, K. (2013). Depression as a psychosocial consequence of occupational injury in the US working population: Findings from the medical expenditure panel survey. *BMC Public Health, 13*(1), 303.

Kim, I. H., Khang, Y. H., Muntaner, C., Chun, H., & Cho, S. I. (2008). Gender, precarious work, and chronic diseases in South Korea. *American Journal of Industrial Medicine, 51*(10), 748-757.

Kobayashi, T., Suzuki, E., Takao, S., & Doi, H. (2012). Long working hours and metabolic syndrome among Japanese men: A cross-sectional study. *BMC Public Health, 12*(1), 395.

Mahmood, S. E., Srivastava, A., Shrotriya, V. P., Shaifali, I., & Mishra, P. (2011). Prevalence and epidemiological correlates of hypertension among labour population. *National Journal of Community Medicine, 2*(1), 43-48.

Marmot, M. G., Bosma, H., Hemingway, H., Brunner, E., & Stansfeld, S. (1997). Contribution of job control and other risk factors to social variations in coronary heart disease incidence. *Lancet, 350*(9073), 235-239.

Patel, V., Chatterji, S., Chisholm, D., Ebrahim, S., Gopalakrishna, G., Mathers, C. & Reddy, K. S. (2011). Chronic diseases and injuries in India. *Lancet, 377*(9763), 413-428.

Ramin, C., Devore, E. E., Wang, W., Pierre-Paul, J., Wegrzyn, L. W., & Schernhammer, E. S. (2015). Night shift work at specific age ranges and chronic disease risk factors. *Occupational Environmental Medicine, 72*(2), 100-107.

Rosengren, A., Hawken, S., Ounpuu, S., Sliwa, K., Zubaid, M., Almahmeed, W. A. & Yusuf, S. (2004). Association of psychosocial risk factors with risk of acute myocardial infarction in 11 119 cases and 13 648 controls from 52 countries (the INTERHEART study): Case-control study. *Lancet, 364*(1), 953-962.

SAGE. (2012). *WHO Study on global AGEing and adult health (SAGE) Waves 0 and 1: Sampling information for China, Ghana, India, Mexico, Russia and South Africa.* World Health Organization.

Steele, R., & Mummery, K. (2003). Occupational physical activity across occupational categories. *Journal of Science & Medicine in Sport, 6*(4), 398-407.

Tong, B., & Stevenson, C. (2007). *Comorbidity of cardiovascular disease, diabetes and chronic kidney disease in Australia.* Australian Institute of Health and Welfare.

Uchiyama, S., Kurasawa, T., Sekizawa, T., & Nakatsuka, H. (2005). Job strain and risk of cardiovascular events in treated hypertensive Japanese workers: Hypertension follow- up group study. *Journal of Occupational Health, 47*(2), 102-111.

Van de Mheen, H., Stronks, K., Schrijvers, C. T., & Mackenbach, J. P. (1999). The influence of adult ill health on occupational class mobility and mobility out of and into employment in the Netherlands. *Social Science & Medicine*, *49*(4), 509-518.

Volkers, A. C., Westert, G. P., & Schellevis, F. G. (2007). Health disparities by occupation, modified by education: A cross-sectional population study. *BMC Public Health, 7*(1), 196.

World Health Organization (WHO). (2001). *Occupational health: A manual for primary healthcare workers*. WHO.

Zygmuntowicz, M., Owczarek, A., Elibol, A., & Chudek, J. (2012). Comorbidities and the quality of life in hypertensive patients. *Polskie Archiwum Medycyny Wewnetrznej, 122*(7-8), 333-340.

Section II

Questions of Women's Health and Reproductive Justice

Sectional Introduction

In the middle of the so-called male-dominated sciences, medicine, which initially accepted gender differences as natural and inherent in the female body, slowly began to accept that not all differences were biological. The recognition that some differences are socially constructed and can be changed through social transformation added many new aspects to public health research. Thus, researches in public health started addressing issues of women's health in communities and the place of women in the health provisioning of services. The rising challenges of women's movement and a gender-conscious public health movement added to the affectivity and promptness with which the role of social determinants of women's health was brought forward (Qadeer, 2014).

This specificity of sex and gender as social constructs by feminist scholars has contributed immensely to understand the complexities and nuances of public health. This new method of analysis has contributed to a better comprehension of health differentials and the distribution of mortalities and morbidities. Independent India created an environment in which population growth was viewed as an economic concern rather than a social development. Other than the Soviet model of development, all capitalist modes of development and so-called mixed economies were ideologically married to Malthusian politics in their understanding of 'limited resources'. Unlikely their counterparts in the Global North, Indian feminists criticized abortion laws liberalization as they saw it as a double-edged sword in the new demographic context. Instead of upholding reproductive freedom in a patriarchal society, it could be used as a tool to oppress women by regulating their sexualities (Arathi, 2016).

The colonial legacy extended even after Independence in India, and legislative measures to bring about the liberalization of abortion law in Britain forced parliamentarians in India to think in this direction, especially in the context of nation building and nationalization, and welfarism began to be influenced by values of modernity like 'small families' and the radical idea of the emancipation of women (to a very limited extent). The main research questions posed to academia in the context of legalizing abortion in India were different from that of Western countries (Arathi, 2016). Here, the frequently asked questions were whether the liberalization of law had any impact in lowering maternal mortality by reducing illegal (surely, unsafe!) abortions and improve the health of women in India; the role of abortion in the context of national population control policies and the quality of services from both the provider and beneficiary perspective (Arathi, 2016).

Globalization's impact on the health of women in India became one of the prominent discourses in the 1990s. The public health policy approach to women's health with an objective to understand the factors that prohibit poor women from accessing healthcare services in the wake of globalization contributed to build a political economy approach in gender analysis of health service provisioning. This economic phenomenon initially seemed very promising for the well-being of humankind, especially for marginalized communities. Many empirical studies focused on the history of engendering public health in India to develop a comparative analysis on the impact of the welfare state as against the neoliberal state on the health of poor women. Those empirical evidences clearly showed that any public health project cannot be effective, while more than 80 per cent adolescent girls are anaemic, more than 40 per cent children are malnourished, the mothers mortality rate is 452, the infant mortality rate is 41 and thousands of children are dying because of respiratory tract infection and diarrhoea (National Family Health Survey IV). The more important agenda for the state in such condition needs to be institutional instead of promotional. The infrastructure of the state cannot deal with the international pressure and priorities while people are dying from curable diseases. The role of the welfare state is needed in a nation like India, with the majority of its population living in poverty.

Neoliberal politics and the retreat of the welfare state started affecting women disproportionately for several reasons. The role of conservative religious forces to reiterate Right-wing family values created a situation that adversely affected women's health needs, particularly reproductive health needs. The context of the re-emergence of nationalist politics clearly created its emphasis on the role of women to confine to reproduce the nation by biologically producing more children. Nationalism, together with neo-Malthusian politics in the form of anti-immigrant and Islamophobia on the one hand, places the burden on 'native' women to reproduce more and restricts reproductive autonomy in terms of access to contraceptives and abortion services and, on the other, restricts immigrant women and minority women accused for being an additional burden on the public health system due to their 'increased reproduction numbers'.

The discourse on abortion within a framework of reproductive justice primarily challenged notions of power and control in family, sexual and procreative relations. The work of Pandey (2014) analyses the Medical Termination of Pregnancy (MTP) Act, 1971, as an example of the intersection of two symbiotically, hegemonic superstructures, patriarchy and law. She argues that the law serves as a major instrument of perpetuation and validation of patriarchy in the Indian context. The legislative process and practices related to the MTP Act remained instruments of perpetuation and validation of patriarchy in India. The Act became an example of the intersection of exploitative structures, patriarchy and law. The debates clearly indicate that the law dealing with the health of women is dominated by perceptions that consider them essentially as reproductive machines and is predictably protectionist. The political imagination of the legislative process considered them as childbearing beneficiaries, and it could hardly capture the idea of women as equal rights-bearing citizens.

Technological interventions in biomedical practices have made the boundaries of both reproductive bodies and nation states porous in a globalized world. While it is an important therapeutic aid in infertility treatments, it is simultaneously integral to the regenerative pharmaceutical industry. Active lobbying for regulation, deregulation and re-regulation of the practice of egg donation and research on bio-cells (human embryonic stem cell) happens at the national level. My unpublished work explores the need and possibilities of an international meta-regulatory framework to understand, negotiate and protect the exploitation of less privileged women in the structure of regulatory practices in egg donation and research on bio-cells.

The history of *Social Change* marks different trajectories of feminist discourses on public health issues covering the spectrum between critiques of the Malthusian ideology of coercive population policies to the commodification of the female body through new reproductive technologies. The studies such as trends in fertility behaviour and status of women (Dandekar, 1974); the importance of female education and the risk of family planning programme in controlling fertility in India (Vig, 1976); family structure and fertility (Reddy, 1978) mark the feminist criticism of the family planning programme in India. The 1980s witnessed the mix of response to both family planning programmes and the MTP Act (C. A. S. Mouli & C. S. Mouli, 1981; Kapoor et al., 1981; Mouli et al., 1981; Prabhakar & Murthy, 1981; Reddy, 1984; Singh, 1981). Chaudhuri (1984) emphasizes the sex bias in nutrition practices and Jayaswal (1985) analyses the concept of health modernity and correlates it in women of south Bihar. The article titled 'Village *Dai* as an Agent for Infant Care' reiterates the tradition wisdom in maternal and infant care (Bhatnagar et al., 1985). Ramalingaswami (1986) traces the impact of social change on the health problems of tribal women and Khan (1987) identifies the productive and reproductive roles of women.

The second section of the volume 'Questions of Women's Health and Reproductive Justice' includes five chapters. Chapter 7 by Ramalingaswami (1986) deconstructs the popular myth of 'awareness creation' among marginalized sections about government welfare programmes and popular nation of the relationship between the underutilization of state-sponsored programmes due to lack of information. Post-Independence state-sponsored plans spent major junk of allocation of fund to improve awareness. In Chapter 7, Ramalingaswami finds that though tribal women were illiterate and living in remote rural areas, far away from urban influence, they showed awareness about these programmes. However, the systemic failure created a situation where programmes did not reach these women nor benefitted them. The study was conducted with a sample consisting of 372 tribal women between 15–45 age groups living in Paderu block of Visakhapatnam district in then Andhra Pradesh. The author considers social change due to changes in social circumstances, a self-awareness of their social conditions and exposure towards available state-sponsored programmes. The study conducted in 1986 still shows the relevance of getting out of the rhetoric of 'creating awareness' for the successful implementation of programmes and points towards the need for fresh empirical enquiries to find real issues why benefits are not reaching marginalized sections of society.

Chapter 8 studies the relationship between the employment of women and the fertility-productive and reproductive roles of women by Khan (1987). Following trends in academic writings prevalent in the late 1970s and the 1980s, this work attempts to understand the role of women and population issues to locate women's role in demographic change. This chapter locates the relationship between different variables such as women's employment and fertility, family planning and health. The author argues that the simplistic approach of dichotomizing women into working/non-working status is reductionist and points towards a holistic approach by mapping all other activities of women. This approach includes nuanced variables such as the definition of labour force, mechanism of division of labour within family in different socio-economic and class systems, the linkage between the division of labour and power base of women and its relationship with reproductive behaviour.

Chapter 9 by Jai Prakash (1999) traces historical views and examines the findings regarding the effect of menopause on women's health, well-being and sexuality. Menopause as a significant biological marker of ageing has several popular and psychological connotations existing in our society. As she notes:

A major transition in the life cycle of women during middle age is menopause. The cessation of menstruation announces, in unequivocal terms, that a woman's reproductive role has come to an end. As dramatic an event as the menarche, menopause is often believed to be a significant event that strains the coping abilities of women. It is a topic that is surrounded not just by old wives' tales but also with 'scientific myths'. (Prakash, 1999, p. 171)

After doing a rich secondary literature review and evaluation of several empirical studies on menopause, the author argues for the necessity of multidisciplinary studies that assess the gynaecological status of women along with their psychological conditions which requires a holistic perspective based on conditions of women in society.

Chapter 10 is a review of literature on female infanticide by Saravanan (2002). Through historical analysis of legal provisions, she identifies the causes behind female infanticide and finds the patriarchal social structure and lower social status of women as a primary cause.

Female infanticide is supported by sanctions and pressures from the family. It is fueled by the evil of the dowry system, which places demands on the girl's family…. It is believed that killing a girl child increases the probability of a male child born in the family. Female infanticide is reported to occur due to lack of scanning centres, as an alternative to foeticide. (Saravanan, 2002, p. 58)

This chapter calls for social mobilization along with political will and awareness generation and community support.

Disability is a highly stigmatized identity and women with disability are viewed as asexual, dependent, in need of care and hence incapable of performing the culturally approved 'womanly' role of a sexual partner and nurturing mother. In Chapter 11, Shubhangi Vaidya examines the experiences of the disabled in the context of sexuality and motherhood. She examines the experiences of disabled women in the context of sexuality and motherhood. By citing a range of cross-cultural studies, the author demonstrates how disabled women engage with sexuality and procreation, and how patriarchal social structures regulate sexuality and fertility of women with disabilities and therefore construct their humanity and personhood. The author argues for a nuanced approach that respects the rights of women with disabilities to bodily integrity and personal dignity. The study proposes their need for support and assistance to protect their bodily autonomy and the right to decision-making regarding their reproductive choices.

REFERENCES

Arathi P.M. (2016). Aborting reproductive justice: An analysis of the legislative process concerning abortions in India, *Indian History*, Volume III, p.129 –159.

Bhatnagar, S., Sharma, U., & Nath, D. H. (1985). Village *dai* as an agent for infant care. *Social Change*, 5(4), 15–19.

Chaudhuri, M. (1984). Sex bias in child nutrition. *Social Change*, *14*(3), 50–52.

Dandekar, K. (1974). Trends of fertility behaviour reflecting the status of women. *Social Change*, *4*(3&4), 36–41.

Jayaswal, M. (1985). Health modernity and its correlates in women of south Bihar. *Social Change*, *15*(2), 7–14.

Kapoor, S. D., Dayal, S. B., Trakroo, P. L., & Roy, S. N. (1981). Medical termination of pregnancy: Present status, policy implications & recommendations. *Social Change*, *11*(3&4), 3–10.

Khan, M. E. (1987). Productive and reproductive roles of women. *Social Change*, *17*(1), 60–65.

Mouli, C. A. S, & Mouli, C. S. (1981). Medical termination of pregnancy: An opinion survey. *Social Change*, *11*(2), 31–34.

Mouli, C., Murthy, A. S., Venkatesha, G. B., & Prabhakar, K. (1981). Abortion demand in India. *Social Change*, *11*(3&4), 65–67.

Pandey, Shruthi. (2014). Women's health and law in India: Trends of hope and despair, in Kalpana Kannabiran (ed), *Women and Law: Critical Feminist Perspectives*, New Delhi, Sage, pp. 206 –239.

Prabhakar, K., & Murthy, V. G. B. (1981). Induced abortion in Karnataka: An analysis. *Social Change*, *11*(3&4), 68–70.

Prakash, J. I. (1999). Menopause: A fresh look at the much misunderstood phenomenon. *Social Change*, *29*(1–2), 171–187.

Qadeer, I. (2014). Limits to Medicine: Social Determinant's of Women's Health. *Samyukta Journal of Women's Studies*, 14(2), 7.

Ramalingaswami, P. (1986). Impact of social change on health problem of tribal women. *Social Change*, *16*(2&3), 100–103.

Reddy, M. (1984). Status of women and family planning behaviour among non-adapters. *Social Change*, *14*(3), 53–57.

Saravanan, S. (2002). Female infanticide in India: A review of literature. *Social Change*, *32*, 58–66.

Singh, K. P. (1981). Status of women and population growth. *Social Change*, 11(3&4), 27–30.

Vig, O. P. (1976). Neglect of female education: A risk for family planning programme in controlling fertility in India. *Social Change*, 6(3&4), 22–29.

Chapter 7

Impact of Social Change on Health Problems of Tribal Women*

Prabha Ramalingaswami

Women in India have always enjoyed a unique position. On one hand, they have been deified, have been praised as being the cornerstone of Indian society and have been depicted as the very personification of moral force that binds the family together. On the other hand, women in real life have been denigrated and have been subjected to many hardships, The reality of this actual status of Indian women had been brought out very vividly by the Government of India (1974).

The polarization that exists between the privileged sections of society and the masses influences the problem of women. It is the women from economically weaker sections that are adversely affected. Women who are the prime producers of the necessities of life, women on whom the society depends so heavily for economic support and family healthcare, are the prime targets of these inequalities and injustices.

When one talks about women from economically weaker sections of society, it is the rural and tribal women that stand out. These women are poor and illiterate. They are working not by choice but by force of circumstances. They are working as agricultural labour, as construction workers, and in agro-based industries such as tobacco and cotton. All the back-breaking jobs in agriculture are done by women. All the jobs

* *Social Change* 16, no. 2–3 (June–September 1986): 100–103.

which are health-hazardous—in tobacco and other industries—are done by women. The wages that are paid to them are very low in comparison to the work of their male counterparts and in comparison with the quantity and quality of work they do. There is a lot written on this (Balasubrahmanyam, 1985; Bardhan, 1985; Dighe, 1985; Gulati, 1981; Mazumdar, 1982; Murali Manohar et al., 1981; Saradamoni, 1982; UNICEF 1980).

Added to these are other problems which these women face. Cow dung and firewood which used to be easily available and which were free of cost have become scarce commodities (Batliwala, 1983; Nagabrahmam & Sambrani, 1983). Kerosene stoves and cooking gas are beyond the means and reach of these women. Another most important problem which these women face is with regard to drinking water. They have to fetch their drinking water sometimes from long distances and sometimes waiting in a long queue which is a time- and energy-consuming chore. The result is that, in addition to work outside the house and inside the house, they are spending more time and energy for getting cooking fuel and drinking water. The work in the house is itself not regarded as important or remunerative. The work they do outside is hard and wages are usually very low. They are usually in a poor state of health. Repeated pregnancies, chronic under-nutrition, hard work, lack of healthcare and basic amenities have sapped all their energies. Yet they are the key person in the family—it is they who take care of the children and every member of the family.

Health and education are two issues which are central to the lives of women.

Table 7.1 Female Literacy and Work Participation All India 1981 Figures in %

	Total	Urban	Rural
Female literacy	24.82	47.82	17.96
Main workers (female)	14.44	7.57	16.49
Marginal workers (female)	75.28	64.00	76.96

Source: Social Change 16, no. 2–3 (June–September 1986): 100–103.

Table 7.2 *Childbirth*

Category	Persons Who Actually Had Their Deliveries		Persons Who Preferred to Have This Category	
	Number	Percentage	Number	Percentage
Family members	304	81.72	188	50.54
ANM	4	1.08	107	28.76
Local *Dais*	58	15.59	77	20.69
Hospital	5	1.34	—	—

Source: Social Change 16, no. 2–3 (June–September 1986): 100–103.

Table 7.3 *Tetanus Toxoid Injection*

	Number	Percentage
Those who received	58	15.59
Those who did not	314	84.41

Source: Social Change 16, no. 2–3 (June–September 1986): 100–103.

A woman is at a disadvantage because of the physiological problem of childbirth. A woman needs special care during her reproductive years. Education is a societal problem in which the government is committed. There are also economic programmes which the government has initiated for the betterment of the poor. What is the effect of these programmes? It is interesting to see the census figures for 1981 which are given in Table 7.1.

The disparity between the urban and rural literacy and the disparity between female workers categorized as main and marginal workers is striking. This itself is an indication of the disadvantages which the rural women are suffering and that the government programmes have not reached them. Literacy has not reached them in the way it should have and in spite of their hard work, they are classified as marginal workers because they do not have continuity of work.

The government has a number of programmes for economic development as well as for rendering basic healthcare. What is the effect of these programmes? Are the women from disadvantaged group aware of these programmes? Have these programmes reached them? In our effort to find answers to the above questions, a study was conducted as part of a major study.

Objectives of the study

1. Are the women from economically weaker sections in rural areas aware of the primary health centre (PHC)?
2. Are the women aware of maternal and child health services rendered by auxiliary nurse midwives (ANMs)? If so, have they utilized their services?
3. Are the women aware about TB, leprosy and malaria?
4. Are the women aware of family planning services and have they utilized them?
5. Are the women aware of economic programmes of the government? If so, have they utilized them?

AREA OF THE STUDY

Six villages near Paderu block in Visakhapatnam district of Andhra Pradesh are included in this study. Paderu has 93 per cent tribal population and is completely rural. It has a female literacy rate of 3.05 per cent. It is the headquarters of the tribal division and is about 150 km from the district headquarters. The nearest town (which has a population of 21,000) is about 74 km. The Integrated Tribal Development Agency which is set up by the government for bringing economic development for the tribal areas has its divisional headquarters at Paderu. Out of the six villages, one village is at about 10 km distance from Paderu, another village 8 km, another village 6 km and two villages are 4 km, and two villages are 3 km from Paderu.

SAMPLE

A total of 372 women in the 15–45 age group were included in the study. For each household, one woman was interviewed. 15 women

Table 7.4 *Awareness about Diseases*

	Number	Percentage
TB	111	29.84
Leprosy	105	28.23
Malaria	368	98.92
*Goitre	121	32.53

*While they were aware about goitre as swelling near the neck, it is only 121 who knew it was a disease and could be prevented by changing the salt, that is, iodized salt.
Source: Social Change 16, no. 2–3 (June–September 1986): 100–103.

Table 7.5 *Family Planning Programme*

Number	Percentage
Persons who were aware of government family planning programme 249	66.94
Persons who used this programme 249	66.94
Persons who said there should be only two or three children 289	77.69
Persons who said that there should be 3 years of difference between children 286	76.88

Source: Social Change 16, no. 2–3 (June–September 1986): 100–103.

were literate without educational level, 20 women had about two to three years of schooling. All of them were married and had at least one child. They were all tribal women. This group was selected for the study because of their illiteracy and poverty, and were living far away from urban areas.

TECHNIQUES USED

The women were interviewed with the help of an interview schedule consisting of open-ended questions. The interviews were conducted in their houses and at times that was fixed by pre-arrangement. This

Table 7.6 *Awareness about Government Programmes*

Programme	Aware		Used	
	Number	Percentage	Number	Percentage
Developmental	186	50.0	186	50.0
PHC	249	66.94	249	66.94
Adult education	25	6.72	5	1.34

Source: Social Change 16, no. 2–3 (June–September 1986): 100–103.

enabled a smooth interview with no rush. After establishing rapport and after collecting data and background information, questions were asked about childbirth, persons who helped them during childbirth and the person they would like to have during childbirth, whether they were aware of the tetanus toxoid injection (part of the immunization programme of the government and which an ANM is supposed to give) which reduces maternal mortality, knowledge about family planning programme, knowledge about diseases such as TB, leprosy, malaria and goitre (which is prevalent in this region), awareness about PHC and awareness about developmental programmes. The attempt here has been to understand the existing factual knowledge they have about these problems. Although health modernity is an important concept (Singh, 1984), this was not used. The emphasis is on understanding the factual knowledge.

ANALYSIS OF DATA

Content analysis was done on the responses. Analysis of data is still in progress. Here, the most important features of the results are presented in Tables 7.2 to 7.6.

Table 7.2 clearly indicates that though the services of the ANM have not reached these people, they are aware about them and nearly 29 per cent have said that they would have preferred to have an ANM attend on them. Although the present group of women are tribal women living in a remote area away from urban influence, their responses are similar to those of rural women studied by Banerji (1982).

The tables presented here bring out one point very clearly that these people are aware of the government programmes. The programmes have not yet reached them. For instance, it is only 4 out of 372 women who had the luxury of having their babies through the hands of an ANM. Yet 107 out of 372 (nearly 29%) were aware about ANM, as a trained person and preferred to have her attend on them.

Likewise, almost everyone was aware of the malaria worker and associated them with fever tablets and blood smear. It is indeed interesting to notice that malaria programme reached these villages, and everyone knew about malaria.

Although this area is an endemic area for leprosy and TB also is quite common, only approximately 29 per cent of the women could mention the important symptoms of these diseases and were aware of the possibilities of treatment.

Family planning/welfare programme reached these women. They were motivated for adopting family planning operation and dutifully mentioned to us that the number of children one should have is two or three and that there should be a gap of 3 years between children, thus reflecting the propaganda of the family welfare programme.

With regard to developmental programmes, 50 per cent of women were aware of two programmes: (a) the agricultural programmes and (b) the houses for weaker sections. Those who knew about them utilized them and those who did not know about them were trying to find out details from our workers. Adult education programme has not really reached these people. This is probably because the developmental programmes and health programmes touch their very lives; they are important for their immediate value. And as such the news about these spreads fast—they try to get benefit out of this. Understanding the importance of education will only come later.

Social change that is being brought about by government programmes has succeeded to an extent in creating awareness about them. The actual services might not have reached them, but women living in a remote area away from urban influence also are becoming aware of them and are desiring these services. Social change that comes about because of circumstances, such as, for instance, the scarcity of firewood due to rapid deforestation, scarcity of cow dung due to the knowledge that it could be used as a manure and for gobar gas plants, have made the already difficult life of these women more difficult. The same thing has happened with cash crops: tobacco and cotton ginning and other industries have made their appearance. It is the women who are mostly employed in these health hazardous occupations thereby undermining the welfare of these women who are already undernourished due to poverty. The knowledge about what they can have and what they are having in basic problems like childbirth is making them aware of their own circumstances and is creating a mixed feeling of sorrow and discontent. Added to this is the inroads made by business groups such as the cool drink companies, the cinema theatres and nylon fabrics, and the consumerism that is coming up. Although the data are not presented in this chapter, almost all the women want to spend at least part of the money (if they can make extra money) on nylon fabrics. It is here that a concentrated effort is needed. In addition to providing avenues for making extra incomes and better healthcare facilities emphasis on education—education for not falling a prey to the influences that are detrimental to their welfare—is needed.

REFERENCES

Balasubrahmanyam, V. (1985). Biology and gender bias: Some issues in discrimination against women at the work place. *Economic & Political Weekly*, *20*(20).

Banerji, D. (1982). *Poverty class and health culture in India* (Vol. I). Prachi Prakashan.

Bardhan, K. (1985). Women's work, welfare and status: Forces of tradition and change in India. *Economic & Political Weekly*, *20*(5).

Batliwala, S. (1983). Women and cooking energy. *Economic & Political Weekly*, *18*(52–53).

Dighe, A. (1985). Women's employment in the urban informal sector—Some critical issues. *Social Change*, *15*(2), 3–6.

Government of India. (1974). *Towards equality: Report of the committee on status of women in India.*

Gulati, L. (1981). *Profiles in female poverty: A study of five poor working women in Kerala.* Hindustan Publishing Corporation, India.

Mazumdar, V. (1982). Another development with women: A view from Asia. *Development Dialogue.*

Murali Manohar, K., Shobha, V., & Janardhan Rao, B. (1981). Women construction workers of Warangal. *Economic & Political Weekly*, *16*(4).

Nagabrahmam, D., & Sambrani, S. K. (1983). Women's drudgery in firewood collection. *Economic & Political Weekly*, *18*(3).

Saradamoni, K. (1982). Women's status in changing agrarian relations: A Kerala experience. *Economic & Political Weekly, 17.*

Singh, A. K. (1984). Health modernity: Concept and correlates. *Social Change, 14*(3), 3–16.

UNICEF. (1980). *Board report on the integration of women in the development process and its impact on the well being of children Part I.* The author.

Chapter 8

Productive and Reproductive Roles of Women*

M. E. Khan

Studies on the relationship between the employment of women and fertility have been reviewed. Although the relationship is mainly situational and not fixed, there is evidence that whenever it exists, it is inverse. However, there is little knowledge about the mechanism which links the two.

Recently, there has been growing interest both among the social scientists and policymakers to understand the interrelationship between the roles of women and population issues (Alman, 1978; Anker et al., 1982; Dixon, 1975, 1976; Marshall, 1972; Safillios-Rothschild, 1979).

The women's main role was traditionally considered to be procreation. However, in the recent literature, various other roles of women are also considered to be equally important and relevant for the study of demographic issues. Oppong (1980) forwarded a model of seven roles of women which provides a framework for the collection and analysis of cross-cultural data, both quantitative and qualitative, on women's role and status in relation to demographic change. According to Oppong, the other six roles of women in addition to her traditional role of mother are conjugal, domestic, occupational, kin, community and individual. Linkages between these roles and the demographic behaviour are yet under investigation and hence are inconclusive.

---

* *Social Change* 17, no. 1 (March 1987): 60–65

One of the major attempts to understand the complex interrelationships between the women's role particularly the female employment and demographic and related variables such as fertility, family planning and health, is that of ILO/UNFPA global research on 'Women's Roles and Demographic Change'. Under this project, a multidisciplinary approach has been adopted, which includes integrated quantitative—qualitative studies, both individual and household survey questionnaires, favoured by economists and statisticians as well as the in-depth qualitative case study approach favoured by anthropologists (Anker, 1980, 1982; Khan, 1980; Nag et al., 1982; Oppong & Church, 1981). The detailed findings of the major studies under this project, which are currently in progress in India, Bangladesh and Egypt are yet awaited. However, some preliminary observations from these studies have shown promising results (Khan & Ghosh 1981; Khan et al., 1982; Khan et al., 1983) and it is expected that on completion of the detailed analysis some more light could be thrown on this subject.

The study of interrelationship between the productive and reproductive roles of women is not new in the demographic literature. However, as we will see in the present chapter, the focus of these studies was rather narrow and hence still we do not have a clear picture about the nature and causal relationships and the mechanism through which they influence each other. In the end, some gaps have been identified which may be of interest for future research.

THE RELATIONSHIP BETWEEN WOMEN'S WORK AND FERTILITY

A review of literature on the subject shows that there are several studies which demonstrate a negative relationship between fertility and women's participation in labour force. For example, Duza (1967) reported a negative association between child women ratio and female participation in labour force in Pakistan. A similar relationship was observed in Bangladesh by Chaudhury (1974) among the women's participation in non-agricultural activities. A few Indian studies also show similar negative association. Some other studies showing negative association between fertility and women's work are reported from the Philippines (Herman , 1970), Latin America (Requena, 1965; Stycos,

1965), Puerto Rico (Carleton, 1965; Nerlove & Schultz, 1970) and Japan (Jaffe & Azumi, 1960; Taeuber, 1960).

Further, analysis by rural–urban residence and occupation categories shows that women working in urban areas have lower fertility than the non-working women (Bindary et al., 1973; Goldstein, 1972; Heer, 1964; Stycos, 1965). The negative relationship between fertility and women's work was less frequently observed in rural areas than in urban areas (Weller, 1977). Similarly, analysis by place of work and occupational categories shows that women who work for wages and salaried income in non-agricultural activities located outside home have lower fertility than other women (Chi & Harris, 1975; Hass, 1971; Jaffe & Azumi, 1960; Kobayashi, 1971; Stycos & Weller, 1967; Taeuber, 1960).

Review of the demographic literature on the subject presents yet another set of observations indicating only small and inconsistent relationships between fertility and women's work (Collver, 1968; Langlois, 1962). For example, Bindary et al. (1973) in Egypt observed a positive relationship between women's participation rate in labour force and Child Women Ratio (CWR) in rural areas and a negative relationship in urban areas. Dube et al. (1975) and Minkler (1970) in urban areas of Delhi did not find any difference in the fertility of uneducated working and non-working women. However, Minkler (1970) also reported that less educated non-working women had a much higher fertility than teachers. On the basis of his review of Indian literature on this subject, he concluded that there is no 'secure basis for ascertaining the nature of the relationship between economic activity and maternal responsibility'. In India, Driver (1963) also did not find any association between fertility and women's work in central India when age of the women was controlled.

Similarly, Chaudhury (1974) from Bangladesh reported a positive relationship between fertility and agricultural activity and negative relationship between fertility and non-agricultural activities. The National Family Planning Board of Malaysia found a *strong negative* relationship between women's work and fertility among those living in metropolitan cities, *a moderately negative* relationship among old women (aged 35–44 years) living in metros and *no relationship* among the women living in rural areas. Stycos and Weller (1967) and Mason

(1972) did not find any association between fertility and women's work. A somewhat similar observation was made by Goldstein (1972) in Thailand.

An interesting observation made by Heer and Youssef (1977) and also personally observed by the present author during his recent visit to the Central Asian Republic of the USSR reveals no association between fertility and women's participation in labour force. In fact, despite a very high proportion of women in the Central Asian Republic of the USSR participating in labour force, their fertility is much higher than that observed in many Muslim countries of Middle East and North America where the proportion of women participating in labour force is reported to be extremely low.

The above review of literature gives the impression that only under *certain* conditions, woman's participation in economic activities has negative relationship with her reproductive role. The causal relationship between these two variables could be due to any of the following four possibilities.

1. The observed relationship is spurious and is caused by common antecedents of both variables.
2. Women's family size affects their labour force participation.
3. Women's labour force participation affects the family size.
4. Both family size and labour force participation affect each other.

It is interesting to note that again the available literature supports all the above possibilities. For example, Terry (1974) showed that much of the negative relationship between fertility and participation in economic activities was explained by education, duration of marriage, farm background and timing of marriage in relation to parenthood. Similarly, there are a number of studies (Elizaga, 1974; Freedman et al., 1959; Mott, 1972) which show that it is the women's family size which affects their labour force participation. Stycos (1965) using his Peru data concluded that employment status is more often a consequence of marital fertility than a cause. Arguing the same point, Dixon (1975) further added that apart from fertility, marriage itself could reduce female's participation in the labour force.

The bulk of the studies explaining the negative impact of women's work on childbearing have taken the stand that it is only the 'opportunity cost' which matters. According to this logic, the rewards associated with employment are largely economic and social while those associated with motherhood are socio-emotional. Women for whom these two roles are incompatible are left with only one option that is to participate in either of the two roles extensively and only marginally in the other one. The women who choose to have many children forgo full or a part of the rewards of participating in economic activities and that becomes the 'opportunity cost' of motherhood. Those who decide to avail the benefits of participating in labour force compromise with childbearing and reduce their number of children by adopting family planning and/or delaying age at marriage. In situations when these two roles are not incompatible, women manage to perform both the roles and hence no association between women's work and fertility is observed.

Few studies also indicate that job satisfaction and commitment to work is yet another important ingredient for reducing fertility. In urban Greece, Safillios-Rothschild (1972) observed that women with high commitment to job had less number of children as compared to those who had low commitment towards the job. Similarly, Pinelli (1971) observed that women who had undertaken a job for self-satisfaction and to be independent had fewer children than those women who had taken job because of economic need. In fact, in this context, self-perception plays a crucial role. A woman who identifies her role with 'traditional values' tends to have a large number of children than those women who identify themselves with 'modern' roles (Blake, 1965; L. W. Hoffman & M. L. Hoffman, 1973).

Yet another mechanism through which labour force participation of women could reduce fertility is the changes in power structure within family and her enhanced role in the decision-making process. Studies show that a wife who contributes substantially to household income through regular economic activities is more independent and exercises considerable influence in family decision-making and hence decides her own family size (Rosen & Simmons, 1971; Weller, 1968).

Female employment also affects fertility by increasing age at marriage. It is argued that as the working daughters contribute to family income, their parents tend to postpone their marriage. Economic contribution from girls may also help in reducing the son preference of parents and hence they may not 'wait' to get two or three sons as generally observed in India and other developing countries. However, in Mauritius, Hein (1983) observed that because of their earnings, some girls working in industries were able to marry sooner than if they waited for their family to provide money for meeting their marriage expenses.

As mentioned earlier, the fourth type of causal relationship between employment and fertility could be that both family size and labour force participation affect each other. Many studies (Blake, 1965; Waite & Stolzenberg, 1976; Weller, 1968) supported this view. However, it is not clear at this moment whether these joint influences are exercised subsequently, simultaneously or both.

CONCLUSION

The complexity of the relationship between productive and reproductive roles as reviewed above clearly indicates that the relationship is multidimensional and each of these dimensions may react differently in different situations. Hence, the relationship between these two roles is situational rather than fixed. The above review also indicates that under certain circumstances, there is a definite negative relationship between women's work and fertility. The intensity of this relationship varies with circumstances and is perhaps strongest when the two roles are incompatible and the opportunity cost for bearing children is high. The relationship perhaps will be weakest in situations where the two roles are not incompatible and/or the opportunity cost is not very high. However, no such information is available to show how the relationship will vary with change in the characteristics of the women, job market and the social structure as a whole.

Some of the factors which could influence and create role incompatibility between productive and reproductive roles are the availability of acceptable arrangements for childcare, the existence of technological aids for performing various tasks, the extent to which each spouse is willing to share in performance of domestic tasks, the normative orientation of employees, husbands and wives towards the employment of mothers, the flexibility of working hours and the extent to which the woman is rewarded socially for working instead of having children (Weller, 1978). However, the available literature again does not throw enough light in which situation one or more types of these factors would be more effective in making the role incompatible and thereby reducing fertility.

We still do not have much knowledge about the *mechanism* through which various factors influence the relationship between the two roles. Similarly, how women's participation in economic activity changes the sexual division of labour within family and shifts her power base? How these shifts in the power base affect her status and her role in family decision-making processes? In fact, there are not many field studies available which could demonstrate that women's domestic authority in family decision-making process is a necessary or sufficient condition for changing reproductive behaviour and fertility ideals (Youssef, 1982).

Similarly, to clarify many of these issues, it is vital that more information should be generated to establish the linkages between woman's work, her status and fertility and, more importantly, the *dynamics* through which these linkages work in different socio-economic and class systems.

Last, but not the least, it is crucial that the simplistic approach of dichotomizing women into working/non-working status should be avoided, and attempt should be made to generate detailed information about women's activities. Such information base could help us in many ways including improvement in the definition of labour force, mechanism of division of labour within family in different socio-economic and class systems, the linkage between division of labour and power base of women and finally its relationship with the reproductive behaviour.

ACKNOWLEDGEMENT

The author acknowledges the help from Mr C. V. S. Prasad for going through the first draft of the chapter and giving useful comments.

REFERENCES

Alman, J. (Ed.). (1978). *Women's status and fertility in the Muslim world*. Praeger Publishers.

Anker, R. (1980). Demographic change and the role of women: A research programme in developing countries. In R. Anker (Ed.), *Women's roles and population trends in the third world*. Croom Helm.

Anker, R., Buvinic, M., & Youssef, N. H. (Eds). (1982). *Interactions between women's roles and population trends in the third world*. Croom Helm.

Bindary, A., Baxter, C. B., & Hollingsworth, T. H. (1973). Urban–rural differences in the relationship between women's employment and fertility: A preliminary study. *Journal of Biosocial Sciences, 5*(2).

Blake, J. (1965). Demographic science and the redirection of population policy. *Journal of Chronic Diseases, 18*, 1181–1200.

Carleton, R. (1965). Labour force participation: A stimulus to fertility in Puerto Rico? *Demography, 2*(1).

Chaudhury, R. H. (1974). Labour force status and fertility. *The Bangladesh Development Studies, 2*, 819–838.

Chi, S. K. P., & Harris, R. (1975). *Interaction between action programmes and social structural variables: A study of family planning and fertility differentials in four Colombian cities* (Paper presented at the annual meeting of the PAA, Seattle, Washington).

Collver, A. O. (1968). Women's work participation and fertility in Metropolitan areas. *Demography, 5*, 55–60.

Dixon, R. B. (1975). *Women's rights and fertility* (Report on Population Family Planning No. 17). New York Population Council.

Dixon, R. B. (1976). The roles of rural women: Female seclusion, economic production and reproductive choice. In R. Ridker (Ed.), *Population and Development: The search for selective interventions*. Johns Hopkins University Press.

Driver, E. D. (1963). *Differential fertility in central India*. Princeton University Press.

Dube, D. C., Bardhan, A., & Garg, D. (1975). *Fertility behaviour of working and non-working women*. National Institute of Family Planning.

Duza, M. D. (1967). Differential fertility in Pakistan. In W. C. Robinson (Ed.), *Studies in demography of Pakistan*. PIDE.

Elizaga, J. C. (1974). The participation of women in the labour force of Latin America: Fertility and other factors. *International Labour Review, 109*, 519–538.

Freedman, R., Whelpton, P. K., & Campbell, A. A. (1959). *Family planning sterility and population growth*. McGraw Hill.

Goldstein, S. (1972). The influence of labour force participation and education on fertility in Thailand. *Population Studies, 26*(3).

Hass, P. (1971). *Maternal employment and fertility in metropolitan Latin America* (PhD dissertation). Duke University.

Heer, D. (1964). Economic development and fertility. *Demography, 3*(2).

Heer, D., & Youssef, N. (1977). Female status among Soviet Central Asian nationalities: The melding of Islam and Marxism and its implications for population increase. *Population Studies, 31*(1).

Hein, C. (1983). Mauritius: Women, factory employment and fertility. In ILO (Ed.), *Women, work and demographic issues: Report of an ILO/UNITAR seminar.*

Herman, A. (1970). *Fertility and economic behaviour of families in the Philippines.* RAND Corporation.

Hoffman, L. W., & Hoffman, M. L. (1973). *The value of children to parents.* In J. T. Fawcett (Ed.), *Psychological Perspectives on Population.* Basic Books.

Jaffe, A. J., & Azumi, K. (1960). The birth ratio and cottage industries in under-developed countries. *Economic Development and Cultural Change, 9*(1).

Khan, M. E. (1980). *Study of inter-relationships between status of women and demographic change in Uttar Pradesh, India* (A research proposal, Working Paper No. 1). Operations Research Group.

Khan, M. E., Ghosh Dastidar, S. K., & Singh, R. J. (1982). *Nutrition and health practices among the rural women—A case study of Uttar Pradesh, India* (Working Paper No. 31). Operations Research Group.

Khan, M. E., Ghosh Dastidar, S. K., & Bairathi, S. (1983). *Accessibility of women to health and family planning services—A case study of sex discrimination* (Paper presented in the International ILO/UNITAR seminar on women's role and demographic behaviour held at Tashkent, 11–19 October 1983).

Kobayashi, K. (1971). Traditions and transitions in family structure in Japan. In A. A. Campbell (Ed.), *The family in transition.* Government Printing Office.

Langlois, E. (1962). The female labour force in metropolitan areas: An international comparison. *Economic Development and Cultural Change, 10,* 4.

Marshall, J. M. (1972). *Studies relating women's non-familial activities and fertility* (Bibliography Series I). Carolina Population Center.

Mason, K. O. (1972). *Turkish fertility: A review of social and economic correlates.* Research Triangle Institute.

Minkler, M. (1970). Fertility and female labour force participation in India. *Journal of Family Welfare, 17,* 31–34.

Mott, F. L. (1972). Fertility, life cycle stage and female labour force participation in Rhode Island. *Demography, 9,* 173–185.

Nag, M., Anker R., & Khan, M. E. (1982). *A guide to anthropological study of women's roles and demographic change in India* (WEP 2–21/WP 1I5). ILO.

Nerlove, M., & Schultz, T. P. (1970). *Love and life between the censuses: A model of family decision making in Puerto Rico, 1950–1960.* RAND Corporation.

Oppong, C. (1980). *A synopsis of seven roles and status of women: An outline of a conceptual and methodological approach* (mimeographed WEP research working paper). ILO.

Oppong, C., & Church, K. (1981). *A field guide to research on seven roles of women: Focussed biographies* (WEP 2–21 | WP 106). ILO.

Pinelli, A. (1971). Female labour and fertility in relationship to contrasting social and economic conditions. *Human Relations, 24.*

Requena, M. (1965). Social and economic correlates of induced abortion in Santiago, Chile. *Demography*, *2*.

Rosen, B. C., & Simmons, A. B. (1971). Industrialization, family and fertility: A structural psychological analysis of the Brazilian case study. *Demography*, *8*(1).

Safillios-Rothschild, C. (1972). The relationship between work commitment and fertility. *International Journal of Sociology of the Family*, *2*, 64–71.

Stycos, J. (1965). Family employment and fertility in Lima, Peru. *The Milbank Memorial Fund Quarterly*, *43*(1).

Stycos, J., & Weller, R. H. (1967). Female working roles and fertility. *Demography*, *4*(1).

Taeuber, I. B. (1960). Japan's demographic transition, re-examined. *Population Studies*, *14*, 28–39.

Terry, G. B. (1974). Rival explanations in the work–fertility relationship. *Population Studies*, *29*, 191–205.

Waite, L. J., & Stolzenberg, R. M. (1976). Intended child bearing and labour force participation of young women. *American Sociological Review*, *41*, 235–252.

Weller, R. H. (1968). The employment of wives, role incompatibility and fertility: A study of lower and middle class residents of San Juan, Puerto Rico. *Milbank Memorial Fund Quarterly*, *46*(4).

Weller, R. H. (1977). *Demographic correlates of women's participation in economic activities* (Paper presented in IUSSP Conference, Mexico).

Youssef, N. H. (1982). The inter-relationship between the division of labour in the household, women's roles and their impact on fertility. In R. Anker (Ed.), *Women's roles and population trends in the Third World*. Croom Helm.

Chapter 9

Menopause*
A Fresh Look at the Much-misunderstood Phenomenon

Indira Jai Prakash

A major transition in the life cycle of women during middle age is menopause. The cessation of menstruation announces, in unequivocal terms, that a woman's reproductive role has come to an end. As dramatic an event as menarche, menopause is often believed to be a significant event that strains the coping abilities of women. It is a topic that is surrounded not just by old wives' tales but also by 'scientific myths'. Menopause, as a field of investigation, presents several interesting contrasts. As an ubiquitous event in the lives of women, it never got the attention it deserved. An experience that millions of women around the world go through is often devoted a page or two in standard gynaecology textbooks. Feminists who were so vocal about premenstrual syndrome were slower to pick up issues related to menopausal women. The psychology of women was so engrossed in disproving psychological differences based on biological sex that it had little time to focus on the developmental issues of middle-aged and older women. With a dramatic increase in life expectancy, women had more than a decade of postmenopausal life to live. Yet the medical profession showed a laissez-faire attitude regarding menopause, and there was a reliance on a physician's subjective 'experience' in managing menopausal 'cases' (McKinlay & McKinlay, 1973). This was seen in the cursory consideration given by the medical profession by prescribing such ineffective treatments as aspirin and/or sleeping pills or equivalents

* *Social Change* 29, no. 1–2 (March–June 1999): 171–187

with little sympathy or using hormonal treatment because of its apparent effectiveness in reducing symptoms (and thus complaints) without weighing the possible dangerous side effects. Traditional psychiatry found it convenient to deal with the psychological problems of older females by pushing them under the label of 'involutional melancholia'.

This chapter briefly traces the historical views on menopause and reviews available literature on different aspects of menopause, with special reference to the Indian scene. An effort is made to bring forward some of the main issues that are relevant for researchers. Considering the paucity of documented studies in India and the difficulty in accessing information from different sources, the chapter does not make any claims to exhaustiveness.

About 100 years ago, Currier presented the first comprehensive discussion of menopause. In this impressive but neglected document, Currier (1897) made the following observations: (a) menopause lacks scientific attention; (b) there is no menopause reported in animals; (c) it is the abnormal which is remembered (i.e., instance of problematic menopause are recalled more often than normal); (d) there is evidence of predisposing factors in women with severe menopausal symptoms; (e) the appearance of symptoms varies: within a society, 'highly bred', 'civilized' women and 'those with many troubles and ills' appeared to be the main sufferers; across societies, Eskimos and Mexican Indians were contrasted with the French and the Irish; (f) there appeared to be no association of parity with menopause, given the available data, and (g) menopause is uneventful for majority of women, he added.

Although Currier's paper attempted to generate scientific interest in menopause, it was only in the 1940s that the subject gained recognition. This interest was due to two principal catalysts. First, with the development of facilities for describing populations (surveys, censuses, etc.), there was a growing interest in describing the health and fertility of populations. Second, the development of hormone therapy, which includes effective extraction and manufacture of oestrogen compounds, provided a method to alleviated the hot flushes and sweating that are frequently associated with menopause. Yet well-formulated scientific studies on menopause have been slow to appear. There was also very little change in physicians' attitudes toward menopause (Bart & Grossman, 1975). In the 18th and 19th centuries Europe, physicians believed that women decayed at menopause. The frequency and seriousness of symptoms during menopause were considered to depend on 'indiscretions of earlier life' and 'transgressions' of nature's laws by women (Haller & Haller, 1975). Bart and Grossman (1975) noted that such pervasive 'sexism' was persisting in gynaecological writings even in the 1970s, and there was a traditional male ambience in medical education (Campbell, 1973). Things obviously have not improved much in medicine over the years. After reviewing research published during 1984–1994, Rostosky and Travis (1996) conclude that there is a dominance of biomedical models, a failure to acquire baseline data, a lack of control groups in studies, vague definitions and blatantly pejorative language in the accepted knowledge base regarding menopause.

Perhaps the most comprehensive and evaluative review of the work in this area was that of McKinlay and McKinlay (1973). They provided an annotated bibliography of the work on menopause from three main sources: general reports of clinical observations or experience; reports of surveys, generally of non-clinical populations that provide descriptive data, and clinical trials aimed at evaluating the effectiveness of proposed treatments of menopausal symptoms. This chapter lucidly presents the methodological problems in each type of study and raises several pertinent questions that influenced subsequent research in this area. It was as late as 1976 when the First International Congress on the Menopause was held in France and the workshop report on international consensus on menopause research was published (Vankeep et al., 1976).

The psychological aspects of menopause, on the other hand, have received even less attention than the physiological ones. Parlee (1974), in her survey of psychological literature on the climacterium, found biased statements about menopausal women that had no empirical grounding. In psychology, focused study on adulthood and middle age and, in turn, menopause developed around the 1970s. Initially, however, there were somewhat unbalanced views of middle age as either a plateau or a crisis (Neugarten & Datan, 1974). Popular literature has declared midlife to be a crisis and menopause in women and retirement in men to be turning points in life. Recent years have brought changes in the medical treatment of menopausal women as well as in social attitudes about menopause. Self-help guides and book on women's health during pre- and postmenopausal years, as well as practical advice for maintaining general health, are becoming popular (Cherry & Runowicz, 1994). There is also a re-examination of the transition period between middle and old age from different theoretical perspectives (Pertat, 1994). Changes in the psychiatric view of menopause and mental illness reflecting a more holistic stance have also been reported (Herrick et al., 1996).

AGE AT MENOPAUSE

Perhaps the most striking event during midlife for females is the menopause. While in male, there is a gradual tapering off of sperm production in old age, females proceed to a fairly abrupt menopause sometime between 42 and 52 years, on average, at which time ova production ceases entirely. The exact age at which menopause occurs varies from population to population. The age of menopause in Japanese, Caucasian, Chinese and Hawaiian women was between 49 and 50 and was unrelated to the age at which the women began menstruating (Goodman et al., 1978), 49.8 years for a sample of US women (MacMahon & Worcester, 1966), 49 years for Israeli women (Maoz et al., 1970), 50 years for New Zealand women (Rutherford, 1978), 51.4 years in a semi-urban community in Holland (Jaszmann et al., 1969), and 48 years for Filipino women (Ramoso-Jalbuena, 1994). Studies on South Indian women have reported the median age at menopause to be around 45 years (Indira, 1979; Prakash, 1989, 1991; Shirokar, 1992; Uma, 1981). This reported age is closer to earlier studies on other Indian samples (Chowdhury, 1969; Rakshit, 1962). This median age at menopause for Indian women is considerably lower than the median age of 50 that is reported for US women.

Determining the most probable age at menopause is not as straight-forward as it appears. Many studies report findings based on clinical groups. Very rarely are samples of 'well' women at risk of a natural menopause surveyed. Another major methodological difficulty is the retrospective nature of the reports. The bulk of such information depends on recall and involves memory factors (McKinlay & McKinlay, 1973). Also, women tend to round off to the nearest five or zero while reporting their age at menopause. There is a tendency to understate the age at menopause, particularly by women who are at least five years postmenopausal (McKinlay & McKinlay, 1972). The findings of these studies may be affected by the age range of the samples selected. Most studies take middle-aged women in the range of 36 to 50 years. If samples were drawn from higher and lower age ranges, there is a possibility of getting a different median age.

There has been inconclusive debate as to whether the age of menopause has increased over the last century or has remained constant. According to Flint (1976), the following factors affect age at menopause: The aspects of reproductive history that affect menopausal age are parity and marriage *versus* non-marriage and abortion, genetic factors such as race and familial patterns, diseases such as diabetes, fibroids, polyps, cancer of the body, the uterus, cervix and breast are associated with late age to menopause, while cancer of the ovaries, vulva, pruritus senilis and hernia are associated with early menopause. The only geographical factor known to affect this age is altitude, and it has been found to accelerate the age. No socio-economic factors have been conclusively correlated with this age. Whether or not there is a secular trend for a later age at menopause is not clear yet.

SYMPTOMATOLOGY OF MENOPAUSE

The questions of what menopausal symptoms are, who experiences what type of symptoms, how frequently they occur, when they reach a peak of occurrence and severity and what extent they are related to past events, personality characteristics and women's social milieu are only partially answered. According to organic aetiological views, symptoms during menopause are primarily due to temporary endocrine imbalances and should be treated by correcting oestrogen deficiency. However, it is more or less accepted that oestrogen depletion alone cannot be responsible for all the symptoms that women complain of. Menopause is said to occur at a time in the life cycle when a woman is facing physical, social and familial stresses. When the cultural underpinnings, myths, beliefs and superstitions are added, it may result in a period beset with many ills.

In a recent review of symptoms associated with menopause, Pearce et al. (1995) report considerable inconsistency in the results of studies of psychological and sexual sequelae of menopause and their treatment. The existence of a large, commonly occurring group of menopausal symptoms has been questioned. There is some general agreement about physical symptoms that may occur with menopause. Of the many symptoms supposed to be related to menopause, vasomotor symptoms such as hot flushes and night sweats have been linked to oestrogen depletion. According to Indian studies, the presence of vasomotor symptoms clearly distinguishes menopausal women from pre- and postmenopausal women (Indira, 1979; Prakash, 1989; Shirokar, 1992).

There continues to be debate and disagreement between gynaecologists and psychiatrists as to which psychological symptoms and disorders, if any, are directly attributable to the normal changes of the menopause and what should be the treatment (Ballinger, 1990). The major reason for this appears to be the methodological issues involved in research in this field. The prevalence of psychological symptoms may indicate a vulnerable population who is likely to develop symptoms in relation to stress.

Cross-sectional studies leave uncertainty about the direction of causation of any associations that are found. There are also inconsistencies in the way menopausal status is defined in different studies. Psychological symptoms have also been assessed from different conceptual perspectives. Some of the studies discuss the impact of control for non-menopausal factors such as the environment and social stress (Ballinger, 1990; Gath & Iles, 1990). These factors should be kept in mind while evaluating the studies on psychological symptoms associated with menopause. Depression is one symptom that is very often associated with symptoms associated with menopause. A slightly significant increase in depressed mood during menopause (Hunter, 1990; McKinlay et al., 1987) has been reported in cross-sectional and follow-up studies. But well-designed prospective studies do not report such an increase in depression or anxiety. To date, there are virtually no studies that have included objective performance tests, and most studies have relied on clinical observation or self-report. When psychological symptoms are present, non-menopausal factors such as psychosocial stresses appear to be relevant (Pearce et al., 1995).

Research suggests that a postmenopausal state increases some aspects of women's physiological responses to psychological stress. Using laboratory stressors such as speech and serial substitutions, higher cardiovascular or catecholamine stress reactivity in postmenopausal women has been reported. It has been suggested that this reactivity is associated with reduced oestrogen level and hormone replacement therapy (HRT) may play an ameliorative role. Since heightened stress reactivity contributes to cardiovascular diseases, HRT may be considered as a health-protective option for postmenopausal women (Burleson et al., 1998). A modest effect on the memory function of women using oestrogen has been reported (Sherwin, 1997). The important role that HRT plays in preventing degenerative diseases such as osteoporosis has been acknowledged. This, in turn, may have a preventive effect on psychological health in later decades (Pearce et al., 1995). The lack of HRT in postmenopausal women may increase the likelihood of dementia of Alzheimer's type and also ischemic vascular dementia (Mortes & Meyer, 1995). Evaluating the use of HRT, Doughty (1996) concludes that its advantages include elimination of hot flashes, reduced risk of calcium depletion, reduced risk of atherosclerotic plaque formation and a possible reduced risk of Alzheimer's dementia (AD). Among the disadvantages are such possible side effects as increased risk of breast cancer, liver or gall bladder disease and growth of uterine fibroids. Henderson (1997), however, suggests caution in interpreting a link between HRT and AD. Reviewing publications on this topic between 1978 and 1996, Henderson points out that even the best epidemiologic studies indicate a modest range of relationships. A number of demographic features and lifestyle choices distinguish oestrogen users from non-users. There is a possibility of undetected selection or observation bias that could account for the reported association.

In Indian studies, Blatt–Kupperman menopausal index, a measure weighted for endocrine related changes, was found to differentiate menopausal women from pre- and postmenopausal women. Fatigue, rheumatic pain, irritability, nervousness and pounding of the heart were the most common symptoms reported. For most women, the appearance of vasomotor symptoms and aggravation of somatic psychological symptoms constitute the menopausal syndrome for most women (Prakash & Murthy, 1982). Increased psychological morbidity is also reported in postmenopausal women, with depression being the most common symptom reported. The curve of morbidity seems to rise and reach its height during the menopausal period, with a slight drop in the postmenopausal period (Prakash & Murthy, 1981). In another study, women in the age group of 41–45 had higher levels of psychological distress. Similarly, women diagnosed as menopausal had higher distress scores than pre- and postmenopausal women (Uma, 1981). A study of adjustment concluded that menopausal women were more maladjusted than other groups (Jamuna, 1984). As assessed on questionnaires (Prakash, 1991), the experience of menopause, however, does not seem to bring about deeper personality changes. Personality patterns appear stable during midlife. Once again, it should be emphasized that most of the Indian studies are cross sectional, based on small samples often drawn from clinics.

There is a considerable lack of clarity in the evidence concerning the effect of menopause on female sexuality. Studies based on samples of women attending gynaecological or special menopausal clinics report a higher incidence of sexual problems than general population studies. Most studies are cross sectional and do not take into account factors such as earlier sexual difficulties, current stress such as marital problems, mood and other psychological changes. More importantly than all these, most studies do not take into account changes in a male partner's sexuality. An older woman's sexuality is influenced by her partner's abilities or interests as much as by changes within herself (Bachmann et al., 1985). Decreased levels of sexual desire, sexual fantasy and activity are often associated with age. However, it is unclear to what extent menopause contributes to such changes. Hawton et al. (1994) conclude that there is no evidence for women developing frank sexual dysfunction at this time or for reduced satisfaction with sexual relationships. Similarly, Cawood and Bancroft (1996) conclude that none of the hormonal parameters significantly predict sexuality. The most important predictors were other aspects of sexual relations, sexual attitudes and measures of well-being. Indian studies show a decrease in sexual activity in middle-aged and older women, mostly due to sociocultural factors. Widowhood and thus lack of availability of a partner affects women's sexuality in our culture to a large extent.

Lack of privacy, married children living in the same house and poor health of the spouse are other reasons for decreased sexual activity in older women rather than menopause *per se* (Indira, 1979; Prakash 1989). Research, however, agrees that vaginal dryness, reduced vaginal lubrication and dyspareunia seen in postmenopausal women may be helped by HRT (Dow et al., 1983). However, oestrogen alone is not beneficial for diminished sexual desire and other sexual problems. Regular and continuing activity appears to protect against such symptoms.

The effect of HRT on psychological symptoms has been studied. Controlled treatment designs using standardized psychological tests have produced conflicting results, with some claiming HRT as superior to placebo in relieving psychological symptoms (Montgomery et al., 1987), while others do not find any such difference (Strickler et al., 1977). Zweifel and O'Bren (1997) in a meta-analysis of the effect of HRT on depression found lower depressed mood in treated women. It has been suggested that oestrogens may help improve cognitive function in postmenopausal women and probably improve mood and well-being but may not be effective as stand-alone anti-depressants for treating depression (Halbreich, 1997). Many well-controlled studies show a modest improvement in memory with HRT. The current opinion seems to be that oestrogen therapy ameliorates psychological symptoms after surgical menopause while the use of HRT is still questionable in case of natural menopause (Pearce et al., 1995).

ARTIFICIAL OR SURGICAL MENOPAUSE

Although it is not clear why menopause occurs, it appears that the ovaries stop resounding to the follicle-stimulating hormones produced by the pituitary; they do not respond by bringing an egg to maturity and do not produce oestrogen. Thus, the cycle stops. A surgical removal of the uterus and ovaries (hysterectomy) would have similar effects. If ovaries are not removed, oestrogen and progesterone will still be produced, but there will be no menstruation, ushering in an 'artificial' menopausal state. Surgical menopause may occur at any age. While menopause is a normal phase of the female life cycle, hysterectomy is a 'non-normative event' and, as such, stressful. As such, surgical menopause merits a separate discussion.

In the psychiatric literature, hysterectomy is often associated with increased morbidity (Ballinger, 1977). An early study by Lindeman in 1941 is widely cited in the literature, suggesting an association between hysterectomy and psychiatric disorders. Martin et al. (1977) studied women undergoing non-cancer hysterectomy. Of the 49 subjects, more than half (50%) were diagnosed as psychiatrically ill before the surgery. The most prevalent disorders were hysteria (27%) and primary depression (18%). After surgery, 16 per cent were judged as not having any demonstrable pelvic pathology. The hysteria group were younger, had more operations and were hospitalized more often. The authors concluded that certain age group may have been placed 'at risk' for hysterectomy due to psychiatric rather than gynaecological illness.

For women undergoing total hysterectomy, HRT is often recommended to compensate for the sudden loss of hormones. Prospective treatment studies of HRT in oophorectomized women have more consistently demonstrated improvements in psychological symptoms (Phillips & Sherwin, 1992; Sherwin, 1988; Sherwin & Gelfand, 1985). Women who did not have any psychiatric problems were followed prospectively through abdominal hysterectomy and oophorectomy (for benign disease). Women given implants of oestrogen and/or testosterone were compared with those given placebos or no treatment at all following surgery. Women under HRT showed a reduction in their depression scores when compared to others, though there was no such effect on anxiety scores. Insomnia and irritability were the most common symptoms found to improve with HRT. Alder (1992) found that when the study design controlled both vasomotor symptoms and non-menopausal social factors, minor stresses and 'hassles' contributed more to the psychological status of oophorectomized women than did either hormone levels or time since insertion of hormone implants. Androgens have been often given as an adjunct to oestrogen to improve the sexual feelings of oophorectomized women. An improvement in the sense of well-being in such women was reported after androgen administration by Sherwin (1988).

In an Indian study on menopausal women, higher psychiatric morbidity was seen in post-surgical menopausal women. As per a screening inventory, nearly 30.77 per cent of women who had hysterectomy were classified as 'possible case'. These subjects also reported more severe symptoms of menopause and a higher number of psychiatric symptoms when compared to natural menopausal women (Indira, 1979). Interestingly, three out of four women in this group had a history of either in-patient or out-patient treatment prior to the interview. The history of preoperative psychiatric disorders is considered one of the main determinants of post-operative psychiatric disorders. Ballinger (1977) contends that women in the early stages of psychiatric illness may present with symptoms for which hysterectomy is a possible treatment. Newton and Baron (1976) also report a 'sleeper effect' with a sequelae developing after the first six months of hysterectomy. In the light of such reports, psychological screening and psychological care for women undergoing hysterectomy are obviously important.

ANDROPAUSE OR MALE MENOPAUSE

There have been debates as to whether there is an andropause in men just as women have a menopause. Technically, the term 'menopause' refers to the cessation of menses, while the term 'climacterium' refers to the loss of reproductive ability. In women, they are two sides of the same coin since, when the menstrual cycle ends, reproductive ability also comes to an end. In men, there is no such abrupt event, but a tapering off of the production of fertile sperm with advanced age. In an early study, Exley and Corker (1966) showed that men too experience cyclical fluctuations in hormone production. Similarly, the level of testosterone in the blood is supposed to vary in a cyclical fashion. With advancing age, there is a change in hormone production in men also. Unlike the marked drop in oestrogen and progesterone in women, in men, the level of testosterone declines gradually with age, eventually reaching a very low level. However, fertility and the production of testosterone are separate phenomena in men and some rather old men who have fathered children. In addition the ability to engage in satisfying sexual relations is unrelated to either hormone level or to fertility in men and women.

McMorrow (1974) coined the term 'midolescence', a dangerous period of turbulent impulse. According to him, 'male menopause' in America coincides with a period in life when a man faces problems with parents, children, spouse and his career. Sheehy (1976) claims that men experience a substantial drop in hormonal levels beginning between 46 and 55 years of age. Complaints of male climacteric include morning fatigue, lassitude, nervousness, diminished sexual potency, psychological instability, circulatory symptoms and a host of other psychological symptoms.

NEW PERSPECTIVES

The media hype in the West projected menopause in women and midlife in both sexes as a crisis in the 1970s. The development of a life cycle perspective, conscious efforts of academicians against sexism and ageism in science and medicines, a growing body of women's focused research, the spread of the women's health movement and self-help groups were largely responsible for a change in perspective. With feminism came the re-examinations imposed on their biological functioning. Women decided to talk and write about their experiences rather than accept what they were told to expect at different stages of their life cycle.

In the 1970s, two women's groups, one in Seattle and the other in Boston, investigated the experience of menopause in women. The publication of the Boston group *Our Bodies, Ourselves* (Boston Women's Health Book Collective, 1971) pioneered the 'women-oriented' approach to female experience. Feminist publications (such as 'Prime Time') started addressing older women's issues. Such efforts have culminated in a large body of literature that tries to demedicalize and demystify menopause. Greer (1992) examined theories about menopause and ageing for the past 200 years. Challenging traditional views, she encourages women to become responsible for their own health and listen to their own perceptions rather than accept common 'truths' about this misunderstood subject. Coney (1994) critically examines the social and medical issues surrounding menopause and the politics behind its 'medicalization'. The success of HRT, according to her, derives from the willingness of vested interests to exploit negative stereotypes of older women. Carolan (1994) points out that traditional views suffer from either a minimalist or maximalist bias. The minimalist view suggests that this phase is a natural process of little consequence, and as such, women can be criticized if they do experience difficulties with menopause. From the maximalist view, women could be treated as if they were undergoing a health catastrophe. Both views fail to consider the influence of the timing of the event, social circumstances and socio-cultural attitudes on the experience.

Gerontologists call for a reorientation within the healthcare system. Studies, collectively named the Women's Health Initiative (WHI), are currently enrolling 164,500 postmenopausal women in several overlapping clinical trials and observational studies. The overall goals of WHI are to understand the determinants of postmenopausal women's health and to evaluate the efficacy of practical interventions in preventing the major causes of morbidity and mortality in older women (Matthews et al., 1997). Butler (1995) suggests that an important goal for managing the healthcare of older women is the prevention of late-life disability, and physicians can integrate several health promotion strategies into their primary care practice. Osteoporosis and heart disease can be prevented through HRT and regular exercise. Weight control and diabetes prevention can result from dietary changes. Vitamin D and calcium play an important role in the avoidance of bone fractures; Pap smears and mammograms prove effective in the early detection of cancer. There are several woman-friendly books that provide information on every aspect of life for middle-aged women (e.g., Culter & Celso-ramon, 1992; Cherry & Runowicz, 1994; Davis, 1996; Pertat, 1994). Such efforts help in disseminating current information and help counter the trend toward making menopause a medical event in women's lives and also encourage new approaches to scholarly research (Callahan, 1993).

Indian studies reveal that menopause is not generally perceived as a crisis by women in our cultural context (Indira, 1979; Parkash, 1989). At the most, it is seen as a period of transitory stress. Vatuk (1975) noted that Indian women do experience the physical changes of menopause but do not regard them as forming a complex. Many studies report that menopause is often welcomed by Indian women as it releases them from many social restrictions (Flint, 1974), taboos and fear of pregnancy

(Indira, 1979). The concepts of loss of femininity or sexuality (as in the West) did not seem to apply in such cases. The presence of self-help groups or menopausal clinics for healthy women is also not noticeable. Nor is the much talked about 'empty nest syndrome' seen in Indian samples where women are likely to have the stress of a 'large full nest' during midlife (Indira, 1979).

There is no doubt that sociocultural factors play a dominant role in perception of and attitude towards menopause. In the West, menopause was often associated with loss of youth, vigour, sexuality and femininity. It was perceived as a threat to the self-image of a women and thus given the status a crisis. Interestingly, in India, most women do not feel that they are less feminine because they are menopausal. Widowhood, familial and financial problems and health concerns seem to influence the well-being of middle-aged women than menopausal status in India. Cross-cultural studies show that African-American women perceive menopause as a natural transition (Padoun et al., 1996). Filipino women (Ramoso-Jalbuena, 1994) accept menopause disorders as unavoidable natural stage of woman's life cycle. Similar findings have been reported from a study of seven Southeast Asian countries, Chinese factory workers, (Tang, 1994), from northeast Thailand (Chirawatkul & Manderson, 1994) and Portuguese women (Fjgueiras & Marteu, 1995). This speaks volumes about the influence of culture on the experience of menopause.

In conclusion, it is not easy to understand the impact of menopause on physical and psychosocial well-being of women. There are several methodological issues that need a closer look. Sample selection, study design, definition of menopause and techniques used to assess psychological status/symptoms affect the findings. There are several non-menopausal factors that need to be controlled in such studies. Longitudinal prospective studies with well-controlled designs and standardized measures are necessary to reach unequivocal conclusions. Similarly, awareness of cultural differences in the perception of menopause is essential to avoid uncritical acceptance of Western findings. Multidisciplinary studies that assess the gynaecological status of the women along with her psychosocial condition are needed. A holistic perspective is needed that examines her condition in society and her life circumstances.

REFERENCES

Alder, E. M. (1992). The effect of hormone replacement therapy on psychological symptoms. In K. Wijama & B. Van Schoultz (Eds.), *Reproductive life*. Camforth Parthenon.

Bachmann, G. A., Leiblum, S. R., Sandler, B., Ainsley, W., Narcessian, R., Shelden, R., & Hymans, H. N. (1985). Correlates sexual desire in postmenopausal women. *Maturitas*, 7(3), 211–216. https://doi.org/10.1016/0378-5122(85) 90042-8

Ballinger, C. B. (1997). Psychiatric morbidly and the menopause, survey of gynaecological out-patient clinic. *British Journal of Psychiatry*, 131, 83–89.

Ballinger, C. B. (1990). Psychiatric aspects of menopause. *British Journal of Psychiatry*, 156(6), 773–787. https://doi.org/10.1192/bjp.156.6.773

Bart, P. B., & Grossman, M. (1975). Menopause. *Women and Health*, 1(3), 3–11. https://doi.org/10.1300/J013v01n03_01

Boston's Women's Health Book Collective. (1971). *Our Bodies. Ourselves*. New England Free Press.

Burleson, M. H., Malarkey, W. B., Cacioppo, J. T., Poehlmann, K. M., Kiecolt-Glaser, J. K., Berntson, G. G., & Glaser, R. (1998). Postmenopausal hormone replacement: Effects on autonomic, neuroendocrine, and immune reactivity to brief psychological stressors. *Psychosomatic Medicine*, 60(1), 17–25. https://doi.org/10.1097/00006842-199801000-00004

Butler, R. N., Collins, K. S., Meier, D. S., Muller, C. T., & Pinn, V. W. (1995). Older women's health: Clinical care in the postmenopausal years. A roundtable discussion part 2. *Geriatrics*, 50(6), 33–6, 39.

Callahan, J. C. (Ed.). (1993). *Menopause: A midlife passage*. Indiana University Press.

Campbell, M. A. (1973). *Why would a girl go into medicine*. Feminist Press.

Carolan, M. T. (1994). Beyond deficiency: Broadening the view of menopause. *Journal of Applied Gerontology*, 13(2), 193–205. https://doi.org/10.1177/073346489401300207

Cawood, E. H. H., & Bancroft, J. (1996). Steroid hormones, the menopause, sexuality and well-being of women. *Psychological Medicine*, 26(5), 925–936. https://doi.org/10.1017/s0033291700035261

Cherry, S. H., & Runowicz, C. D. (1994). *The menopause book: A guide to health and well being for women after forty*. Macmillan.

Chirawatkul, S., & Manderson, L. (1994). Perception of menopause in North East Thailand contested meaning and practice. *Social Science and Medicine*, 39(11), 1545–1554). https://doi.org/10.1016/0277-9536(94)90006-x

Chowdhury, N. R. (1969). Menopause and its problems. *Journal of the Indian Medical Association*, 53(1), 16–17.

Coney, S. (1994). *The menopause industry: How the medical establishment exploits women*. Hunter House Publishers.

Currier, A. F. (1897). *The menopause*. Appleton.

Culter, W. B., & Celso-Ramon, G. (1992). *Menopause: A guide for women and the men who love them* (Revised). W. W. Norton.

Davis, S. (1996). *The healthy women: Menopause and other things we don't talk about.* Brunner/Mezel.

Doughty, S. E. D. (1996). Menopause: A holistic look at an important transition to the last and best third of life. *Topics in Geriatric Rehabilitation, 11*(4), 7–15. https://doi.org/10.1097/00013614-199606000-00004

Dow, M. G. T., Hart, D. M., & Forrest, C. A. (1983). Hormonal treatment of sexual unresponsiveness in postmenopausal women. A comparative study. *British Journal of Obstetrics and Gynaecology, 90*(4), 361–366. https://doi.org/10.1111/j.1471-0528.1983.tb08924.x

Exley, D., & Corker, C. S. (1966). The human male cycle of urinary oestrone and 17-oxosteroids. *Journal of Endocrinology, 35*(1), 83–99. https://doi.org/10.1677/joe.0.0350083

Fjgueiras, M. J., & Marteu, T. M. (1995). Experiences of the menopause: A comparison between Portugal and the UK. *Journal of Reproductive and Infant Psychology, 13*(2), 93–100. https://doi.org/10.1080/02646839508403239

Flint, M. (1974). Menarches and menopause of Rajput women. *Abstract International, 34*(12), 5791B.

Flint, M. (1976). Cross cultural factors that affect age of menopause. In A. Vankeep, R. B. Greenblat & M. Albeaux-Ferent (Eds.), *Consensus on menopause research MTP.* Lancaster.

Gath, D., & Iles, S. (1990). Depression and the menopause. *British Medical Journal, 300*(6735), 1287–1288. https://doi.org/10.1136/bmj.300.6735.1287

Goodman, M. J., Grove, J. S., & Gilbert, F., Jr. (1978). Age at menopause in relation to reproductive history in Japanese, Caucasian, Chinese and Hawaiian women living in Hawaii. *Journal of Gerontology, 33*(5), 688–694. https://doi.org/10.1093/geronj/33.5.688

Greer, G. (1992). *The change: Women aging and the menopause.* Alfred A. Knopf.

Haller, J. S., Jr., & Haller, R. M. (1975). *The physician and sexuality in Victorian America.* University of Illinois Press.

Halbreich, U. (1997). Role of estrogen in postmenopausal depression. *Neurology, 48*(5) (Suppl. 7), S16–S19. https://doi.org/10.1212/wnl.48.5_suppl_7.16s

Hawton, K., Gath, D., & Day, A. (1994). Sexual function in a community sample of middle-aged women with partners: Effects of age, marital, socioeconomic, psychiatric, gynecological, and menopausal factors. *Archives of Sexual Behavior, 23*(4), 375–395. https://doi.org/10.1007/BF01541404

Henderson, V. W. (1997). The epidemiology of estrogen replacement therapy and Alzheimer's disease. *Neurology, 48*(5), S27–S35. https://doi.org/10.1212/wnl.48.5_suppl_7.27s

Herrick, C. A., Douglas, V., & Carlson, J. H. (1996). Menopause and hormone replacement therapy from holistic and medical perspectives. *Issues in Mental Health Nursing, 17*(2), 153–168. https://doi.org/10.3109/01612849609035003

Hunter, M. S. (1990). Emotional well-being sexual behaviour and hormone replacement therapy. *Maturitas, 12,* 217–228.

Indira, S. N. (1979). *Midlife crisis: A psychosocial study of menopause* [Thesis]. Bangalore University.

Jamuna, D. (1984). *A study of some factors related to adjustment of middle aged and old women* [Doctoral Dissertation]. S. V. University.

Jaszmann, L., Van Lith, N. D., & Zaat, J. C. A. (1969). The age of menopause in the Netherlands. The statistical analysis of a survey. *International Journal of Fertility, 14*(2), 106–117.

MacMahon, B., & Worcester, J. (1996). Age at menopause: United States 1960–1962. *US Vital and Health Statistics Series II, 19.*

Maoz, B., Dowty, N., Antonovsky, A., & Wijsenbeek, H. (1970). Female attitude to menopause. *Social Psychiatry, 5*(1), 35–40. https://doi.org/10.1007/BF01539794

Martin, R. L., Roberts, W. V., Clayton, P. J., & Wetzel, R. (1977). Psychiatric illness and non-cancer hysterectomy. *Diseases of the Nervous System, 38*(12), 974–980.

Matthews, K. A., Shumaker, S. A., Bowen, D. J., Langer, R. D., Hunt, J. R., Kaplan, R. M., Klesges, R. C., & Ritenbaugh, C. (1997). Women's health initiative. Why now? What is it? What's new? *American Psychologist, 52*(2), 101–116. https://doi.org/10.1037//0003-066x.52.2.101

McKinlay, S. M., & McKinlay, J. B. (1972). An investigation of the age at menopause. *Journal of Biosocial Science, 4*(2), 161.

McKinlay, S. M., & McKinlay, J. B. (1973). Selected studies of the menopause. *Journal of Biosocial Science, 5*(4), 533–555. https://doi.org/10.1017/S0021932000009391

McKinlay, J. B., McKinlay, S. M., & Brambilla, D. (1987). The relative contributions of endocrine changes and social circumstances to depression in mid-aged women. *Journal of Health and Social Behavior, 28*(4). https://doi.org/10.2307/2136789

McMorrow, F. (1974). *Midolescence: The dangerous years.* Strawberry Hill Press.

Mortes, K. F., & Meyer, J. S. (1995). Lack of post menopausal estrogen replacement therapy and the risk of dementia. *Journal of Neuropsychiatry and Clinical Neuroscience, 7*(3), 334–337.

Montgomery, J. C., Appleby, L., Brincat, M., Versi, E., Tapp, A., Fenwick, P. B., & Studd, J. W. (1987). Effect of oestrogen and testosterone implants on psychological disorders in the climacteric. *Lancet, 1*(8528) 297–299.

Neugarten, B. L., & Datan, N. (1974). The middle years. In Areniti (Ed.), *American handbook of psychiatry/Vol I.* Basic Books.

Newton, N., & Baron, E. (1976). Reactions to hysterectomy: Fact or fiction? *Primary Care, 3*(4), 781–801. https://doi.org/10.1016/S0095-4543(21)00580-7

Padoun, G., Holmes-Rovner, M., Rothert, M., Schimitt, N., Knoll, J., Rovner, D., Talarczyk, G., Breer, L., Ranson, S., & Gladney, E. (1996).

African-American Women's perception of menopause. *American Journal of Health Behavior, 20*(4), 242–251.

Parlee, M. B. (1974). Psychology sings: *Journal of Women in Culture and Society, 1*(1), 119–138.

Pearce, J., Hawton, K., & Blake, F. (1995). Psychological and sexual symptoms associated with the menopause and the effects of hormone replacement therapy. *British Journal of Psychiatry, 167*(2), 163–173. https://doi.org/10.1192/bjp.167.2.163

Phillips, S. M., & Sherwin, B. B. (1992). Effects of estrogen on memory function in surgically menopausal women. *Psychoneuroendocrinology, 17*(5), 485–495. https://doi.org/10.1016/0306-4530(92)90007-t

Prakash, I. J. (1989). *Life cycle changes in aging Indian women.* Career award report submitted to University Grants Committee.

Prakash, I. J. (ed.). (1991). Psychological profile of aging Indian women. *Quality aging, collected papers.* Association of Gerontology (India).

Prakash, I. J., & Murthy, V. N. (1981). Psychiatric morbidity and the menopause. *Indian Journal of Psychiatry, 23*(3), 242–246.

Prakash, I. J., & Murthy, V. N. (1982). Menopausal symptoms in Indian women. *Journal of Personality and Group Behaviour, 2,* 54–58.

Pertat, J. R. (1994). *Coming to age: The craning year and late life transformation. Studies in Jungian psychology by Jungian analysts.* Inner City Book.

Rakshit, S. (1962). Reproductive life of some Maharashtrian Brahmin women. *Man in India, 42*(2), 139–159.

Ramoso-Jalbuena, J. (1994). Climacteric Filipino women: A preliminary survey in the Philippines. *Maturitas, 19*(3), 183–190. https://doi.org/10.1016/0378-5122(94)90070-1

Rostosky, S. S., & Travis, C. B. (1996). Menopause research and the dominance of the biomedical model 1984–1994. *Psychology of Women Quarterly, 20*(2), 285–312. https://doi.org/10.1111/j.1471-6402.1996.tb00471.x

Rutherford, A. M. (1978). The menopause. *New Zealand Medical Journal, 87*(609), 251–253.

Sheehy, G. (1976). *Passages: Predictable crisis of adult life.* E. P. Dutton.

Sherwin, B. B. (1988). Affective changes with estrogen and androgen replacement therapy in surgically menopausal women. *Journal of Affective Disorders, 14*(2), 177–187. https://doi.org/10.1016/0165-0327(88)90061-4

Sherwin, B. B. (1997). Estrogen effects on cognition in menopausal women. *Neurology, 48*(5), S21–S26. https://doi.org/10.1212/wnl.48.5_suppl_7.21s

Sherwin, B. B., & Gelfand, M. M. (1985). Sex steroids and affect in the surgical menopause: A double-blind, cross-over study. *Psychoneuroendocrinology, 10*(3), 325–335. https://doi.org/10.1016/0306-4530(85)90009-5

Shirokar, A. (1992). *A psychosocial study of men and women at middle and later life* [Doctoral Thesis]. Bangalore University.

Strickler, R. C., Borth, R., Cecutti, A., Cookson, B. A., Harper, J. A., Potvin, R., Riffel, P., Sorbara, V. J., & Woolever, C. A. (1977). The role of oestrogen replacement in the climacteric syndrome. *Psychological Medicine*, 7(4), 631–639. https://doi.org/10.1017/s0033291700006280

Tang, G. W. K. (1994). The climacteric of Chinese factory workers. *Maturitas*, 19(3), 177–182. https://doi.org/10.1016/0378-5122(94)90069-8

Uma, H. (1981). *Study of some variables influencing psychological symptoms in middle aged women* [Master's Dissertation]. Bangalore University.

Vankeep, P. A., Greenblatt, R. B., & Albeaux-Fernet, M. (Eds.). (1976). *Consensus on menopause research: A summary of international opinion*. MTP Press.

Vatuk, S. (1975). The aging women in India. Self perception and changing role. In A. De Souza (Ed.), *Women in contemporary India*. Manohar.

Zweifel, J. E., & O'Brien, W. H. (1997). A meta-analysis of the effect of hormone replacement therapy upon depressed mood. Psychoneuroendocrinology, 22(3), 189–212. https://doi.org/10.1016/S0306-4530(96)00034-0

Chapter 10

Female Infanticide in India*
A Review of Literature

Sheela Saravanan

Foeticide and infanticide are fatal forms of child abuse. There are other passive forms of child abuse which lead to illness of the female child, like neglect, sustained nutritional deprivation, delayed healthcare for female infants or, in other words, an unequal allocation of household resources detrimental to the health of the girl child.

HISTORY OF INFANTICIDE

Female infanticide and foeticide have not only occurred in several cultures across history, but it is also known to occur in contemporary societies as well. Several scholars have documented female infanticide in British Colonial rule. The first recorded instance in India dates to 1789 when Jonathan Duncan, a British resident at Benares (at present, Varanasi in Uttar Pradesh state, North India) detected the practice in a Rajput clan. In 1870, the British passed the Infanticide Regulation Act. Subsequently, a special Census was taken in 1881 in the Western Provinces and Oudh to detect female infanticide (Negi 1997: 4). Post-Independence, the practice has been reported as occurring in many parts of the country, including Tamil Nadu, where it was not

* *Social Change* 32, no. 1–2 (March 2002): 58–66.

This paper was written as part of the Gender Planning Network (1998–2001) funded by the International Development Research Centre (IDRC) Canada and coordinated by the Institute of Social Studies Trust (1SST), New Delhi.

known to have occurred earlier (Chunkath and Athreya 1997). While evidence from British records and other historical sources shows that female infanticide was confined to Northern and Western regions of the country including present-day Rajasthan, Punjab, Uttar Pradesh and Bihar, in Tamil Nadu, it is essentially a post-Independence phenomenon. Interviews with village elders in Tamil Nadu confirm this (Chunkath and Athreya 1999: 4).

In 1986, when the practice of female infanticide in Madurai district of Tamil Nadu first received major media attention, the focus was on the caste group known as 'Pramalai Kallar' and it was held that the practice was confined to this caste. Over the past two decades, the region has attracted wide attention due to the prevalence of the practice of female infanticide in Usilampatti taluka. This region has a predominant large population of Kallars (Negi 1997: 4). Female infanticide in Tamil Nadu had been reported as occurring also among the Toda tribe of Tamil Nadu. Chunkath and Athreya, who confirm that the practice of female infanticide is widespread in Dharmapuri, Salem and Madurai districts, arrived at this conclusion after preparing a table on the distribution of blocks by number of female infanticide deaths as per public health centre records. They observe that there is a contiguous cluster of blocks where female infanticide occurs and what should be of a cause for particular concern is that the phenomenon is spreading from the core area to a much wider neighbouring periphery area and beyond (Chunkath and Athreya 1997: WS25).

LEGAL PROVISIONS

The Constitution of India contains certain provisions that guarantee the welfare and development of children. The Indian Penal Code (IPC) also has defined infanticide as murder. The deliberate act of causing a miscarriage or injury to the newborn child, exposure of the infant and concealment of births are covered under Sections 312–318 of the IPC. The intention of preventing a child from being born and causing bodily harm to the infant are covered under IPC Sections 315 and 317. This makes the concealment of the birth and secret disposal of the dead body an offence (Negi 1997: 24). Yet it is a well-known fact that technologies like amniocentesis[1] and ultrasound have been extensively misused for determining the sex of the foetus so that it can be aborted if it happens to be a female. To prevent female foeticide and to restrict the misuse of ultrasound facilities, the Prenatal Diagnostic Techniques (Regulation and Prevention of Misuse) Act was passed on 20 September 1994 to forbid the communication of the sex of the foetus (Negi 1997: 26). Despite legislation in certain states to regulate the tests, amniocentesis[1] continues to take place in many parts of the country. Even if there is a restriction on the doctor communicating the sex of the child to the woman or her family members, it is very difficult to monitor this communication. Apart from this, abortion was legalized with the Medical Termination of Pregnancy Act of 1971. Ironically, the Act was meant purely to safeguard the rights of women and doctors who performed abortion. It was conceived as a health measure: where there is danger to the life or risk to physical or mental health of the woman; on humanitarian grounds such as when a lunatic woman was raped, etc., and eugenic grounds, where there is substantial risk that the offspring would suffer from deformities and disease (Ramaseshan 1998: 46).

SURVEY FINDINGS

Carefully confirmed primary data on infanticide cases and social variables related to infanticide are difficult to obtain. There is also a problem of gathering data on direct or indirect infanticide through any brief field trip. It makes it even more difficult to obtain data when people remain tight-lipped. With the practice recognized as a crime by the law and media coverage, people tend to hide the reality. However, some selected survey findings have been discussed below.

One of the key points that emerges from the findings of Chunkath and Athreya (1997) is that there is hardly any gender differential in post-natal infant death rates in most of the districts surveyed in Tamil Nadu. On the other hand, mortality rates are considerably higher for females as against male infants in the entire neo-natal phase[2] (Chunkath and Athreya 1997: WS25) indicating that the girls are killed almost as soon as they are born.

Sabu George, Rajaratnam Abel and B. D. Miller carried out their research in 12 villages of K. V. Kuppam block, North Arcot Ambedkar district, Tamil Nadu state and South India for four years beginning in September 1986. All pregnancies in the 13,000 population during this period were followed. After about five months following the establishment of excellent rapport with the study families, the field team had knowledge of the intent of infanticide even before the birth occurred in many cases. The main findings of the survey conducted by George and his associates were that in the study population of 13,000, there were a total of 773 birth outcomes recorded, involving 759 live births, of which 378 were male and 381 were female. Among the cohort of live births, 56 died in the period of two and a half years (from 1 April 1987 to 30 September 1989) and of these, 23 were males and 33 females. Thus, the female–male ratio was about 3:4. Of the 23 male deaths, there was no infanticide. Among the 33 female deaths, there were 19 infanticides. Thus, more than half the female deaths in the 12 study villages were due to direct or indirect infanticide. In the six villages in which infanticide occurred, it constituted 72 per cent of female child mortality (excluding the only case of the female infanticide to an unwed mother). In the 12-village study population, the overall sex ratio (females per male) at the time of the study was 977.5. In the village where female infanticide was practised, the sex ratio was 939.8, while in the other villages, it was 1018.6 (George, Abel, and Miller 1992: 1155).

In the study by George et al., in 1992 in Tamil Nadu, of the 18 cases of female infanticide (of the daughters of married mothers) that they came across, 17 were among the Gounders. The remaining one case occurred among the Arunthati, a cobbler Scheduled Caste (George et al. 1992: 1155). Adithi, a local NGO in Katihar district, Bihar, in its survey report of 35 *dais* says, the practice originally began among Rajputs but spread to many castes including the Bhumihars, Brahmins, Kayasthas, Yadavas and some Scheduled Castes. This, the report says, is similar to the case in Tamil Nadu, where it originally began with the Gounder caste and has now spread to almost all castes. What makes the practice important in the contemporary society is that there are indications of its increase in occurrence.

In Tamil Nadu, hospital records are a major source by which one can speculate that female infanticide has occurred. Negi states that in a number of cases, especially in hospital delivery, the female infants are sent home in good health. Subsequently, within a few hours after reaching home, the family claims that the child has died due to various causes. This leads to speculate that a case of infanticide has occurred. Even the ritual that is normally observed on death in the family is never followed in cases of female infanticide (Negi 1997: 19). There are also survey findings to show that babies and mothers vanish from hospitals when the newborn is a girl child. George and his associates in their study recorded that nearly 600 girls are born into the Kallar caste in the Usilampatti government hospital every year, out of which an estimated 570 babies vanish from the hospital with their mothers. Hospital sources estimate that nearly 80 per cent of these vanishing babies, that is, more than 450, become victims of infanticide (George et al. 1992: 1154). Hospital records however only report the births that take place in hospitals. It is a common practice in rural India that the delivery is done by the midwives and at home. It is also known through various surveys that midwives are themselves perpetrators of this violence.

Adithi, a local NGO in Katihar district, Bihar, conducted a survey in four districts of Bihar state and found that Katihar district alone accounts for over 1,000 infanticide cases per year. The survey, based on interviews with 35 midwives in the district, reveals that each kills at least three to four babies every month. A similar situation was found in Sitamarhi, Gumla and Pumia districts. In Bihar, it is primarily the *dais*, at the behest of the parents, who kill the newborn girls. They receive an amount of ₹25–₹30 for the deed (*Times of India* 1995).

The child is normally killed within the first three days or the first week of its birth, after which the chances of its survival increase. It is only in rare instances that the child is killed after the first week (Negi 1997: 23). According to the survey done by George et al. (1992: 1155), 17 of the 19 female infanticides occurred within seven days of birth, one on the ninth day after birth, and the remaining one on the sixteenth day. In the entire study population, there were a total of 18 female infant deaths during the first seven days after birth.

CAUSES OF FEMALE INFANTICIDE

The lower status of women is one of the main reasons for these ruthless killings of infant girls. Dowry, given at the time of the daughter's marriage, has influenced the status of women. The daughter is considered to be a liability as her contribution to the family is temporary, up to the time she is married and sent to another family. Dowry is not the only transaction as far as the daughter's marriage is concerned. There is a series of ceremonies in South India, Tamil Nadu, associated with the girls in the family: gifts in cash and kind to the husband's family during ceremonies connected with pregnancy, childbirth and ceremonies for piercing the ear of the girl child and so on. It is the inability to meet the dowry-related demands from the in-law's family which is a major cause for female infanticide.

Chunkath and Athreya (1997: WS27) shows the occurrence of female infanticide as widespread among the poorer and socially disadvantaged community including the Thevars, Vaniyars and the Scheduled Castes. In contrast, Adithi and Community Services Guild, 1992, has suggested that several communities, including the wealthy Gounder community, the landed caste in Salem district, Tamil Nadu, also practice female infanticide (Negi 1997: 12).[3] Thus, the practice cuts across all classes.

Negi (1997: 18), in her report, has mentioned that the society and families having used coercive tactics to ensure that female infanticide continues limit the scope for outside influences in arresting the problem. The view of Negi (1997) and others who have researched this issue is that there is a social sanction for the deed. The familial and social situations seem to outweigh personal reactions and, therefore, women opt to kill their newborn girl children. The Indian Council for Child Welfare, Tamil Nadu, has mentioned that the feeling of guilt and trauma is almost absent in the community that perpetrates the practice, although there is grief among the mothers (Negi 1997: 19).

According to one of the *dais* interviewed, in the survey conducted by Adithi, Bihar, 'mothers are never willing, but the men force them' (*Times of India* 1995). The same study holds that the men generally take the decision to carry out the killing of the newborn babies with females being reluctant participants (Upadhyay 1995).

One mother justifies her action by saying that they have hardly any access to medical care. All deliveries take place at home and often the mother is left to bleed after a particular difficult childbirth. They categorically state that they do not wish to expose their girls to such harsh conditions. Mothers sometimes kill their babies as an act of 'mercy' so that they may be saved from sexual abuse, molestation or other kinds of violence. They feel justified in killing their girl child so that she is saved from all the suffering she may have to undergo all her life (Negi 1997: 19).

According to a study in Tamil Nadu, the first female infant is, in a majority of cases, not a victim of female infanticide. The second female infant also has a chance of escaping infanticide. Thereafter, the girl infants are at a high risk of facing infanticide. The survey finding by George and others mentions 19 female infanticides and 18 of the victims had birth orders greater than 1 and the remaining one involved a first-born daughter. Each of these families had at least one surviving female child at the time and usually they had two. In their study, they also found that no twin died as a result of direct infanticide, but they also say that they are subject to more neglect than a male twin and a female infant born after a set of twin girls is very likely to be killed (George et al. 1992: 1155). The results show that birth order does influence the chances of child's survival.

Negi (1997: 19), after conducting interviews and discussions with people and NGOs closely working in Madurai district (Tamil Nadu), indicates the prevalence of a superstition that killing a newborn girl child increases the probability of a male child being born in the family.

Some of the other findings of the survey conducted by George and his associates in 1989 are that the villages in which female infanticide occurs tend to be even more remote and have less educated people than the villages with no cases of infanticide (George et al. 1992: 1155). Lack of scanning centres has also been cited as reason for infanticide. As people do not have this facility, they kill the child after it is born. According to Soma Wadhwa, every year, 50,000 female foetuses are aborted in India. These perpetrators of the deed are not very different from those who kill the baby after it is born. The latter, she says, simply do not have enough money or facility to kill the baby when it is in the womb (Wadhwa 1995). Another analyst observes that scanning centres exist even in the so-called remote, less-developed areas (Negi 1997: 23).

Negi cites modernization of the traditional way of cultivation as one of the reasons for a decline in the overall status of women and increase in the forms of violence against them, for instance, female infanticide. Earlier, women had the knowledge of how to cultivate seeds in the traditional way, when to start collecting them, when to sow them and how to store them. They also had the knowledge of what kinds of fertilizers are necessary and should be used and so on. With modernization of agriculture and given restrictions on female mobility in the public sphere, it was the man who started going out to government offices to get loans, bring seeds and pesticides and sell the crops, and overlook the irrigation. Women became mere liabilities with their knowledge having become redundant and men aspired to marry only those women whose families could afford to offer more dowry. Modernization has brought about these changes in the traditional systems and thereby lowering the status of women in the society (Chunkath and Athreya 1997: WS22). This has happened in Madurai district of Tamil Nadu where infanticide has a high occurrence.

CONCLUSIONS

It is very important that an attempt is made at eradicating the evil of female infanticide and foeticide. Social mobilization along with political will and widespread awareness generation can make a difference. Apart from bringing about awareness among people, fear of community ostracism has known to make a difference in people's attitude and behaviour. It is very important to have community support and political will to bring about any change in the present situation.

NOTES

1. Amniocentesis is the technique developed for the detection of genetic abnormalities at an earlier stage of pregnancy so that complications, if any, could be rectified with ease. But currently, this technique is being mainly used to cater to parents wanting to know the sex of the forthcoming baby. Generally, this test is done in the 14–16 weeks of the pregnancy. However, now it has become possible to detect the sex of the foetus in the first trimester.

2. Early neo-natal (0–6 days), other neo-natal (7–27 days), post-natal 28–364 days.
3. Although the Gounders live in remote villages, they own a significant proportion of land and are the upper social stratum of their villages in the North and South Arcot districts in Tamil Nadu (George et al. 1992: 1155).

REFERENCES

Chunkath, Sheela Rani, and V. B. Athreya. 1997. 'Female Infanticide in Tamil Nadu.' *Economic & Political Weekly* 32, no. 17.

———. 1999, 7 March. 'The Unwanted Child.' *The Hindu*, p. 4.

George, Sabu, Rajaratnam Abel, and B. D. Miller. 1992. 'Female Infanticide in Rural South India.' *Economic & Political Weekly* 27, no. 22.

Negi, Elizabeth Francina. 1997. *Death by Social Causes: Perceptions of and Responses to Female Infanticide in Tamil Nadu*. Chennai: M. S. Swaminathan Research Foundation.

Ramaseshan, Geeta. 1998. 'Some Reflections on Women and Health under the Law.' In *In the Name of Justice: Women and Law in Society*, edited by Swapna Mukhopadhyay. New Delhi: Manohar Publishers.

Upadhyay, Navin. 1995, 13 November. 'Female Infanticide in Rise in Bihar: Study.' *The Pioneer*.

Wadhwa, Soma. 1995, 29 March. 'Thank Heavens for Little Girls: Do Not Kill Them.' *The Times of India*.

Chapter 11

Women with Disability and Reproductive Rights*
Deconstructing Discourses

Shubhangi Vaidya

INTRODUCTION

In recent years, debates around gender and sexuality in contemporary India have gained salience and visibility. The activism around the contentious Article 377 of the Indian Penal Code, the mobilization of sexual minorities, the sexualization of the body facilitated by the spread of globalization and mass media and the bold and unconventional depiction of sexuality in some recent mainstream films exemplify this trend. At the same time, sexual violence against women, the most notorious example of which was the December 2012 Delhi gang rape followed by days of angry street protests, has assumed increasingly brutal and blatant forms. The watchdog role of the 24 × 7 electronic media has resulted in sexist statements by politicians and other public figures to become the headlines of the day. The opening up of this discourse is also accompanied by attempts to regulate and police female sexuality, as can be seen in the so-called 'honour killings', acid attacks and other forms of structural violence perpetrated upon women who challenge patriarchal norms and exercise choice and agency.

In this paradoxical scenario, the situation of women with disabilities raises several critical and delicate issues. Women with disabilities are a

---

* Social Change 45, no. 4 (December 2015): 517–533.

particularly vulnerable section of society, devalued and discriminated against both on account of their gender and their physical or intellectual impairments. Addlakha (2008a) writes that the multiple barriers (physical, social, attitudinal, economic, legal and so on) experienced by persons with disabilities magnify manifold in the case of women with disabilities, rendering them a stigmatized and neglected category. According to the 2011 Census, there are 26.8 million persons with disabilities in India, of which 11.8 million, that is, 44 per cent, are women with 8.2 million living in rural areas and 3.6 in urban areas. This is believed to be a highly conservative estimate by scholars and activists, and does not capture the ground reality.

The disability rights movement worldwide has campaigned on the rights of persons with disability for full inclusion and participation in all aspects of social life. The major thrust has been on removing physical and architectural barriers, provision of services, education and employment. However, when it comes to the specific issues of women with disabilities, particularly their experiences of sexuality, conjugality and parenthood, both the disability rights movement and the women's rights movement seem to talk past each other. While the disability movement in India is largely male dominated, the women's movement has not paid adequate heed to disability as an axis of discrimination and marginalization. Contemporary feminist scholarship has sought to address this issue and bring to light the lived experiences of women with disability facing both patriarchy and 'ableism'.[2] The work of feminist scholars such as Addlakha (2008a, 2008b, 2013), Davar (1999, 2001), Dhanda (2000, 2008), Ghai (2002, 2003), Hans and Patri (2003), Hans (2015), Limaye (2008, 2015), Ghosh (2013), Mehrotra (2004, 2006, 2013), Mehrotra and Nayar (2013, 2015), to name a few, can be cited in this context. The recent edited volume by Hans (2015) situates itself against the backdrop of changing gender relationships, emerging 'trajectories of power' and a global human rights regime exemplified by treaties such as the United Nations Convention on the Rights of Persons with Disabilities (2006) and the Convention on the Elimination of All Forms of Discrimination Against Women (CEDAW). While mainstream social science in India is yet to engage with disability with the same urgency as other categories of oppression such as caste, gender and class, there is no denying that disability is no longer a soft issue to be wrapped in the tissue of charity but rather a political category that speaks the language of rights.

Despite the social and cultural aversion towards disability, the fact is that it is a great leveller that can strike anyone, anytime. The link between poverty and disability is well established and it is estimated that 80 per cent of the world's disabled population lives in the poorest countries.[3] However, populations in affluent societies, too, face age-related disabling conditions of body and mind; disability scholars remind us that with the increase in life expectancy and medical technologies, most of us are bound to face disabling conditions during our life course.

This chapter attempts to open up the category of disability from a gendered lens with a specific focus on reproductive rights. Motherhood is a social role with tremendous cultural and ideological heft; the bringing forth of new life from one's body through the processes of conception, gestation and birthing, sustenance through lactation, nurturing and the practices of care are surrounded by webs of meaning that shape and transform the embodied experience of mothering. When the mother in question is a disabled woman, the discourse of motherhood gets complicated. Sexuality, conjugality and motherhood are associated with normative, desirable, fertile bodies, whereas the disabled body is regarded as defective, undesirable and, thus, devalued. The very juxtaposition of 'motherhood' and 'disability' is viewed as a contradiction in terms—an 'oxymoron reality' in the words of Haldar (2015). Motherhood denotes caregiving, while disability suggests a woman in need of care herself and thus unfit to assume the caring role for another.

The multiple discrimination faced by women with disabilities and their erasure from discourses around sexuality and reproduction will be explored with the help of empirical studies from different parts of the world. The implications of the experiences of motherhood for the gender identity of disabled women, which pose a challenge to feminist understandings of reproductive and caring roles as oppressive and disempowering, will be discussed. Two well-known cases in India, frequently cited in the context of debates on sexual and reproductive rights of institutionalized women with mental disabilities, will also be highlighted. In the 'Pune hysterectomies case' of 1994, mentally disabled women, in a state-run institution near Pune, underwent the surgical removal of their wombs, supposedly as a social service to prevent unwanted pregnancies and the discomfort of monthly periods. The second case took place in 2009. It relates to the pregnancy after the custodial rape of a young, intellectually disabled, destitute woman in a Nari Niketan, a women's shelter, in Chandigarh and the ensuing debates on her right to give birth to the baby in the light of her marginal and precarious status. The chapter highlights some of the major themes surrounding the categories of disability and motherhood, examining cultural notions of what constitutes 'good' and 'bad' mothering and how disabled mothers negotiate this discourse.

DISABILITY AND REPRODUCTIVE RIGHTS

The experience of disability across cultures and through history has by and large been viewed in negative terms; persons with disability have been viewed as accursed beings or victims of fate, a burden to be stoically borne by the affected individual and the family. Negative social attitudes are internalized by disabled persons themselves; their own self-worth suffers and they come to view themselves as inferior and inadequate. Disability is frequently deployed in cultural representations as a metaphor to connote moral flaws or weaknesses; everyday language is replete with disability metaphors. For instance, Mehrotra (2013) illustrates the local proverbs and folk tales used in Haryana that depict persons with disabilities as being hot-tempered, erratic, cunning and sexually incompetent.

The disability rights movement and the interdisciplinary area of disability studies, which emerged in the UK and the USA in the 1970s and 1980s, overturned the conventional understanding of the category of disability from an individual affliction or deficit to a *social* product, the consequence of disabling environments, and social and attitudinal barriers that constrain and exclude persons with impairments from participating in the life of society and, thus, marginalize them. The 'social model' of disability, which is the theoretical and ideological fulcrum of the disability rights movement and the discipline of disability studies, thus, focuses on identifying and transforming 'disabling' practices and policies so that people with impairments enjoy full human rights and are not discriminated against on the basis of biological or physiological differences.

The similarities with the core ideas of the women's movement are too obvious to be missed, as both challenge biological determinism and the social differentiation of persons based upon their sexual identity or their ability/disability. Kallianes and Rubenfeld (1997) point out that the women's movement has a long history of fighting for women's rights to self-determination and bodily integrity and supports their right to make decisions about their bodies, sexuality and childbearing. Yet, according to disabled feminists, neither the women's movement nor the disability rights movement has adequately addressed reproductive freedom for disabled women.

The term 'reproductive rights' broadly refers to the rights of women and men to be informed and have access to contraception, rights of women to have a safe and legal abortion, to control her fertility and not to be forced to undergo an unwanted pregnancy (TARSHI, 2010). However, in speaking of disabled women, reproductive rights have a broader connotation. Morris (1995) writes that having sexual relationships (homosexual or heterosexual), family relationships, bearing and rearing children and making a home are all considered important human and civil rights that, if denied to non-disabled women, would cause an outcry. However, since women with disabilities have traditionally been seen as undesirable sexual partners and incapable mothers, for them, reproductive rights also include the right to engage in consensual sexual relationships and bear and rear children. While the women's movement focuses on societal expectations and pressures on non-disabled women to marry and become mothers within patriarchal structures and, in a sense, aims to liberate women from these expectations, ironically, women with disabilities are routinely denied their 'right' to become mothers, if they so desire, by the negative attitudes and values of mainstream culture and society, and even by the legal system in some cases. Women with disabilities, thus, view their reproductive rights as more than just the right to choose not to bear a child; they include the right to be recognized as sexual beings, to bear children even if the children are also disabled, to be seen as fit to mother and to refuse the use of genetic technologies (see Kallianes & Rubenfeld, 1997 for references to feminist perspectives). In the

Indian context, Addlakha (2007) observes that the focus of disability policy is confined to medical rehabilitation, provision of education and employment. The rights of persons with disabilities to sexuality, conjugality, family life and parenthood remain unacknowledged and unaddressed. The Working Paper by TARSHI (2010) underscores the bleak situation of people with disability in India with regard to sexuality and reproductive rights.

DISABILITY, SEXUALITY AND WOMEN'S BODIES

Women with disabilities are regarded either as asexual beings incapable of becoming sexual companions or as hyper-sexual and unregulated ones who must, therefore, be put out of sight so that their sexuality can be controlled and contained. Writing about her experience of growing up as a disabled girl in a Punjabi family, Ghai (2002) narrates that the restriction imposed on male and female cousins sleeping in the same room was not observed in the case of disabled girls, sending the clear message that they were not sexual beings in the same way as non-disabled girls of their age. Disabled activist Chib (2015) observes that the personal and sexual needs of disabled women are constantly hidden and ignored because they fail to live up to the notion of the feminine body, being the embodiment of sexuality. They are socialized into feeling ashamed about their bodies and thus deny their sexual feelings and needs.

> [However, in reality,] disability does not hamper a person's emotional need to be touched and loved on an emotional and physical plane just like everyone else. Our sexual organs are not damaged or affected, and hence we do long for and are able to enjoy pleasurable sexual experiences. (Chib, 2015, p. 105)

In her recent autobiographical narrative, Gupta (2013), paralysed after a road accident as a young woman in her early 20s, writes of her experiences of romantic love, marriage and intimacy. Her narrative captures the ambivalent feelings and insecurities about her changed body, its needs and limitations, and the ongoing struggles with a world that regards disabled bodies as defective and worthless.

Stereotypes in popular culture also reinforce the idea of the pitiable and tragic disabled woman, as captured in Bhambani's (2009) description of the disabled 'heroines' in mainstream Hindi cinema. Challenging this dominant narrative, a recent film by Shonali Bose, *Margarita with a Straw* (2015), depicts the story of Laila, a young woman with cerebral palsy and her search for love, sex and romance. Her experiments with sexuality, masturbation, pornography, a lesbian love affair with another disabled woman and casual sex with a male friend turn on the head received notions of the asexual and repressed disabled woman. The film received praise from some quarters for challenging traditional notions of sexuality and disability, and simultaneously criticism for 'over-sexualizing' the disabled subject. An 'open letter' to the director of the film by a television actress Sonal Vengurlekar (Gera, 2015), widely publicized on social media, expressed the view that opined sex was the last thing on the minds of disabled women in India, as they faced so many other barriers and obstacles in their lives. She pointedly asks whether the film-maker would take the responsibility if 'sick' men were to molest and take advantage of disabled women after seeing the film. Here again, we note the two extremes of asexuality and hyper-sexuality between which the construction of disabled sexualities fluctuate.

Empirical research by Addlakha (2007) provides insights into the sexual needs, dreams and aspirations of young people in urban India with disabilities, capturing their ambiguous feelings about their bodies and sexualities. Their poor body image emerges due to the lack of 'fit' with culturally idealized images of healthy, strong independent and beautiful bodies, resulting in low sexual self-esteem. Since they have been taught to think of themselves as unattractive and undesirable, they may not take the risk of initiating and communicating sexual interest, fearing ridicule and rejection. Living in institutions for disabled persons or living restricted lives within the four walls of their homes reduces their opportunities for social interaction and developing relationship skills. Limaye's (2008) case studies of two young, hearing impaired adolescent girls highlight how the 'communication bottlenecks' they face in a world which privileges the hearing affects their self-worth and the pressures to 'fit in'. Radha and Hasina resent the restrictions and limitations imposed on them by their families owing to their gender and disability, and actively strive to forge friendships and romantic relationships with other hearing impaired people, revealing their need to engage with the world in the same way as their non-disabled peers.

SEXUAL VIOLENCE

Domestic and sexual violence is a harsh reality in the lives of women with disability, especially because it is believed that they cannot resist their tormentors nor communicate what has happened to them because of their disabilities. Women with mental or cognitive disabilities are at special risk. The report on Violence against Women with Disabilities in India submitted to the UN Special Rapporteur by the Women with Disabilities India Network in April 2013 highlights their plight.[4] The horrific gang rape and murder of an intellectually disabled woman near Rohtak, Haryana, in February 2015, where unspeakable torture meted out to the victim was widely reported in the media but failed to generate the kind of public outrage and anger witnessed after the Delhi gang rape of 2012. The protests that took place were largely by the community to which the woman belonged. With regard to sexual violence, the lot of disabled women like their non-disabled sisters in India is bleak indeed; their disability marks them out as the 'other', subjecting them to further humiliation and inhuman treatment.

MARRIAGE AND DOMESTIC LIFE

As regards to marriage and domestic life, we find that women with disabilities are frequently given away in marriage to men who are much older, widowers and are unable to secure non-disabled wives due to economic or social reasons. Mehrotra's (2004, 2006) ethnographic work in rural Haryana reveals that women with mild-to-moderate disabilities that do not interfere much with their ability to perform reproductive and domestic tasks have to work as hard as other women—fetching water from the well, cutting fodder, cooking and cleaning. Few concessions are made for their impairment and if they receive any help or support, it is from their natal kin. Domestic violence and wife beating are common. Disabled men, on the contrary, find it easier to get wives due their structural superiority in the gender hierarchy.

Mehrotra (2013) also brings out the role of 'sorority' or sisterhood as it operates through highly feminized domestic spaces, allowing women to manipulate kin ties and draw upon physical and emotional support from sisters, sisters-in-law, daughters and daughters-in-law to manage issues that arise from their disabilities. She cites cases where disabled women are married off into the same family as their female kin and can, thus, rely on them for support. Elderly women with age-related disabilities similarly expect care from daughters-in-law and grandchildren.

A study by Khanal (2013), detailing the reproductive health experiences of disabled women in Nepal, reports that disabled women are more likely to get married to disabled men due to the perception that their common experience of disability enables them to understand each other. However, a few disabled women also got married to non-disabled men because they were supportive, helpful and understanding of their disability. In some cases, disabled mothers were abandoned by disabled husbands, who later got married to able-bodied women at the behest of the man's family. The study revealed that disabled mothers experience violence within the family, both emotional and severe physical violence in some cases. Haldar's (2015) essay on married women with disabilities in West Bengal also highlights the violence and exploitation that these women face. One of Haldar's sources, with a disabling accident, was told by her husband, as she lay on the hospital bed, that he wanted a divorce as she would no longer be able to tend to his needs or give him sexual satisfaction. In another case, a non-disabled man who married a disabled woman made it clear that his reasons were strictly practical: unemployed, he expected his wife to avail of the reservation in jobs granted to persons with disability and take care of him! (Haldar, 2015).

Disability management within the structures of South Asian kinship, thus, is of a qualitatively different order from the framework of medicalization and segregation that has emerged in the West. At the same time, with the growth of urbanization, migration and the shrinking of extended family support and entrenchment of a neoliberal capitalist order, traditional structures of support for the elderly, infirm and disabled are disintegrating (Mehrotra & Vaidya, 2008). The role of the state as the guardian of these marginalized and vulnerable categories, thus, assumes significance, as we shall see later in the chapter.

DISABLED MOTHERS AND 'IDEAL MOTHERING'

We now shift the lens to the complex discourse of motherhood and how the embodied experience of disability enables us to consider it in new ways. It is in these discourses that societal and cultural attitudes towards disability and the 'othering' of women with disability resonate with great force. At the same time, through the lens of disability, we can reconceptualize mothering as an experience that confers agency on a person who is otherwise viewed only as a dependent. As givers of care rather than mere recipients, disabled women attempt to assert or reclaim their identities as 'competent' women. This certainly complicates feminist critiques of the female body as a vessel or the receptacle controlled by men through which patriarchal structures reproduce themselves.

The importance given to motherhood in India can best be summarized in the following quote from Sudhir Kakar:

> Whether her family is poor or wealthy, whatever her caste, class or region, whether she is a fresh young bride or exhausted by many pregnancies and infancies already, an Indian woman knows that motherhood confers upon her a purpose and identity that nothing else in her culture can. Each child born and nurtured by her safely into childhood, especially if the child is a son, is both a certification and redemption. (Kakar, 2008, p. 56)

Becoming a mother is supposed to make a woman complete and fulfilled; a childless woman is referred to as a barren field (*baanjh* in Hindi). Her moral power in nurturing and training her children is acknowledged and celebrated. Thus, it is not merely the biological act of giving birth but the process of nurturing that constitutes the experience of motherhood. The mother as the source of selfless love and sacrifice is celebrated in myth and folklore; under conditions of globalization, the 'super mom' who combines career and care seamlessly is the stuff of consumerist fantasy and the backbone of the advertising industry. Disabled women do not fit into these stereotypes. Moreover, the fear that a disabled woman can transmit her 'defects' to her child can adversely affect her own marriage chances and those of her relatives.

The valourized mothering role across cultures leads to judgemental attitudes and suspicion towards women with disabilities who aspire to become mothers. Thomas' ([1997]2009) sociological study of women with a variety of disabilities and chronic medical conditions in the UK reveals how these women are incorporated into the medical and social discourse around reproductive risks to their own health and well-being and, more significantly, to their unborn babies. If they give birth to a baby with impairments, they are viewed as being irresponsible and made to feel guilty. They also feel fearful about not being 'good mothers' and are under constant surveillance by professionals and 'experts' who judge their performance as good or bad mothers and potentially wield the power to take custody of the child. The medicalization of pregnancy and childbirth under Western biomedicine is starkly evident in the case of disabled women whose impairments are seen as additional complications to be managed by professionals: their reproductive journeys are characterized by material, ideological and attitudinal barriers that exemplify the devaluation of the disabled identity.

In their study of Norwegian women with a range of disabilities, Grue and Laerum (2002) employ a Foucauldian framework to show how these women resist the dominant discourse of disability as dependence by situating themselves within the discourse of motherhood, thereby constructing themselves as social actors capable of *providing* care and becoming responsible for the welfare of another human being.

> When disabled women have children, they make themselves known as something other than disabled women, as dependent, rather than responsible for others. Becoming a mother and thereby entering the discourse of motherhood can be seen as a way of challenging and resisting widely held views in relation to what kinds of statuses disabled women are expected to have in society. (Grue & Laerum, 2002, p. 674)

Among the important themes highlighted by the authors was the empowering nature of the experience of motherhood and the difference it made to their perceptions of their bodies. They were not viewed merely as impaired bodies in need of medical treatment and improvement but rather as valuable persons capable of producing new life. For those women who had been disabled since childhood, having a child meant that for the first time in their life, they were given the status of adults and not just disabled people. Their motherhood enabled them to 'stage their lives as gendered persons, as women' (Grue & Laerum, 2002, p. 676). Building upon Thomas' ([1997]2009) discussion on the need for disabled mothers to show that they are 'good enough mothers', Grue and Laerum (2002) demonstrate the care and the stress that goes into the 'performance' of competent motherhood and the self-policing that these women do to make sure their performance is perfect. Sometimes, the harsh and unforgiving glare of society refuses to account for the practical difficulties they undergo and the strategies they adopt. The authors cite the case of a wheelchair-using mother monitoring her toddlers at the beach. Because she could not run after them to keep them safe, she tied a long rope around the children and attached it to her wheelchair. As tying a leash on a child is considered unacceptable in that society, and only a 'bad mother' would do such a thing, someone reported to the police that she was mistreating her children! Disabled mothers must always be mindful and vigilant of the fact that the safety, health, well-being and psychological adjustment of their children are evaluated against the backdrop of their disabilities and the blame for anything that may go wrong is likely to be laid at their door. The performance of mothering is, thus, a tightrope walk that is carefully negotiated and always tricky.

In her qualitative study of Canadian mothers with disability, Malacrida (2009) examines the contradictions and tensions embedded in the disabled mothers' performances of ideal motherhood and how women with disabilities reconcile the demands of ideal mothering against the realities of their disabilities. The 'ideal mother' is one who performs her multifaceted role as caregiver, teacher, playmate, optimally and perennially. As such, it is a construct that can never be lived up to by mothers, thus amplifying their sense of guilt and disempowerment. She attempts to show how disabled women perform motherhood in ways that will undermine or challenge the perceptions of others and the ways that normative constructs of femininity and motherhood structure their interactions with their peers, professionals, experts and welfare delivery systems. She notes that 'women with disabilities go to creative and extraordinary lengths in order to be seen as complying with ideal motherhood, perhaps as a way to lay claim to a maternal and sexual identity that society denies them' (p. 99). The experiences of mothers with disabilities, as they negotiate the tensions of ideal motherhood, hold up a mirror to the challenges that the mothering ideology raises for all women and the need for a feminist politics that will account for the lived experiences of all mothers and attempt to change it.

These mothers' stories, regardless of their marital status, socio-economic positions or geographical locations, inevitably acknowledged how their mothering practices reflected their awareness of the ideology of ideal motherhood. Malacrida's respondents too spoke of how they felt judged and evaluated by non-disabled society and, thus, had to become 'over-conscious' of their motherhood performance and of living up to the image. While most women spoke about the difficulties in the performing ideal motherhood role, some of them, particularly those whose children also had disabilities, described their disabilities as enhancing their mothering, as they could intuitively understand what their children were going through.

'Mother's intuition' is regarded as an important ingredient of the idealized mothering ideology and these mothers felt that they could lay claim to it because of their own disabled state. While narrating how their bodily differences often interfered with their performance of ideal motherhood, the mothers also demonstrated remarkably creative ways of getting around these barriers. One of the mothers who was housebound and unable to access public spaces and, thus, unable to do many of the things with her son, like taking him to the park or the playground, worked around the problem by providing free day care facilities to her neighbours' children. In exchange, her neighbours helped her out with her son, thus fostering strong community networks and supports that helped her provide all that an ideal mother was expected to. The disabled mothers consciously performed 'compensatory mothering' by ensuring that their children were always clean, tidy and well turned out or by pushing themselves beyond their limits in order to overcome the stigma attached to being a mother with disabilities. At the same time, hegemonic discourses of the 'good mother'—ever present, endlessly nurturant and always available—were internalized and never questioned. Malacrida speculates that it is perhaps the denial of sexuality and procreation as legitimate experiences for disabled women that make them so eager to be seen as conforming to such an over determined construct that is fundamentally oppressive for all women, disabled or otherwise. Like the women in Grue and Laerum's (2002) study, Malacrida's respondents also experienced motherhood as ultimately a fulfilling and enabling experience, helping them to occupy the status of an adult women rather than dependents in need of care.

Limaye (2015) has opined that Indian mothers with disabilities, like their Western counterparts, also have faced similar issues of stigma, pressure to conform to the concept of ideal motherhood and various kinds of oppression by family members. In her study of seven mothers with various disabilities, she found that during their pregnancies, the women experienced tension (reinforced by the attitudes of family members and doctors alike) that their children too would be born with impairments. After the delivery of 'normal' babies, they felt a sense of great joy and satisfaction. Their parenting experiences revealed their struggle to cope with the stress and strain of raising young children and their innovative strategies to cope with situations. For instance, a mother with visual impairment tying an anklet with a bell on her child's feet to know where the child went and another mother with hearing impairment rigging a bell with a light bulb near the bed so that she could be alerted by her mother-in-law in the next room when the child cried at night. The author highlights how mothers could draw upon support from their parents, in-laws and friends, and the children too who were certainly affected by the negative perceptions society had towards their mothers but over time came to accept their mothers' disabilities as a part of their lives. She underscores the need for disability organizations to provide services and support for mothers with disabilities, particularly in rural areas.

While the studies discussed above reveal the ways in which disabled women attempt to exercise agency and empowerment through motherhood, the following section moves the debate to another entirely different social and situational context where agency over the body and consent for the things done to it are appropriated by medical, legal and social practices that challenge the very personhood and humanity of the disabled person.

DISABILITY, AGENCY AND PERSONHOOD:
CASE STUDIES OF INSTITUTIONALIZED WOMEN[5]

The reproductive capacities of persons with disabilities are perceived as a threat to 'normal' society and various means have been used to control them. Writing on the history of sterilization of women with disabilities in several European countries, Tilley et al. (2012) remark upon its continuance with the tacit support of the medical system even in present times. A much cited case in India is the mass hysterectomies or womb removal surgeries conducted on 11 women students from the Government Certified School of Mentally Deficient Girls in Shirur, Maharashtra, in February 1994. The women whose chronological ages ranged between 15 and 35 years reportedly functioned at the level of three- or four-year-old children. The justification given for the procedures by the facility's authorities was that this would safeguard the women from unwanted pregnancies and the inconvenience of menstruation. Activists protested against what they believed to be a violation of the rights and bodily integrity of women under state control; they felt that conducting such a major surgical procedure was unwarranted and could not possibly guarantee of the safety of the women from sexual assault. The facility was described by activists as a horrific hellhole, reeking of urine and excrement where inmates led bleak, dreary lives, devoid of any kind of stimulation or engaging activity. No training in self-help skills, basic literacy or vocational skills was imparted that would help them lead a dignified life. The girls and women suffered from anaemia, skin infections and other clear indicators of poor care and bad hygiene. The absence of staff compounded the problem further. A report prepared by a group of non-governmental organizations, *In The Guise of Human Dignity* (Forum for Women's Health, 1994), was a damning indictment not only of abysmal conditions at the Shirur centre but also the appalling and callous attitude towards persons with disability in general. Given this state of affairs, it is hardly surprising that the women residents were seen as troublesome bodies to be managed and controlled rather than as persons with rights and entitlements to a dignified and comfortable life despite their cognitive limitations.

The voices of the affected women did not find a place in the discourse; it was the doctors, activists and administrators who battled out the ethical, medical and legal aspects and offered contradictory understandings (Sunder Rajan, 2005). The activists' perceptions of the feelings and emotions of the women were countered by the versions of the officials running the facility who highlighted the difficulties experienced by the women in managing their periods and the risks of pregnancy. The lack of engagement, the subjectivities and consciousness of experts, who took decisions on the behalf of the women, were a testimony to the devaluation and dehumanization of the disabled subject.

A report in *The Indian Express* (22 January 2008) published in *The Punekar*, revisiting the events of 1994, painted a less dismal picture. The running of the centre was handed over to social workers in 1997. Conditions had improved—there was more staff available to run the home and the women who had undergone the procedure in 1994 were reported to be doing well with no medical complications. The nun, who was in charge of the centre, felt that for some women with profound disabilities, a surgical removal of the womb was necessary and humane, as they were just not able to manage their periods. For many non-disabled women too, monthly periods are frequently painful and debilitating, and if they wish to opt for womb removal, they are free to do so. The jury continues to be out on the vexed issue of rights over bodily integrity and reproductive freedoms, on the one hand, and the very real difficulties and dilemmas of caregivers of disabled persons (usually women), on the other hand, who must assist their charges in maintaining menstrual hygiene, changing soiled clothing and so on. The experiential reality of the reproductive female body cannot be captured clinically within a medical or legal discourse; the voices of diverse women must be taken into account.

The Chandigarh Nari Niketan case further complicates these debates. The custodial rape and resultant pregnancy of an intellectually disabled 19-year-old woman in March 2009, at a government-run home for destitute women, by staff working in the facility created a public outcry. The issue of whether the young woman who suffered from several physical ailments, in addition to her mental impairment, and had no family or any other means of social support, was fit to carry and give birth to a baby was a sensitive and contentious one. The Chandigarh administration and the Punjab and Haryana High Court had to weigh the legal issues of informed consent and the ability of mentally disabled persons to make decisions about their futures and those of their unborn children (see Rastogi & Yadav, 2010). A three-member committee was formed by the director of the Government Medical College and hospital to assess the young woman's mental condition: she was reported to be 'mildly mentally retarded' with the mental capacity of a 9-year-old. A multidisciplinary medical board, constituted a few days later, then went into the details of the case. The board felt that the woman's physical ailments and impairments were such that they might be genetically transmitted to the foetus or endanger the health of the mother. The mental condition of the woman was such that she was not deemed capable of understanding how she came to have a baby inside her. Her destitute status and the bleak future prospects of a child of a victim of sexual abuse were also considered. The board, therefore, recommended the medical termination of the pregnancy. The High Court, however, appointed yet another committee consisting of three doctors, including a psychiatrist with a judge as a coordinator. According to the committee, there were no serious physical risks involved in the pregnancy. However, they felt that the woman was neither socially nor emotionally capable of understanding what motherhood meant. She thought of her unborn baby as a future playmate and seemed quite unaware of the precariousness of her situation. The committee was unable to ascertain whether the woman's surroundings were conducive to her making an informed choice about herself and her unborn child. On 17 July 2009, the High Court ordered the Chandigarh administration that the pregnancy be terminated. The case took a new turn when an advocate took an interest in the case and helped the young woman move the Supreme Court to seek the protection of her unborn child.

After listening to arguments on both sides, the Supreme Court stayed the decision of the High Court. The woman was permitted to go ahead with the pregnancy. The Supreme Court's decision was based on the following considerations. First, whether it was correct on the part of the High Court to direct termination of pregnancy without the consent of the woman in question. Second, even if the woman was assumed to be mentally incapable of making an informed decision, what were the appropriate standards for a Court to exercise *parens patriae* jurisdiction? If the intent was to ensure the 'best interests' of the woman in question, the Court held that the direction for termination of pregnancy did not serve that objective (Tripathi, 2014). It is also pertinent to note that the woman's pregnancy was perilously close to the legal limit for medical termination, that is, 20 weeks.

The Nari Niketan case is cited as a crucial landmark in moving the discourse around disability and the lack of agency of the subject to one driven by recognition of personhood and rights. The labelling of institutionalized women as 'inmates' suggested that they were on par with prisoners in a jail or dangerous persons who deserved to be locked away from public view rather than 'residents' of shelters or rehabilitation homes where they were entitled to receive care and services by virtue of being citizens. Ironically, the institution mandated with her care and safety was the site of her violation and its own employees actively colluded in the crime. The presumed inability of the young woman to understand the enormity of what had happened to her and the presumption that having the child could result only in further deterioration of her situation were compelling reasons for ordering a termination. Her resistance prompted the legal system to review the ruling and restore the girl her rights over her body and reproductive decisions. Her disability was not deemed to disqualify her as a potential mother; at the same time, it was acknowledged that she would need support and help in discharging her functions as a mother and that it was the duty of the state to provide her with adequate and appropriate help.

On 2 December 2009, a baby girl was born. A recent article by Tripathi (2014) suggests that both mother and child are doing well. According to the report, a special educator visits them regularly; the mother is imparted basic self-help and vocational skills and the child attends a playschool. The young woman, after initial hesitation, learned to handle and care for her child and is reportedly an affectionate mother. The little girl is likely to be admitted to a residential school when she is older. The circumstances around her birth brought into view the pathetic condition of state-run institutions and the need to make them more open and accessible to public scrutiny so that the routine and unreported abuse taking place behind their walls would be exposed and prevented.

The need to engage disabled 'inmates' to integrate them into the life of the community and to make available to them a range of life experiences is underscored. India is a signatory to the United Nations Convention on the Rights of Persons with Disabilities (UNCRPD-2006) that views disabled people as equal and contributing members of society. Apart from recognizing persons with disabilities as equal holders of all rights, the UNCRPD places them at the centre of all rights. It is for this reason that even though families are seen as the major support for persons with disabilities, the rights and entitlements still belong to the person (UNCRPD-2006). While the exercise of their rights may be problematic for persons with profound disabilities, the attempt as far as possible should be to ensure that they receive support and help to make informed decisions and their personhood and agency be respected.

The young woman in Chandigarh was reported to have a 'mental age' corresponding to that of a 9-year-old, and thus she was deemed unfit to take appropriate decisions regarding her well-being and that of the child she was carrying. The equating of 'fitness to mother' to a Western biomedical construct, namely the Intelligence Quotient, denies a whole realm of emotional experience and is a reductive and simplistic way of measuring ability and competence. It exemplifies the application of the medical model of disability to the hilt and sidelines the role of social and community structures in fostering or impeding competence.

CONCLUDING REMARKS

The experience of disability complicates the understanding of motherhood as a 'natural' and normative rite of passage signalling a girl's entry into the adult world and her incorporation into a gender regime where her role as a reproducer and nurturer is paramount. The disabled, deficient female body is viewed as an abomination which is itself in need of care and incapable of giving or receiving sexual pleasure or bringing forth new life. While women with physical disabilities are regarded as 'asexual' and unattractive, women with mental or cognitive disabilities are seen to be sexually unregulated and vulnerable to abuse and, therefore, in need of medical and social interventions ranging from sterilization to confinement in institutions where their sexuality and reproductive capacities may be controlled if not erased. Scholarship at the intersections of gender and disability studies has sought to illuminate the ways in which women with disabilities challenge these understandings, and thereby complicate and enrich discourses on embodiment and motherhood. At the same time, hegemonic, patriarchal ideological constructs of 'good' and 'bad' mothering practices appear well entrenched and internalized, and disabled women attempt to reclaim agency and feminine identity by conforming to these constructs to the best of their ability. The growing medicalization of disability in contexts like India has resulted in Western constructs of ability and intelligence being mechanically applied. Disabled women's bodies become the objects of medical and legal discourses about reproduction and sexuality, often at the cost of lived, experiential realities and diverse socio-cultural contexts. This compels us to reflect upon the disciplining and punitive power of patriarchal social structures and the modern state over non-normative bodies and will hopefully lend urgency and a critical edge to our understandings of what constitutes humanness and personhood.

NOTES

1. Some of the ideas in this chapter have earlier been discussed in the 'Self-Learning Instructional Material' (teaching module), *Disability, Sexuality and Motherhood* (Vaidya, 2013), prepared by the author for MA in Women's and Gender Studies Programme (Open and Distance Learning mode) offered by the School of Gender and Development Studies, Indira Gandhi National Open University, New Delhi. This chapter is thoroughly revised and updated. This chapter forms a part of a larger study on the theme awaiting publication as a book.
2. 'Ableism' is a term coined to describe ideas, practices, social relations and institutions that are based on the assumption of able-bodiedness and therefore views persons with disabilities as being inferior.
3. http://www.disabled-world.com/disability/statistics/
4. http://www.wwdin.org/pdf/Report%20by%20WWDIN%20India%20Network%20for%20SRVAW_22nd%20April%202013.pdf
5. These case studies have also been discussed in the IGNOU teaching module *Disability, Sexuality and Motherhood* (Vaidya, 2013) referred to in note 1.

REFERENCES

Addlakha, R. (2007). *Gender, subjectivity and sexual identity: How young people with disabilities conceptualise the body, sex and marriage in urban India* (Occasional Paper). CWDS.

Addlakha, R. (2008a). Introduction: Disability, gender and society. *Indian Journal of Gender Studies, Special Issue, 15*(2), 191–207.

Addlakha, R. (2008b). *Deconstructing mental illness: An ethnography of psychiatry, women and the family.* Zubaan Books.

Addlakha, R. (Ed.). (2013). *Disability studies in India: Global discourses, local realities.* Routledge.

Bhambani, M. (2009). Societal responses to women with disabilities in India. In R. Addlakha, S. Blume, P. Devlieger, O. Nagase & M. Winance (Eds.), *Disability and society: A reader* (pp. 233–245). Orient Blackswan.

Chib, M. (2015). I feel normal inside. Outside, my body isn't! In A. Hans (Ed.), *Disability, gender and the trajectories of power* (pp. 93–112). SAGE.

Davar, B. (1999). *Mental health of Indian women: A feminist agenda.* SAGE.

Davar, B. (2001). *Mental health from a gender perspective.* SAGE.

Dhanda, A. (2000). *Legal order/mental disorder.* SAGE.

Dhanda, A. (2008). Sameness and difference: Twin track empowerment for women with disabilities. *Indian Journal of Gender Studies, Special Issue, 15*(2), 209–232.

Forum for Women's Health. (1994). *In the guise of human dignity.* http://www.unipune.ac.in/snc/cssh/HumanRights/07%20STATE%20AND%20GENDER/12.pdf

Gera, S. (2015). TV actress Sonal Vengurlekar not happy with 'sexuality' in *Margarita, with a straw*, writes open letter to Shonali Bose. indianexpress.com/article/entertainment/entertainment-others/tvactress

Ghai, A. (2002). Disabled women: An excluded agenda of Indian feminism. *Hypatia, 17*(3), 49–66.

Ghai, A. (2003). *(Dis)embodied form: Issues of disabled women.* Har-Anand Publications.

Ghosh, N. (2013). Bhalo Meye: Cultural construction of gender and disability in Bengal. In R. Addlakha (Ed.), *Disability studies in India: Global discourses, local realities.* Routledge.

Grue, L., & Laerum, K. T. (2002). Doing motherhood: Some experiences of mothers with physical disabilities. *Disability & Society, 17*(6), 671–683.

Gupta, S. (2013). *No looking back.* Rupa Publications.

Haldar, S. (2015). Tale of married women with disabilities: An oxymoron reality? In A. Hans (Ed.), *Disability, gender and the trajectories of power* (pp. 121–132). SAGE.

Hans, A. (Ed.). (2015). *Disability, gender and the trajectories of power.* SAGE.

Hans, A., & Patri, A. (Eds). (2003). *Women, disability and identity.* SAGE.

Kakar, S. (2008). *The inner world: A psycho-analytic study of childhood and society in India* (3rd ed.). Oxford University Press.

Kallianes, V., & Rubenfeld, P. (1997). *Disabled women and reproductive rights.* Disability & Society, 12(2), 203–222.

Khanal, N. A. (2013). *Status of reproductive health and experience of motherhood of disabled women in Nepal* (Report submitted to the Social Inclusion Research Fund [SIRF] Kathmandu, Nepal). Social Inclusion Research Fund (SIRF). http://www.socialinclusion.org.np/new/files/Neeti%20Aryal%20 Khanal_1380089047dW5d.pdf

Limaye, S. (2008). The inner world of adolescent girls with hearing impairments: Two case studies. *Indian Journal of Gender Studies, Special Issue, 15*(2), 387–406.

Limaye, S. (2015). A disabled mother's journey in raising her child. In A. Hans (Ed.), *Disability, gender and the trajectories of power* (pp. 133–154). SAGE.

Malacrida, C. (2009). Performing motherhood in a disablist world: Dilemmas of motherhood, femininity and disability. *International Journal of Qualitative Studies in Education, 22*(1), 99–117.

Mehrotra, N. (2004). Women, disability and social support in rural Haryana. *Economic & Political Weekly, 39*(52), 5640–5644.

Mehrotra, N. (2006). Negotiating gender and disability in rural Haryana. *Sociological Bulletin, 55*(3), 406–426.

Mehrotra, N. (2013). *Disability, gender and state policy: Exploring margins.* Rawat Publications.

Mehrotra, N., & Nayar, M. (2013). Women and psycho-social disabilities among the urban poor. In N. Mehrotra (Ed.), *Disability, gender and state policy: Exploring margins* (pp. 208–236). Rawat Publications.

Mehrotra, N., & Nayar, M. (2015). Women with psycho-social disabilities: Shifting the lens from medical to social. In A. Hans (Ed.), *Disability, gender and the trajectories of power* (pp. 72–90). SAGE.

Mehrotra, N., & Vaidya, S. (2008). Exploring constructs of intellectual disability and personhood in Haryana and Delhi. *Indian Journal of Gender Studies, Special Issue, 15*(2), 317–340.

Morris, J. (1995). Creating a space for absent voices: Disabled women's experience of receiving assistance with daily living activities. *Feminist Review, 51*(Autumn), 68–93.

Rastogi, P., & Yadav, M. (2010). Issue of consent for MTP by orphan, major and mentally retarded: A critical review. *Journal of the Indian Academy of Forensic Medicine, 32*(3), 267–274.

Sunder Rajan, R. (2005). Beyond the hysterectomies scandal: Women, the institution, family and state. In K. Kannabiran (Ed.), *The violence of normal times* (pp. 121–171). Women Unlimited.

TARSHI. (2010). *Sexuality and disability in the Indian context* (Working Paper). TARSHI.

The Punekar. (2008). At peace in Shirur, site of mass hysterectomies. *The Indian Express.* http://www.thepunekar.com/at-peace-in-shirur-site-of-mass hysterectomies/2008/01/

Thomas, C. ([1997]2009). The baby and the bath water: Disabled women and motherhood in social context. In R. Addlakha, S. Blume, P. Devliger, O. Nagase and M. Winance (Eds.), *Disability and society: A reader* (pp. 246–270). Orient Blackswan.

Tilley, E., Walmsley, J., Earle, S., & Atkinson, D. (2012). The silence is roaring: Sterilisation reproductive rights and women with intellectual disabilities. *Disability & Society, 27*(3), 413–426.

Tripathi, D. (2014). Her story. http://www.frontline.in/social-issues/general-issues/her-story/article5601365.ece?homepage=true

Vaidya, S. (2013). *Disability, sexuality and motherhood* (Unit-2, Block-2 Course MWG004, MA in Women's and Gender Studies). Indira Gandhi National Open University, School of Gender and Development Studies.

Section III

Nutrition: A Social Determinant of Health

Sectional Introduction

P. M. Arathi

'Malnutrition is the biological translation of a social disease with historical roots (Schuftan, 1989, p. 34). Historically, distribution of food has been a collective initiative, either by groups of food gatherers or the family. Food availability in more complex social formations was constrained by social factors such as class and caste/ethnic positions and gender. As Ghosh and Qadeer (2017) observe, the entry of science into the scene takes place later, when the state emerged as a key actor and needed to ensure order in productive processes and a dependable stream of workforce in times of war and peace. Deciding on quantities, types of foods and supply systems for the common man were a product of this striving.

Nutrition is primarily a physiological process that reflects the interaction between food intake, providing energy and nutrients, and the metabolic demands of the body, which are required to establish and maintain body function, as well as the nutritional processes that take place against a wide range of environmental factors such as access and availability, which are linked to economic, sociological (caste and gender), organizational, cultural and ecological context. Nutrition is defined as 'the sum total of the processes involved in the taking in and the utilization of food substances by which growth, repair and maintenance of the body are accomplished'. It involves consumption and assimilation. 'Nutrients are stored by the body in various forms and drawn upon when the food intake is not sufficient.' Lately, there has been an aggressive projection of the falling levels of poverty in India by national as well as international agencies (Qadeer et al., 2016).

In India, the pervasiveness of anaemia in women is a relatively well-documented and researched area. However, other dimensions of the nutritional status of women, as well as the linkage between those and women's socio-economic status, intra-household food consumption and so on, have so far remained relatively less explored. The study (2018) conducted jointly by the Council for Social Development, Nutritional International and Care India on the nutritional status of women in India clearly indicates that under-nutrition and malnutrition continue to be a major problem, particularly among adult women and adolescent girls. The most recent data of the National Family Health Survey (NFHS), 2015–2016, and the National Nutrition Monitoring Bureau, 2011–2012, show that the vast majority of women in India are undernourished. Despite certain improvements in terms of reducing acute under-nutrition in India, this study shows that the vast majority of women are still suffering from under-nutrition in current times and require our urgent attention. The condition of poorer women and the socially marginalized (SC/STs) is even worse in terms of nutritional indicators compared to their well-off counterparts (Council for Social Development, 2018).

Women from socio-economically vulnerable sections bear a much higher risk of under-nutrition than their relatively more privileged counterparts. Special attention is required for them, which also includes identifying nutritionally deprived regions. Food intake is an important determinant of nutritional status. There should be a thorough review and re-strategizing of India's food policy. The provision of adequate basic food without any barriers to access should be the minimum mandate of the government. Reduction of food intakes in India over the last two decades is a distressing fact, which needs to be corrected. Increasing people's access to a minimum level of basic food is the first step towards addressing early-age under-nutrition.

Social Change carries 18 chapters in the time span studied under the theme of nutrition and malnutrition covering a wider spectrum of the issues. Fifty years of research and academic writings on nutrition marks a dearth of macro-level data in later periods as compared to the earlier one. More empirical studies at the regional level have unfolded the social realities of nutrition and food disparities in India. Chapters from previous issues highlight the important analysis-related role of NGOs in examining the nutrition and the health status of women and children (Tikku, 2004); the social dimension of child nutrition among the economically disadvantaged (Khandekar & Kini, 1974); infant nutritional practices in the urban community (Nirmalamma & Reddy, 1990); macro- and micro-determinants of hunger and malnutrition (Schuftan, 1989); paediatric nutrition and population growth (Ramalingaswami, 1971); non-cognitive correlates of malnutrition (Dutta & Das, 1981); the role of individuals, institutions and social groups (Schuftan, 1990); levels of food consumption among rural labour households (Dasaradha Rama Rao, 1974); the effect of supplementary food on motor development rural infants (Bhogle, 1979); awareness of private practitioners and pharmacists on oral rehydration therapy (Nagi, 1990); availability of traditional food systems and well-being (Shankari, 2015); strong participation of people to improve supplementary nutrition to women and children in tribal areas of Gujarat (Ratnawali, 2010); comparison of tribes and others in mid-Indian tribal region on child nutrition (Das, 2008) and cultural determinants of malnutrition in urban India (Acharya, 2005).

The third section, 'Nutrition: A Social Determinant of Health', has four selected chapters. Chapter 12 by Mankekar (1971) claims that 80 per cent of India's rural population lives on a subsistence diet and required calories and the necessary nutrients are lacking in the daily food of this segment, which is largely poor in protein content. The only exceptions she finds are people living in and around riverbanks or the coastal region, where sometimes fish forms a part of the regular diet. 'The diet in the rural areas varies in pattern and nutritive content, according to the geographical regions, agricultural produce available in the area and the financial status of the people' (Mankekar, 1971, p. 40). She criticizes the fact that the actual practice of this awareness has been reduced to symbolic rituals only and the same pattern continues till today.

Chapter 13 in this section by Rastogi and Dwivedi (2014) uses the NFHS Third Round data analysis of eight metropolitan cities and examines the impact of maternal employment on the nutritional status of children. Rapid urbanization, poverty and in-migration all have an impact on the standard of living of households, compelling women to work outside their homes. Changing living and working conditions of women also have an impact on child feeding and rearing practices, adversely affecting child nutrition practices, though the study admits that other socio-demographic variables are also detrimental to the nutritional status of children. This study uses the statistical tool of multiple logistic regressions and finds that maternal employment, living in slums and a low maternal education significantly affects the nutritional status of children in richer sections. However, this factor does not affect the nutrition of children from the poorer strata. The authors suggest a better coverage by the Public Distribution System (PDS) and Integrated Child Development Services (ICDS) as a way to address this issue of malnutrition among children of working-class women.

Chapter 14 by Qadeer et al. (2016) is a macro-level data analysis and critique of trends in declining calorie intake. Using food consumption data of successive rounds of the National Sample Survey (NSS), the authors show that the post-liberalization era in India has witnessed a steady decline in calorie intake. The dominant and popular 'scientific' and other explanations to this phenomenon are increasing prosperity, declining morbidity and technological advancement, which has reduced hard physical labour, resulting in a lower human energy requirement. The analysis of the NSSO round makes the authors sceptical about the popular argument that emphasizes a noticeable increase in calorie intake. To develop a deeper understanding of this paradox, the authors make different estimates of food consumption by different social sections in India. The findings of this analysis clearly show that increasing levels of under-nourishment are due to reduced access to food for a larger section of people. The authors argue that the strengthening of redistribution policies can make improvements by citing minor improvement during the 2011–2012 period. This chapter also reiterates the importance of welfare schemes such as the PDS and the ICDS mid-day meal system in schools and relevance of better wages through the National Rural Employment Guarantee Act and a comprehensive primary healthcare approach towards the dream of inclusive development and strong democratic India.

In Chapter 15, Murty (2018) discusses the vicious cycles of poverty, social exclusion, deprivation and marginalization of tribal community in India and argues that their lower social status adversely affects access to information, supplies and essential services. The study further points that the 'degraded conditions of natural resources paucity of land combined with unskilled human resources within the tribal communities have brought their economy to the brink. The tribals seek various options with their own initiative, but these offer very little security or long-term sustainability' (Murty, 2018, p. 217). The study focuses on the crucial aspect of a tribal's right to food from the lens of availability, accessibility, adequacy and affordability. From a rights framework, the author suggests that measures to reduce poverty and steps to respect human rights have to be evolved in tandem, sharing the same in the overall goal of an increased human well-being.

REFERENCES

Acharya, P. K. (2005). Cultural determinants of malnutrition in an urban slum. *Social Change*, *35*(2), 1–12.

Bhogle, S. (1979). Effects of supplementary food on motor development of rural infants. *Social Change*, 18–22.

Council for Social Development. (2018). *Strategy for enhancing women's nutritional status via programmatic interventions* [Unpublished].

Das, S. (2008). Childhood undernutrition: A comparative analysis of Scheduled Tribes and others in the mid-Indian tribal region. *Social Change*, *38*(1), 64–83.

Dasaradha Rama Rao, G. (1974). Levels of food consumption among rural labour households. *Social Change*, 19–23.

Dutta, T., & Das, J. P. (1981). Noncognitive correlates of malnutrition. *Social Change*, 9–12.

Khandekar, M., & Kini, S. (1974). The social dimension of child nutrition among the economically disadvantaged in Greater Bombay. *Social Change*, 24–35.

Mankekar, K. (1971). Diet habits in rural areas. *Social Change*, *1*(3), 40–47.

Murty, R. K. (2018). Food security eludes tribals of Andhra Pradesh. *Social Change*, *48*(2), 208–221.

Nagi, B. S. (1990). Oral rehydration therapy: Level of awareness among private practitioners and pharmacists. *Social Change*, *20*(4), 92–99.

Nirmalamma. N., & Reddy, P. R. (1990). Infant nutritional practices in an urban community. *Social Change, 20*(3), 92–97.

Qadeer, I., Ghosh, M. S., & Arathi, P. A. (2016). India's declining calorie intake: Development or distress? *Social Change, 46*(1), 1–26.

Ramalingaswami, V. (1971). Paediatric nutrition and population growth. *Social Change, 1*(3), 23–27.

Rastogi, S., & Dwivedi, K. L. (2014). Child nutritional status in metropolitan cities of India: Does maternal employment matter? *Social Change, 44*(3), 355–370.

Ratnawali. (2010). Supplementary nutrition to women and children: A situational analysis of *Aanganwadis* in tribal areas of Gujarat. *Social Change, 40*(3), 319–343.

Schuftan, C. (1989). Hunger and malnutrition: Macro- and micro-determinants. *Social Change, 19*(4), 33–44.

Schuftan, C. (1990). Activism to face world hunger: Exploring new needed commitments. *Social Change, 20*(4), 45–50.

Shankari, U. (2015). Wellbeing by eating well. *Social Change, 45*(1), 145–157.

Tikku, N. (2004). NGOs in three North Indian states—Evaluation of NGOs working in the areas of nutritional and health status of women and children. *Social Change, 34*(3), 34–52.

Chapter 12

Diet Habits in Rural Areas*

Kamala Mankekar

The rural population of India—and 80 per cent of the total population of the country in the villages—still lives, by and large, on a subsistence diet. The required calories and nutrients are lacking in their daily food, which is markedly poor in its protein content. Except in a couple of agriculturally rich states, the consumption of milk or milk products is either totally absent or negligible. Most of the rural communities are vegetarian, but even those who are non-vegetarian hardly eat any meat products as the purchasing power of these people is very low. The only exceptions in this matter are villages on riverbanks or along the coast, where sometimes fish forms part of the regular diet of the people.

The diet of expectant and nursing mothers is no better. There is awareness of the need for special and nutritious diet for an expectant mother practically among all castes and communities. In fact, there are some rituals and social customs emphasizing this point. In Maharashtra and along the West coast, there is a custom whereby the pregnant mother is invited by friends and relatives who feed her on special and rich dishes. However, in actual practice, this awareness has been reduced to symbolic rituals only. The main reason for the neglect of the diet of expectant and nursing mothers again is poverty—the poor purchasing power of the family.

The diet in the rural areas varies in pattern and nutritive content, according to the geographical regions, agricultural produce available in the area and the financial status of the people. But basically the

* *Social Change* 1, no. 3 (December 1971): 40–47

pattern is more or less the same all over the country. There are two main meals in the day. Besides, in the working seasons, that is, sowing and harvesting periods, generally the leftovers from the night meal are consumed early in the morning before the people set out for work and the remnants of the mid-day meal are consumed early in the evening as the people round up the day's activities.

A major portion of the income of the rural communities is spent on food. It is sometimes as high as 88 per cent of the total earnings of a family. The lower the income, the higher is the proportion of earnings spent on food requirements.

We are giving here some examples of the food habits of people of different regions in villages selected at random. The observations and information are based on the Village Survey Monographs of the Census of India, 1961.

The Gonds of Jaitpur district in Uttar Pradesh (UP): There has hardly been any change in the diet of these people during the last 50 years or so. Most *Gond* families live on *Pej*, a gruel of rice and/or a millet locally called *Kutki*. According to Russell (1916, p. 125), 'The common food of the labouring Gond is gruel of rice and a small millet boiled in water, the quantity of water increasing in proportion to their poverty.' This *pej* is drunk, and not really eaten. This is perhaps the cheapest kind of food on which man can live and the quantity of the grain used is astonishingly small. Naturally, the *Gond* has to 'eat' his food many times a day, sometimes every three hours.

The subsidiary foods of these people include *mahua* fruit, which grows wild in the jungles and *makka* or maize. *Gond* women collect *mahua* from the forests, dry and preserve it. When other food stocks are depleted, *mahua* comes to the people's rescue. It is powdered and mixed with some other flour. *Mahua* is also distilled to make a heady liquor.

A strange habit of the *Gonds* is not to eat salt in their food. After taking the food, they round off the meal with a few chillies and a pinch of salt. By and large, *Gonds* are non-vegetarians but few among them have the money to buy meat or meat products even occasionally.

Another of their food items is *Birra*, a mixture of wheat and gram. *Jowar* is also used for making rotis.

Such poor people can hardly be expected to give special diet to an expectant or nursing mother. In fact, after the delivery of the child, the mother is kept without any food for several days—usually till the dropping of the naval cord. She is, however, given a concoction of the bark of the *Kankar* tree, *ajvayan* and turmeric to cleanse her system during this period. After the fifth or sixth day, she gets a meal of rice, jaggery and dried ginger.

Richhari village in district Datia of Madhya Pradesh: The general pattern in most villages in this area is two meals a day with one or two subsidiary meals according to the financial capacity of the household. Richhari village follows the same pattern. However, the ingredients of the meal vary significantly according to the financial status of the family which in turn is closely linked with the caste divisions.

Brahmins, for instance, have wheat and *juar* as the staple grain. They are strict vegetarians and their meal includes one dal and one vegetable. They take milk with overnight chapati in the morning, two main meals and sometimes another small meal of some snack in the afternoon.

Ahirs—Their staple food is *juar* roti which is eaten either with dal or just an onion and a pinch of salt.

Maheris—*Juar* and a gruel of *juar* flour boiled with salt and some chillies are the common items of the food of these people. Dal is cooked only sometimes and if possible a little buttermilk is used in preparing the *juar* flour gruel.

Chamars: Their food is the same as that of Maheri people. They also consume homemade liquor. No milk or milk products are consumed by Chamars, Maheris or even Ahirs. The three castes are meat-eaters, but that is only in name, as they are too poor to buy meat. Wheat is a luxury and is used only to feast guests or for the family on special occasions.

Rajderwa Tharu, a village in Gonda district of UP: This village is in the forest area and all the inhabitants except Brahmins are meat-eaters.

Rice and dal are the staple foods of the people, but the forests provide some game and the rivulets, some fish. In fact, most village homes have their fishing nets and for young boys of the family, fishing is a daily chore. Their diet also includes eggs and chicken as most families raise poultry. They hunt and eat rabbits, boar, fox, etc.

Another group of semi-tribal people of Pipalgota in Hoshangabad district have *kutki* and *pej* as their main diet. But they get some fruit, such as berries, *jambul, gular, semal* petals and tender roots from the nearby forests to supplement their diet. Maize and dal are eaten when available. The restrictions on game hunting by forest authorities have restricted eating of meat by the people but they fish whenever possible.

Rafiulnagar village of Bijnor district: The majority of the inhabitants are meat-eaters but they cannot afford to buy meat.

However, fishing in local ponds and rivulets is common and fish forms part of the daily diet of most families.

Their staple food is an inferior quality of rice and some coarse grains like millet. About 70 per cent of the inhabitants have three meals a day, while the rest live on two meals.

This is a fertile area with plenty of fruits in the village orchards. In season, even poor people can get some mango, watermelon and melons.

Kalath village in Simla district of Himachal Pradesh: The staple food of these people like most people in the hill districts is maize and a millet, *Koda*. These are supplemented occasionally with rice. Some pulses too are used in the area and in summer months there are green vegetables grown around homesteads. A popular item of daily meals is *Kheru*, gramflour mixed in buttermilk and cooked into a thin paste.

Although winter months demand more calories, people live generally on two meals in the cold season. In summer, when the days are long, people eat three meals. Tea is a much desired beverage and most families drink it at least once a day. The only milk consumed is in tea or in buttermilk of *Kheru*.

The pregnant and expectant mothers do not get any special diet, but they are fed *Panjiri* and halwa, prepared with ghee, sugar and wheat flour, during the first five days following childbirth.

Tandi village in Lahaul and Spiti district: Racially, the people of this area are a mixture of Mongol and Aryan stocks. Many of their food habits have been influenced by Tibet which is in close proximity.

Although buckwheat and barley form the main ingredients of their diet, the people observe no taboos where food is concerned and eat various meats and are fond of fermented drinks. Potatoes, vegetables, meats and a variety of soups form part of the daily diet of the people. Missionaries working in the area have introduced a variety of vegetables such as peas, cabbage, greens and beans.

Baking is another popular culinary practice among these people and they make a variety of simple cakes and pancakes. They ferment their own wines and, like the Tibetans, use salt and butter in their tea. Sugar is scarce and is rarely used.

The people eat three main meals beginning with pancakes in the morning, porridge and vegetables for lunch and wheat cakes and meat soup or curds at night. In the beginning of winter, practically every household slaughters five or six goats. The meat is dried and preserved for the long winter months.

The expectant mothers engage themselves in routine tasks and are not given any special diet. After the childbirth, the mother is fed on barley porridge, *saktoo* boiled in butter and plenty of meat soups. This special diet is given to her for 15 days. The child is breastfed for a year to a year-and-a-half but after eight months his food is supplemented with goat milk and bone soup.

Kunran village in Sangrur district of Punjab: Over 90 per cent of the inhabitants in this area eat wheat and only less than 10 per cent eat maize and millet. Rice too is available but is not used much.

The daily diet of the people includes plenty of vegetables such as carrot, cauliflower, turnips, potato, gourd, brinjal, ladies' finger, cabbage, tomato, peas and green leafy vegetables. In winter, people eat a good deal of sag with maize chapati and *khichdi*. Harijans use oil as the cooking medium but the rest of the people use ghee, butter and vegetable oils.

About 90 per cent of the inhabitants are non-vegetarian. They eat meat at least once a month and in winter hunt quails and partridges and raise poultry. Eggs are consumed regularly and surplus is sold in the market; jaggery is made locally and sugar is brought from market towns.

The people eat two main meals and two subsidiary meals. The first meal consists of overnight chapati eaten with butter, buttermilk and pickles. Lunch consists of chapati, dal, vegetable and buttermilk. In the afternoon, the leftover from lunch is eaten in the field itself. The night meal is more or less the same as lunch. Most people take milk before retiring to bed at night.

The pregnant mother is put on special diet of milk and ghee about two months before the delivery. She is generally not allowed to do strenuous physical work. After delivery, she is given jaggery, honey, milk, *panjiri*, *khichdi* with butter and ghee, etc. The baby is fed on goat's milk for the first two days and later is breastfed. Cow's or buffalo's milk is given to the child after six months. Weaning is with chapati and dal. For mother and baby, it is rich food, but not scientific.

Raibaghini village in West Bengal: Rice is the staple food in this area. People take two or three meals depending on their financial resources. About 30 per cent of the inhabitants can afford only two meals.

Different castes have their own food habits. For *Bauris*, the morning meal consists of overnight stale rice kept in water which is drained off in the morning and rice is taken with a couple of chillies and an onion.

Hot rice is cooked for the mid-day meal and is eaten with *gugli* (water snail), *saak* (leaf vegetable), *pasto* (poppy) or some vegetable available. The same sort of meal is eaten at night and whatever is left is kept for the next morning.

Bagdis generally take three meals a day, morning, mid-day and night. The day begins with roti or parched rice, the mid-day meal means rice, *gugli* and potato or a pulse, if available, and rice and a curry at night.

Caste Hindus have parched or fried rice for the morning meal and rice, fish (for richer families) dal and/or a green vegetable for the lunch and same type of meal for the evening. When the price goes up, people cut out pulses from the food.

Bagdis and *Bauris* are non-vegetarians but, again, they are too poor to purchase fish, meat or eggs.

There is no special diet for the expectant mother. After the delivery of the baby, the mother is fed on flattened rice and ghee for the first three days after which she is given normal food. Children are weaned on rice. Few families can afford milk, even for children.

Ghatampur in Hoogli district: The staple diet of the people is rice. People here are poor. Some families live on just one meal plus a subsidiary meal of puffed rice. The richer section, about one-third of the total inhabitants, has fair nourishment. The agricultural labour is most undernourished.

In the Kamnara village in Burdwan district: The meal patterns follow the caste pattern, which means roughly the financial pattern of the different family groups.

Out of the 150 families in the village, 70 live on two meals only. They are mainly Santals, Namasudras, Bauris and Bagdis.

The 42 cultivator families have three meals and another six well to do cultivators take four meals a day. However, two of these meals generally consist of *mudi* or parched rice. Very few households take fish or eggs.

The main diet is rice, dal or a vegetable. Sixty per cent of the families may be taken as undernourished.

Para village in Gazipur district: Of the 95 households in this village, 42 have only two meals a day. These include Harijans, Chamars, etc. The rest have three meals a day.

Most families live on coarse grain. In summer, gur sharbet is a popular drink and people take it with or without parched gram as the morning meal. They eat thick chapatis with tur dal or some locally available vegetable. Mango is available in season.

Bhadkar Uparhar village in Allahabad district: The majority of the inhabitants here are *mallahs* (boatmen). Practically, all inhabitants live on *bajra* and barley roti eaten with dal. Wheat is used for festive occasions only. A good deal of spices are used with mustard oil as the cooking medium. The majority of the people are vegetarian, though the *mallahs* catch and eat fish. Milk and ghee are scarce and even children seldom get milk. Local fruits such as mango and melon are available in season.

Vokkaleri village in Kolar district of Mysore state: Rice and ragi, a kind of millet, are the staple food of the people of this area. Many families eat both rice and ragi, but the quantity of rice eaten depends upon the means of the individual families. Groups such as Adikarnatakas, Adidravidas and Besthas live mainly on ragi. Ragi is either cooked as a gruel or the dough is made into lumps and cooked. *Saru*, a kind of spicy soup, goes with these lumps as a side dish.

The Brahmins among the residents are strict vegetarians. Others eat meat, mutton being the most popular, but few can afford it. Adidravidas eat beef which is from the caracasses they are asked to dispose of.

Most cultivator families grow vegetables such as gourds, pumpkins, greens, chou-chou and beans. But they do not always use them in their daily food, as these are marketed in the cities. People take tea and coffee once or twice daily.

MADRAS STATE

The food habits of the people of Madras state can clearly be divided according to the grain-producing zones of the state. Those are the rice zone, the millet zone and the rice millet mixed zone.

The state is surplus in cereals but deficient in pulses and proteinous foods such as eggs and meat. Hence, the latter ingredients in the diet depend strictly on the purchasing power of the people.

Income level is the decisive factor in the food practices of the people. According to a study conducted, a balanced diet per head per day cost ₹1.24 paise; in actual practice, the average expenditure was 0.45 paise per head per day. The people in the lower income groups spent 33 to 70 paise, the ₹400 income group spending as much as 86 paise which was still far below the balanced diet cost.

Taking a few samples district wise, Salem grows more millet than rice and hence the poorer sections live on the former. Ragi, cooked into a paste, is their main food item.

In Coimbatore, *cholam* is grown in abundance and hence forms the major item of food of a majority of people. But in this district, millets are cooked as solid food and not in the form of gruel or paste.

In the Nilgiris, plantation labourers eat rice but the labouring class in other fields subsist on ragi and other millets. This is one of the few southern areas where wheat is accepted as a major item of food. People eat bread and coffee for breakfast, and some take chapatis for the mid-day meal.

Thanjavur: This is a fertile land, predominantly rice growing. Many people live on rice as the staple food while some others also eat maize and *cholam*. The morning meal generally consists of cold rice and pickles while hot rice is freshly prepared and eaten with sambar, vegetables, curds, etc., at mid day. The same type of meal is repeated at night.

Kanyakumari: People eat mainly rice but the low-income people cannot afford rice twice a day. They have one rice meal and the other consists of tapioca gruel. Tapioca is used in large quantities throughout this area.

REFERENCE

Russell, R. V. (1916). *Castes and tribes of central India* (Vol. III). Laurier Books.

Chapter 13

Child Nutritional Status in Metropolitan Cities of India*
Does Maternal Employment Matter?

Saumya Rastogi and Laxmi Kant Dwivedi

INTRODUCTION

Health of the children is reflected by their nutritional status which in turn is determined by various factors such as early childhood care, mothers' employment status, infant feeding practices, quality of food intake and illness prevention. Nutritional status of children is measured by weight-for-age, height-for-age and weight-for-height which are the standardized anthropometric z scores devised by the WHO (Cogill, 2001). These are also the most common indicators of health and social development. Around half of all the children under the age of 5 in India are underweight and the burden of underweight children in India is one of the highest in the world. It is also nearly double the prevalence of underweight children in sub-Saharan Africa (Gragnolati et al., 2005). When this burden is disaggregated at the level of cities, it is found that among the eight metropolitan cities in India, one-fourth of the children are stunted, the highest number being in Mumbai (45%), followed by Meerut (44% and Delhi (41%). The prevalence of wasting is as high as 29 per cent in Indore. The proportion of underweight children in these cities is also high with 39 per cent in Indore. The situation is

* *Social Change* 44, no. 3 (September 2014): 355–370.

even worse for the population in slums and in the poorest section of these cities (Gupta et al., 2009).

Urban cities are a disadvantaged lot as opposed to the rural areas (Fry et al., 2002). In a review of studies performed in developing countries, it was found that the nutritional status was worse in poor areas of cities than in rural areas in India (Atkinson, 1993). The metropolitan cities of developing countries like India have double burden of ill health as two very different types of populations are living in these. On one hand, there is a population living in upscale areas of the city (non-slum area) with fully equipped modern health facilities and there are others who live in slums, struggling for basic health facilities. This divide, based on slum and non-slum, is not very well-defined in most cities. According to a recent report, a large proportion of population living in the non-slum areas of cities particularly in Indore, Hyderabad and Chennai areas was found to be poor. In Mumbai, Delhi and Kolkata, poor mostly lived in the slum areas (Gupta et al., 2009).

Families living in the poor neighbourhoods cannot afford even basic health services, sanitation, housing, etc., required for appropriate growth of the children. They have been trapped in poverty for many years and, in order to break this cycle of poverty, women are compelled to work for money away from their houses. It is hypothesized that working mothers as compared to non-working ones spend less time with their children because of the nature of job which usually requires them to be out of the house (Sivakami, 1997). Poor women from slums usually work as rag pickers, manual scavengers, construction labourers, farm workers and domestic helps, etc. On the other hand, women in non-slum areas are involved in occupations such as managers, teachers, clerks and salespersons. Being involved in such activities leaves them with little time to take care of the children. These women get less time for child rearing practices, such as feeding, preparing food, breastfeeding and taking the child for immunization. When these important practices suffer due to shortage of time, the child is predisposed to illnesses and to poor nutritional status (Desai & Jain, 1994; Girma & Timožiows, 2002; Morrill, 2009; Pandey, 2007; Ukwuani & Suchindran, 2003). Women who work are more likely to stop breastfeeding and use milk substitutes and may have to leave their children to substitute caretakers (Levine, 1988; Nakahara et al., 2006; Ukwuani & Suchindran, 2003).

On the other hand, some studies conclude that there is only a little evidence of a negative effect of maternal employment on child nutrition (Leslie, 1988). In the same vein, a study showed maternal employment as a protective factor for child nutrition (Ulijaszek & Leighton, 1998). With this background, the primary objective of the present study is to assess the impact of maternal employment on child nutritional status in the eight metropolitan cities of India by poor and non-poor status of household. Second, we have also tried to explore whether there is any systematic difference in relation to the factors responsible for child nutritional status among poor and non-poor families.

METHODS

This study used the data from the third round of the National Family Health Survey (NFHS-III), conducted in the year 2005–2006. The main objective of the survey was to collect reliable and up-to-date information on family planning, fertility, mortality, maternal and child health to provide national as well as state-level estimates. The analysis is based on the information of 2,396 children born within five years prior to the survey in non-slum areas of eight Indian cities and 2,633 children from the slum areas of the same cities (IIPS & Macro International, 2007). It was the first time that the information for eight metropolitan cities in relation to slum and non-slum was made available.

For the present study, covariates such as socio-economic variables, parents' employment status and child's morbidity were analysed for their impact on child's nutritional status. The child's nutritional status comprised of the standardized z scores for weight-for-age, height-for-age and weight-for-height. The dependent variable was classified in the following way—children who were more than 2 SD below the reference median (z score < -2) were considered to be stunted, wasted or underweight. Children with measurements above 2 SD were considered to be having normal height-for-age, weight-for-age and weight-for-height (WHO Expert Committee, 1995). The various covariates which were a part of logistic regression were place of residence (slum, non-slum), region of residence (Delhi, Meerut, Kolkata, Indore, Mumbai, Nagpur, Hyderabad, Chennai), mother's employment type (Not working, Prof/Tech/Manag., Clerical/Sales,

Agri./Manual, Services), mother's education (Illiterate, Primary, Secondary, Higher), sex of the child (Female, Male), size of the child at birth (Larger than average, Average, Smaller than average) and recent experience of diarrhoea or acute respiratory infections (ARI) (No, Yes).

Statistical tests such as independent sample t-tests and one-way ANOVA were carried out on the data with the purpose of comparing the means of the different variables in relation to the anthropometric measurements of the children. In the final phase of analysis, multiple logistic regression analysis was performed to find the net effect of each explanatory variable on child nutritional status after controlling the important covariates. For logistic regression analysis, the data set was divided based on the wealth index quintiles. The first two quintiles of poorer and poorest populations were grouped to form poor, the last two quintiles of richer and richest were combined to form rich and the middle-income group remained as such. This was done with the aim of controlling the effect of different wealth indices because wealth is an important predictor of the children's nutritional status. The results of multiple logistic regression were reported for the two extreme wealth indices (poor and rich), leaving out the middle-income group. P-value of < 0.10 and < 0.05 were considered to be significant. Data analysis was done using SPSS-15 software.

RESULTS

General Profile

The socio-economic and demographic profile of the children aged 0–59 months is presented in Table 13.1. Majority of children in both slum and non-slum areas were Hindus followed by Muslims. Most of the children were born to mothers who had completed at least secondary schooling in both slum (48.4%) and non-slum areas (47.2%). The proportion of illiterate mothers in slum areas (28.4%) was more than their non-slum counterparts (17.5%). The distribution of children by wealth index shows that about 77 per cent children were in the top two wealth quintiles compared with about 6 per cent in the lowest two wealth quintiles in the slum areas of these eight cities. The same result was also found in the case of non-slum areas of these cities.

Table 13.1 *Socio-economic, Demographic and Health Status of Children aged 0–59 Months in the Eight Indian Cities: 2005–2006*

Variables	Slum Per cent	Slum No.	Non-slum Per cent	Non-slum No.
Region of residence				
Delhi	10.8	284	15.7	376
Meerut	18.2	480	18.2	436
Kolkata	11.4	299	7.7	185
Indore	13.7	361	13.3	318
Mumbai	9.2	241	6.4	154
Nagpur	12.0	317	12.9	310
Hyderabad	14.4	380	16.2	387
Chennai	10.3	271	9.6	230
Religion				
Hindu	68.1	1,794	70.7	1,693
Muslim	26.6	701	23.2	557
Others	5.2	138	6.1	146
Caste				
SC & ST	26.1	686	14.8	354
OBC	32.3	850	33.1	794
Others	40.4	1,064	51.2	1,227
System missing	1.3	33	0.9	21
Mother's education				
Illiterate	28.4	747	17.5	419
Primary	13.1	345	9.0	215
Secondary	48.4	1,275	47.2	1,130
Higher	10.1	266	26.4	632
Wealth index				
Poorer + Poorest	5.8	152	3.0	73
Middle	17.4	457	9.3	222
Richer + Richest	76.9	2,024	87.6	2,101
Child's age (in months)				
<12	17.5	462	17.0	408
12–23	20.1	529	19.2	459
24–47	41.7	1,099	43.4	1,039
48 +	20.6	543	20.5	490
Sex of child				
Female	46.6	1,226	47.5	1,139
Male	53.4	1,407	52.5	1,257

(Continued)

(Continued)

Variables	Slum		Non-slum	
	Per cent	No.	Per cent	No.
Mother's age at birth (in years)	15.3	403	11.2	268
<20	46.3	1,219	41.9	1,003
20–24	27.0	710	33.3	798
25–29	11.4	301	13.6	327
>= 30				
Birth order				
1	35.7	941	40.4	969
2	31.6	831	34.4	824
3	16.2	427	13.8	331
>= 4	16.5	434	11.4	272
Mothers' work status				
Not working	80.5	2,119	81.6	1,955
Professional/technical/	2.3	61	4.7	113
manager	2.1	55	2.3	56
Clerical/sales	9.9	261	7.3	175
Agricultural employee/ skilled and unskilled manual labour	5.2	137	4.0	97
Services				
Fathers' work status				
Not working	0.9	24	1.0	23
Professional/technical/	7.6	199	15.1	361
manager	27.3	720	33.0	790
Clerical/sales	55.8	1,469	43.8	1,049
Agricultural employee/ skilled and unskilled manual labour	8.4	221	7.2	173
Services				
Recent diarrhoea or ARI episodes	83.2	2,191	86.8	2,079
No	16.8	442	13.2	317
Yes				
Total	100.0	2,633	100.0	2,396

Source: Social Change 44, no. 3 (September 2014): 355–370.

Age-wise distribution of children in both slum and non-slum areas confirmed that highest proportion was in the age group of 24 to 47 months. Most of the children were in the birth order two or below. Majority of mothers in the households were not working at the time of the interview. The most common occupations of the mothers in the slum were agriculture/manual labour (9.9%) and service (5.2%). On the other hand, in the non-slum areas, most of the mothers were employed as agriculture/manual labourers (7.3%) followed by professionals/managers (4.7%).

Work Profile of the Mothers

The index children have been classified on the basis of their mothers' current employment status as shown in Table 13.2. The four categories of work that they were involved in are as follows:

1. Professional/technical/managerial
2. Clerical/sales
3. Agriculture/skilled and unskilled labour
4. Services

The idea behind categorizing the work status of the mothers in the four above-mentioned categories was that it should help in capturing other work-related details such as money earned, educational level

Table 13.2 *Distribution of Employment Types*

Types of Employment	Percentage Non-slum	Slum	Number Non-slum	Slum	Total Number
Not working	48.0	52.0	1,955	2,119	4,074
Prof/Tech/Manag.	64.9	35.1	113	61	174
Clerical/Sales	50.5	49.5	56	55	111
Agri./Manual	40.1	59.9	175	261	436
Services	41.5	58.5	97	137	234
Total	47.6	52.4	2,396	2,633	5,029

of the respondents, whether working from home or away from home and seasonality of the work. Among both slum and non-slum dwellers, the category of professional/technical/managerial occupations included mostly teachers (59.3% in non-slum and 59.0% in the slum areas) and nurses or other healthcare professionals (10.6% in non-slum and 13.1% in the slum areas). Among non-slum residents, the most common occupations in the category of clerical/sales were salespersons at shops (25.0%) and clerks (17.9%), whereas in the slum inhabitants it was mainly salespersons at shops (47.3%). The third category of agriculture/skilled and unskilled labour mainly included occupations such as tailors and sewers (47.4%), weavers (9.1%) in the non-slum residents; whereas this category among the slum dwellers was mostly constituted by tailors and sewers (45.2%) followed by agricultural labourers (6.5%). Finally in the category of services, the non-slum dwellers were employed as domestic helps (54.6%), waitresses and bartenders (12.4%), hairdressers (12.4%), whereas in the slum dwellers this category was most commonly constituted by domestic servants (69.3%) alone. When looking at the distribution of different types of employments across slum and non-slum areas, it was found that the proportion of professional workers, technical workers and managers (64.9%) was the highest in non-slum areas, whereas women involved in agriculture, skilled and unskilled labour (59.9%) and service (58.5%) were predominant in the slum areas (table not shown).

Among the non-slum dwellers, women involved in services (14.4%) possessed most Below Poverty Line (BPL) subsidy cards, whereas among the slum residents, it is the workers in agriculture and skilled/unskilled labour (12.6%) that have most of the BPL cards (Table 13.3). Overall, mothers living in slum (9.4%) had more BPL cards than those who lived in non-slum areas (6.3%). Majority of women in both slum (76.6%) and non-slum areas (82.3%) worked round the year. Professionals, women in technical and managerial jobs, worked away from home in both slum (91.8%) and non-slum (82.3%) areas. On the other hand, an increasing number of agricultural labourers and skilled/unskilled manual labourers worked at home in slum (66.5%) and non-slum (74.9%) areas. Most of the women worked for someone else in both the slum (71.3%) and non-slum areas (67.1%). An equal number of women worked for someone from family in both slum (13.5%) and

Table 13.3 *BPL Cardholders in Slum and Non-slum Areas*

Types of Employment	BPL Cardholders	
	Non-slum (%)	Slum (%)
Not working	5.8	9
Prof/Tech/Manag.	4.4	8.2
Clerical/Sales	8.9	10.9
Agri./Manual	7.4	12.6
Services	14.4	9.5
Total	6.3	9.4

non-slum areas (13.6%). 19.3 per cent are self-employed in non-slum areas as compared to 15.2 per cent in slum areas.

Anthropometric Measurements of Children by Selected Background Characteristics

The results of the *t*-test and ANOVA (table not shown) show that except mean height-for-age z score (−2.05 ± 1.85) in slum in Delhi, no other city had any mean anthropometric measure less than the critical −2 SD. Table 13.4 shows the percentage children undernourished according to selected background characteristics. Percentage of underweight was highest in Indore in both slum (49.0%) and non-slum areas (37.4%). Stunting was found to be highest in the slums of Delhi (50.7%) and non-slums areas of Meerut (42.0%). Percentage wasted was highest both in slum (33.8%) and non-slum regions (28.6%) in Indore. Children born to illiterate mothers in non-slum areas were stunted (mean: −2.08 ± 1.61) and also in the slum areas the height-for-age z score was very close to being stunted (mean: −1.97 ± 1.69). Percentage of underweight and stunted children was highest among mothers who were illiterate in both the slum (41.2% underweight, 52.3% stunted) and non-slum regions (44.2% underweight, 54.4% stunted). The children born to poor families were stunted in both the slum (mean: −2.16 ± 1.93) and non-slum regions (mean: −2.40 ± 1.37) of cities. Also, in both slum and non-slum, the poorer population

Table 13.4 Per Cent Children (0–59 Months of Age) Undernourished by Selected Background Characteristics

Variables	Slum			Non-slum		
	Under weight[1] (%)	Stunted[2] (%)	Wasted[3] (%)	Under-weight[1] (%)	Stunted[2] (%)	Wasted[3] (%)
Region of residence						
Delhi	35.2	50.7	14.8	25.0	38.6	16.5
Meerut	26.5	45.8	9.6	30.5	42.0	9.6
Kolkata	26.4	32.4	16.7	14.6	22.2	13.5
Indore	49.0	39.3	33.8	37.4	30.2	28.6
Mumbai	35.7	47.3	15.8	26.0	41.6	16.2
Nagpur	42.0	48.3	18.0	28.4	26.8	15.2
Hyderabad	26.1	32.6	11.1	18.6	32.0	9.6
Chennai	31.0	27.3	22.9	21.3	25.7	17.8
Mother's education						
Illiterate	41.2	52.3	17.8	44.2	54.4	15.8
Primary	30.7	43.5	14.5	33.5	39.5	19.5
Secondary	33.3	38.0	18.7	25.1	32.1	15.0
Higher	17.7	15.8	14.3	12.8	18.8	14.7
Wealth Index						
Poorer + poorest	50	58.6	21.1	56.2	68.5	17.8
Medium	39.2	50.8	15.8	42.8	48.6	18.5
Richer + richest	31.1	36.9	17.5	23.1	30.3	15.0
Sex of child						
Female	33.8	39.9	16.2	24.6	32.2	13.7
Male	33.5	41.2	18.5	27.2	34.0	17.0

Women's work status						
Not working	32.2	39.4	17.1	25.3	31.9	15.5
Prof./tech./manag.	19.7	23.0	21.3	12.4	24.8	8.8
Clerical/sales	29.1	23.6	14.5	14.3	25.0	19.6
Agric. employee/skilled and unskilled manual	43.3	52.1	19.5	37.1	45.7	17.1
Services	44.5	51.1	17.5	41.2	51.5	16.5
Recent diarrhoea or ARI episodes						
No	33.5	40.8	16.9	26.3	34.2	15.3
Yes	34.2	39.6	20.1	23.7	26.8	16.1
Total	33.6	40.6	17.4	26.0	33.2	15.4

Notes: [1] Weight-for-age Z score < –2; [2] Height-for-age Z score < –2; [3] Weight-for-height Z score < –2.

fared the worst for all the growth indicators. Sex-wise, none of the children were found to be with poor nutritional status in either slum or non-slum regions. With respect to mother's occupation, only children of agricultural employees and skilled and unskilled manual labourers were found to be stunted in the slum areas (mean: −2.05 ± 1.51) and the mean of other anthropometric scores were not found to be below normal either in slum or non-slum areas. Per cent underweight was highest among mothers who were employed in the service sector in slums (44.5%) as well as non-slums (41.2%). Children of agricultural employees/skilled and unskilled manual labourers had the highest stunting in slums (52.1%), whereas it was again the mothers involved in service sector in non-slum regions (51.5%) whose children were most stunted. Recent diarrhoea or ARI episodes seemed to have had no effect on the nutritional status of the children.

Results of Logistic Regression Analysis

A substantial number of poor in the eight metropolitan cities, specifically Indore Hyderabad and Chennai, lived in non-slum areas. In the rest of the cities, majority of the poor lived in slum areas (Gupta et al., 2009). However, even in those cities, proportion of the poor living in non-slum areas was large; therefore, for the final logistic regression analysis, the data set was divided based on the wealth index groups and not based on whether they lived in slum/non-slum areas. The analysis was carried out by dividing the population into three subgroups based on wealth quintiles. The results of the analysis are presented only for the two subgroups of extreme wealth quintiles, that is, richer + richest and poorer + poorest in Table 13.5. For the dependent variable, weight-for-age (underweight) z score is used for analysis as it is a composite score reflecting both the height-for-age and weight-for-height measures.

Among the richer group, the children in slum areas were more likely to be underweight (OR = 1.32, 95% CI: 1.12, 1.55) as opposed to non-slums. The underweight measures were not found to be significantly different in the poorer group when a slum versus non-slum comparison was made. Among the different cities, Chennai as compared to Delhi city had less chance of having underweight children (OR = 0.28, 95%

Table 13.5 Logistic Regression Results for Weight-for-age

Explanatory Variable	Poorer + Poorest				Richer + Richest			
	Odds Ratio	95% Conf. Interval		P-Value	Odds Ratio	95% Conf. Interval		P-Value
		Lower	Upper			Lower	Upper	
Place of residence								
Non-slum®	1.000	–	–	–	1.000	–	–	–
Slum	0.811	0.397	1.65	0.560	1.325	.1129	1.556	0.001
Region of residence								
Delhi®	1.000	–	–	–	1.000	–	–	–
Meerut	0.566	0.202	1.580	0.279	0.887	0.659	1.194	0.428
Kolkata	0.564	0.167	1.910	0.358	0.597	0.413	0.861	0.006
Indore	0.523	0.133	2.059	0.354	2.262	1.682	3.040	0.000
Mumbai	0.999	0.980	1.020	0.999	1.123	0.802	1.573	0.499
Nagpur	1.463	0.465	4.598	0.515	1.612	1.174	2.213	0.003
Hyderabad	1.549	0.402	5.961	0.525	0.747	0.546	1.021	0.067
Chennai	0.280	0.073	1.073	0.063	0.860	0.603	1.224	0.402
Mother's employment type								
Not working®	1.000	–	–	–	1.000	–	–	–
Clerk	1.571	0.232	10.636	0.643	0.875	0.496	1.542	0.644
Agriculture	0.789	0.348	1.788	0.569	1.440	1.100	1.884	0.008
Service	2.974	0.968	9.140	0.057	1.302	0.881	1.922	0.185
Professional	NA				0.738	0.458	1.190	0.212

(Continued)

(Continued)

Explanatory Variable	Poorer + Poorest				Richer + Richest			
	Odds Ratio	95% Conf. Interval		P-Value	Odds Ratio	95% Conf. Interval		P-Value
		Lower	Upper			Lower	Upper	
Mother's education								
Illiterate®	1.000	–	–	–	1.000	–	–	–
Primary	0.487	0.163	1.455	0.198	0.668	0.498	0.897	0.007
Secondary	0.878	0.372	2.073	0.766	0.611	0.492	0.759	0.000
Higher	NA				0.276	0.206	0.368	0.000
Sex of the child								
Female®	1.000	–	–	–	1.000	–	–	–
Male	1.503	0.812	2.785	0.195	0.925	0.791	1.081	0.327
Size of the child								
Larger than average®	1.000	–	–	–	1.000	–	–	–
Average	1.623	0.665	3.965	0.288	1.167	0.951	1.432	0.140
Smaller than average	1.969	0.641	6.047	0.236	1.924	1.463	2.531	0.000
Experience of diarrhoea or ARI								
No®	1.000	–	–	–	1.000	–	–	–
Yes	0.648	0.259	1.620	0.353	0.873	0.690	1.105	0.258

Note: NA denotes that cases in the categories of professional and higher were not available in the poorer group.

CI: 0.07, 1.07) in the poorer group and this difference in underweight measures was found to be significant ($P < 0.10$). On the other hand, in the richer group, Kolkata (OR = 0.59, 95% CI: 0.41, 0.86) and Hyderabad (OR = 0.74, 95% CI: 0.54, 1.02) had better chance of having underweight measures than Delhi. The difference was significant for Kolkata ($P < 0.05$) and Hyderabad ($P < 0.10$). In the same richer group, Indore (OR = 2.26, 95% CI: 1.68, 3.04) and Nagpur (OR = 1.61, 95% CI: 1.17, 2.21) had worse underweight measures than Delhi. In the poorer group, women working in the service sector had worse underweight indicators than those women who were not working (OR = 2.97, 95% CI: 0.96, 9.14). The difference between these two is also significant ($P < 0.10$). In the richer section, the children of those women who were working in the agricultural or skilled/unskilled manual labour were more likely to have worse underweight indicators than those who were not working (OR = 1.44, 95% CI: 1.10, 1.88). For richer group, the prevalence of underweight measures was found to be less among children of those mothers who were educated up to primary level (OR = 0.66, 95% CI: 0.49, 0.89) and secondary level (OR = 0.61, 95% CI: 0.49, 0.75) than those mothers who were illiterate. Rest of the other variables such as sex of the child, size of the child at birth, recent diarrhoea or ARI episodes did not have any significant impact on the underweight measures.

DISCUSSIONS

Maternal employment affects the nutritional status of the children through several ways. Poverty forces the women out of their houses to seek employment. Working women get much less time at home and more so with their children for childcare practices such as feeding, preparing food, breastfeeding, taking the child for immunization than their non-working counterparts (Sivakami, 1997). Thus, the child suffers from illnesses and poor nutritional status, when these essential activities are not performed due to shortage of time.

This chapter explored the possibility of interlinkages between maternal employment and child nutritional status by poor and non-poor households in the eight metropolitan cities of India. This study utilized the data from third round of National Family Health Survey

(NFHS-III), conducted in the year 2005–2006. The analysis was based on the information of 2,396 children born within five years prior to the survey in non-slum areas of eight Indian cities and 2,633 children from the slum areas of the same cities. Covariates such as socio-economic variables, parents' employment status and children's morbidity were analysed for their impact on children's nutritional status. Findings indicate that the only category of employment variable showing significant association with nutritional status of child in the poorer population of the cities was employment of the mother in the service sector. The service sector comprised mainly of women working as domestic helps. This relationship indicated that the children of those women who worked as domestic helps and who were also poor were more prone to be underweight than children of those mothers who did not work. This finding is substantiated by another study in which, compared to non-working women, women working as domestic servants spent much less time at home with the children resulting in their poor nutritional status (Rastogi, 2011). The work timings of these domestic servants were not found to be rigid, but they were out of their houses on an average for six to seven hours daily, often working in several homes everyday (Rastogi, 2011). In the richer group, the employment variable which was found to have a significant association with the child's nutritional status was employment of the mother in the agricultural/skilled and unskilled manual labour. This category included agricultural labourers working on daily wages, tailors, sewers and weavers, etc. This association meant that the children of farmers and labourers in the richer section of the cities had higher chance of being underweight as compared to those children whose mothers did not work. This can be explained by the same reasoning that agricultural labourers work outside their homes usually for the entire length of the day; as a result, they do not find enough time to rear their children. Tailors, weavers and sewers may work from home, but these are labour-intensive jobs, which may not leave enough time with mothers to take care of their children's needs. These results are consistent with the results of several studies from India and other developing countries which state that maternal employment is adversely associated with child weight-for-age measures (Desai & Jain, 1994; Girma & Timotiows, 2002; Pandey, 2007).

Not only employment, this study also found several other variables having significant association with child's nutritional status. Among the poorer sections, there were no statistically significant differences between slum and non-slum with regards to their weight-for-age measures. However, children belonging to the richer sections who lived in slums seemed more prone to develop underweight than their non-slum counterparts. This finding seems reasonable as poor population would remain in poverty whether in slum or non-slum and poverty being a major limiting factor the nutritional status of the children would also remain the same, whereas among the richer group, living in slums adds to their disadvantage. The living conditions and access to healthcare are poor in slums compared to non-slums, which is why the richer section fares worse with respect to weight-for-age measures when living in slums. Living in different cities also had different effects on the underweight measures of the child. On one hand, where Indore and Nagpur had a higher proportion of underweight children, Kolkata had fewer underweight children. This difference could be attributed to the difference in availability and accessibility of healthcare facilities in these cities. Possibly, Indore and Nagpur being smaller cities as compared to Kolkata did not have the necessary healthcare infrastructure. On similar lines, a study performed in Cameroon has reported that children living in larger cities had better nutritional status as compared to smaller cities for the same reasons (Pongou et al., 2006). Mother's education also cast an important effect on the nutritional status of the children in the richer group. The mothers who had education up to primary or secondary level had less underweight measures in their children than those mothers who were illiterate (Girma & Timotiows, 2002; Kabubo-Mariara et al., 2006; Mahgoub et al., 2006; Mishra & Lahiri, 1999; Rastogi, 2011). It is important to note here that in the present study, gender of the child did not predict their nutritional status in any socio-economic class. In India and other developing countries, girl child has since long been discriminated against in feeding practices and healthcare. This discrimination has resulted in the poor nutritional status of the girl child (Abeykoon, 1995; Bairagi, 1986; Visaria, 1987). Our results point towards an encouraging trend that girl child is no longer discriminated in Indian cities in terms of feeding practices and her nutritional status is at par with the boy child.

Even though the slums had poorer nutritional status among children for most of the variables, the finding which emerged from the above analysis was that among the poorer section only a few variables mattered as far as children's nutritional status was concerned. The reason is that poorer people, because of their poverty and deprivation, already suffer from ill health and malnutrition (Arnold et al., 2009; Giashuddin et al., 2005; Kanjilal et al., 2010), so there were no significant associations when variables other than poverty—place of residence, city, education, etc., were examined for their impact on children's nutritional status. Among the richer sections, there were a number of determinants that clearly impacted the nutritional status of the children even at $P < 0.05$, it is because richer people have the basic minimum resources to meet their needs and it is the other variables such as maternal employment, mother's education and place of residence (slum/non-slum, city) which significantly affect the nutritional status of the children.

In previous similar studies, the presence or absence of maternal employment has been considered as a covariate and it is for the first time that the effect of type of maternal employment on child's nutritional status has been assessed (Desai & Jain, 1994; Girma & Timotiows, 2002). Thus, this study may prove instrumental in specifically pointing at the types of employment activities, in which when the mothers are involved, affect the nutritional status of the children. Also, this study has been able to capture the seasonality of maternal work which other studies have not. Having said that, maternal employment negatively affects the nutritional status of the children; it is important to judiciously use this information to devise policies. Merely withdrawal of women from the job markets may lead to a drop in the family income, making the nutritional status of the children even more precarious. Supportive measures such as better coverage and implementation of Integrated Child Development Services (ICDS) programme and its outreach towards families where mothers are employed may help to bring down child undernutrition in such families. Other than maternal employment, several other socio-demographic variables too caused significant variation in the nutritional status of children among the non-poor population in the cities. These findings may help in devising fine-tuned policies that focus at the particular causes of poor nutritional status in different income groups.

REFERENCES

Abeykoon, A. T. P. L. (1995). Sex preference in South Asia: Sri Lanka an outlier. *Asia Pacific Population Journal, 10*(3), 5–16.

Arnold, F., Parasuraman, S., Arokiasamy, P., & Kothari, M. (2009). *Nutrition in India: National Family Health Survey (NFHS-3), India, 2005–06.* International Institute for Population Sciences; ICF Macro.

Atkinson, S. J. (1993). Urban–rural comparisons of nutrition status in the Third World. *Food Nutrition Bulletin, 14*(4), 337–340.

Bairagi, R. (1986). Food crisis, nutrition, and female children in rural Bangladesh. *Population and Development Review, 12*(2), 307–315.

Cogill, B. (2001). *Anthropometric indicators measurement guide.* Food and Nutrition Technical Assistance Project, Academy for Educational Development.

Desai, S., & Jain, D. (1994). Maternal employment and family dynamics: The social context of women's work in rural south India. *Population and Development Review, 20*(1), 115–136.

Fry, S., Cousins, B., & Olivola, K. (2002). *Health of children living in urban slums in Asia and the Near East: Review of existing literature and data.* Environmental Health Project, US Agency for International Development.

Giashuddin, M. S., Kabir, M., & Hasan, M. (2005). Economic disparity and child nutrition in Bangladesh. *Indian Journal of Pediatrics, 72*(6), 486.

Girma, W., & Timotiows, G. (2002). *Determinants of nutritional status of women and children in Ethiopia.* ORC Macro.

Gragnolati, M., Shekar M., Das Gupta, M., Bredenkamp, C., & Lee Y. (2005). *India's undernourished children: A call for reform and action.* World Bank.

Gupta, K., Arnold, F., & Lhungdim, H. (2009). *Health and living conditions in eight Indian cities. National Family Health Survey (NFHS-3), India, 2005–06.* International Institute for Population Sciences; ICF Macro.

International Institute for Population Sciences (IIPS) & Macro International. (2007). *National Family Health Survey (NFHS-3), 2005–06: India.* IIPS.

Kabubo-Mariara, J., Ndenge G. K., & Mwabu, D. K. (2006, March). *Determinants of children's nutritional status in Kenya: Evidence from demographic and health surveys* (Paper presented at Centre for the Study of African Economies [CSAE] Conference, Oxford, United Kingdom).

Kanjilal, B., Mazumdar, P. G., Mukherjee, M., & Rahman, M. H. (2010). Nutritional status of children in India: Household socio-economic condition as the contextual determinant. *International Journal for Equity in Health, 9*(1), 19.

Leslie, J. (1988). Women's work and child nutrition in the Third World. *World Development, 16*(11), 1341–1362.

Levine, N. (1988). Women's work and infant feeding: A case from rural Nepal. *Ethnology, 27*(3), 231–251.

Mahgoub, S. E. O., Nnyepi., M., & Bandeke, T. (2006). Factors affecting prevalence of malnutrition among children under three years of age in

Botswana. *African Journal of Food Agriculture Nutrition and Development*, 6(1), 2–15.

Mishra, V. K., & Lahiri, S. (1999). *Child nutrition in India: National Family Health Survey subject reports*. International Institute for Population Sciences (IIPS).

Morrill, M. (2009). *The effects of maternal employment on the health of school age children* (Working Paper). North Carolina State University, Department of Economics.

Nakahara, S., Poudel, K. C., Lopchan, M., Ichikawa, M., Poudel-Tandukar, K., & Jimba, M. (2006). Availability of childcare support and nutritional status of children of non-working and working mothers in urban Nepal. *American Journal of Human Biology*, 18(2), 169 -181.

Pandey, A. (2007). *Mother's status in the family and nutritional status of their under five children*. Regional Leprosy Training and Research Institute.

Pongou, R., Ezzati, M., & Salomon, J. A. (2006). Household and community socioeconomic and environmental determinants of child nutritional status in Cameroon. *BMC Public Health*, 6(4), 98.

Rastogi, S. (2011). *Feeding patterns and nutritional status among children 1–3 years of age in urban slum of Lucknow, India* (Unpublished master's thesis). Tata Institute of Social Sciences.

Sivakami, M. (1997). Female work participation and child health: an investigation in rural Tamil Nadu, *India*. *Health Transition Review*, 7(1), 21–32.

Ukwuani, F., & Suchindran, C. (2003). Implications of women's work for child nutritional status in sub-Saharan Africa: A case study of Nigeria. *Social Science and Medicine*, 56(10), 2109–2121.

Ulijaszek, S., & Leighton, D. (1998). Maternal employment and child nutritional status in a very poor population of residents and migrants from Bangladesh in Calcutta, India. *Anthropological Science*, 106(3), 253–263.

Visaria, L. (1987). *Sex differentials in nutritional status in a rural area of Gujarat state: An interim report* (Working Paper No. 7). Gujarat Institute of Area Planning.

WHO Expert Committee. (1995). *Physical status: The use and interpretation of anthropometry* (Technical Report Series No. 854). World Health Organization.

Chapter 14

India's Declining Calorie Intake*
Development or Distress?

Imrana Qadeer, Sourindra Mohan Ghosh and P.M. Arathi

INTRODUCTION

Nutrition is defined as 'the sum total of the processes involved in the taking in and the utilization of food substances by which growth, repair and maintenance of the body are accomplished.' It involves consumption and assimilation. 'Nutrients are stored by the body in various forms and drawn upon when the food intake is not sufficient' Brookover (n.d.). Although primarily a physiological process that reflects the interaction between food intake, providing energy and nutrients, and the metabolic demands of the body that are required to establish and maintain body function, nutritional processes take place against a wide range of environmental factors, such as access and availability linked to economic, sociological (caste and gender), organizational (productive and intervention programmes) and a cultural and ecological context.

The complexity of this aspect of health is immense. It not only involves understanding the balance and synergy between nutrients, their requirements for different levels of growth and activity, the processes of adaptation by the body to lower/higher states of nutrition and their manifestations, individual variations and age and sex

* *Social Change* 46, no. 1 (March 2016): 1–26.

differences but also relates to intra-family distribution. Policymaking then is challenging as it requires simple, though not simplistic, principles for planning, critical knowledge of nutrition and its complexity and a political commitment to equity and inclusive development. The 1993 National Nutrition Policy document though starting with the Integrated Child Development Scheme (ICDS) emphasized food grain production targets of 250 metric tonnes (MTs) by 2020 and a distribution system to ensure food security to further reduce chronic energy deficiency (Government of India [GoI], 1993).

The Tenth Five-Year Plan in 2002, in contrast, took a U-turn: from focusing on household universal food security, it focused on individual nutritional security. Screening to identify the vulnerable and their appropriate management became the key, thus restricting a major public health problem into an issue amenable to programmatic strategies. As a result, the extent of food shortage was downplayed despite the National Sample Survey Organisation (NSSO) data showing very low intakes and also the relative stagnation of nutrient intakes (fat being the only exception) over the period 1983–2000 within households from the lowest calorie consumption groups (Qadeer & Priyadarshi, 2005). Prevention of obesity, however, appeared as a concern for action (GoI, 2002). The current draft on India's National Health Policy while accepting the importance of nutrition and its implications on people's health leaves the matter of non-medical welfare inputs into health to different departments (GoI, 2014a). It does not even mention the ICDS nor does it articulate clearly the minimum requirement of non-medical inputs. This is a matter of concern as the current debate on nutrition often tends to get diverted from the core challenges of a national food security system, which in today's context is absolutely necessary.

DEBATES: PAST AND PRESENT

The availability of food grains (defined as net output plus imports, minus addition to stocks and minus exports) improved in independent India until the mid-1960s when it stagnated for a while though at a higher level. It again improved from the mid-1970s until the early 1990s when a second phase of stagnation set in followed by a definite decline from 1997 onwards (Patnaik, 2007). The planning process and the professional debates on these trends are interlinked and are briefly highlighted here.

Planning for Food Security

While the first three Five-Year Plans (1951–1956, 1956–1961 and 1961–1966) emphasized land reforms, agricultural development, food production and the emergence of a public distribution system (PDS), the Fourth Five-Year Plan initiated a separate chapter on food and nutrition in 1969. It laid out strategies for equitable distribution, food stocks, price and market regulation, restrictions over exports of food grains and a universal PDS (GoI, 1970). The Fifth Five-Year Plan (1974–1978) introduced the concept of minimum needs along with a long-term strategy of strengthening food security. Special provisioning of food was envisaged through programmes, such as the ICDS and mid-day meals for schoolchildren (GoI, 1976). By the Ninth Five-Year Plan (1997–2002), though the problem of acute and severe under-nutrition reduced, chronic under-nutrition persisted. Assuming that sufficiency of production and per capita availability were adequate indicators of the success of planning, supplementation programmes were initiated to tackle chronic under-nutrition, anaemia (iron and folic acid deficiency), iodine and vitamin A deficiencies. Also, newer problems, such as obesity and non-communicable diseases, especially among the urban middle- and upper-income groups, drew the planner's attention. Over time, the weaknesses of supplementation programmes were dealt with by individualized treatment for specific micronutrient deficiencies, and the responsibility of tackling residual nutritional issues was passed on to the intersectoral cooperation between the departments of health, family welfare, women and child development and education (GoI, 1997).

By the Tenth Five-Year Plan (2002–2007), the way out was seen in limiting PDS through more targeting of the poor, screening, fortification of food rather than supplementation, food processing and individualized/clinical approaches to macro- and micro-nutrient deficiency (GoI, 2002).

Contribution of Nutritionists

In the 1970s when the UN was talking of 'International Action to Avert Impending Protein Crisis' (Sukhatme, 1972) and the need to mobilize resources for the production of protein-rich food to handle it, Sukhatme, the then director of the Food and Agriculture Organization (FAO), on the basis of his analysis of Indian diets, argued that India primarily needed more of its traditional diet based on cereal and pulses. He contended that the very composition of an Indian diet provided an adequate balance of nutrients if taken in sufficient quantities (Sukhatme, 1972). To this was added the special needs of children and the minimum needs of basic calories for adults by the Indian Council of Medical Research (ICMR) (1978). The nutritionists played a key role in working out the cheapest (vegetarian) diet following the logic of feasibility (Shatrugna, 2010). A bare minimum agricultural wage was also calculated in 1982, which was based on inaccurate assumptions of an ideal family size of four, 270–300 days of work in a year, two working members and a wage differential in male and female agricultural workers (Gopalan, 1982).

Over time, instead of food baskets, calories became the basis of the strategy to ensure cheap, basic minimum food to the maximum possible numbers. Evidence of a decline in the level of severe under-nutrition and malnutrition in the initial decades and some lowering of chronic under-nutrition from 1979 to 1997 through the measurements of body mass index (BMI) of adults and the height and weight of children under 6 years of age (Radhakrishna, 2006) from the National Nutrition Monitoring Bureau (NNMB) tended to rationalize the use of the cheapest sources of calories in policymaking. Persistent deficiencies of specific nutrients were then sought to be tackled by experiments with fortification of food with micro-nutrients and food-processing technologies as reflected in the Tenth Five-Year Plan (GoI, 2002).

Shatrugna in her review of the history of nutrition sciences in India holds the nutritionists responsible for the 'close stitching' (Shatrugna, 2010) of nutrition sciences and governmental policies focusing on the cheapest solutions that acted against the interests of the poor. She points to the shift in attention to be applied rather than basic nutritional science, policy imperatives, cultural biases and lack of critical distancing (Shatrugna, 2010).

On the other hand, Gopalan, reviewing the current nutritional scene, sees the success of Indian policy in containing severe forms of malnutrition but accepts the persistence of chronic under-nutrition and laments the isolated focus on wheat and rice that has neglected pulse production and its distribution through the PDS. He is now concerned with the emergence of 10–15 per cent of obesity in rural and urban areas after the 1990s, which he proposes could be an outcome of metabolic disorders arising because of the low birth weights of babies, which are the outcome of maternal under-nutrition in an undernourished population (Gopalan, 2013). These levels of obesity (BMI over 30), however, are doubtful as the National Family Health Survey makes a distinction between overweight and obesity: the former, among women and men, aged between 14 and 49 years, being 10 per cent and 8.5 per cent, respectively, while the latter is 2.8 per cent and 1.3 per cent, respectively (GoI, 2007).

Another concern of Gopalan is the 'hidden hunger' reflected as micro-nutrient deficiencies. These deficiencies, according to him, are critical for growth as well as healthy immune responses of the body. Based on the failures of long-standing programmes (iron and vitamin A supplementation programmes being prime examples), he concedes the limitations of stand-alone supplementation by one or the other micro-nutrients and stresses 'food-based approaches' as there is increasing evidence that micro-nutrients function synergistically within the human body. He locates these shifts in population pressure, increasing urban migration leading to changing dietary patterns (more sugars and oils) and increased mechanization due to which 'lifestyles became more sedentary' (Gopalan, 2013). Yet he has no satisfactory answers for the persistence of chronic hunger in the face of declining population growth rates and impressive economic growth. For Gopalan, obesity and micro-nutrient deficiency are the emerging issues, while chronic under-nutrition is residual.

For Shatrugna, scientists/bureaucrat planners over the years 'discovered the cheapest source of calories that was cereals and expected populations to consume enough (about 450–500 gms) so that they get 2,400 calories; and thus cereals begin to find a central place in discussions on calorie requirements and planning of diets' (Shatrugna, 2010).

Debates among Economists

Meanwhile, economists, too, have been debating the decline in calorie consumption. Patnaik (2007) has shown that the decline in food availability in India over the 1990s was worse than sub-Saharan Africa with the annual per capita availability of food grains coming down to 151 kg in 2001. She argues that reducing the total availability of food grain not only reduces direct consumption of cereals and pulses but also makes the increasing consumption of animal products—milk, meat and eggs—impossible because of the reduction in the availability of animal feed. The declining availability of food grains from the mid-1990s, Patnaik argues, is rooted in impoverishment and lowered purchasing capacity. A direct relationship of income with demand for total food grain and animal feed was also pointed out earlier (Yotopoulos, 1985). Others searched for economic explanations of this 'calorie consumption puzzle', that is, the declining average calorie consumption and rising expenditures (Basu & Basole, 2013; Chandrasekhar & Ghosh, 2003). There are some who have attempted to open up the complexities of nutritional requirements and ecological shifts and argued that the decline in calories over the decades (from 1983–1984 to 2004–2005) was more due to decreased requirements borne out of better health environments and reduced levels of physical activities (Deaton & Dreze, 2009). In the process, they have questioned the logic of declining availability of food grains as the reason behind the decline of calories. They also doubt the standards used for calories and calorie-based nutritional assessments. Their evidence, however, resolves none of the issues raised and the authors themselves end up by accepting that 'nothing we have said justifies downplaying of calorie deficiencies among poor households' (Deaton & Dreze, 2009, p. 60). They set up no new criteria or levels of requirements as standards to measure the proportion of the poor about whom they are concerned and end up rationalizing the official lowering of pre-existing standards. They also argue that 'although the number of calories is important so are other factors, such as, a balanced diet containing reasonable proportions of fruits, vegetables and fats' (Deaton & Dreze, 2009, p. 43). Interestingly, the 'other factors' do not include pulses that actually are an important source of proteins and calories.

The release of the Global Hunger Index (Grebmer et al., 2014) elevated India's ranking from 66 to 55 among the emerging economies of 76 countries. This index is based on three indicators—an insufficiency in the average calorie intake, the prevalence of underweight children and child mortality—and has tended to distract from the nature of food crisis in India where child survival is not synonymous with improved child nutrition (Gopalan, 1987) and where minor nutritional gains mask the extent of food deprivation. The expectation of a positive relationship between the nutritional status of children and demographic indicators (life expectancy and infant and child mortality) induces Panagariya to doubt the malnutrition figures from India (Panagariya, 2013). With the decline of mortality in developing countries with poor services, morbidities may in fact rise (both infectious and nutritional) given the negative relationship between morbidity and nutritional status. Disregarding this, the well-established indicator of 'wasting' (weight deficit for height, irrespective of age) is rejected as 'anomalous' to bring down India's under-nutrition figures. The logic offered is 'A child who is both stunted and underweight could still be classified as free of wasting; likewise, progress in reducing stunting without a corresponding progress in alleviating underweight problems would imply increasing wasting' (Panagariya, 2012). Nutrition, however, is a complex dynamic physiological process not recognizing mutually exclusive statistical categories. A child, both underweight and stunted, is physiologically 'adapted' at a nutritional cost and is, therefore, still undernourished. Wasting, as a result of reduced stunting in the healing process of such a child, will only change his description but not his undernourished status which is determined by biological needs, activity levels, food availability, environmental stresses, etc. Extensive critiques have been presented of this view by several authors (Gupta et al., 2013; Jayachandran & Pande, 2013; Lodha et al., 2013).

These debates within a majority of nutritionists and economists miss the point that the state has failed to make even the most basic foods available for the majority of its population. Indeed, they have influenced policy, sometimes adversely, as far as the interests of the poor are concerned. The poor, however, oblivious of these debates, continue to struggle to survive. They are constantly making choices on the basis of their life experiences. Have policies really pushed them into changing their dietary practices or do they still continue to manage as best as they can within their meagre resources? What practices are reflected in the patterns of food consumption among different groups over time and what lessons can be drawn from those? To explore these questions, this chapter takes forward an earlier analysis of the NSSO data from 1983–1984 to 1999–2000 (Qadeer & Priyadarshi, 2005). The need for this analysis was rooted in the examination of various explanations for the economic 'puzzle' that was given a nutritional hue and the ensuing policy choices then offered. The following sections present our methodology, the emerging trends over the period of study and a discussion of the issue to draw conclusions.

METHODOLOGY

The unit-level data of five large sample Consumption Expenditure Surveys (CES), each covering approximately 100,000–120,000 households, spanning the years from 1993–1994 to 2011–2012 and published by the NSS, have been used for the analysis. From the quantity of 150 individual food items consumed, six broad categories of foods—cereals, pulses, milk, vegetables, edible oils and non-vegetarian foods—were studied.[1] We have done some approximate aggregation for some items. Milk and different milk products were aggregated omitting 'ice cream' and 'other milk products' as only their value in rupees is available and not their consumption quantity. All vegetables, including roots and tubers, were aggregated under vegetables; the only omission is lemon. Eggs, recorded in numbers, have been assumed to weigh 50 g. These household-level consumption quantities have then been divided by household size to get per capita per month (PCPM) consumptions. We have then calculated the proteins, fats and calories derived from foods and added up at the household level to get total household intakes. From these, total levels of calorie, protein and fat intakes per capita per day (PCPD) were derived. Calorie is expressed in kilocalorie (kcal) and protein and fat in grams.

Calories, and allowances, officially recommended for rural areas at two points of time have been used, 2,400 kcal PCPD (GoI, 1979) and 2,200 kcal PCPD (GoI, 2014b). For urban areas, we used 2,100 kcal as the minimum requirement, recommended by both the committees. We have considered the minimum protein requirement of 55 g PCPD of an average female (not pregnant or lactating) as prescribed by the ICMR to be the average cut-off for the whole population. That level of protein intake also comes approximately to 10 per cent of the minimum calorie requirements. We follow the ICMR norm of approximately 48 g of PCPD fat intake (providing 20% of the minimum calorie intake) (ICMR, 2009).

Adjustments, suggested by Sen and Himanshu, were incorporated to compensate for the relative overestimation of consumption data in the 1999–2000 NSS round due to its methodological shift. They point out that the problem of overestimation may have persisted in some of the food items even after adjustments (Sen & Himanshu, 2004a, 2004b). We have analysed time trends through monthly per capita consumption expenditure (MPCE) quintiles (i.e., dividing the sample households into five equal-sized groups from the lowest to the highest MPCE) as well as through calorie intake groups based on different levels of sufficiencies/insufficiencies.

EMERGENT TIME TRENDS

In this section, we examine some time trends, ranging from those of per capita food and nutrient intakes in each of the five MPCE quintiles over the period from 1993–1994 to 2011–2012 of the extent of combined deficiency of calorie and protein, proportion of calories from different nutrients and the expanding proportion of people in low-calorie groups. These trends help us interpret the nature of deprivation suffered by a large majority and the social processes at work.

DECLINING FOOD INTAKE

The last two decades, from 1993–1994 to 2009–2010, witnessed a steady decline in the consumption of cereals, pulses and vegetables but the average consumption of fish/meat/egg (non-vegetarian food) remained almost stagnant. Even in 2011–2012, the consumption levels of non-vegetarian food were as low as 0.43 kg and 0.55 kg PCPM for rural and urban areas, respectively, which in daily calorie terms convert approximately to 16 kcal and 21 kcal, respectively. It was even lower for previous years. While milk intake remained stagnant in rural areas, in urban areas it saw a slight increase during this period. Only the consumption of oil unambiguously increased in both rural and urban areas over the last two decades, where the declining trends of other foods have reversed recently in 2011–2012 in all MPCE quintiles, except the higher quintiles where cereal intake either falls marginally or stagnates (Figures 14.1a and 14.1b).

The average food consumption trends seen through MPCE quintiles in rural areas are striking. All MPCE quintiles show an arrest of the declining cereal consumption post 2009–2010. The lowest three MPCE quintiles in rural areas started with 11.3, 12.9 and 13.6 kg PCPM consumption, respectively, which came down to 10.4, 11.1 and 11.4 kg, respectively, by 2009–2010. At this point, the cereal consumption of the lowest two MPCE quintiles actually fell below the levels recommended in the cheap vegetarian diet prescribed by the ICMR (11.3 kg PCPM).[2] The cereal consumption of the highest two rural quintiles declined from 14–15 kg to 11.8–12 kg PCPM by 2009–2010 and then the decline was arrested in 2011–2012. Pulse consumption was never sufficient (0.96 kg PCPM being the given minimum) over this period except in the highest MPCE quintile. In 2009–2010, the amount of pulses even in this quintile became insufficient. Vegetables were sufficient in 1993–1994 for all quintiles except the lowest but declined significantly in all quintiles subsequently; by 2009–2010, even the highest quintile was consuming less than the minimum levels (3.9 kg PCPM). Milk and edible oil consumptions in rural areas improved over the period but never entered sufficient levels for the three lowest MPCE quintiles. The top two quintiles reveal sufficient milk consumption throughout the period with the highest quintile consuming approximately 1.5 times more than the preceding quintile. For edible oil consumption, the trend was revealing as, though all quintiles show improvement in consumptions, none enter sufficiency levels ever.

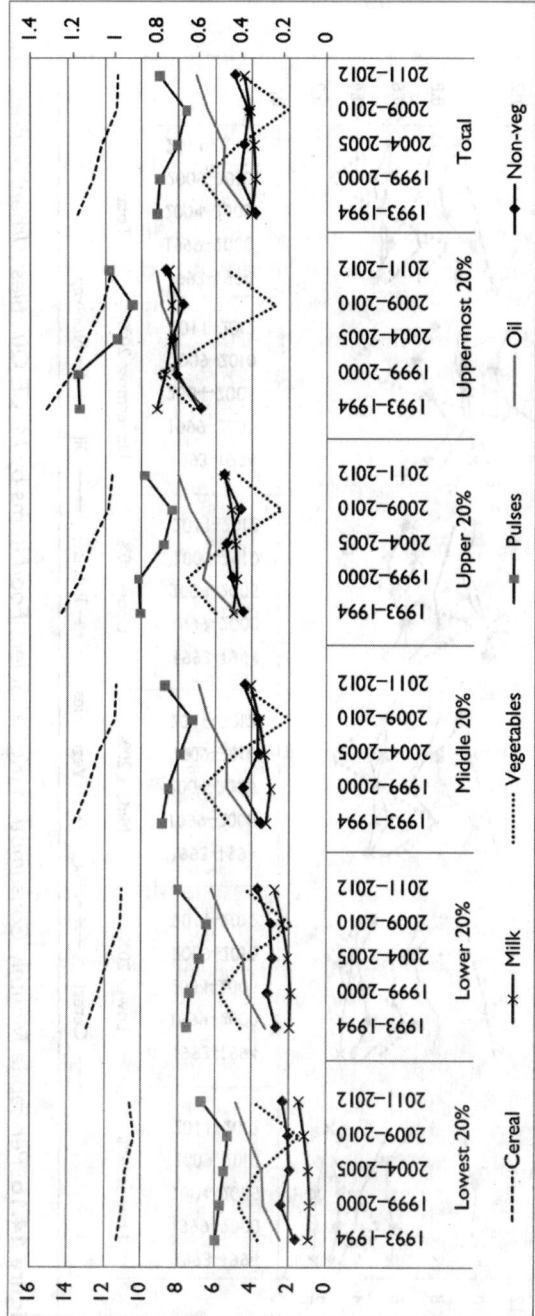

Figure 14.1a *Per-capita Monthly Consumption (Kg) of Select Food Items by MPCE Quintiles (Rural) [Pulses, Oil and Non-veg Are Measured in Secondary Axis]*

Source: Authors' calculation from unit-level data, NSSO various rounds.

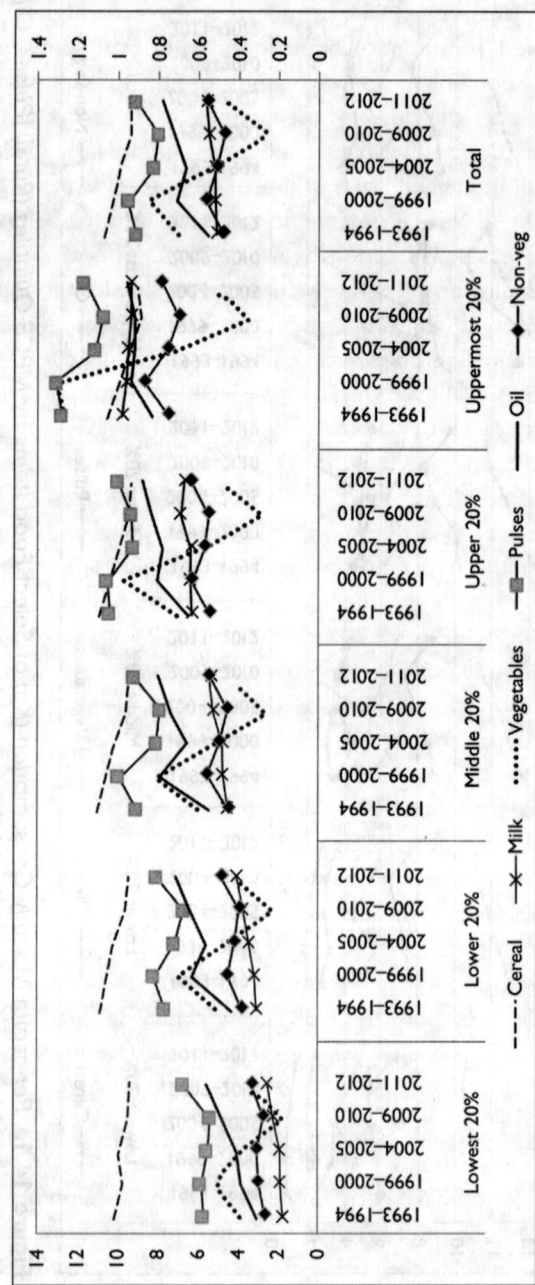

Figure 14.1b *Per-capita Monthly Consumption (Kg) of Select Food Items by MPCE Quintiles (Urban) [Pulses, Oil and Non-veg Are Measured in Secondary Axis]*

Source: Authors' calculation from unit-level data, NSSO various rounds.

In urban areas, as we move up from lower to higher MPCE quintiles, cereal consumption initially increases over some quintiles and then declines. For the first two points of time in our analysis, this decline starts after the third lowest quintile, while in the next three points of time it came after the second lowest quintile itself. The peak cereal consumption achieved by the five quintiles was never beyond 11 kg PCPM. All MPCE quintiles in the urban area fell below 10 kg PCPM of cereal consumption by 2009–2010. This is a matter of concern especially for the poorer sections given their low consumption levels of other food items. In terms of time trends, pulse consumption in the lowest three quintiles declined from a range of 0.57–0.91 kg to 0.54–0.79 kg PCPM by 2009–2010. Vegetable consumption declined from sufficient levels to below sufficiency for all MPCE groups. Milk consumption has increased in the lowest four quintiles over the period entering sufficiency except for the lowest quintile. The highest quintile in the initial year was consuming 1.5 times more milk than the preceding quintile: over time, this group showed a slight decline staying well above sufficiency. Edible oil consumption has increased over the period but only the highest quintile entered sufficiency levels by 2009–2010. These trends reveal that a large number of people were eating less than recommended quantities of food.

There is a sharp shift in the trends observed above in both rural and urban areas in 2011–2012. The decline in cereal consumption was arrested, while that of pulses and vegetables reversed. The consumption of milk increased in all MPCE quintiles (except in the topmost MPCE quintile in rural areas and top two quintiles in the urban areas). Consumption of non-vegetarian food items increased for all MPCE quintiles and that of oil continued its upward trend.

Translating the dietetic pattern into nutrient intake, we take our analysis further to understand dietetic sufficiency and balance as well as the patterns of shifts in different sets of populations.

Implications of Trends in Food Intake for Levels of Nutrients

It is evident from the data that visible increase in food consumption in 2011–2012 still does not give the majority food adequacy. A balance in diet requires that around 60–70 per cent of calories come from carbohydrates, 10–15 per cent from proteins and 20–30 per cent from fats. The decade of the 1980s saw stagnation in intake of both calories and proteins (Qadeer & Priyadarshi, 2005), but, in the next phase, starting from 1993–1994 to 2009–2010, both calorie and protein intakes fell steadily until 2009–2010. Again a turnaround came in 2011–2012 when intakes of both increased from their previous levels. While the decline in protein intake from 1993–1994 to 2009–2010 is evident in all the MPCE quintiles, it is relatively sharper in the higher quintiles. The lowest quintile did not show any decline in calorie intake, while the rest show gradually increasing declines. This, more than anything else, shows that there is an increasing compulsion to not let consumption go below a certain level as we move from higher to lower quintiles. This matches the trend of cereal intake as the poor depend on it to maintain their minimal calorie levels. In terms of trends alone, the intake of total fat over all these years increased steadily across quintile groups; however, all except for the highest quintile continued to remain below the minimum recommended levels (of 2,200 kcal PCPD) in rural areas, whereas in urban areas, the third lowest MPCE quintile entered sufficiency level (of 2,100 kcal PCPD) only in 2009–2010 (Figure 14.2).

Trends of Overlap in Protein and Calorie Insufficiency

An analysis of 10 exhaustive and mutually exclusive categories of calorie–protein insufficiencies (Table 14.1) shows that from 1993–1994 to 2009–2010, the percentage of population with severe calorie insufficiency (less than 1,800 kcal PCPD) along with protein insufficiency (less than 55 g PCPD) increased to cover more than one-third of the population in 2009–2010 and came down only in 2011–2012 (Table 14.1).

The percentage of people with different degrees of calorie and protein insufficiency (taking all three groups under 2,200 kcal, along with protein intake of less than 55 gm, per day) has increased over time in the last two decades to reach 56.0 per cent and 58.4 per cent in rural and urban areas, respectively, before declining in 2011–2012. On the other hand, the percentage of people with only calorie insufficiency or those with only protein insufficiency is small. Pure calorie insufficiency

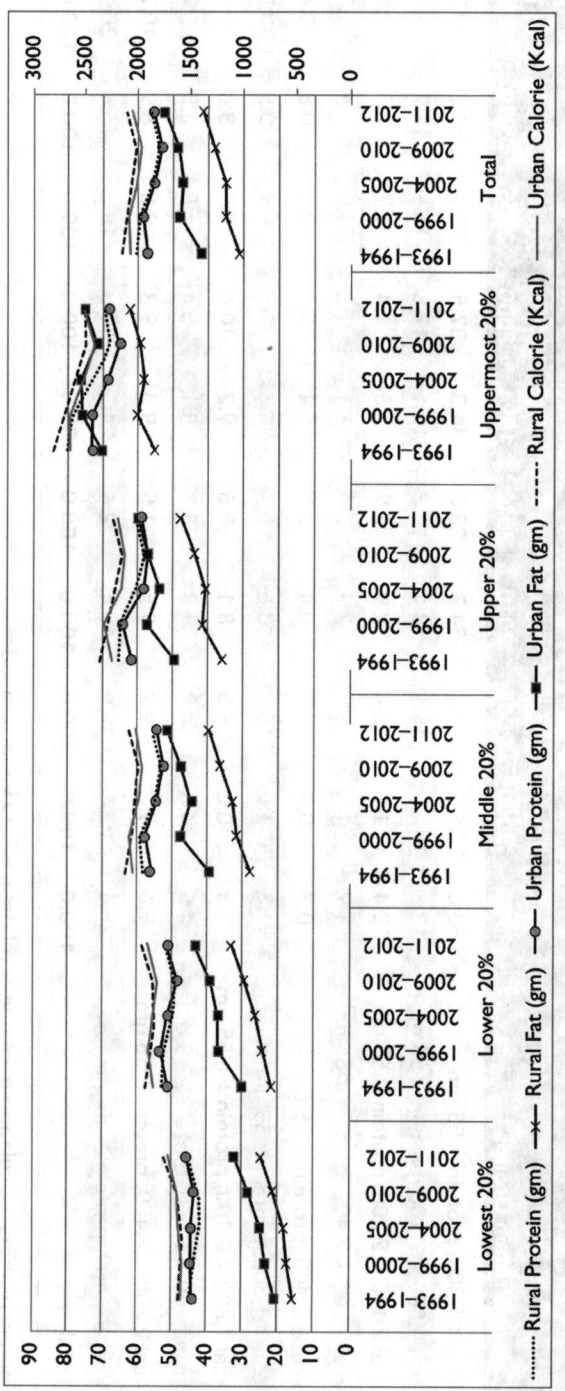

Figure 14.2 Per-day Per-capita Consumption of Key Nutreints by MPCE Quintiles [Calories Measured in Secondary Axis]

Source: Authors' calculation from unit-level data, NSSO various rounds.

Rural Protein (gm) ····· Rural Fat (gm) ✕ Urban Protein (gm) ■ Urban Fat (gm) ● Rural Fat (gm) ● Rural Calorie (Kcal) ----- Urban Calorie (Kcal)

Table 14.1 *Distribution of Combined Calorie–Protein Deficient Groups*

Calorie Protein Groups	Rural					Urban				
	1993–1994	1999–2000	2004–2005	2009–2010	2011–2012	1993–1994	1999–2000	2004–2005	2009–2010	2011–2012
kcal < 1,800, protein < 55 gm	30.0	35.3	35.8	34.7	28.0	34.3	37.5	37.2	38.2	32.3
kcal 1,800 < 2 100, protein < 55 gm	12.3	12.6	15.1	18.4	18.2	13.1	12.8	15.9	17.9	17.2
kcal 2,100 < 2,200, protein < 55 gm	2.4	1.9	2.4	2.9	2.9	1.8	1.4	1.7	2.2	2.1
kcal 2,200 < 2,400, protein < 55 gm	1.9	1.6	2.0	2.3	2.4	1.1	1.2	1.2	1.4	1.5
kcal ≥ 2,400, protein < 55 gm	0.3	0.3	0.3	0.4	0.3	0.4	0.4	0.4	0.8	0.6
kcal < 1,800, protein ≥ 55 gm	1.3	1.6	0.9	0.6	0.4	1.3	1.7	0.9	0.5	0.5
kcal 1,800 < 2,100, protein >= 55 gm	9.3	10.2	9.5	8.1	8.6	9.2	10.6	9.9	8.8	9.3
kcal 2,100 < 2,200, protein ≥ 55 gm	4.5	4.8	4.9	4.8	5.3	5.1	5.4	4.8	4.5	5.7
kcal 2,200 < 2,400, protein ≥ 55 gm	9.6	9.2	9.2	9.5	11.5	9.5	9.3	9.8	8.9	10.7
Kcal ≥ 2,400, protein ≥ 55 gm	28.4	22.5	19.9	18.4	22.4	24.3	19.8	18.2	16.8	20.1
Total	100.0	100.0	100.0	100.0	100.0	100.0	100.0	100.0	100.0	100.0

Source: Authors' calculation from unit-level data, NSSO various rounds.

remained approximately 13–17 per cent and pure protein insufficiency did not exceed 4.5 per cent in both rural and urban areas over the period. And here too, those who may be protein sufficient in diets may end up with protein deficiency as they burn it to get their calories (Figure 14.3). These overlaps show a close link between calorie and protein insufficiency that is embedded in the availability of food and prevailing dietetic practices. We explore this relationship in the next section.

Trends in Dietetic Balance: Proportion of Calories Derived from Nutrients

From 1993–1994 to 2011–2012, for all MPCE groups in both rural and urban areas, the percentage of calories from protein intake has remained at approximately 11 per cent, while that from fat is steadily rising, from an average of 18 per cent to 22 per cent in urban and from 13 per cent to 18 per cent in rural areas. In rural areas, the consumption levels of fat that provide the required minimum share of calories from fat have never been reached in this period except in 2011–2012 when the topmost quintile touched this level. In urban areas, even the second lowest MPCE quintile entered this level in 2011–2012 (Figure 14.4).

First, these trends prove that people do their best to achieve balance in their diets if they have access to food. This is clear from the fact that (a) as we move from the lower to higher MPCE quintiles, not only does the calorie intake increase (Figure 14.2) but so does the consumption of high-value food items, such as pulses, milk and non-vegetarian food (Figures 14.1a and 14.1b) and (b) peoples' diets maintain a proportion of protein which is balanced and constant across all MPCE quintiles over the period of study (Figure 14.4). Second, even the lowest three MPCE quintiles, whose diets are primarily based on a higher proportion of carbohydrates (mostly cereals) to give them their calories (72–82% in rural areas and 68–77% in urban areas), maintain a relatively balanced proportion of calories from proteins. Hence, the challenge is to ensure access to basic food and ensure conditions through which they could add vegetables, milk, fish, meat and fruits as choices—as done by the higher quintiles.

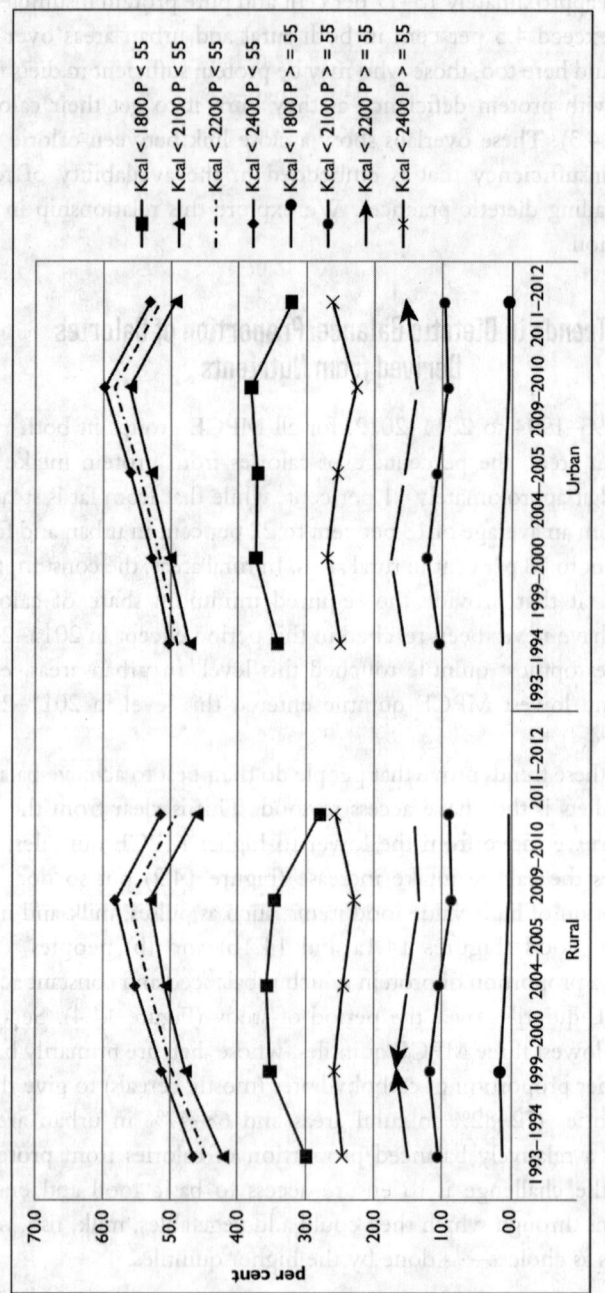

Figure 14.3 Percentage of Persons by Type of Combined Calorie-Protein Deficiency Groups, Rural and Urban All India

Source: Authors' calculation from unit-level data, NSSO various rounds.

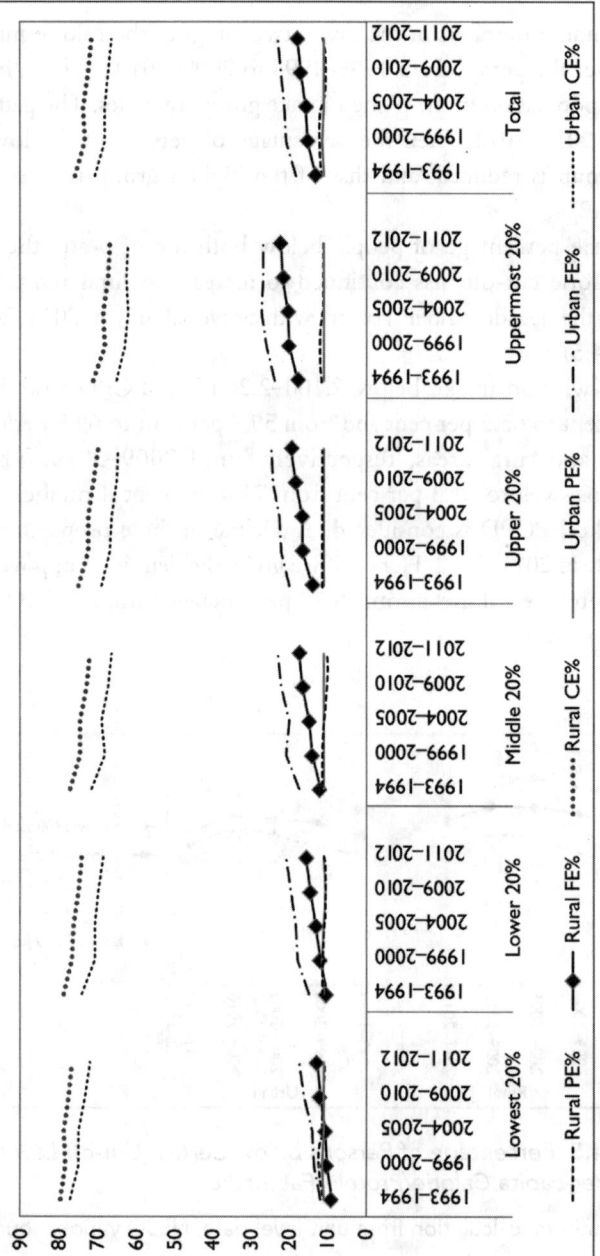

Figure 14.4 *Percentage of Energy/Calorie Contributed by Protein, Fat & Carbohydrate over Time by MPCE Quintiles*

Source: Authors' calculation from unit-level data, NSSO various rounds.

Expanding Population with Low-calorie Intakes

The expanding numbers in the lower two rungs of the calorie intake groups over the period from 1993–1994 to 2009–2010 are significant while the population in the highest intake group dwindles. The pattern breaks in 2011–2012 when the percentage of persons in the lowest calorie group is reduced, and that of the highest group is increased (Table 14.2).

Also, the percentage of people below both the new and the old official calorie cut-offs has continued to increase in rural and urban areas over the decades under scrutiny with a reversal only in 2011–2012 (Figure 14.5).

Those with an intake below 2,100–2,200 kcal PCPD rose from 57.9 per cent to 65.5 per cent and from 59.9 per cent to 69.5 per cent in urban and rural areas, respectively, until 2009–2010. These populations swell to 81.3 per cent from 71.4 per cent if rural cut-off of 2,400 kcal PCPD is considered. A decline in these proportions is visible only in 2011–2012. Hence, if we go by the definition of poverty, according to the calorie norm, these percentages surpass the official poverty levels.

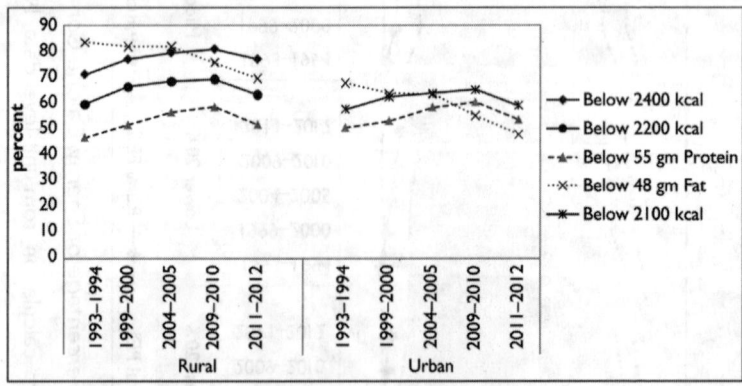

Figure 14.5 *Percentage of Persons below Certain Cut-off Levels of Per-day Per-capita Calorie/Protein/Fat Intake*

Source: Authors' calculation from unit-level data, NSSO various rounds.

Table 14.2 Percentage of Persons by Per Capita Per-day Calorie Intake Groups, All India

Calorie Groups (kcal)	Rural					Urban				
	1993–1994	1999–2000	2004–2005	2009–2010	2011–2012	1993–1994	1999–2000	2004–2005	2009–2010	2011–2012
0 < 1800	31.3	36.9	36.7	35.3	28.4	35.6	39.2	38.1	38.8	32.79
1,800 < 2,100	21.6	22.8	24.6	26.5	26.8	22.3	23.4	25.8	26.7	26.49
2,100 < 2,200	6.9	6.8	7.3	7.7	8.2	6.9	6.8	6.5	6.8	8
2,200 < 2,400	11.6	10.7	11.2	11.8	13.9	10.6	10.5	10.4	10.3	12.17
2,400 and above	28.7	22.8	20.2	18.8	22.8	24.7	20.2	16.6	17.5	20.7
Total	100.0	100.0	100.0	100.0	100.0	100.0	100.0	100.0	100.0	100

Source: Authors' calculation from unit-level data, NSSO various rounds.

DISCUSSION

Our analysis highlights the association between the declines in cereal intake over time with the decline of pulse and vegetable intake and the direct implication for declining calories, proteins and other nutrients, except oils. These findings along with the strong positive relationship between the total calorie intake and the consumption of high-valued foods reiterate that calorie intake can be an adequate thumb rule for policy framers to ensure sufficiency of food consumption and also quality of diet in our given context.

As far as time trends are concerned, the percentage of people below minimum calorie and protein cut-offs continued to increase from 1993–1994 to 2009–2010, and then came down in 2011–2012. On the contrary, those below the minimum cut-off of total fat intake have steadily declined and yet the deprivation levels remain quite high—70 per cent in the rural and 48 per cent in the urban population—as of 2011–2012 (Figure 14.5).

The high correlation between calorie intake and both proteins and high-value foods, taken with increasing percentage of people falling below the minimum calorie cut-offs, strongly indicates increasing food deprivation—the root cause of persisting under-nutrition. The highest MPCE quintiles remain an exception as the calorie intake never comes below the recommended levels. Any reluctance in accepting this interpretation can be set aside by examining the vulnerability of people in different MPCE groups by looking at the percentage of population with less than the required calorie intake (Figure 14.6).

The differential shifts speak for themselves. The lowest three MPCE quintiles do not only have a very high proportion of calorie-deprived people but also continue to show their increase until 2009–2010, more so in rural than in urban areas. It is interesting to note that while the rise in the calorie-deprived population is comparatively less among the lower quintiles (because these are already loaded with the deprived), even the highest and second-highest quintiles show a rise of the calorie-deprived by 13 and 15 percentage points. This indicates a situation of compulsive dietetic shifts even among people who were earlier getting sufficient calories.

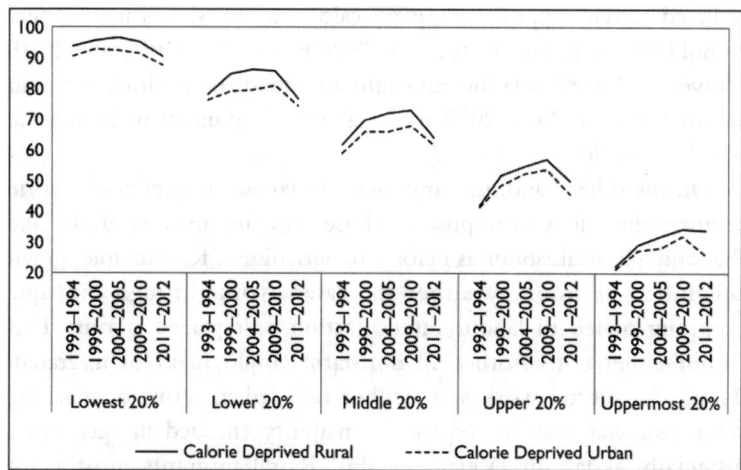

Figure 14.6 *Percentage of Calorie Defficient Persons by MPCE Quintiles*

Source: Authors' calculation from unit-level data, NSSO various rounds.

De-emphasizing the seriousness of low consumption levels and focusing on factors other than availability and access, we have three alternative explanations as already mentioned in the introduction: (a) reduction in calorie requirement due to a reduction of physical activity and increased mechanization, (b) improvement in health environment and basic facilities, such as better access to clean drinking water and sanitation leading to better absorption, and hence less wastage—all resulting in a lower requirement of intake and (c) diversification of diet leading to people choosing costlier sources of calories. We examine these arguments individually.

'Reduced' Requirements of Calories

If the argument of a reduction in calorie requirement via a reduction of physical activity, due to an increased use of technology, is valid, then this contention should apply to all sections that have benefitted from technological improvements. While sedentary lifestyles and reduced activity appear to explain calorie declines, this may appear to hold true only for our topmost MPCE quintiles until 2009–2010. However, this explanation runs into a contradiction with the rise in calorie intake in 2011–2012 across all MPCE quintiles including the highest quintile.

On the other hand, this argument, in favour of a reduced calorie requirement, does not apply to those who in any case undertake the same physical labour as before. In agriculture, for example, green revolution technology either increased work through multiple cropping or led to labour intensification or replaced labour. This labour either got absorbed in non-farm employment or migrated. Thus, agricultural work was neither reduced in terms of working hours nor was it lightened for the majority engaged in agriculture especially as labour (Verma, 2005). Rural migrants mostly got absorbed in the expanding unorganized sectors such as construction, the unorganized manufacturing, trade, hoteliering, transport and the service sectors (Bhalla, 2003). It is well known that the working conditions of this 'footloose labour' (Breman, 2013), the hours of work, etc., remain harsh (Hariss-White & Gooptu, 2001). Any lowering of activity, if at all, is limited to the service sector professionals— the IT sector, bureaucracy and politicians who largely fall in the top MPCE quintiles.

Our data demonstrate that even the second lowest MPCE quintile shows a reduction of calorie intake during the period 1993–1994 and 2009–2010 by 60 and 40 kcal PCPD for rural and urban areas, respectively, from the initial levels of only 1,912 and 1,849 kcal. We would like to underline the fact that these initial levels were far below the new reduced norms of calorie adequacy, yet they declined further. The persistence of low intakes—less than 1,800 kcal PCPD in one-third of the population; 63 per cent and 59 per cent of the population consuming less than 2,200 and 2,100 kcal PCPD in rural and urban areas, respectively, and the expansion of underfed groups— across all MPCE quintiles—reflects the seriousness of the problem. It appears as if the listlessness/inactivity of the chronically hungry and unemployed is being mistaken for the reduced activity of the fully employed. However, by no stretch of the imagination does this decline in intakes reflects decreasing calorie requirements.

Improved Environment

It is indeed historically true that with an improved environment (water sanitation, housing and health services), the prevalence of disease, especially infectious morbidities, comes down and the nutritional status of populations improves (McKeown, 2009). Environment shifts, if significant, do reduce morbidities and excess calorie requirements, thus improving the absorption and assimilation of nutrients leading to a better nutritional status. To argue that this has happened in India, to the extent that morbidity levels have come down, however, has problems. We underline the well-accepted epidemiological pattern that where mortalities come down, initially morbidity increases (Panikkar & Soman, 1984) and that with lagging health services and epidemiological transition, a new set of diseases leads to a double burden of disease (GoI, 2011). The health surveys of the NSSO show that the prevalence of morbidity in India has increased significantly between 1995–1996 and 2003–2004 (Arokiasamy & Yadav, 2014). Second, to believe that an improved health environment lowers morbidity and hence calorie requirements is in itself wrong as the standard requirements for nutrients are set for healthy human beings and not diseased populations which, in fact, requires factoring in their additional calorie requirements. To say, therefore, that an improved disease status has further lowered requirements in India is incorrect.

'Diversification' of Diet

Dietary diversification means meeting required nutritional levels sourced from a variety of food items over a period of time. Diversity, however, is but one component of overall dietary goals and may not, in itself, ensure the achievement of all other goals, such as calorie sufficiency, nutrient adequacy and dietary quality which includes all these and more (concentration of nutrients, adequate roughage, etc.). Diversity thus does not necessarily mean quality even though it is so assumed. It may in fact be acquired from an undesirable variety of foods and may be there even when the total calories consumed are inadequate, depending upon easy availability, prices of food and cultural dietetic patterns. It is considered to be the key to ensure micro-nutrients and is greatly emphasized for poor countries assuming that the diets there are based on starchy cereals. Measurement of diversity varies from simple methods of counting food items to more exacting ones such as the number of helpings of specific items (dietary scores) or developing scores for number of servings of specific foods, service scores—ideally over 3 days. Such studies, in fact, showed a direct relationship between dietary diversification and nutrient adequacy (Ruel, 2002).

Diversification is also measured through a food diversification index (FDI). It is argued that increasing diversification reflected by FDI can explain declines in calories (Gaiha et al., 2013). This index, however, is based on *relative* proportions of different food items/food groups or the share of expenditure on these foods. Other than diversity, it does not reflect absolute quantities and, therefore, adequacy or any other quality of diet. A rising index of diversification, if confused with the quality of diet, creates a false impression.

Diversification with high-quality foods (with high nutrient concentration) may reduce the total quantity of food intake but it does not reduce total calorie consumption. Thus, increasing diversification neither unequivocally indicates nor explains the decline of total calorie consumption. Our analysis shows that though the quantities people take in different MPCE quintiles vary markedly, given the six groups of foods we have examined, all MPCE categories consume them; hence, it appears that diversification in terms of the variety of food groups has not increased markedly, though there may be diversification within each food group.

The real issue underlining the trend of calorie decline thus remains the quantities of intake. The steady decline (between 1993–1994 and 2009–2010) in the consumption of cereals, pulses and vegetables, the stagnating consumption of milk and fish/meat and the increasing deprivation of both calories and protein intakes when taken together point out that for the majority of the population, there was an overall decline in food consumption. This limits the possibilities of diversification of diet. On the other hand, it will be pertinent to note that in the past, around the 1970s and 1980s, we have seen the beginning of diversification of diet along with an increase in quantities when the reduction in cereal consumption was accompanied by non-cereal consumption on a wide scale, which led to an increase in per capita calorie consumption as well (Radhakrishna, 2006).

Contemplating the possibility that there may have been a squeeze in the food budget due to the increasing cost of meeting minimum non-food requirements, Sen (2005) opines that even with the lower share of food expenditure, the calorie-deprived households could have opted within their current food budget for cheaper sources of calorie, like their poorer counterparts, and fulfilled the required calorie gap, if they had wished to do so. In other words, he expects people to be guided by calorie norms and buy more cereals rather than buying other groups of foods. He misses the fact that in India, pulses, vegetables, fish/meat/eggs and some milk products to some extent act as compliments to cereals and not as their substitutes. This is exactly what our data show.

Such technical perspectives to the dietary practices of people who do not eat calories but food within their given cultural context have added to the obfuscation of the real issue of availability and access. We argue that neither by hiding behind inadequate explanations of calorie decline, blaming people for not achieving sufficiency in calories through cheaper diets and attempting some balance in it nor by harping about the need for enhancing diversification can we take our understanding forward. One needs to recognize two things: the capacity of people to improve their diets, if given a chance, and the challenges of building food security and addressing the real issues of production of food grains and pulses versus cash crops, which would enhance the purchasing capacity of the majority by paying attention to ensuring minimum wages, controlling food prices, distribution systems and programmes for protection of the vulnerable.

IMPLICATIONS FOR POLICY

Persistence on non-availability of food and high levels of under-nourishment despite rising expenditure on food and non-food items when seen through the trends in development expenditure underlines the role that the state plays. The decline in food intake with an increasing undernourished population over the decades under study matches the period of decline followed by stagnation in development

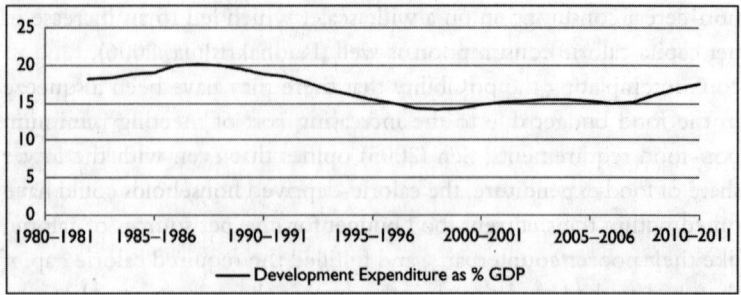

Figure 14.7 *Trends in Development Expenditure as Percentage of GDP (3-year Lagged Average)*

Source: Authors' calculation from (a) Handbook of Statistics on State Government Finances, Reserve Bank of India and (b) Central Statistical Organisation.

expenditure[3] as a proportion to gross domestic product (GDP). It begins to rise only around 2007–2008 (Figure 14.7) and is associated with the later reversal of declining food consumption trends in 2011–2012.

The importance of crucial welfare programmes cannot be ignored in the context of the latest revival of food consumption. The initiation of rural employment guarantee scheme, though far from playing its role to the desired extent, may have given some buffer to rural poor. Evidence has started trickling in of its positive impact on infant and maternal nutrition (Dev, 2011; Nair et al., 2013). In the context of high rural-to-urban migration rates, with the migrant urban labour having familial ties in rural areas, such rural welfare schemes have positive effects on urban areas as well. Other important components of the welfare system, such as the Food Corporation of India (FCI) and PDS, are also threatened as the new Expert Committee is advocating dismantling of the PDS. The PDS, even in its truncated, 'targeted' form as compared to the previous 'universal' form has improved in efficiency since mid-2000 (Basu & Das, 2015). While the National Rural Employment Guarantee Scheme is showing signs of getting weakened with expenditure cuts, the latest Land Acquisition Act is further undermining people's control over food security. The Rehabilitation and Resettlement Act, 2013, remains unimplemented and the Mid-day Meal Scheme is suffering with expenditure cuts. The Draft National

Health Policy document is simultaneously pushing privatization of medical care, undermining comprehensive *primary health care*, and its complete silence on the ICDS is yet another indication of the state's lack of concern about vulnerable populations. If this policy direction continues, then the 2011–2012 food consumption revival may only be short-lived. These policy shifts are dangerous and do not auger well for the dream of inclusive development as the basis for a strong and democratic India.

ACKNOWLEDGEMENT

The authors would like to acknowledge the financial and institutional support provided by the Council for Social Development for carrying out the research for this chapter.

NOTES

1. While considered for calorie and nutrient calculations, we excluded the consumption of fruits, nuts, beverages, sugars and eating out from our analysis of different food categories as we were interested in key food items. Eating out is recorded in monetary terms only and hence quantity analysis is not possible.
2. A typical Indian vegetarian diet providing 2,223 kcal and 55 g of protein (nutrient level being close to rural minimum norms if we consider the new lower norm of 2,200 kcal PCPD) would consist of 375 g of cereal, 32 g of pulses, 32 g of visible fat (oil), 130 g of vegetables and roots/tubers and 120 g of milk and milk products (ICMR, 2009, p. 113). We have simply adjusted by a factor of 2,100/2,200, the numerator being urban minimum calorie norm and the denominator being the rural one, to get the urban quantities that correspond to 2,100 kcal.
3. Developmental expenditure of the government comprises expenditure on various social and economic schemes and programmes in sectors such as education, health, nutrition, social security, agriculture and rural and urban development.

REFERENCES

Arokiasamy, P., & Yadav, S. (2014). Changing age patterns of morbidity *vis-à-vis* mortality in India. *Journal of Biosocial Science, 46*(4), 462–479.

Basu, D., & Basole, A. (2013). *An empirical investigation of the calorie consumption puzzle in India* (Working Paper No. 3). Department of Economics, University of Massachusetts.

Basu, D., & Das, D. (2015). A flawed approach to food security. *The Hindu*. http://www.thehindu.com/opinion/op-ed/commenta-flawed-approach-to-food-security/article6902377.ece

Bhalla, S. (2003). *The restructuring of the unorganised sector in India* (Report on a project funded under the Planning Commission Scheme of Socio-Economic Research). Institute for Human Development.

Breman, J. (2013). *At work in the informal economy of India: A perspective from the bottom up*. Oxford University Press.

Brookover, A. (n.d.). What is the definition of nutrition? *Health Guidance*. http://www.healthguidance.org/entry/9975/1/What-Is-the-Definition-of-Nutrition.html

Chandrasekhar, C. P., & Ghosh, J. (2003). The calorie consumption puzzle. *The Hindu Business Line*.

Deaton, A., & Dreze, J. (2009). Food and nutrition in India: Facts and interpretations. *Economic & Political Weekly, 44*(7), 42–65.

Dev, S. M. (2011). *NREGS and child well being* (Working Paper No. 4). Indira Gandhi Institute of Development Research. www.igidr.ac.in/pdf/publication/WP-2011-004.pdf

Gaiha, R., Kaicker, N., Imai, K., Kulkarni, V. S., & Thapa, G. (2013). *Has dietary transition slowed in India? An analysis based on the 50th, 61st and 66th rounds of the National Sample Survey*. International Fund for Agricultural Development.

Gopalan, C. (1982). *Minimum wage for agricultural labour* (NFI Bulletin). Bulletin of the Nutrition Foundation of India.

Gopalan, C. (1987). Combating under-nutrition: Basic issues and practical approaches. In C. Gopalan (Ed.), *Collection of papers from bulletin of NFI from 1980–1987* (pp. 80–88). National Foundation of India (Special Publication Series).

Gopalan, C. (2013). The changing nutrition scenario. *Indian Journal of Medical Research, 138*(3), 392–397.

Government of India (GoI). (1970). *The Fourth Five-Year Plan of India*. Planning Commission. http://planningcommission.nic.in/plans/planrel/fiveyr/4th/4planch10.html

Government of India (GoI). (1976). *The Fifth Five-Year Plan 1974–79*. Planning Commission.

Government of India (GoI). (1979). *Report of the task force on projections of minimum needs and effective consumption demands*. Planning Commission.

Government of India (GoI). (1993). *National nutrition policy*. Department of Women & Child Development, Ministry of Human Resource Development.

Government of India (GoI). (1997). *The 9th Five-Year Plan 1997–2002*. Planning Commission. http://planningcommission.nic.in/plans/planrel/fiveyr/9th/vol2/v2c4-3.htm

Government of India (GoI). (2002). *Tenth Five-Year Plan 2002–2007* (Vol. 2). Planning Commission. http://planningcommission.nic.in/plans/planrel/fiveyr/10th/volume2/v2_ch3_3.pdf

Government of India (GoI). (2007). *National Family Health Survey (NFHS) III (2005–2006)* (Vol. I, pp. 304, 307, Table Nos: 10.22.1 &10.22.2). Indian Institute of Population Sciences and Ministry of Health and Family Welfare.

Government of India (GoI). (2011). *Report of the working group on disease burden for the Twelfth Five-Year Plan.* Planning Commission.

Government of India (GoI). (2014a). *National Health Policy (2014, draft).* Ministry of Health & Family Welfare. http://www.mohfw.nic.in/showfile.php?lid=3014

Government of India (GoI). (2014b). *Report of the expert group to review the methodology for the measurement of poverty.* Planning Commission.

Grebmer, K. V., Saltzman, A., Birol, E., Wiesmann, D., Prasai, N., Yin, S., Yohannes, Y., & Menon, P. (2014). *Global hunger index: The challenge of hidden hunger.* International Food Policy Research Institute.

Gupta, A., Patnaik, B., Singh, D., Sinha, D., Holla, R., Srivatsan, R., Jain, S., Garg, S., Dand, S., Nandi, S., Prasad, V., & Shatrugna, V. (2013). Are child malnutrition figures for India exaggerated? *Economic & Political Weekly, 48*(34), 73–77.

Hariss-White, B., & Gooptu, N. (2001). Mapping India's world of unorganised labour. *Socialist Register, 37,* 89–118. http://socialistregister.com/index.php/srv/article/view/5757/2653#.Vl2Mm9KrRdg

Indian Council of Medical Research (ICMR). (1978). *Recommended dietary intakes for Indians* (Report of an Expert Group). ICMR.

Indian Council of Medical Research (ICMR). (2009). *Nutrient requirements and recommended dietary allowances for Indians.* ICMR.

Jayachandran, S., & Pande, R. (2013). Choice not genes: Probable cause for the India-Africa child height gap. *Economic & Political Weekly, 48*(34), 77–79.

Lodha, R., Jain, Y., & Sathyamala, C. (2013). Reality of higher malnutrition among Indian children. *Economic & Political Weekly, 48*(34), 70–73.

McKeown, R. E. (2009). The epidemiologic transition: Changing patterns of mortality and population dynamics. *American Journal of Lifestyle Medicine, 3*(1 Suppl.), 19–26.

Nair, M., Ariana, P., Ohuma, E. O., Gray, R., De Stavola, B., & Webster, P. (2013). Effects of the Mahatma Gandhi National Rural Employment Guarantee Act (MGNREGA) on malnutrition of infants in Rajasthan, India: A mixed methods study. *Plos One.*doi:10.1371/journal.pone.0075089

Panagariya, A. (2012). *The myth of child nutrition in India* (Presented at a conference on India: Reforms, economic transformation and socially disadvantaged, Columbia University, 20–22 September).

Panagariya, A. (2013). Does India really suffer from worse child malnutrition than sub-Saharan Africa? *Economic & Political Weekly, 48*(18), 98–111.

Panikkar, P. G. K., & Soman, C. R. (1984). *Health status of Kerala.* Centre for Development Studies.

Patnaik, U. (2007). *The republic of hunger.* Three Essays Collective.

Qadeer, I., & Priyadarshi, A. P. (2005). Nutrition policy: Shifts and logical fallacies. *Economic & Political Weekly, 40*(5), 358–364.

Radhakrishna, R. (2006). *Food consumption and nutritional status in India: Emerging trends and perspectives.* Indira Gandhi Institute of Development Research. www.igidr.ac.in/pdf/publication/WP-2006-008.pdf

Ruel, M. T. (2002). *Is dietary diversity an indicator of food security or dietary quality? A review of measurement issues and research needs.* International Food Policy Research Institute.

Sen, A., & Himanshu. (2004a). Poverty and inequality in India: I. *Economic & Political Weekly, 39*(38), 4247–4263.

Sen, A., & Himanshu. (2004b). Poverty and inequality in India: II: Widening disparities during the 1990s. *Economic & Political Weekly, 39*(39), 4361–4375.

Sen, P. (2005). Of calories and other things: Reflections on nutritional norms, poverty lines and consumption behaviour in India. *Economic & Political Weekly, 40*(43), 4611–4618.

Shatrugna, V. (2010). The career of hunger: Critical reflections on the history of nutrition science and policy. In A. Zachariah, R. Srivatsan, & S. Tharu (Eds.), *Towards a critical medical practice reflections on the dilemma of medical culture today.* Orient BlackSwan.

Sukhatme, P. V. (1972). India and the protein problem. *Ecology of Food and Nutrition, 1*(4), 267–278.

Verma, S. R. (2005). Impact of agricultural mechanisation on production, productivity, cropping intensity income generation and employment of labour. In K. Tyagi, H. Bathla, & S. Sharma (Eds.), *Status of farm mechanisation in India* (pp. 133–153). Indian Agricultural Statistics Research Institute.

Yotopoulos, P. A. (1985). Middle-income classes and food crisis: The 'new' food-feed competition. *Economic Development and Cultural Change, 33*(3), 463–483.

Chapter 15

Food Security Eludes Tribals of Andhra Pradesh*

K. Radhakrishna Murty

STATEMENT OF THE PROBLEM

Talking about the meaning of the right to food, the International Covenant on Economic, Social and Cultural Rights says that the right to adequate food is realized when every man, woman and child has physical and economic access to adequate food at all times or means for its procurement. A society is said to be food secure when there is access to adequate food for all thus enabling them to lead active and healthy lives. Food security can be assured by a regular supply of food where required, that is, physical access to food and adequate individual purchasing power, that is, economic access to food. Lack of either of these two factors results in food insecurity. In the welfare framework within which Indian democracy works, the state is responsible for ensuring food security to all citizens. Improving food security at the household level is an issue of considerable importance for a developing country like India where millions of people suffer from hunger and malnutrition. It is now widely recognized that food security is not only linked to quality food production but also, more importantly, to the ability of people to access food and utilize effectively so as to lead a healthy life. It is imperative to also recognize that nutrition security is an important dimension of food security.

* *Social Change* 48, no. 2 (June 2018): 208–221.

India has the world's largest officially supported food and nutrition security programme. The most noteworthy aspect of the programme is the public distribution system (PDS). It was launched as a programme to help the country cope with emergency situations such as droughts, floods and cyclones, and distribute food items at fair prices to all vulnerable people while also guaranteeing remunerative prices to the farmers. However, until the late 1970s, it was confined mainly to urban food deficit areas with an emphasis primarily on price stabilization. The welfare dimension of the programme, however, became prominent during the 1980s during which time its coverage was extended to rural and tribal areas suffering from a high incidence of poverty. It was during the Ninth Five-Year Plan period (1997-2002) that PDS targets were shifted to focus on people living below the poverty line or BPL and to increase the availability of food to them. All these changes assigned a new role to the PDS by making it not only an instrument of sustaining food production but also a mechanism for supplying food grains to consumers at subsidized rates. The significance of this system increased manifold in the case of the tribal poor as their habitations were often difficult to access. Further, their low purchasing capacity prevented them from opting for local market purchases. The volatility of the market further reduced their chances of depending on the market. The role of the state in such circumstances assumed greater significance in providing food security to the tribal poor at the household level.

Despite the elaborate network that is involved in handling massive quantities of food items, the performance of PDS has not been free from criticism. Its universal coverage has drawn adverse comments because of the large subsidy burden on the exchequer. Many researchers have reviewed the system from different angles; its relevance was also questioned on the basis of its urban bias (Dreze & Sen, 2002; George, 1996; Suryanarayana, 1996); inclusion and exclusion errors due to definition problems (Cornia & Stewart, 1995; Dutta & Ramaswamy, 2001; Sen, 1995); large leakages and diversion of PDS commodities to open markets (Dev, 2008; Indrakanth, 1997; Radhakrishna & Rao, 1993; Swaminathan, 2000); lack of timely supplies to the needy (government-issued ID cardholders) resulting in less intake of subsidized food grains (Dreze & Khera, 2012; Mooij, 1999); lack of proper infrastructure and storage facilities (Dev, 2000; Meenakshi,

2001) and malpractices and corruption of PDS staff at various levels (Dev, 2008; Indrakanth, 1997; Swaminathan, 2000). A quick scan of these studies reveals that they covered mostly the cost–benefit aspect of the PDS operating in different states in India, but no research or study has focused on this problem exclusively in any tribal pockets in the state of Andhra Pradesh (undivided) in an integrated and holistic manner, especially in the context of right to food and food security. This gap in existing research has encouraged and motivated the current researcher to take up this problem for the present study. Such a study is needed especially in the context of widespread problem of under-nutrition and malnutrition prevalent among the Indian tribal population who live at BPL- levels, suffering from deprivation, exclusion and marginalization. Caught in cycles of poverty, the poor struggle to survive, while opportunities to access needed resources such as food, health and education eludes them. In this type of environment, moving out of poverty and exclusion lies beyond their personal effort.

OBJECTIVES AND METHODOLOGY OF THE STUDY

Given the above scenario, the present study intends to evaluate and assess the overall implementation process of government-run PDS in select tribal areas of Andhra Pradesh against the background of their social exclusion, food security and right to food. In other words, the study examines the role of PDS in terms of providing food security to a selected population in the form of accessibility of the commodities, their availability and affordability for consumers targeted. While identifying their problems in making use of the PDS operations in their communities, the study is also meant to suggest feasible and possible measures for an effective implementation of the programme. In line with the stated objectives, the present study (conducted in 2013 and tailored under an evaluation research design) intended to cover the tribal pockets of Visakhapatnam district in Andhra Pradesh with the help of a multi-stage sampling device. The rationale behind selection of this district is that it is one of the more backward districts in the north coastal Andhra region, inhabited predominantly by a tribal population that accounts for 14.5 per cent of the total population of the district (4.3 million) according to the 2011 Census. While 57 per cent of the district comes under forest (agency) area, the remaining 43 per cent is a plains area. Further, the district is an abode for about 14 major tribes, the population of which lives in a tropical forest environment under extreme economic backwardness. Only about 30 per cent of the arable and cultivable area of the district is brought under cultivation with the help of minor and medium irrigation systems. The rest of the cultivable area is covered by dry crops depending on the vagaries of the Indian monsoon.

Of the three revenue and administrative divisions of the selected district with a combined total of 43 *mandals* (sub-districts), Paderu is one such division with 11 *mandals,* all solely inhabited by tribal folk. In the second stage, while selecting *mandals* from among these 11 *mandals,* consideration was given to the literacy rate prevailing in these *mandals,* since one of the proxy indicators for assessing development is the level of literacy. Accordingly, the researcher selected two *mandals,* namely Araku *mandal* (with the highest literacy rate at 50.8%) and G. Madugula *mandal* (with the lowest literacy rate at 33 per cent). In the third stage of the sampling design, the researcher selected, on a random basis, two villages from each one of the two selected *mandals.* Thus, in all, the study covered four selected villages in the tribal pocket. They are Siragam and Bondam from Araku *mandal,* and Korapalli and Vanjari from G. Madugula *mandal.* In the final stage, the researcher again has randomly selected 30 households from each of the four selected villages. Thus, in all, the present study covered a sample of 120 households (120 white ration cardholders under the BPL category). The needed field data have been generated by structured-interview schedules prepared for this purpose and canvassed among the selected 120 white ration cardholders, usually among the heads of the households. The data so generated have been pooled, classified, tabulated and analysed keeping in view the aims and objectives of the study. In doing the fieldwork, the researcher, as an outsider, encountered many difficulties such as an inaccessible topography, poor transportation facilities, low levels of cognitive capacity and awareness in the respondents and different subcultures. However, with the help, assistance and cooperation offered by the field staff at the *mandal* and village levels, the researcher has ultimately succeeded in completing the fieldwork despite difficulties.

BRIEF PROFILE OF THE STUDIED AREA AND THE SELECTED RESPONDENTS

The major tribes found in the studied area are as follows: Bagata, Konda Dora and Konda Kapu. The economy of these tribes is agroforest in nature and is largely influenced by the habitat and the level of knowledge accumulated about the natural resources and skills for exploiting them from the forest. Farmers practise both settled and shifting cultivations *(podu)*. However, the settled cultivation is found mainly on the sides of hill streams and on plain lands. The wet cultivators grow paddy (rice) in the *kharif* (monsoon) season only, whereas the shifting cultivators grow mixed crops such as millet, pulses and oilseeds. Since these farmers still use crude, primitive tools and technology in their agricultural operations, their yields are low giving them food security for about only six months in a calendar year. Those who collect forest produce such as *adda* leaves, honey and tamarind sell to the government-run Girijan Cooperative Corporation. Their staple food used to be *ragi* gruel (millet-based), but they are now shifting to rice consumption. Men and women drink alcohol in the form of *sara* (arrack), *jeelugu kallu* (sago palm extract) and *maddi* (rice beer). The food items supplied under the PDS are rice, wheat, sugar and edible oil at subsidized rates. The intake of protein food items is much less than recommended since the consumption of milk and milk products is almost insignificant among them. Similarly, oil consumption is less than optimal. The problems of food and water contamination, nutritional deficiency and inadequate public health facilities contribute in turn to morbidity, mortality and loss of working capacity. In other words, these tribal populations have limited knowledge about health and hygiene, and are adamantly resistant to changing their food and drinking habits. Under the Integrated Child Development Scheme (ICDS), Anganwadi centres (local community centres) were established in these areas with a view to increase the nutritional status among pregnant women and children below six years of age by providing some additional high nutritive-value food. But this scheme, just like other government schemes meant for tribal welfare and development, is a failure since the functionaries associated with it are neither paying much interest nor focusing attention on obtaining fruitful results. The Integrated Tribal Development Agency (ITDA) is trying to increase the energy base in the area by introducing horticulture and commercial crops such as turmeric, ginger and maize by providing irrigation through check dams, seeds, chemical fertilizers and pesticides. It is also taking needed steps to reduce soil erosion by means of land levelling and discouraging shift cultivation. Unfortunately, the attitudes of the tribal people towards the efforts initiated by the agency are not favourable, as they oppose any innovation. In short, the tribals lack motivation to participate in the developmental activities and programmes meant for their own improvement. The result is that the available food resources are not sufficient to meet the subsistence levels of the tribals in view of their population growth and simultaneously a stagnation in the resource base.

All studied respondents were males distributed within the age range of 25-65 years, their mean age being 42 years. While 58.3 per cent of them were illiterate, 36.7 per cent studied up to the elementary school level and the rest (5%) studied up to the high school level and beyond. Data related to their main occupations revealed that 49.3 per cent were cultivators, 26.7 per cent were agriculture labourers, 18 per cent belonged to the food gathering and hunting category and the remaining 6 per cent were engaged in traditional service occupations. While a majority (51.7%) of the respondents had no land at all, 28.3 per cent owned less than 1 acre and the remaining 20 per cent had 1 to 2 acres each. Respondents' monthly family income ranged between ₹2,000 and ₹4,500, the average being ₹3,100. All the respondents possessed white ration cards and when specifically asked to show their cards, every respondent reacted positively and showed the card with pride. While about 70 per cent live in *kaccha* (makeshift) houses, 23.3 per cent had semi-pucca (semi-permanent) houses and the rest (6.7 %) had *pucca* abodes. Regarding family type, as many as 66.4 per cent of the respondents live in and maintain nuclear families, and the remaining 33.6 per cent maintain extended family living. When calculated, the respondents' average family size equalled 4.8 members. The adoption of small family norm was negligible among these tribals since the parents posited positive values on their children.

PDS' FUNCTIONING: FROM THE RIGHT HOLDERS' VIEWPOINT

The effectiveness and usefulness of the PDS can be assessed directly from the views and experiences expressed by the consumers of the system. Ration cardholders are the real consumers (right holders) who receive the subsidized food grains of PDS through fair price shops. Therefore, what follows is an analysis and interpretation based on the responses and views of the respondents. An administrative function related to the PDS that needs strengthening is the empowerment of all citizens by making them aware of their entitlement to nutritious food to begin with. A rights-based approach to public services argues that knowledge about entitlements enhances the ability to garner collective action and serves as a 'weapon in the battle for government accountability' (Jenkins & Goetz, 1999, p. 606). In this context, it is heartening to note that our respondents are clearly aware of the main objectives of the PDS and have correct perceptions about its goals since a majority (56.7%) feel that serving the poor and vulnerable sections of the population is the main objective behind this programme. While28.3 per cent perceive that supplying essential commodities at fair prices is the goal, the remaining 15 per cent believe that facilitating easy accessibility of the essential commodities to the needy at a single delivery point is the main objective of the PDS (Table 15.1). Also, most of the respondents (86%) consider the benefits offered under the PDS as their right, not a privilege. The procurement and consumption pattern of people mostly gets affected by the location of PDS fair price shops (ration shops), especially in tribal areas. If such a shop is located far away from the village or hamlet, regular PDS purchases from the ration shop become difficult and inconvenient for purchasers. According to the present data shown in Table 15.1, as many as 63.3 per cent state that their ration shops are located outside their hamlets or villages, often at a distance of about 4 to 5 km away from them. The basic problem in tribal belts is that cardholders have to commute mostly by foot and without any protective footwear to reach these shops and this exercise becomes much more difficult if all the items are not available at a time, especially in the rainy season. Mainly for this reason, while about 42.8 per cent express their satisfaction with the location of their shops, the remaining 57.2 per cent feel unhappy and inconvenienced.

In interior tribal areas, easy accessibility of ration shops and their supply of essential items is still a distant dream. Poor roads, an uneven terrain and a lack of proper transport facilities prevent smooth access to these areas. Given this situation, it becomes difficult for the salesmen even to reach and open their shops daily. According to the official circular, it is mandatory for salesmen to open their shops located anywhere at least twice a week. In tribal areas, these shops are also expected to be opened compulsorily on local market days as per instructions given with such markets occurring four times a month. This arrangement is made since all the people in and around the fair price shop area flock together with money on weekly shanty days to purchase the needed goods and services in addition to ration items. In contrast to the policy, only 21.7 per cent of the respondents reveal that shops are open twice in a week, and then, only when the ration items are available. While 48.3 per cent feel that their shops are open once in a week, the remaining 30 per cent report no such regularity (Table 15.1). Most respondents also report that ration items are available only on some market days and in the remaining shanty days the ration shops are kept open but the much-needed ration items are often out of stock as reported by salesmen. Vital information such as which days ration shops are open and the list of available ration items is not known

Table 15.1 Respondents' Responses on the Objectives of PDS

Main Objectives of the PDS	To Serve the Poor and Vulnerable Section	To Supply Essential Commodities at Fair Prices	To Provide Accessibility of Essential Items to Needy	Total
FR (%)	68 (56.7%)	34 (28.3)	18 (15.0)	**120 (100.0)**
Location of Fair	Within their Hamlets/ Villages	Outside their Hamlets or Village		**Total**
FR (%)	44 (36.7)	76 (63.3)		**120 (100.0)**
Frequency of Opening Fair Price ShopPrice Shops	Twice in a Week	Once in a Week	No Such Regularity	**Total**
FR (%)	26 (21.7)	58 (48.3)	36 (30.0)	**120 (100.0) Total**

Source: Based on field data.

to the public in advance since there is no guarantee on the supply side on account of transportation problems, apathy and the indifferent attitude of concerned personnel involved in the supply chain at the district and *mandal* levels. This problem is more acutely felt by the public during the rainy season when the demand for supplies increases because it is the off-season for local production and total dependency on the food items supplied by PDS.

Almost all respondents report that their traditional staple food, prior to the introduction of the PDS, was white maize or *chollu* or *ragulu* (millet), along with vegetables. Since they used to mainly cultivate these crops and cereals, they were available at much cheaper rates in the local markets. But now they have changed their food habits radically, shifting totally to rice, since rice is available under the PDS at subsidized rates. Local cultivators also have switched over from these traditional dry crops to cash crops. Hence, for these people, the PDS is directly associated with their food security. Despite this, only about 69 per cent of our cardholders are making full use of the PDS by buying their full eligible quota monthly. The remaining 31 per cent are not making use of this facility every month due to various constraints.

The major problem for them as reported before is a lack of much-needed advance information about the days and times that the ration shops are open and the availability of ration items. Usually, such information is passed only by oral communication and thus there is a high probability that many will miss such information. To further complicate matters, ration items are often not available in the PDS shops when the local people possess the needed money to purchase them. In addition, all ration items are not available on any one single day, and the ones that are available (rice) are supplied in two instalments since these tribal people cannot purchase everything at one time. To purchase each item supplied to them on an instalment basis and on different days and times is a tedious and inconvenient process to manage and plan for local tribal populations. Hence, most of our respondents expressed their inability and helplessness in making use of the PDS fully and regularly. When our respondents were probed further to identify specifically the reasons for the non-availability of rations to some cardholders every month, they responded clearly (here multiple responses were allowed). An analysis revealed that for as many as

Table 15.2 *Reasons for Non-availability of Ration to Cardholders*

Reasons	FR	%
1. Lack of all items at a time	84	70.0
2. Lack of availability of supply when money is available	66	55.0
3. Lack of money when ration items are available	54	45.0
4. Irregular supply by the dealer	98	81.7
5. Salesmen's indifferent attitude and lack of their cooperation	42	35.0
Total	120	–

Source: Based on field data.
Note: Multiple answers allowed.

70 per cent, the lack of availability of all items at one time is one of the reasons. While 55 per cent feel that a lack of availability of supplies when they have the money is another reason; for 45 per cent, it is the lack of money at the time of availability of the supplies. For 81.7 per cent, the reason is the irregular supply by dealers and 35 per cent complained against the indifferent attitudes of salesmen in not passing on information about the supplies to them on time (Table 15.2). Due to this sad circumstance, most respondents reveal their anguish by stating that every month the stock supplied under every item is not sold to the cardholders completely. The dishonest dealers successfully divert this stock balance to local merchants through the black market, earning easy and quick profits for themselves. This game is going on with the collusion and nexus between vigilance personnel, local black marketeers, dealers and local political leaders for the advantage of all. As a result, the irony of this situation, repeated by all the respondents, is that the stock sold by the local retail merchants is actually what is meant for the PDS. Those unfortunate enough to require an additional quantity of rice or kerosene on special occasions, or those who cannot purchase the quota in time, are forced to purchase these items at local shops at higher prices. So finally the stock meant for targeted beneficiaries is not reaching them and most of the time the effected cardholders feel that they are victims of the system.

Under the targetted PDS, each white cardholder is provided with a maximum of 20 kg of rice, 2 kg sugar, 3 litres of kerosene and 2 litres of edible oil per month at subsidized prices. But only 28.3 per cent are satisfied with the quality of items supplied and their weights. While a majority of 56.7 per cent are totally dissatisfied both with the quality and weight of the items provided, the rest 15.0 per cent could not say anything about the issue. Their dissatisfaction and frustration is due to pilferage, the underweighing of items, as well as the inferior quality of supplies. When questioned, the dealers/salesmen blame officials at higher levels for substandard quality and attribute the underweight problem to leakages occurring during transportation between the district headquarters and the village end point leading consumers bearing the burden and sharing the loss caused on the supply side. The analysis of data further revealed that as many as 71.7 per cent are not satisfied with the quantity of quota fixed for all the items under the PDS. Again, of those dissatisfied respondents, 48.8 per cent had a family size of six or more members, followed by 32.6 per cent who had four to five members each; the remaining 18.6 per cent had only three or less each. Thus, the respondents' family size seems to have a direct bearing on their dissatisfaction regarding the fixed quantity of items being supplied as expected. Similarly, of those 71.7 per cent who are not satisfied with the fixed quantity of quota being supplied, a significant majority (66.7%) had a monthly family income of less than '4,000 each and the remaining 33.3 per cent belonged to the income category of '4,000 and above each per month. This also explains the fact that the respondent's income level has a bearing on the levels of dissatisfaction with the quantity of items being supplied as expected. It is also pertinent to note that for 62.8 per cent of the respondents, price variationsof the items supplied between the local markets and ration shops alone acts as a major impetus for them to opt for ration (PDS) items. However, the remaining 37.2 per cent feel that the prices are low since the quality is poor and, hence, they see no advantage in procuring ration items.

Data regarding problems frequently encountered by respondents while purchasing ration items at the PDS fair price shops as presented in Table 15.3 reveal unexpected responses. While for 38.3 per cent, repeat visits to these shops for each item is the main problem, 30.8 per cent

Table 15.3 *Respondents' Problems while Purchasing Ration Items*

Problems Perceived	FR	%
Heavy rush and long queues	22	18.4
Delays, corruption and favouritism	15	12.5
Repeated visits for each item	46	38.3
Irregular supplies	37	30.8
Total	120	100.0

Source: Based on field data.

feel that irregular supplies and open times as practised by dealers and salesmen is the main irritant. About 18.4 per cent complain that a heavy rush and long waiting lines at fair price shops when delivering goods is a common problem. The remaining 12.5 per cent report that delays, corruption and favouritism on the part of salesmen are the most crucial problems they experience at the shop levels.

Customer satisfaction on prices, supplies and service is the main expectation from PDS. In this context, one notices from the data that while a significant majority, 73.3 per cent of respondents, expressed their satisfaction on the price front, 81.6 per cent were not satisfied with the supply and another 85 per cent were displeased and unhappy with the service provided (Table 15.4). This is quite an important and pertinent finding which ultimately suggests that all is not well with

Table 15.4 *Respondents' Opinions on the PDS*

Opinions	On Price Front		On Supply Front		On Service Front	
	FR	%	FR	%	FR	%
Satisfied	88	73.3	17	14.2	18	15.0
Can't say	12	10.0	5	4.2	–	–
Not satisfied	20	16.7	98	81.6	102	85.0
Total	120	100.0	120	100.0	120	100.0

Source: Based on field data.

the PDS in tribal pockets. It reveals that even though the intentions of the government in operating a PDS appears to be admirable, problems associated with its implementation at the final distribution point or at the shop level are coming in the way of reaping positive benefits by the targeted poor and needy. As a result of all these problems, a significant number of the tribal population, especially children and mothers, are experiencing acute malnutrition due to food scarcity and the lack of a nutritious diet. The data collected reveals that 29 per cent of children below 14 years of age and 36 per cent of mothers are suffering from malnutrition ranging from mild to severe levels.

When asked the question: 'In the past 30 days did you feel worried because there was not enough food in the household?', a sizeable majority of the respondents (68%) responded in the affirmative. Similarly, while 35 per cent reveal that they and their children ate food which is not adequate at all two or three times during the last month, 28 per cent confess that they have borrowed food several times from their neighbours to meet their needs during the same reference period.

All respondents reveal their lack of knowledge and awareness about the recent Food Security Bill passed by the Indian Parliament and subsequent changes being contemplated by the government in the PDS. When asked, some respondents offer useful, practical and pertinent suggestions for improving the overall functioning of the PDS: ration shops should be housed in *pucca* buildings with separate doors for entry and exits; ration items to be pre-packed after a weight check and kept ready for delivery at the shop level to control pilferage and underweighing; number of fair price shops to be increased wherever needed and both the quality and the quantity of food items to be improved.

Discussion and Suggestions

The study focuses on food security among the tribal poor and throws light on the crucial aspects of the socio-economic situation of people which reflects their long- and short-term food security situations. It is they, with their resilience and culture, who can survive harsh conditions. Degraded conditions of natural resources and paucity of land combined with unskilled human resources within tribal communities have brought their economy to the brink. The tribals seek various options with their own initiative, but these offer very little security or long-term sustainability. They have walked a tightrope of subsistence for centuries, and it would be a huge mistake to take for granted that they will continue to accept to do so. Even though a strong kinship system prevails among these tribal folk, its support structure in crisis situations is weak since all of them experience problems similarly with no significant difference among them. These tribals have a weak political voice with poor articulation, made worse by a lack of education which deprives them of any measure of confidence in countering the hegemony of the upper class elite who have entrenched themselves in tribal pockets. Despite provisions for local governance and opportunities they get because of protective discrimination policies adopted by the government, the participation of tribal populations in decision-making is very poor. Government intervention has had little positive or constructive impact on the food security situation of this unfortunate lot. Some innovative schemes and programmes have been thought of by administrators, but due to a lack of control at the time of implementation, these innovations are often countered by new methods of misappropriation and exploitation. This is truly a sad state of affairs, as much can be done if there is a real effort on the part of the government and the officials involved in India's PDS.

Food security has become a new strategy for development planners. There are many formulas, plans and calculations for food security. But in the tribal regions, it is important to understand the real causes behind their food insecurity. There is a substantial gap between what the state (PDS) is offering and what the local people actually need. Even though a significant majority of the respondents were satisfied on the price front of the commodities being supplied, they were not happy on the supply front as well as on the service front. Hence, in the food security debates, the analysis offered by pundits generally focuses on the supply side. In the rights approach, one has to go beyond the supply side and focus more on the demand side. In other words, the supply of food and nutrition is important but, as a right, the demand side is more important. Unless citizens demand the right to food, governments may not fulfil their obligations (Parikh, 2013). What is really needed is a well-concerted and coordinated effort and activities among citizens, rights activists, NGOs and related national and international organizations to achieve these goals. However, the absence of such coordination cannot justify the non-fulfilment of an obligation by individual governments (Agarwal & Mander, 2013). Therefore, to improve the food security situation among the tribals in general, and in the studied area in particular, some of the specific suggestions are indicated here.

It is recognized and accepted by tribals that the PDS is one of the most important welfare programmes to protect them from food insecurity in adverse conditions. At the same time, they are dissatisfied with the quantity of food grains being supplied and its quality. Hence, in addition to rice, each cardholder should also be provided with a minimum quantity of maize, *chollu and ragulu* (millets) according to their choice so that they will be ensured with sufficiency as well as adequate nutritional efficiency. Since wheat consumption is low as reported by these tribals, most of them are not purchasing it as supplied under PDS. In its place, the rice quota may be increased to meet the demand.

Also to be considered is that PDS should be supported and supplemented with other linked programmes, such as employment generation programmes and food for work programmes, to ensure food security while improving their purchasing capacity. In the studied area, these programmes, for reasons not known to them, have not yet been introduced. When asked, local leaders reacted by saying that these programmes are on the cards and will be introduced soon as promised by the district and state leaders. There is a need also to coordinate efforts and activities of PDS with NGOs, Girijan Cooperative Corporation, the ITDA and ICDS by networking with them to ensure regular delivering of services and supplies to those in the needy, isolated and excluded category.

The salesmen of fair price shops (duty bearers) form an important link between dealers at *mandal* (sub–district) levels and local consumers at shop levels, and they are key to managing effectively all the activities associated with running the shops. But their low wages, lack of incentives for working in interior forest agency areas, combined with tedious government procedures involved in operating the PDS shops in such tribal areas, all contribute to their lack of interest and motivation in performing their duties properly. These very same reasons instead often compel them to indulge in malpractices for their own personal gain and survival. The suggestions they offered to improve the PDS apparatus and its efficiency are as follows: a minimization of political interference at all levels; timely delivery of the stocks of all ration items on a regular basis and on stipulated dates; improvement of their wages/allowances/incentives; allowance to sell non-rationed items needed by the locals to improve the economic viability in maintaining these shops; introduction of pre-packed and pre-weighed sales of the ration items and assistance in tackling corruption of and harassment by their supervisors and vigilance personnel. Concerned authorities should take these suggestions into account to revamp the system for improving its efficiency. However, as long as the apparatus used by the PDS is the same with no reforms made, it is not possible to ensure food security to the needy even when additional benefits under the new Food Security Bill are introduced with new labels and nomenclatures. By its conception, the PDS is competent enough in providing food security to the needy, but due to its mismanagement coupled with malpractices in its implementation along the supply chain, it is unable to fulfil its intended objectives. Hence, there is an urgent need to reform the existing apparatus to improve its efficiency in delivering goods.

The restriction of the PDS to BPL households has proven to be quite problematic, since there is currently no reliable way of identifying them in this category. There is therefore a growing pressure for a more inclusive and universal PDS as suggested by Himanshu and Sen (2011) and Dreze and Khera (2012). Reforms to the PDS in Chhattisgarh state that focused on extending coverage, improving delivery and increasing transparency and accountability has led to its remarkable revival (Raghav, 2012). Perhaps other states should also follow these reforms along similar lines as soon as possible.

Ultimately, there is an immediate need to adopt a multifaceted approach for improving food and nutrition security in the country, especially among tribals. Apart from policies at the national level, there is an urgent necessity for conceiving and implementing location-specific policies and programmes at state, district and regional levels as problems of hunger and food insecurity may differ from place to place. However, achieving freedom from hunger still remains one of the highest challenges in democratically free India. To conclude, the present study shows that the issue of food security needs to be seen with a holistic perspective, taking into account both the micro- and macro-aspects of hunger and nutrition. In such a comprehensive food security system, the state is responsible for ensuring that every needy person has economic as well as physical access to food and nutrition, thereby realizing every person's right to food.

It is hoped that this study and its findings will be useful in placing the issue of food security on centre stage as well as in formulating appropriate strategies and policies in moving towards a more food-secure India. In this context, there is need to bring together human rights thinking, exemplified by food as a human right and development thinking through poverty reduction efforts. Therefore, measures to reduce poverty and steps to respect human rights have to be evolved in tandem, sharing the same in the overall aim of increased human well-being, even though they might have different frameworks and tools for reaching this goal. Ultimately, it is to be acknowledged that right to employment is crucial for achieving right to food and that without achieving right to food, it is difficult to achieve food security.

ACKNOWLEDGEMENT

This chapter is a product of the major research project: Taking Public Distribution System to the Tribal and Rural Poor: A Study in the Context of their Right to Food and Food Security, funded by the University Grants Commission and carried out by the author during his Emeritus fellowship period, the report of which was submitted to the UGC. The author is grateful to the UGC in this regard.

REFERENCES

Agarwal, A., & Mander, H. (2013). Abandoning the right to food. *Economic & Political Weekly*, *48*(8), 21–23.

Cornia, G., & Stewart, F. (1995). Two errors of targeting. In D. Van de Walle & K. Nead (Eds.), *Public spending and the poor: Theory and evidence*. John Hopkins University Press and World Bank.

Dev, S. M. (2000). Agricultural development and public distribution system: Lack of major initiatives. *Economic & Political Weekly*, *35*(13), 1046–1049.

Dev, S. M. (2008). *Inclusive growth in India*. Oxford University Press.

Dreze, J., & Khera, R. (2012). The bill that asks too much of the poor. *The Hindu*.

Dreze, J., & Sen, A. (2002). *India: Development and participation*. Oxford University Press.

Dutta, B., & Ramaswamy, B. (2001). Targeting and efficiency in the public distribution system: Case of Andhra Pradesh and Maharashtra. *Economic & Political Weekly*, *36*(18), 1524–1532.

George, P. S. (1996). Public distribution system, food subsidy and production incentives. *Economic & Political Weekly*, *31*(39), A140–A144.

Himanshu, P., & Sen, A. (2011). Why not a universal food security legislation? *Economic & Political Weekly*, *46*(12), 38–47.

Indrakanth, S. (1997). Coverage and linkages in PDS in Andhra Pradesh. *Economic & Political Weekly*, *32*(19), 999–1001.

Jenkins, R., & Goetz, A. M. (1999). Accounts and accountability: Theoretical implications of the right to information movement in India. *Third World Quarterly*, *20*(3), 603–622.

Meenakshi, S. S. S. (2001). Public distribution system: Safety net for the poor. In M. D. Asthana & P. Medrano (Eds.), *Towards hunger free India: Agenda and imperatives* (pp. 141–153). Manohar Publishers.

Mooij, J. (1999). Dilemmas in food policy: About institutional contradictions and vested interests. *Economic & Political Weekly*, *34*(52), A114–A120.

Parikh, K. S. (2013). Right to food and food grain policy. *Economic & Political Weekly*, *48*(11), 23–27.

Radhakrishna, R., & Rao, K. H. (1993). *Food security, public distribution and public policy* (Working Paper No. 26). Centre for Economic and Social Studies.

Raghav, P. (2012). Reforming the public distribution system: Lessons from Chhattisgarh. *Economic & Political Weekly*, *47*(5), 21–23.

Sen, A. (1995). The political economy of targeting. In D. Van de Walle & K. Nead (Eds.), *Public spending and the poor: Theory and evidence* (pp. 104–120). John Hopkins University Press and World Bank.

Suryanarayana, M. H. (1996). *PDS: Beyond implicit subsidy and urban bias: The Indian experience* (Discussion Paper No. 217). Indira Gandhi Institute of Development Research.

Swaminathan, M. (2000). *Weakening welfare: The public distribution of food in India*. Left Word Books.

Section IV

Malthusian Spectre and Indian Public Health History

Sectional Introduction

P. M. Arathi

The rapid increases in the population and the consequent pressure on the limited resources available have brought to the forefront the urgency of problems of family planning. The main appeal for the family planning is, however, based on consideration of the health and welfare of the family. All progress in this field depends first on creating a sufficiently strong motivation in favour of family planning in the minds of the people and next, on providing the necessary advice and service…but these presuppose intensive studies concerning attitude and motivation affecting the sizes of families and about techniques and procedures for the education of the public on family planning as well as medical technical research. (Government of India, 1953, p. 218)

Population control and policies have always been a political statement of nation states about their perspective and commitment on resource reallocation in societies based on social stratifications. India is the first country in the world to adopt a national family planning policy as an integral part of its development plans. The close perusal of population policies of India shows the aggressive nature of the state through coercive measures. Recent development in population policy discourses is strongly determined by communal values, othering of minority communities as well as islamophobia. Tracing of the history and political economy of the demographic politics of policymaking gives more clarity about the present.

Changes in the agrarian sector in the last two decades through neoliberal policies have led to an acute yet unnoticed deprivation in rural India. This deprivation, rooted in the growth-led developmental ideology, has impacted the agrarian sector severely, reducing the size of cultivable land, migration to urban location and has influenced the fertility choices of married women. The different components of power structure and their confluence (intersectional dynamics) influence the participation of women in the decision-making process regarding the number of children. Therefore, it varies from region to region.

The availability of contraceptives is limited and method of spacing became expensive due to private provision in India. Male/rich/upper caste-centric policies which are seemingly gender-responsive and caste-neutral are dominant and a camp approach for family planning is only one such policy. Institutional and structural failures and restricted demands for their resurrection contribute to the weakening of social justice mechanisms and legal capacity to resist the expansion of deprivation and disparities. This has created a situation of skewed choice for rural poor women who have little option, but to seek the only available method of population control, female sterilization and that too provided in the mass sterilization camps often violating all the national and international prescribed standards.

However, it has remained primarily a programme of controlling numbers rather than focused on reproductive and human rights that India had affirmed at the International Conference on Population and Development (ICPD) in 1994 that took place in Cairo and in its National Population Policy (NPP), 2000 (PFI et al., 2014, p. 3). Although as policy, both these documents speak about doing away with targets and incentives in the FPP, in practice, it still continues despite major tragedies in the past (Hartmann & Rao, 2015). The ambitious goals of family planning policies and counting numbers, not people and their lives, pushes coercion of women and compromises on quality. India's commitment to family planning 2020 is based on the argument that to provide contraceptive service to 48 million couples, there is no other way for policymakers, but to continue with crude camp approaches and target more and more vulnerable women (Das & Contractor, 2014).

Social Change carried over 41 articles on different aspects of population policies. Many of the articles studied the regional variations or region-specific impact of family planning and fertility transitions. Critical engagement with demographic transition theories with evidences from developing countries; the impact of socio-religious thoughts and a son preference; a correlative study on family planning acceptance and adoption assimilated the critical writings on family planning programmes in India. The aspect of the quality of care in family planning programme is examined by Khan et al. (1994). The discussions before and after the ICPD to ensure universally accepted human rights standards in population control programmes are reflected in *Social Change* as well. Issues such as the importance of male involvement in male contraceptive measures; contraceptive transitions in Asia; pan-Indian fertility transition trends since Independence; reproductive goals of couples and their policy relevance (Singh et al., 2006) are also covered under this theme over five decades.

Section IV of this volume, 'Malthusian Spectre and Indian Public Health History', contains three chapters. Chapter 16 by Kamala Gopal Rao (1974) gives an account of the early concerns about the research and policy attempts of family planning in India. The author takes a critical position towards the kind of research happening then in the field of family planning with support of the state's coercive population policies, though she approves of the kind of research happened in 1950s when little was known about the attitudes, beliefs, values, knowledge and practice of contraception among India's population. She reiterates the issue of a lack of proper and effective communication and feedback between researchers and programme–planners, which has been mentioned by several commissions and individuals in their evaluations of Indian family planning programme. The author calls for better forms of communication between researchers and planners and '…to have [a] meaningful quantum of research on vital policy issues and to disseminate the research findings in time' (Rao, 1974, p. 31).

Balakrishnan in Chapter 17 focuses on how children are valued in the family seen in three Asian countries (India, Bangladesh and Thailand) and discusses the notion of role of children as a vital source of welfare for the aged. 'Children versus land as sources of old age security, and the "demand" for children *vis a vis* the demand for "other commodities," are among other theme'. The author discusses the fertility implication of the value of children as well.

Chapter 18 in this section by Srinivasan does a comprehensive analysis of population policies since their inception and enumerates the salient achievements and shortcomings of the programme. The author discusses at length the target approach and its consequences. He analyses the nuances of the Swaminathan Committee Report, reproductive and child health programmes and the NPP, 2000, which signifies a marked departure in the government's approach towards population and related issues in India. It underplays the role of targets, brings into focus gender and reproductive health issues and recognizes the need for participatory and need-based planning at local levels. But evidence indicates that several state policies do not reflect the national policy concerns. She concludes that there is a general consensus that the population programme in India has failed in achieving its specific targets as was the main aim of the programme and bringing about improvement in the health and well-being of women.

REFERENCES

Das, A. and S. Contractor (2014). India's Latest Sterilisation Camp Massacre. *British Medical Journal*, 349: g7282

Government of India. (1953). *First Five-Year Plan*. The author.

Hartmann, Betsy and Rao, Mohan (2015). India's Population Programme. *Economic and Political Weekly*, L (44), 10–13.

Khan, M. E., Prasad, R., Patel, B. C., & Ram, R. B. (1994). Quality of care in family welfare from programme user's perspective. *Social Change*, 24(3&4), 147–155.

Koenig, A. M., & Simmons, R. (1994). Constraints on supply and demand for family planning: Evidence from rural Bangladesh. *Social Change*, 24(3&4), 135–145.

Population Foundation of India, Parivar Seva Sansthan, Family Planning Association of India and Common Health (2014). Robbed of Choice and Dignity: Indian Women Dead After Mass Sterilisation: Report of Situational Assessment of Sterilisation Camps in Bilaspur District, Chhattisgarh, New Delhi.

Rao, G. K. (1974). Policy makers and research in family planning. *Social Change*, 26–33.

Singh, A., Faujdar, R., & Rajeev, R. (2006). Couple's reproductive goals in India and their policy relevance. *Social Change*, *36*(2), 1–18.

Chapter 16

Policymakers and Research in Family Planning*

Kamala Gopal Rao

INTRODUCTION

India is the first country in the world to adopt a national family planning policy as an integral part of its development plans. The interaction of high population growth and the various essential ingredients of development planning was recognized in the First Five-Year Plan launched by India in the post–Independence period. The draft of First Five-Year Plan statement in its enunciation of the policy stated:

> The rapid increase in population and the consequent pressure on the limited resources available have brought to the forefront the urgency of problems of family planning. The main appeal for family planning is, however, based on consideration of the health and welfare of the family. All progress in this field depends first on creating a sufficiently strong motivation in favour of family planning in the minds of the people and next, on providing the necessary advice and service…. But these presuppose intensive studies concerning the attitude and motivation affecting the size of families and about techniques and procedures for the education of the public on family planning as well as medical and technical research.[1]

* *Social Change* 4, no. 2 (June 1974): 26–33.

The views expressed in this chapter are those of the author and do not represent the views of the organization where she is working.

In the statement regarding programmes, the document stated seven items of which five pertained to research. This indicates that ever since the inception of the national family planning programme in the early 1950s, research has been considered as an integral part of the policy and was expected to provide suitable guidelines to the planning, strategy, implementation and evaluation of the programme. This approach is understandable and rational because when the family planning programme began in 1952, little was known about the attitudes, beliefs, values, knowledge and practice of contraception among the Indian population.

In the report of the Second Five-Year Plan (1956–1961), more emphasis was laid on the need for research into biological and medical aspects of reproduction and of population problems, demographic research, including investigations of motivation in regard to family limitation as well as studies of methods of communication and evaluation and reporting of progress.[2]

During this intervening period, several crucial steps were undertaken to strengthen the programme. Several clinics were opened, institutions for training of family planning workers were started, a contraceptive testing unit was established and an autonomous Central Family Planning Board was created to advise government about family planning and population problems.

In the report of the Third Five-Year Plan (1961–1966), the stabilization of population growth was recognized as the very core of planned development. '"Family Planning has to be undertaken not merely as a major development" programme, but as a nationwide movement which embodies a basic attitude towards a better life for the individual, the family and the community.'[3]

During this plan period, a major breakthrough in the programme was achieved through the adoption of an extension approach calling for greater community involvement in the family planning efforts, promotion of biomedical research, establishment of research centres in different regions of the country for demographic and communication-action research, establishment of central and state family planning boards, increased involvement of voluntary organizations and private medical practitioners, augmentation of resources and facilities in primary health centres and indigenous production of contraceptives.

It is noteworthy that the entire programme was reorganized in 1966 by setting up a separate Department of Family Planning and by the creation of a Mass Education Media Section within the Department to organize education and communication aspects of the programme.

The Fourth Five-Year Plan memorandum (1966–1971) laid special stress on the sterilization programme and an increase in indigenous production of contraceptives.

COMMITTEES FOR RESEARCH

As a counterpart of the policy and programme of family planning enunciated through the five-year plan documents, research strategies and institutions grew up concomitantly.

In the early 1950s, the Government of India appointed a Family Planning Research and Programmes Committee to make recommendations on needed research and experimental programmes in the country. This Committee had two subcommittees—one on socio-economic and cultural studies of the population and the other on biological research. Since the beginning of the programme, considerable importance has been given to research, the findings of which have always been expected to provide cues to programme planning and implementation. The research advisory task of the Research Programme Committee was later handed over to three advisory committees—one each in the fields of demography, communication action research (covering social science research) and the biology of human reproduction. In 1968, the Demographic and Communication—Action Research Committees were merged to form the Demographic, Communication and Action Research (DCAR) Committee. Recently, a coordination committee has been set up (in place of DCAR Committee) with five panels concentrating on research on the various aspects of the programme. One of the committees is concerned with socio-economic studies. This Committee has taken up most of the functions of the DCAR Committee.

The DCAR Committee at their meeting held in 1961 delineated the broad approach and focus of research to be research-cum-action (i.e., action should flow from the knowledge gained from research, because due to the urgency of the programme, it cannot await, research results indefinitely). The twofold objectives of the research programme under this scheme were to (a) provide a better understanding of the basic factors that influence the acceptance of family planning and (b) use this understanding as well as available education, knowledge and skills to develop a more effective family planning programme. In addition to fixing responsibilities for coordination and technical support to research programmes, the Committee prescribed the following major research areas for the communication research centres:

1. Background study of factors influencing family size
2. Study of specific problems that hinder family planning programmes
3. Study of specific educational techniques
4. Development of broad action programmes over a period of time, making full use of the educators' skills, *plus* the findings of these research studies, under conditions of maximum flexibility[4]

While setting up the communication action research programmes, the Committee also identified general guidelines for developing action research by dividing it into three interrelated activities:

1. *Diagnostic studies* which would aim at discovering clues for improving upon the present family planning programme efforts; such diagnostic studies would have to be necessarily conducted on a small or micro scale which would not be normally amenable to quantitative, statistical assessment

2. *Action programmes* should be developed which make use of clues derived from diagnostic studies and which also have the advantage of close, expert technical guidance, combined with high flexibility of execution. Diagnostic studies should be continued as an intrinsic part of the action programme in order to improve it continuously and achieve maximum impact.

3. *Statistical assessment of programme result*, the three basic statistical indicators being (a) increase in knowledge and awareness of family planning through indirect planning and communication, (b) an increase in the number of those practising contraception, including sterilization and (c) a decline in the pregnancy rate or the birth rate.

Each action programme was allowed to use a technique or groups of method in a 'package' form that was deemed best for the particular population under study to induce social pressure, foster the felt need for a small family, provide family planning knowledge and make contraceptives easily available in order to promote their adoption. The action programme thus was based on the extension methodology.

As a result of the impetus given to research by this Committee, eight communication action research centres funded by the Ministry of Health and Family Welfare were established. They have been conducting research on the varied aspects of the family planning programme since 1972. In addition to these centres, a number of studies have also been conducted by researchers located in University of Social Sciences departments and other research, training and service organizations. It is estimated that over 500 studies have hitherto been conducted on the aspects of the family planning programme related to the social sciences. They have their varied lessons for the ongoing family planning programme. In a programme in which research is sponsored by the government and definite expectations are entertained about the results of the research as a guide to programme planning, a careful scrutiny is needed to assess the extent to which the findings of research have been utilized hitherto for administrative action and policy formulation, the problems and lacunae in such utilization, the causes of underutilization and the strategies needed for promoting a better utilization of research findings by policymakers for taking rational decisions. This scrutiny is both timely and essential.

PRESENT SITUATION ON THE UTILIZATION OF RESEARCH

The lack of proper and effective communication and information feedback between researchers and programme planners have been mentioned by several commissions and individuals in their evaluation of the Indian family planning programmes.

The Second United Nations Advisory Mission,[5] in their evaluation of the Indian Family Planning Programme in 1968, carefully considered the types and amount of research carried out within the family planning administration itself or by agencies more directly linked with it. The mission concerned itself both with the selection of research topics and the machinery channelizing findings into the relevant organs of the programme administration. They observed:

No amount of research can, however, be meaningful, unless it is carried out with an administrative and organisational framework that provides for both the best possible determination of research priorities and an efficient system of channelising research findings into the action programmes.... Research topics do not always appear to be selected with adequate knowledge, or regard for questions that need answers as guidelines to policy and policy implementation.

A careful look at programme implementation and policymaking indicates several instances where there is a visible communication gap between researchers and policymakers, the practitioners and users of the findings. Atal[6] identifies two types of lags—one is the *information lag* which is caused by the inability of researchers to cover a wide territory as they propose to or what the programme needs. The other lag is the *application lag* which has two aspects, namely (a) the time lag between data collection and its presentation and between report writing and its publication and (b) the communication gap between the researchers and consumers either due to the research findings not reaching the consumer or even when accessible, the disinclination of the consumer to buy them.

Several instances can be quoted as illustrative of the findings of research not being properly utilized to promote the needs of programme and policy. The association between educational attainment of couples and the adoption of contraception to achieve a small family norm has been repeatedly demonstrated by several studies dating back to the early 1950s. But for anyone who has witnessed the progressive budget cuts for education, the inconsistency at the macro-level policy formulation is too obvious. Arguing the case for considering family planning as an integral part of the national effort towards social and economic development, Simmons[7] recognizes the two-day benefits of investment in education—increase in the pool from which skilled family planning workers become available and increasing the responsiveness of the general population to family planning. As he says, investments in education are not at all independent of investments in family planning, and, ideally, with enough information we would be able to deal explicitly with some of the interdependencies.

Recently, there has been an increasing emphasis on alternative strategies in population policy, apart from the direct interventionist approach of crash birth control programmes. These measures—'beyond family planning', as suggested by some economists[8,9]—indicate the need for policies that change the parents' inherent preference for children by reducing the utility of additional children and raising its cost. This is definitely an area where policymakers ought to have commissioned researches. One of the surer methods of altering the scale of preference is education. A somewhat insular approach to family planning with no concern for education is one of the glaring instances of the poor utilization of research findings for policy decisions. Another noticeable case is the report of a summary of findings of over 26 attitude studies conducted up to 1961 by S. N. Agarwala,[10] which clearly highlighted insufficient involvement of males (husbands) in communication and service efforts as a cause of the limited success of family planning. Even the family planning workers are mostly females. From 1961 up to now, at least no worthwhile attempt has been made to involve the male more fully in the family planning efforts. This apathy is not only a reflection of the failure to take cognizance of research findings but also of sheer indifference to sociological power structure realities of Indian families in which man is the prime decision-maker. Subsequently, several studies[11] have also reflected the fact that the husband's non-cooperation is a cause of unsuccessful or sporadic use of contraceptives. We still do not see the male being involved in the family planning programme efforts.

Similar is the case with the findings reported in several attitude studies that people have asked for treatment for sterile/barren women as a prerequisite to any family planning work. Even years after the reporting of this fact, infertility services are far from satisfactory.

Another drawback is that policymakers do not find it possible to ask for research at the time when new programme strategies are to be implemented. In fact, often such steps are taken with meagre information base and little research backing. The ushering in of 'extension education' is a case in point. The much-publicized extension education approach launched in the early 1960s resulted in the recruitment of an army of 'extension educators' at district and block levels. Principally, this is sound enough as the policy is based on awareness of group dynamics and a recognition of the strength of group forces and procedures in effecting behavioural change. The extension educators were expected to perform duties such as contacting individuals and families for communication education, motivation and referrals. After more than 10 years of experience with this category of workers, they still are the most ill-spoken of ambiguous functionaries in the programme. One state totally abolished their posts.

But to date there are no large-scale, systematic studies to indicate the role, expectation and role-perception of extension educators, the content of their training and the ways and means of utilizing them effectively. They are at the bottom of the hierarchy and there is very little consideration anywhere for their career problems. A contradiction to their effective role performance is the large-scale organization of mass sterilization camps with cash incentives—a method of operation in which extension education has hardly any place.

The classical case of this communication gap is provided by the Indian experience of introducing intra-uterine device (IUD) into the programme. The IUD programme launched in 1965, after clinical trials, did not have the community/recipient reaction component built into it. Even after the programme was launched, very little hard data were available regarding complications experienced by IUD users and the retention rates. The programme operators and policymakers badly needed information on adverse reaction to particular aspects of the programme. A more comprehensive and quick feedback on the reaction of users would have successfully countered the spate of rumours that ultimately damaged the programme beyond recovery. As Simmons says, 'The demise of the IUD programme can be in large measure attributed to the informational vacuum in which, the Government was operating...one of the major results of the information gap is that important decisions are made too late or not at all.'[12] It is indeed paradoxical than even after recognizing the validity of the extension philosophy and the need for community involvement in programmes, community reaction studies were never recognized as a vital prerequisite to launching a mass IUD programme in the country.

The cost to the programme as a result of this neglect of oversight is too obvious to need elaboration.

For quite some time, the need to strengthen the management components of the huge family planning programme has been recognized and extensively discussed by several experts. The Second UN Advisory Mission emphasized the need to improve management at the district level and to review the replacement of medical officers by general administrators to take care of critical management functions. The need for conducting research in this area was emphasized by them when they said:

> Provision for management research and measures to ensure the optimum use of available human and material resources present vital missing components in the organisation of the programme.... The recent comprehensive review of studies in family planning in India indicates that relatively little research has been done specifically on administrative or management aspects of the programme, although much of it has relevance to administration.[13]

Over the last three years, though there is increasing concern for research on the management aspects of the programme, in practice, very few such studies have been conducted. The existing institutes of management and administrative institutes may be profitably deployed for this purpose.

Looking at the other side of the picture, one is appalled by the huge mass of essentially repetitive, small-scale, non-generalizable programme-unrelated research. In the author's experience[14] of reviewing available Indian studies in family planning in the context of reviewing their relevance to the ongoing programme, it appears that the three or four points of programme and policy relevance emerging from 250 and odd knowledge, attitude and practices (KAP) studies would have been equally well obtained from fewer, but better designed studies. The abundance of *ad hoc* survey type of studies and the dearth of proper experimental designs of studies have resulted in numerically large but qualitatively poor studies. Apart from quality, the researchers do not always seem to be sensitive to the programme needs. As the Second UN Mission to evaluate the family planning programme stated:

> In a programme aiming for rapid results and involving large expenditures, the need for wise decisions on the allocation of funds among alternative purposes is obvious. Should money be spent on training personnel more fully or on extension of current operations with less fully trained workers; on mass motivational activities or on evaluation activities.... Unfortunately the Indian programme like most,

and perhaps all family planning programmes lacks the basic cost and market research necessary to provide this guidance.[15]

Often, such information gaps in research occur due to the policymakers' inability to identify and conceptualize problems to the researchers. During the deliberations of the seminar on social sciences organized by National Institute of Health Administration and Education in 1970 in the context of identifying the problems of utilization of research findings, the experts said, 'the health administrator provides a broad-based and generalised health problem cutting across personality, culture and organisation to the social science researcher and his expectations from the social scientist are vague and diffused.'[16] The suggested solution was for both the social scientist and the health administrator to see the problem as it is operationalized.

ROLE OF RESEARCHERS

It would not be fair to throw all the blame on the policymakers. There have been several instances where policy formulation has been guided by research findings. The Direct Mailing study[17] of the National Institute of Family Planning highlighted the potentiality and feasibility of using this simple, inexpensive method of disseminating family planning information to remote villages. The methodology tested in this study has provided useful guidelines in the set-up and functioning of the Mass Mailing Unit in the Department of Family Planning. Another study[18] by the same Institute gave an impetus to the idea of distributing condoms through retail outlets with a marginal profit to the retailer. When the mass vasectomy camps were undertaken in 1972, the Institute was commissioned to undertake sociological, psychological and evaluative studies.

Recently, these dialogues between research organizations and policymakers have increased, which is a hopeful sign. But a more systematic and persistent effort is needed (a) to have a meaningful quantum of research on vital policy issues and (b) to disseminate the research findings in time.

ACTION URGENTLY NEEDED TO MAKE POLICYMAKERS IN FAMILY PLANNING TAKE NOTE OF RESEARCH FINDINGS

1. Policymakers at all levels must have a perspective of the long- and short-term objectives and overall goals of the programme. The various means of attaining the goal and the inputs and facilities needed must be clearly identified. The components that need the backing of research must be isolated while the short- and long-term research needs of the programme must be sorted out. It is important that policymakers understand that all problems need not depend upon research findings for their solution and that suitable use has to be made of available data before commissioning new studies. As the majority of the policymakers do not have any specific training in research, seminars and workshops may be organized to orient them to research, its problems and how best to use research for policy formulation and programme implementation. Such workshops wherein policymakers closely interact with researchers will go a long way in reducing the 'social distance' between policymakers and researchers, apart from the obvious gain in terms of their appreciation of research.

    In the selection of research topics and priorities, a continuous communication is needed between researchers and policymakers. As the Second UN Advisory Mission stated:

    > Programme Administrators need to indicate to the research workers the type of questions to which they seek answers; at the same time, researchers must organise their work in such a manner that they are able to respond to the expressed needs of the programme administrators and even to anticipate those needs.... Research workers must not function in isolation from, or be only peripherally concerned with, the realities of programme operation.[19]

    The policymakers should be able to indicate their problems in reasonable terms and even in the selection of research topics the views of research workers must be taken into account.

2. A few factors have been recognized as impeding the effective feedback of research findings into the programme. The different

orientations of researchers and policymakers lead to a clash in approaches. 'The pressure of time and need to meet performance expectations are realities of an administrator's daily life, while for those engaged in scientific research, the wish to present accurate and reliable data predominates the need to meet administrative deadlines.'

All too often the action-oriented policymakers get impatient about the time involved in the research process and tend to view researchers and research findings with cynicism or scepticism. They must understand that research, however short the term, is a scientific process and, therefore, consumes time and that faulty findings reported in haste and implemented without caution may endanger the programme rather than help its progress.

3. Policymakers must appreciate the professional orientation and aspiration of researchers. Programme-oriented research is eternally faced with interim and final report deadlines. For researcher, the demand for a report means intensified work and often a sense of frustration that quality has been sacrificed for lack of time to do their best. While the researcher wants to design rigorous scientific studies, the policymakers insist on 'quickies' so that results may be obtained soon for application. In this context, it is suggested that the possibility of using secondary data and taking advantage of 'natural experiment' situations to provide programme insights must be more seriously explored. Above all, policymakers must have a basic appreciation of the 'value' of research. One of the suggested ways of doing this is to effect an 'exchange of roles'. For some time, senior competent researchers may be allowed to formulate policy by occupying positions as policymakers. Some young, dynamic policymakers may be posted to research departments. The impact of the 'research culture' on the policymaker may then be expected to be favourable.

Policymakers must share their thinking on programme objectives and goals with the researchers and there must be a continuous dialogue between policymakers and researchers. This dialogue would help in identifying priority problems, and an appreciation of the scope and limitations of research findings in terms of generalization and applicability.

4. As regards the manner and content of reports, the researcher must keep in mind the needs of the consumer. The presentation of research findings should answer specific questions as clearly and unequivocally as possible. Research workers need to realize that their training in utilizing scientific data is not necessarily shared by all readers. The solution to overcome this problem, suggested by the UN Mission, is to utilize well-trained journalists to assist in the preparation of research reports which are to be read, comprehended and utilized by laymen. The researchers, however, should be encouraged to publish comprehensive, detailed reports in relevant scientific journals to satisfy their professional aspirations.

CONCLUSION

In their report, titled 'Social Science Research in India', Andrew Shonfield and Cherns while suggesting strategies for developing research identified diffusion of research results relevant for the formulation of public policy as of great relevance. They said:

> The common attitude of researchers is to leave matters to the normal academic channels of diffusion. The general expectation is that any impact on the world of action will be remote and long term but many academics have undertaken problem-oriented research, often at the instance of, and sometimes supported by, administrative organisations. The motives in these cases have been both the advancement of knowledge and the contribution towards the solution or amelioration of a practical problem. Yet once the research was done and the report completed, we found that the academics often had little knowledge of what use, if any, was made of the results. Where they did know, the study was not too encouraging. There seems little readiness among academics to recognise that they have a responsibility for ensuring the utilisation of their research and little interest in the intricate social processes whereby research affects action.[20]

Researchers' silence towards diffusion or application of their findings sometimes results from an understandable unwillingness of policymakers to accept findings that highlight the shortcomings of their programme. Negative findings, which are equally valid as positive findings from the viewpoint of scientific accuracy, are not accepted objectively by policymakers. Policymakers must appreciate that research is needed for the programme in order to identify both successes and shortcomings.

One way of facilitating communication between researchers and policymakers is to set up a coordinating agency which must undertake the task of translating the research findings to the policymakers and ensure rapid feedback to the researcher for further research needed.

Such coordination and liaison functions were expected of the former Demographic Research Committee and the Communication Action Research Committee and their merger, the Demographic and Communication Action Research Committee of 1968. Until 1968, the annual communication–action research workshops performed this function effectively. But later this function has been lost. In reality, however, the later committees primarily concerned themselves with scrutinizing research proposals and making recommendations for funding to the Ministry of Health and Family Welfare. As such, the coordinating task of bridging the wide gap between researchers and programme administrators received only their marginal attention and interest. The urgent need then is to establish a documentation centre for storage, analysis and retrieval of research information on a regular basis to administrators. The establishment of this service may stimulate policymakers to use research for action.

NOTES

1. Government of India, *First Five-Year Plan* (New Delhi: GOI, 1953), 218.
2. Government of India, *Second Five-Year Plan* (New Delhi: GOI, 1956), 553–554.
3. Government of India, *Third Five-Year Plan* (New Delhi: GOI, 1961), 675.
4. Government of India, *Proceedings of the Family Planning Communication Motivation Action Research Committee* (second meeting; New Delhi: Directorate General of Health Services, 1964).
5. UN Advisory Mission, *An Evaluation of the Family Planning Programme of Government of India* (Report No. TAO/IND/50; UN Commission for Technical Cooperation, Department of Economic and Social Affairs, 1969), 62.
6. Yogesh Atal, 'Utilisation of Behavioural Research Findings for Programme Development: Problem and Mechanism for Effective Utilisation' (mimeographed, Paper presented at the Seminar on Behavioural Research in Health and Medical Care, ICMR, March 1972), 15–18.

7. George B. Simmons, *The Indian Investment in Family Planning* (New Yor, NY: The Population Council, 1971).

8. Ibid.

9. Joseph J. Spengler, 'Values and Fertility Analysis', *Demography* 3, no. 1 (1966).

10. S. N. Agarwala, 'Some Random Thoughts on Attitude Surveys in India: A Summary', *Journal of Family Welfare* 6, no. 4 (1960): 33–35.

11. S. N. Agarwala, 'A Family Planning Survey in Four Delhi Villages', *Population Studies* 15, no. 2 (1961): 110–120; D. Anand, 'Knowledge and Sources of Information—Indoor Patients', Report on Family Planning through Hospital Care' (Part IV, Family Planning Research Project; New Delhi: Lady Hardinge Medical College, 1965 [mimeographed]); K. Dandekar, *Demographic Survey of Six Rural Communities* (Publication No. 7; Pune: Gokhale Institute of Politics and Economics, 1959); Lillian Khan, 'Attitude of Health Visitors towards Family Planning', *Family Planning News* 3, no. 2 (1962).

12. Simmons, *The Indian Investment in Family Planning*.

13. UN Advisory Mission, *An Evaluation of the Family Planning Programme of Government of India*.

14. Kamala Gopal Rao, *Studies in Family Planning in India: A Review for Programme Implications* (New Delhi: Central family Planning Institute, 1968 [mimeographed]).

15. UN Advisory Mission, *An Evaluation of the Family Planning Programme of Government of India*.

16. NIHAE, 'Seminar on Social Sciences: A Brief Report', *NIHAE Bulletin* 3, no. 3 (1970).

17. B. Bhatia, D. C. Dubey, and A. K. Devgan, 'A Study in Family Planning Communication', *CFPI Monograph Series*, no. 1 (1966).

18. B. L. Raina, R. R. Wake, Eugene Weiss, 'A Study in Family Planning Communication, Meerut District', *CFPI Mimeographed Series*, no. 3 (1967).

19. UN Advisory Mission, *An Evaluation of the Family Planning Programme of Government of India*.

20. A. Shonfield and A. B. Cherns, 'Social Science Research in India', *ICSSR Occasional Monographs*, no. 3 (1971).

Chapter 17

Fertility and the Value of Children in Three Asian Countries*
A Review of Salient Themes

Rajiv Balakrishnan

The phenomenal population growth India has witnessed in this century has roots in a fall in mortality going back to the 1920s; with mortality's baleful glare challenged on an unprecedented scale, numbers increased as never before. In earlier times, birth and death rates remained at high levels, and such population increments as accrued from the difference between the two were periodically decimated by war, epidemic and famine (Davis 1968: 24–25, 33–34). 1918, the year of the Great Influenza epidemic, a milestone in the country's demographic history, marked a turning point in the age-old pattern; it signalled the beginning of a new demographic regime of sustained mortality decline, induced in part by the diffusion of life-saving medical technology, which made possible the containment of fatal disease (Cassen 1979: 81–88; Davis 1968: 41, 45–51), and by the control of famine, facilitated by irrigated agriculture; a shift from subsistence to commercial food production and a greater scope to famine relief measures following the diffusion of rail and road links (Cassen 1979: 79–81; Davis 1968: 39–40). Fertility remained high, fostering a burgeoning growth of population (Davis 1968: 85).

* *Social Change* 26, no. 2 (June 1996): 74–86.

Recent decades have seen a relatively new demographic phenom-enon in the country, namely fertility decline (Adlakha and Kirk 1974; Jain and Adlakha 1982; Mari Bhat 1994; Mari Bhat et al. 1984; Preston and Bhat 1984; Rele 1987; Visaria 1995). Evidence suggests that this has marked remarkable changes in the way children are valued in the family; whereas earlier, a large number of children were desired, that is no longer the case (Nag and Kak 1984). The preference for 'small' families is now overwhelming, according to a national survey in which 85 per cent of respondents in rural areas said that it is advantageous to have 'few' children (NCAER 1984). Increasing child expenses are likely to be integral to the picture in that as the perception that children are 'costly' gains currency, parents more and more deem it advanta-geous to have smaller families. The phenomenon, reported internation-ally (Knodel et al. 1984), can be traced to the spread of schooling and related child expenses and to growing perceptions of child costs relative to the costs of 'other commodities'. A decline in the demand for child labour may have also contributed to the preference for 'few' children.

THE 'COSTS' OF CHILDREN

Child Costs Relative to the Costs of 'Other Commodities'

Data from a national survey, which indicate that households in 10 Indian states had a higher mean number of modern possessions when contraceptives were used, suggest that family limitation is a function of consumer aspiration (Jejeebhoy 1984: 193). The opportunity cost of children, measured against consumer goods, is likewise believed to underlie the value of children in Thailand (Knodel et al. 1984) and has been documented also with data from Taiwan (Mueller 1972: 394f). Further evidence comes from rural Maharashtra, where respondents in a survey (women aged 25–44 and their husbands) widely reported that child-related costs inhibited them from making 'other purchases' (Jejeebhoy 1984: 472–473).

The pattern, it is argued, derives from the monetization of the economy, for it is only when commodities can be bought and sold that conflicts arise between alternative expenditure outlays. Caldwell and his associates argue on the basis of fieldwork in a rural South Indian locale that in the traditional *jajmani* system, 'monetary transactions were few and economic transactions retained a large element of social relations.' Food was procured from the family farm or as periodic payments accruing in a system of reciprocal rights and obligations, and clothes were mostly hand me downs. But with monetization and the diffusion of concepts of child dependency, families have tended to spend more on food and healthcare for children, with the result that the costs of children have increased (Caldwell et al. 1982: 696, 699, 716).[1]

Schooling as a Source of Child Costs

Micro-data from Manupur, a North Indian village, shows that the commercialization of agriculture and the emergence of modern credit systems had fostered the conviction that schooling was necessary to comprehend and grapple with the new world (Nag and Kak 1984: 673, 675). The demand for schooling was additionally fuelled by growing opportunities in the non-agricultural sector for which schooling attainment was a requirement (Nag and Kak 1984: 676). This has been reported also from a drought-prone South Indian locale where schooling was seen as a route to the non-farm sector and as an escape from the insecurity of dependence on agriculture. In this South Indian setting, daughters were educated so as to make them better wives to husbands in non-farm employment. They were sent to school also because it was felt that as educated mothers, they would be better at child rearing; and because it was felt that education would help them find better jobs. Moreover, education for girls means a reduction of the dowries parents have to pay when their daughters marry (Hatti and Ohlsson 1983: 12–13; Nag and Kak 1984: 675). But less pragmatic considerations come into play as well. Thus, schooling is desired for its own sake, as a source of gentility and betterment.

With the spread of schooling, children become increasingly expensive. Schooling is critical in fuelling child costs, as minimum standards of clothing, food and health are expected of school-going children, with peer pressures and expectations from teachers coming into play in this regard (Caldwell et al. 1982: 716). Expenditures on clothing and textbooks can be quite burdensome for the poor (Nag and

Kak 1984: 676), and educating a child for white-collar employment can mean additional costs to be incurred on bribes that must be paid before a job can be secured (Caldwell et al. 1982: 718). With schooling expenditures a drain on the family coffers, parents are motivated to have fewer children. Indicating this, over 50 per cent of sterilized couples interviewed in a survey in South India said that the costs of educating and finding jobs for children had motivated them to curtail the size of their families. There is also another route through which schooling can boost child cost through the impact it has on the child when he or she becomes a parent. Mueller found in a study in Taiwan that sensitivity to child cost was a positive function of husband's schooling and, to a lesser extent, of mother's schooling. She argues that this reflects schooling aspirations for children and among educated parents (Mueller 1972: 394).

THE DEMAND FOR CHILDREN AS A SOURCE OF FAMILY LABOUR

In Manupur, the North Indian village studied by Nag and Kak (1984), the sweep of the Green Revolution meant that fallow land, originally used for cattle grazing, increasingly came under the plough. This led to a decline in the demand for child labour since cattle grazing and the collection of cow dung from the field have traditionally been the work of children (Nag and Kak 1984: 670, 673). Moreover, the use of chemical weedkillers had obviated the need to employ children for de-weeding operations (Nag and Kak 1984: 670). A general social context of institutional change militated against child labour as well. In Manupur, the market economy had grown to the detriment of the *jajmani* system under which *harijans* and service-providing castes were traditionally obligated to serve the land-owning *jats* in return for a share of the crops produced. So onerous were the terms of the traditional arrangement for the labourers and providers of services that the lower castes had to rely not only on the labour of adult males but also on that of womenfolk and children. But with the eclipse of the *jajmani* system and the growing salience of wage transactions in the market, the labour of children had become inconsequential (Nag and Kak 1984: 670, 675).

Yet there is evidence of a disturbingly high presence of child labour in the country. It has been suggested that the low wages at which children can be put to work and the ease with which they can be exploited are key factors working to promote child labour, with social attitudes rather than economic factors underlying its continuing prevalence (Bhatty 1996). Children's work *within* the household is another facet of child labour which deserves attention. Data from a Delhi slum shows that the labour which children, particularly girls, contribute to household tasks, is impressive (Rosenzweig 1981, cited in Basu 1992). Participation of girls in household work has been well documented also by another study of slum households in the capital city (NCERT n.d.). The phenomenon is widespread in South Asia (Rosenzweig 1981; World Bank 1991) and may be a vital factor operating to limit family size declines or with the potential to do so. Finally, the demand for children as eventual sources of adult labour to be deployed on the family farm or in activities that augment family incomes is another consideration that factors into the perceived value of children. An ethnographic study of a Rajasthan village (Patel 1994) underscores this dimension and suggests that children can be central to a household's material welfare and economic prosperity.

CHILDREN AS A BULWARK

Studying rural society in Bangladesh, Cain (1978) found that *purdah* and constraints to women's involvement in productive activity meant that males played an important role in sustaining the household's resource base. More specifically, the labour of sons and their experience in managing agricultural operations was vital during periods of crisis such as floods or the death of the patriarch, when mature sons in the household could avert distress land sales. A greater number of male earners in the household also meant more opportunities for income diversification. This helped in times of weather-related disasters that potentially undermined agricultural yields. Frequent disputes over that vital asset in this agrarian society— land—and the absence of efficient dispute settlement mechanisms meant, moreover, that widows, bereft of the protection of mature sons, were vulnerable to the risk of property loss. In rural Bangladesh, sons thus played a crucial role in coping with and mitigating the consequences of weather-induced disasters, widowhood and the general environment of lawlessness and insecurity of property rights.

Contrasting the Bangladeshi village Char Gopalpur with three drought-prone Indian villages (two in Maharashtra and one in Andhra Pradesh), Cain (1981) argues that children in the Indian villages were 'largely redundant' in strategies for coping with difficult times. While 'environments of risk' (perhaps with the exception of weather-related ones) were far less severe in the Indian villages, means of risk insurance other than children—institutional credit and public relief employment—functioned adequately in the Indian setting, while comparative mechanisms had not evolved in Char Gopalpur. It is in this context, Cain argues, that Bangladeshi households, faced with the burden of risk, bank on sons.

Cain's comparison of the Bangladeshi setting and the Indian villages however glosses over the considerable regional disparities that can be found within the Indian scene. Thus, a recent ethnographic study of a Rajasthan village has parallels with Cain's depiction of the Bangladesh experience; it was found that the strength of numbers to which sons contribute was essential to a family's security from threats of depredation and to the preservation of its local influence (Patel 1994: 82ff, 101ff). It might be argued that 'environments of risk' are likely to be far more acute in states such as Bihar and Rajasthan as compared to other parts of the country and that disparities such as these may contribute significantly to the considerable spatial variation in Indian fertility; regions less well placed in terms of the security environment may thereby be susceptible to brakes on sustained fertility decline.

Moreover, Cain downplays the role of networks of extended kin as a source of help in emergencies (Cain 1981: 461).[2] The role of relatives in providing assistance in times of distress can however be crucial. Thus, data from a sample of drought-prone Indian villages attest to consumption smoothing arrangements whereby shortages that a household is prone to as a consequence of crop failure are compensated by transfers from a marital household located elsewhere and not similarly affected by local agricultural conditions. Commitments hinging on kinship links between the households that enter into these implicit contracts, it is argued, make the arrangement work and make it work in circumstances where enforcing and monitoring agreements between parties bound only by the letter of the law is not feasible (Rosenzweig 1988; Rosenzweig and Stark 1989). This evidence of the role of the family in mitigating risks also underscores the salience of ties of marital kinship and underscores the value of daughters. Such a role for daughters is in fact explicitly recognized; it was found in a field study in Rajasthan that daughters were perceived to be useful in augmenting a household's network of kinship relationships via the establishment of affinal alliance (Patel 1994: 103).

CHILDREN AS A SOURCE OF OLD-AGE WELFARE

A distinction can be made between children as a source of insurance and children as a source of welfare for the aged. Cain argues that in South Asia, where institutional social security mechanisms for the elderly are lacking, there would be an incentive 'for one son or possibly two' and that the need to compensate for child mortality would not justify 'unrestricted fertility'. But if a high 'environment of risk' is added to the balance, 'the precision of these calculations would blur under the numbing effects of uncertainty' (Cain 1981: 466). When 'environments of risk' cease to be overwhelming, though, it can be expected that the role of children as a source of old-age welfare will begin to exert an influence independent of the insurance role. Thus, it is useful, for analytical purposes, to distinguish between the value of children as a source of insurance and the value of children as a source of old-age welfare. This section discusses aspects of the old-age welfare provisioning the role of children.

A study of the Lous of Karateng, Western Kenya, shows that transfers from children were an important component of elderly parents' income. Transfer incomes were largely provided by 'absent' sons who sent in remittances, or from 'adjacent' sons living in separate households within Karateng itself. Apart from monetary or material assistance (food and goods), a high proportion of households were assisted with tasks such as provision of water and meals, and the collection of firewood. Assistance was provided mainly by resident and, to a lesser extent, by 'adjacent' sons, daughters-in-law and grandchildren. Mean amounts of money and goods as well as time transfers from offspring were found to increase with the number of the elderly's living children and more specifically with the number of living sons. Moreover, a large number of children made it easier for elderly parents to 'allocate' their children to both monetary transfer and task assistance rotes (Hoddinott 1992).

Similarly, Knodel et al. (1992) find that in Thailand, the level and type of support from children depends on family size. The more children an elderly couple has, the greater the chance of their receiving one or the other type of support. While non-married children living locally were most likely to provide food and/or clothes, children living further away were most likely to contribute money. It was found also that the number of children providing support depended on how many of them were there in a family (Knodel et al. 1992: 85). But fewer children can permit higher investments in child education and the earning capacity of better educated children can mean that if fewer children provide support, this does not imply a reduction in the *amount* provided (Knodel et al. 1990; Knodel and Wongsith 1991).

In respect of that vital aspect of the welfare of the aged, co-residence with a child, the role of children as sources of old-age care and security is not diminished when fertility falls. Thus, in Thailand, a drastic fall in the number of children per elderly couple, from 5.1 to 2.2, involved only a marginal reduction of the elderly coresident with or in daily contact with a child, from 88 per cent to 80 per cent (Knodel et al. 1992). The evidence also suggests another reason why having more children is not necessarily better from the point of view of old-age support; while some respondents thought that having many children increased the chances that at least one child would be dependable, it was felt also that the obligation to provide support and the amount that is deemed appropriate may be inversely associated with the number of children (Knodel et al. 1992: 92–95).

A central feature of the Thai experience is that it is predicated on a strong cultural expectation that children will support elderly parents. This typically involves co-residence (Knodel et al. 1987; Wongsith 1990). The scenario is one that has strong echoes in the Indian setting. Data suggest that if co-residence of the elderly with their children is an index of family-provisioned welfare for the aged, the family in India as an old-age care provider has suffered no erosion; with improvements in life expectancy and increases in the proportion of the aged in India's population, it appears that more elderly now co-reside with their offspring, with the result that household size has increased (Shah 1996). But unlike in the Indian case, elderly Thais tend to be flexible in the matter of the sex of the child with whom they reside (Knodel et al. 1992: 96). The pre-eminence of the son is by comparison a key feature of the family in India. This can be inimical to fertility decline and son preference in India has in fact been ascribed such a consequence.

CHILDREN AND LAND AS SOURCES OF SECURITY

The propensity of children to perform the old-age care function, it is argued, is enhanced when inheritable assets induce assistance from children to aged parents in an implicit quid pro quo. A study of rural Bangladesh by Cain (1982) is illustrative. Cain found evidence of arrangements within the family whereby a married son sets up a separate household and independently cultivates a portion of the family land, which he eventually inherits, but the title to which is meanwhile retained by his father. The father's retention of the title confers a measure of control, and assistance from the son in illness and old age can in general be expected (Cain 1982: 171). A study in rural Maharashtra likewise shows that optimism with respect to old-age support from children, or the expectation of it, is a positive function of land owned (Vlassoff and Vlassoff 1980: 493). For land inheritance to be a significant inducement, though, it should outweigh the incomes that can be gained from other sources. Thus, it was found in a study of rural South India that labour markets which have emerged in recent decades provide work opportunities to sons and so erode patriarchal authority on family farms, with the result that fathers fear lest their sons migrate to greener pastures (Caldwell et al. 1982: 715). This could fuel the need for material inducement to ensure that sons stay at home and support aged parents.

A key factor working to *strengthen* the inheritance inducement is the number of potential beneficiaries. Analysing data in an econometric model, Hoddinott finds that land inheritance as an inducement to monetary transfers from sons becomes stronger with an increase in the number of beneficiaries. In societies where land is a scarce and valuable asset, Hoddinott argues, the possibility of parents altering bequeaths in favour of a beneficiary from whom assistance is anticipated can effectively promote the care of the aged by their children. This goes to buttress the argument that the overwhelming reliance on children for old-age security in the less developed world exerts an upward influence on family size. The question arises also as to whether, when sources of financial support other than children become increasingly available, this translates into fertility decline. Micro-data from South Indian tea estates suggest that there is in fact some evidence of this (Ridker 1980). At a macro level, international evidence in support of the relationship indicate that fertility is an inverse function of national pension expenditure (Entlewise and Winegarden 1984).

SUMMARY AND DISCUSSION

The chapter deals with how children are valued in the family in three Asian countries: India, Bangladesh and Thailand. Evidence from India suggests that fertility decline in the country has been accompanied by a growing perception that children are 'expensive'. Child expenses associated with the spread of schooling and growing perceptions of child costs relative to the costs of other 'commodities' are salient factors involved. The shift to smaller families may have to some extent been induced also by a decline in the demand for child labour. Child labour however persists, partly in terms of the contribution of female children to household tasks and partly in the context of the continuing employment of children in the informal sector. Moreover, the demand for children as an *eventual* source of family labour is likely to weigh in the balance as well.

Evidence from Bangladesh is cited to the effect that the labour and skills of sons are a human resource bulwark against crises confronting the family and that, in the absence of alternative mechanisms for coping with misfortune, children are perceived as sources of insurance. By contrast, in three Indian villages studied by Cain, two in Maharashtra and one in Andhra Pradesh, children were 'largely redundant' in strategies for coping with difficult times. Cain's comparison of the Bangladeshi setting and the Indian villages however glosses over the considerable regional disparities that can be found within the Indian scene. Thus, a recent ethnographic study of a Rajasthan village has parallels with Cain's depiction of the Bangladesh experience;

it was found that the strength of numbers to which sons contribute was essential to a family's security from threats of depredation and to the preservation of its local influence. It might be argued that 'environments of risk' are likely to be far more acute in states such as Bihar and Rajasthan as compared to other parts of the country and that disparities such as these may contribute significantly to the considerable spatial variation in Indian fertility; regions less well placed in terms of the security environment may thereby be susceptible to brakes on sustained fertility decline.

Moreover, Cain downplays the role of networks of extended kin as a source of help in emergencies. The role of relatives in providing assistance in times of distress can however be salient. Thus, data from a sample of drought-prone Indian villages attest to consumption smoothing arrangements whereby shortages that a household is prone to as a consequence of crop failure are compensated by transfers from a marital household located elsewhere and not similarly affected by local agricultural conditions. Commitments hinging on kinship links between the households that enter into these implicit contracts, it is argued, make the arrangement work and make it work in circumstances where enforcing and monitoring agreements between parties bound only by the letter of the law is not feasible. This evidence of the role of the family in mitigating risks also underscores the salience of ties of marital kinship and underscores the value of daughters. Such a role for daughters is in fact explicitly recognized; it was found in a field study in Rajasthan that daughters were perceived to be useful in augmenting a household's network of kinship relationships via the establishment of affinal alliance.

Also noteworthy is the role of children in providing social security to the aged, a function that is crucial in underdeveloped country settings, where there are no credible alternatives to children as sources of old-age welfare. Evidence from Thailand suggests that in respect of that crucial aspect of the care of the aged by their children, co-residence, the role of children as sources of old-age care and security is not diminished when fertility falls. The pattern is corroborated also by evidence from India. A central feature of the Thai experience is that it is predicated on strong cultural expectations that children will support elderly parents, and this typically is expected to involve co-residence. The scenario has strong echoes in the Indian setting, with the difference that elderly Thais tend to be flexible in the matter of the sex of the child with whom they reside. The pre-eminence of the son is by comparison a central feature of the family in India. This can be inimical to fertility decline and son preference in India has in fact been ascribed such a consequence.

Studies suggest also that the propensity of children to care for aged parents is strengthened by inheritable assets, which operate to induce quid pro quo assistance from children to aged parents. For land inheritance to be a significant inducement, though, it should outweigh the incomes that can be gained from other sources. It was found in a study of rural South India that labour markets which have emerged in recent decades provide work opportunities to sons and so erode patriarchal authority on family farms, with the result that fathers fear lest their sons migrate to greener pastures. This could fuel the need for material inducement to ensure that sons stay at home and support aged parents.

NOTES

1 Data suggest also that sensitivity to the costs of children need not diminish as income levels rise. Thus, Mueller (1972) found that sensitivity to child cost in Taiwan was a rather weak function of income. Mueller argues that child expenses deemed necessary rise with income so that the perceived costs of children do not vary appreciably across income gradations (Mueller 1972: 392, 394).

2 He does however indicate that regional and cultural differences operate. Thus, in the Bangladesh setting, in contrast to the Indian villages of Cain's sample, distress land sales were largely between brothers or patrikin. This suggests that these categories of kinfolk in Bangladesh functioned poorly as sources of mutual aid in troubled times.

REFERENCES

Adlakha, Arjun, and Dudley Kirk. 1974. 'Vital Rates in India, 1961–1971'. *Population Studies* 28 (3): 381–400.

Bhatty, Kiran. 1996. 'Child Labour: Breaking the Vicious Cycle'. *Economic & Political Weekly* XXXI (7): 384–386.

Cain, Mead. 1978. 'The Household Life Cycle and Economic Mobility in Rural Bangladesh'. *Population and Development Review* 4 (3): 421–438.

———. 1981. 'Risk and Insurance: Perspectives on Fertility and Agrarian Change in India and Bangladesh'. *Population and Development Review*.

———. 1982. 'Perspectives on Family and Fertility in Developing Countries'. *Population Studies* 36 (2): 159–175.

Caldwell, John C., P. H. Reddy, and Pat Caldwell. 1982. 'The Causes of Demographic Change in Rural South India: A Micro Approach'. *Population and Development Review* 8 (4): 689–727.

Cassen, R. H. 1979. *India: Population Economy, Society*. New Delhi: Macmillan.

Davis, Kingsley. 1968. *The Population of India and Pakistan*. New York, NY: Russell and Russell.

Entlewise, B., and C. Winegarden. 1984. 'Fertility and Pension Programs in the LDCs: A Model of Mutual Reinforcement'. *Economic Development & Cultural Change* 32: 331–354.

Hatti, Neelambar, and Rolf Ohlsson. 1983. 'Age at Marriage in India: A Study of Sirsi Taluk, Karnataka, during the Period 1961–1979—Some Preliminary Results'. Lund: Ekonomisk - Historiska Institutionen, Lunds Universitet.

Hoddinott, John. 1992. 'Family Size and Support for the Elderly in Western Kenya'. In *Fertility, Family Size and Structure: Consequences for Families and Children*, edited by Cynthia B. Lloyd. New York, NY: The Population Council.

Jain, Anrudh K., and Arjun L. Adlakha. 1982. 'Preliminary Estimates of Fertility Decline in India During the Early 1970's'. *Population and Development Review* 8 (3): 589–606.

Jejeebhoy, Shireen J. 1984. 'The Shift from Natural to Controlled Fertility: A Cross Sectional Analysis of Ten Indian States'. *Studies in Family Planning* 15 (4): 191–198.

Knodel, John, Aphichat Chamratrithirong, and Nibhon Debavalya. 1987. *Thailand's Reproductive Revolution*. Madison, WI: University of Wisconsin Press.

Knodel, John, Napaporn Chayovan, and Siriwan Siriboom. 1992. 'The Impact of Fertility Decline on Familial Support for the Elderly: An Illustration from Thailand'. *Population and Development Review* 18 (1): 79–104.

Knodel, John, Napaporn Havavon, and Anthony Pramualratana. 1984. 'Fertility Transition in Thailand: A Qualitative Analysis'. *Population and Development Review* 10 (2): 297–328.

Knodel, John, Napaporn Havavon, and Weerasit Sittirai. 1990. 'Family Size and the Education of Children in the Context of Rapid Fertility Decline'. *Population and Development Review* 16 (1): 31–62.

Knodel, John, and Malinee Wongsith. 1991. 'Family Size and Children's Education in Thailand: Evidence from a National Sample'. *Demography* 28: 119–132.

Mari Bhat, P. N. 1994. 'Levels and Trends in Indian Fertility: A Reassessment'. *Economic & Political Weekly* XXIX (51&52): 3273–3280.

Mari Bhat, P. N., Samuel Preston, and Tim Dyson. 1984. 'Vital Rates in India, 1961–1981'. Washington, DC: National Academy Press. National Research Council, Committee on Population and Demography (Report no. 24).

Mueller, Eva. 1972. 'Economic Motives for Family Limitation: A Study Conducted in Taiwan'. *Population Studies* 26 (3): 383–417.

Nag, Moni, and Neeraj Kak. 1984. 'Demographic Transition in a Punjab Village'. *Population and Development Review* 10 (4): 661–678.

NCAER. 1984. *Demographic Report, Rural Economic and Demographic Survey, 1981–82*. New Delhi: NCAER.

NCERT. n.d. *Factors for the Continuance and Discontinuance of Girls in Elementary Schooling*. New Delhi: Department of Women's Studies, NCERT.

Patel, Tulsi. 1994. *Fertility Behaviour: Population and Society in a Rajasthan Village*. Delhi: Oxford University Press.

Preston, Samuel H., and P. N. Mari Bhat. 1984. 'New Evidence on Fertility and Mortality in India'. *Population and Development Review* 10 (3): 481–503.

Rele, J. R. 1987. 'Fertility Levels and Trends in India, 1951–1981'. *Population and Development Review* 13 (3): 513–530.

Ridker, Ronald G. 1980. 'The No Birth Bonus Scheme: The Use of Savings Accounts for Family Planning in South India'. *Population and Development Review* 6 (1): 31–46.

Rosenzweig, Mark R. 1981. 'Household and Non Household Activities of Youth: Issues of Modelling, Data and Estimation Strategies'. Geneva: International Labour Office.

———. 1988. 'Risk, Implicit Contracts and the Family in Rural Areas of Low Income Countries'. *The Economic Journal* 98: 1148–1170.

Rosenzweig, Mark, and Oded Stark. 1989. 'Consumption Smoothing, Migration and Marriage: Evidence Tram Rural India'. *Journal of Political Economy* 97 (4): 905–926.

Shah, A. M. 1996. 'Is the Joint Household Disintegrating?' *Economic & Political Weekly* XXXI (9): 537–542.

Visaria, Pravin. 1995. 'Demographic Transition and Policy Responses in India'. *Demography India* 24 (1): 1–12.

Vlassoff, M., and Carol Vlassoff. 1980. 'Old Age Security and the Utility of Children in Rural India'. *Population Studies* 34 (3): 487–499.

Wongsith, Malince. 1990. 'Altitudes towards Family Values in Thai Society' (Paper presented at the Nihon University National Symposium on Family and the Contemporary Japanese Culture: An International Perspective, Tokyo, 20–24 October 1990).

World Bank. 1991. *Letting Girls Learn: Promising Approaches in Primary and Secondary Education* (World Bank Discussion Paper No. 133). Washington, DC: World Bank.

Chapter 18

Population Policy and Programme in India*
A Review

Sukanya Srinivasan

INTRODUCTION

India was the first country to launch a family planning (FP) programme in 1952. The Indian programme has now existed for more than five decades. This chapter seeks to trace the programme at the national level from the time of its inception to recent times as well as enumerate the salient achievements and shortcomings of the programme.

RATIONALE AT THE TIME OF INDEPENDENCE

The Five-Year Plans in India have never failed to comment that India's development or growth has been the best possible with the given resources, but uncontrolled population growth has acted as a retrogressive factor.

At the time of Independence, the crude birth rate (CBR) was 45/1,000 (i.e., over 45 children born for 1,000 people per year). The total fertility rate (TFR; number of children a woman would have in her lifetime) was 6. At this time, the government set a target to bring the CBR down to 27/1,000 by 1990 and 21/1,000 by 2000, with a target TFR of 2.1.

---

* *Social Change* 37, no. 1 (March 2007): 125–136.

During the first three Five-Year Plans, FP was considered more a measure for improving the health of couples than a means for achieving the demographic goals of the country. Over time, however, the achievement of demographic goals became the principal and perhaps the only focus of the programme.

TARGET APPROACH AND ITS CONSEQUENCES

The target approach which fixed method-specific numerical targets for contraceptive acceptance for each worker was adopted during the mid-1960s. Annually, the FP performance of each state, district and primary health centre and its targets were set by the central government and passed on to the state government, with the community having little or no say in the fixing of these targets. Targets for districts were allocated almost exclusively on the basis of population size, rather than existing contraceptive practice or level of unmet need. Rural development staff, inexperienced in FP counselling or service provision, were entrusted with the task of recruiting FP users. Traditionally, half the district target was allocated to non-health staff.

The target-based approach was adopted because it was considered an effective tool to intensify the level of effort of the programme, use all available resources to achieve the population goal, ensure that the programme was moving in the desired direction and place pressure on the workers to increase the couple protection rate (Khan and Townsend 2001).

Another method of population control was devised when the Medical Termination of the Pregnancy Act came into being in 1972. The important reason for the enactment of this Act was to counter the hazards of the large number of illegal abortions. The Commission, however, stated: '...abortion also can be used as a means to control family size...in which case family planning or contraception and abortion are in two parallel categories, both of which lead to population control' (Ministry of Health and Family Planning 1966: 40).

At the 1974 Conference on Population and Development held at Bucharest, the Indian government argued that 'development is the best contraceptive' and urged for funds for development rather than population control (Bose 1995: 1–29). The new approach was lauded by liberal population experts and 'integrated development' became the watchword.

But at home, the Indian government did a volte face by launching a massive coercive population control programme by forcibly rounding up mainly poor and illiterate men and getting them vasectomized. In 1976–1977, an all-time high of 8.26 million sterilizations were performed on men (Singh and Singh 1998). The coercive, oppressive techniques adopted by the then government did not go down well in a democratic country like India and became one of the major issues in bringing down the government.

In 1976, the first National Population Policy (NPP) talked of integrating FP with healthcare and maternal and child healthcare. It also noted the influence of education, employment, age of marriage and the effect of infant mortality rate (IMR) on family size which needed to be tackled. But these suggestions remained on paper.

The new government which came into power in 1977 issued a statement emphasizing the voluntary nature of the programme. Wary of publicly promoting FP, the name of the department was changed from 'FP' to 'Family Welfare'. But Gupta (2000) says, 'Nothing else really changed. The target approach and the system of incentives and disincentives continued.' The only change was that vasectomies were replaced by female sterilization.

The emphasis on population control continued through the fifth, sixth and seventh plans, with the outlay for FP increasing with every successive plan. In fact, the outlay for FP in the Seventh Plan was more than double that of the Sixth Plan, and the outlay for the Eighth Plan was double that of the Seventh Plan.

However, in the 1980s, though the emphasis was on population control, several states paid attention to the maternal and child health (MCH) approach, with a view to improving the health and nutritional status of mothers and infants. The National Health Policy of 1983 emphasized the need for 'securing the small family norm, through voluntary efforts and move towards the goal of population stabilization'.

By this time, internationally, the rationale for population control had shifted from hunger and famine to ecological and environmental issues. Improving the quality of life, it was argued, hinged on a nation's ability to stabilize its population at a manageable level. Reflecting this, the 1991 Report of the National Development Council Committee on Population recommended the formulation of a NPP with a long-term and holistic approach to development, population, growth and environmental protection.

Around this time, it also became increasingly acknowledged that in the zeal to achieve targets, inadequate attention was given to the quality of FP services. Some of the major limitations of the programme that were repeatedly reported, both in government policy documents and independent studies, included poor counselling, lack of informed choice for clients and poor follow-up services for FP acceptors. It was also observed that, over time, target achievement had become an end in itself, rather than a means to effectively implement and monitor the programme (Khan and Townsend 2001).

SWAMINATHAN COMMITTEE REPORT

In 1993, the Swaminathan Committee Report was submitted which recommended withdrawing the target-based approach, empowering women by increasing their opportunities to participate in the paid labour force, shifting programme emphasis from achieving national demographic targets to helping couples to achieve their reproductive goals, promoting male methods and to bring about a more equitable gender balance in the provision of FP services (Khan and Townsend 1999a, b). This draft foreshadowed many of the ideas expressed at the International Conference on Population and Development at Cairo, Egypt, in 1994. Subsequently, a constitutional amendment was made in 1993, which shifted the control of health and family welfare to the local governments.

In 1994, the International Conference on Population and Development, held at Cairo, described as a historic meeting, managed to shift the meeting's agenda from population control to reproductive health, due to pressure from international women's health organizations. As a befitting sequel to this, India abandoned the target approach in 1996 in the country as a whole and took a crucial step towards evolving a people-centred, inclusive programme.

REPRODUCTIVE HEALTH PROGRAMME

The Reproductive Health Programme was launched with much fanfare in 1997. The Reproductive and Child Health (RCH) programme 'aims to provide need-based, client-centred, demand driven, high quality integrated RCH services'. It was adopted as the national policy and includes the conventional maternal and child health services, including immunization of children, contraceptive services to couples, treatment for reproductive tract infections and sexually transmitted diseases, provision of reproductive health services for adolescent boys and girls, screening of women of menopausal age for cervical and uterine cancer and treatment where required (Khan and Townsend 2001; Srinivasan 2003). Essential components of the programme strategy include community participation in planning for services, multi-sector approach in implementing and monitoring services, a client-centred, gender-sensitive approach to service provision, upgraded facilities and improved training, emphasis on quality of care and the absence of contraceptive targets and incentives.

Operationally, the RCH programme is an alternative integrated approach to the vertical programmes aimed at improving the health status of young women and children. It incorporates all the components covered under the Child Survival and Safe Motherhood Programme and includes two additional components, one relating to sexually transmitted disease and another relating to reproductive tract infection. Further, it emphasizes the provision of services in a manner which is client-centred, demand-driven, high quality and based on the needs of the community, arrived at through decentralized participatory planning without target (GOI 1997). Thus, the RCH programme seeks to increase the efficiency of the earlier programmes, bring about a holistic approach to programme implementation and produce a paradigm shift in implementation based upon clients' needs. Under the new 'target-free' approach, local outreach health workers are to be active in the planning process, since they are in a position to analyse the health needs of the specific communities they work with. They are expected to device targets on the basis of these needs. This community needs assessment (CNA) approach involves micro-level planning and target setting for a range of MCH activities as against the earlier macro-level target setting for contraceptive methods. Essentially micro-planning is used to establish local targets for a range of health indicators based upon local needs. Goals are to be established primarily at the district level, rather than at the state and central government levels (Karkal 1998).

The controversial decision to withdraw contraceptive targets continues to generate discussion. Some, particularly advocates of women's health, have applauded the removal of targets. Donors in general have been supportive of target-free initiatives. Others view the debate on targets as a distraction from the more important issues of health financing and broader social development policy (Jain 1997). Demographers have maintained that dispensing with targets is ineffective.

Many have dismissed the change in stance from 'population control' to 'reproductive health' as 'old wine in new bottles'. Karkal (1998) says, 'Though India is a party to the decision (referring to the ICPD, Cairo provisions), the condemnation on paper has not meant a change in the behaviour...decisions such as "no targets" are on paper, but women are oppressed to accept family planning.'

NATIONAL POPULATION POLICY, 2000, AND AFTER

The NPP 2000 signifies a marked departure in the government approach towards population and related issues in India.

It underplays the role of targets, brings into focus gender and reproductive health issues and recognizes the need for participatory and need-based planning at the local levels. But evidence indicates that several state policies do not reflect the national policy concerns. They are inward looking and largely demographically driven, suggesting the marginalization of this document (Sen 2003).

There are major differences between the states with regard to their current population size as well as the rate of population growth. It is projected that the five states of Bihar, Uttar Pradesh, Madhya Pradesh, Rajasthan and Orissa which constitute 44 per cent of the total population of India in 1996 will constitute 48 per cent of the total population of India in 2016. These states will contribute 55 per cent of the total population increase of the country during the period 1996–2016. In all these states, performance in the social and economic sector has been poor which is the outcome of poverty, illiteracy and poor development. At the other end of the spectrum are states such as

Kerala and Tamil Nadu where the TFR has dropped sharply to below replacement level. These differences among states in demographic and other indicators have made them adopt a separate State Population Policy in order to meet their individualized needs.

In divergence with the policies laid down by the NPP, which stressed heavily on non-coercion and voluntary adoption of contraception, the National Population Commission circulated a note recommending a strict implementation of the 'two-child' norm. The states were directed to introduce disincentives as per local need (*Economic & Political Weekly* 2002). The mandatory two-child norm for panchayat members that exists in many Indian states is proving to be more divisive than productive, with many women being forced to step down from their posts despite having little say in the number of children they have. This directive was later withdrawn, but the damage had already been done, as many states refused to comply and continued with the disincentives.

Thus, the basic mindset of the planners, policymakers, service providers and a large section of decision-makers is still influenced by the old thinking favouring the promotion of population control as an urgent need (Ramachandran and Visaria 1997).

SOME MAJOR CONCERNS

Some major concerns and issues arising out of the above policies and programmes are listed here.

- Policy planners sidelined India's basic problems of poverty, illiteracy, unemployment, social and economic inequalities and ill health and sought to reduce fertility rates by means of a massive birth control programme.
- In their efforts to lower fertility rates, the programme adopted the 'machine theory of implementation', wherein the FP programme is reduced to a mechanical delivery system, in which clients are the 'receptacles for the services delivered'.
- The entire FP programme 'is viewed as a "technological fix," with the aim being on promoting a particular method of contraception—first IUDs, then vasectomies, then tubectomies and now a range of provider-controlled hormonal contraceptives' (Srinivasan 2003).

- The 'cafeteria principle' where a wide number of contraceptive methods are available for clients to make an independent, voluntary, informed choice is not a reality, as the method recommended and even 'pushed' is female sterilization, which is borne out by the high level of female sterilization seen in the data for all India.
- The use of 'incentives' and 'disincentives' to lure people to go in for sterilization is one of the controversial aspects of India's population programme.
- Although targets have been abolished on paper, they have made an insidious return in the form of the CNA approach.
- Another allegation against the Indian programme is that it has encouraged research into potentially hazardous, long-acting, provider-controlled contraceptives targeting women, which could cause irreversible damage to the health of women and children (Srinivasan 2003).
- The government's bid to push for a small family and the strong preference for the male child has skewed the sex ratio against the girl child. The preference for sons has led to discrimination against the girl child, lower female literacy, sex-selective abortion (in spite of the enactment of the law against prenatal sex detection and sex-selective abortion, which imposes stringent action against medical professionals as well as clients who resort to these measures) and higher mortality levels for females up to the age of 45. The 2001 census shows a slight improvement in the sex ratio to 933, but sex ratio of children in the age group of 0–6 has gone down from 962 girls per 1,000 boys in 1981 to 945 in 1991 to 927 in 2001, which is indicative of female foeticide, female infanticide and neglect of the girl child (Registrar General of India 2001).
- There is ever-increasing evidence to show that general health has been sidelined and 'primary healthcare is hijacked by reproductive healthcare' (Rao 2000).
- Investment in the health sector over the years has been negligible compared to funds allocated for contraceptive acceptance and research. Investments in social sectors such as health (particularly primary health) and education are negligible compared to FP.
- The population policy is more concerned with population stabilization and has ignored the fundamental needs of women such as reproductive and sexual health and their right to reproductive choices.

- The major shortcomings and inadequacies relate to poor quality of services, non-availability of staff, lack of empathetic counselling and poor management.
- The difference in performance of different states in the programme is evident with states such as Tamil Nadu and Kerala showing a lower TFR, as well as better performance in antenatal care, delivery and immunization services, as against states such as Uttar Pradesh, Madhya Pradesh, Rajasthan and Bihar.
- Data from national surveys on FP and unmet need for contraception reinforce the assumption that there is a significant demand for FP that is not being met under the current system (Registrar General of India 1993). It is estimated that approximately 30 million women have an unmet need for FP.
- Even though the IMR has almost halved in 50 years, it is still very high and is a contributing factor in high fertility rate.
- In spite of differences in approaches to political, economic and ideological issues, all parties are still guided by the demographers, and stabilization of population is said to be the main objective of population policy. It is believed by critics of population control that the bogey of 'overpopulation' is raised to provide a 'smokescreen' to cover up the failures of the political leadership to keep its promises of bringing about change in the social and economic field (Banerji 1980; *Political Will* 1998).

MILESTONES OF INDIAN FAMILY WELFARE PROGRAMME

Year Events/Significance

1949:   Establishment of Family Planning Association of India

1952:   FP programme was officially initiated as the first step towards improvement of health, especially of mothers and children. Demographic objectives of population control were marginal.

1956–1961:   The Second Five-Year Plan emphasized need for promoting FP for health. Broad programmes including information, education and communication (IEC), education, marriage counselling and child guidance were underlined.

1963:	Integration of FP activities with health programme and shift from clinic-based approach to extension approach
1965–1966:	Introduction of incentives to acceptors and motivators of sterilization and IUD
1966–1967:	Introduction of method-specific target approach. Achievement of demographic goals under strict time schedule became the main focus.
1971:	Introduction of mass vasectomy camp approach; stopped in 1973
1972:	Medical Termination of Pregnancy Act thereby legally approving abortion
1975–1977:	Coercion for accepting sterilization under the Emergency rule. It gave a major setback to the programme.
1983:	Introduction of concept of net reproduction rate (NRR) of one as principle guiding target of FP. Increased emphasis on sterilization targets
1993:	Setting up of Dr M. S. Swaminathan Committee to draft population policy
May 1994:	Submission of Swaminathan draft population policy, strongly recommending withdrawal of method-specific targets, need for enhancing access and quality of FP and reproductive health services, right to informed choice and a broad-based approach to population and development
1994:	India became signatory to ICPD Plan of Action.
1995:	Withdrawal of FP targets from one to two district(s) of each state
April 1996:	Withdrawal of target approach from the entire country
1997:	Launching of Reproductive and Child Health Programme
1999:	Submission of NPP to Cabinet, Government of India
2000:	NPP agenda was declared. It sought to underplay the role of targets and stressed on reproductive health and need-based planning.
2000:	National Commission on Population set up to review, monitor and give direction to NPP with a view to population stabilization (*Source:* Khan and Townsend [1999]).

PERFORMANCE OF FAMILY PLANNING PROGRAMME

The performance of family welfare programmes since inception in the country is given in Table 18.1.

Table 18.1 *Performance of Family Welfare Programme since Its Inception in India*

Sl. No.	Parameter	1951	1981	1991	Current Level
1.	CBR (per 1,000 population)	40.8	33.9	29.5	25.8 (2000)
2.	Crude death rate (per 1,000 population)	25.1	12.5	8.5	8.5 (2000)
3.	TFR	6.0	4.5	3.6	3.2 (1999)
4.	Maternal mortality rate (per 100,000 live births)	NA	NA	437 (NFHS -I 1992–1993)	407 (1998)
5.	IMR (per 100,000 live births)	146 (1951–1961)	110	80	68 (2000)
6.	Child mortality rate (0–4 years) per 1,000 children	57.3 (1972)	41.2	26.5	20.4 (1999)
7.	Couple protection rate (%)	10.4 (1971)	22.8	44.1	48.2 (NFHS -II 1998–1999)
8.	Expectation of life at birth (in years) Male Female	37.1 36.1	54.1 54.7	60.6 61.7 (1991–1996)	63.87 66.91 (2001–2006)

Source: Office of Registrar General of India, National Family Health Survey (NFHS) 1 and 2.
Note: NA = Not available.

CONCLUSION

There is general consensus that the population programme in India has failed both in achieving its specific targets (which was the main aim of the programme) and in bringing about an improvement in the health and well-being of the women.

In spite of the abolition of the target approach on paper, the programme seems to adhere to this aim insidiously. Despite the use of words such as 'choice', 'freedom', 'autonomy' and the pledge to improve women's health, well-being and status, the achievement of demographic goals and targets are still the mainstay of the programme.

REFERENCES

Banerji, D. 1980. 'A Manipulated Programme'. *Economic & Political Weekly* 25: 151–154.

Bose, Ashish. 1995. *The Family Welfare Programme in India: Changing Paradigm*, edited by Hari Mohan Mathur. Noida: Vikas Publishing.

Economic & Political Weekly. 2002. 'Editorial'. *Economic & Political Weekly*.

Gupta, Jyotsna Agnihotri. 2000. *New Reproductive Technologies: Women's Health and Autonomy*. New Delhi/London: SAGE Publications.

Jain, A. 1997. 'Consistence between Contraceptive Use and Fertility in India'. *Demography India* 26 (1): 19–36.

Karkal, Malini. 1998. *Population Control: State Sponsored Violence against Women*. Mumbai: CEHAT.

Khan, M. E., and T. W. Townsend. 1999a. 'An In-depth Analysis of Changes in Population Policy and its Impact on the Family Welfare Programme in India'. *Demography India* 30 (1): 73–100.

———. 1999b. 'Target Free Approach: Implementing a Reproductive Health Agenda in India', edited by Saroj Pachauri. New York, NY: Population Council.

———. 2001. 'Reproductive and Child Health Programme: An In-depth Analysis of Changes in Population Policy and Its Impact on the Family Welfare Programme in India'. *Demography India* 30 (1): 73–100.

Ministry of Health and Family Planning. 1966. *Report of the Committee to Study the Question of Legalisation of Abortion*. New Delhi: MOHFW, GOI.

Political Will. 1998. 'Population Stabilisation Figures in Agenda of All Major Parties in Focus'. *Political Will* XII (1): 4–7.

Ramachandran, Vimala, and Leela Visaria. 1997. 'Emerging Issues in Reproductive Health'. *Economic & Political Weekly*: 2244–2247.

Rao, Mohan. 2000. 'Family Planning Programme: Paradigm Shift in Strategy'. *Economic & Political Weekly*.

Registrar General of India. 1993. 'Census of India: Final Population Totals, Brief Analysis of Primary Census Abstract' (Paper II of 1992, Series I). New Delhi: Controller of Publications.

———. 2001. *Census of India, 2001*. New Delhi: RGI, GOI.

Sen, Ragini. 2003. *We the Billion: A Social Psychological Perspective of India's Population*. New Delhi: SAGE.

Singh, Omkar, and A. K. Singh. 1998. 'Population Growth and Family Planning in India: An Analysis'. In *Strategies in Development Planning*, edited by Singh et al. Mumbai: SNDT.

Srinivasan, Sandhya. 2003. 'National Population Policy, Editorial'. *Indian Journal of Medical Ethics*.

About the Editors and Contributors

SERIES EDITOR

Manoranjan Mohanty retired as Director, Developing Countries Research Centre and Professor of Political Science, University of Delhi in 2004. A political scientist, China scholar and a peace and human rights activist with a special interest in China, India and global transformation, he is the Editor of *Social Change* and Distinguished Professor, Council for Social Development, New Delhi. He is Chairperson, Development Research Institute, Bhubaneswar, and Honorary Fellow and former Chairperson of the Institute of Chinese Studies, Delhi. He has taught or researched in many universities, including those in California, Oxford, Copenhagen, Moscow, Lagos and Beijing. He is the author of many publications, including *China's Transformation: The Success Story and the Success Trap, Ideology Matters: China from Mao Zedong to Xi Jinping* and edited or co-edited many publications, including *People's Rights, Class, Caste and Gender, India: Social Development Report, 2010, Exploring Emerging Global Thresholds* and *China at a Turning Point*.

VOLUME EDITOR

P. M. Arathi is Assistant Professor at the School of Indian Legal Thought, Mahatma Gandhi University, Kottayam, India. She completed her doctoral research on 'Gendered Bodies, Medicine and Law: A Study of Selected Case Laws from India' and an MPhil thesis on 'Aborting Gender Justice: Legislating Abortion in Selected Countries of South Asia—A Preliminary Analysis' from the Centre of Social Medicine and Community Health, School of Social Sciences, Jawaharlal Nehru University, New Delhi. She was a Global Fellow (2015) at the Berlin Social Science Center, which was funded by the WZB and the International Social Science Council, Paris. Dr Arathi co-edited the book *Universalising Healthcare in India: From Care to*

Coverage. Her postdoctoral academic work and publications cover the areas of public health laws, the politics of reproductive technologies, social determinants of health and the regional modernity of Kerala. She was book review editor of the journal *Social Change* (2018–2019).

CONTRIBUTORS

Rajiv Balakrishnan was Associate Fellow at the Council for Social Development, New Delhi, and is currently an independent consultant based in Gurgaon, Haryana.

Premananda Bharati, Professor, Biological Anthropology Unit, Indian Statistical Institute, Kolkata

Sharmila Borkar, Associate Professor of Economics at the Sridora Caculo College of Commerce and Management Studies, Goa, India

Laxmi Kant Dwivedi, Professor, Department of Mathematical Demography & Statistics, International Institute for Population Sciences (IIPS), Mumbai

Sourindra Mohan Ghosh, Consultant at the Council for Social Development and Research Scholar at the Centre for Economic Studies and Planning, Jawaharlal Nehru University, New Delhi

M. E. Khan was the Chief Consultant, Population, Health and Women Studies, Operations Research Group, Baroda, and currently is the President, Centre for Operations, Research & Training.

Dolly Kumari was a Research Scholar at IIPS, Mumbai, and is currently working as Assistant Professor at the Centre for Economic Policy and Public Finance, Asian Development Research Institute, Patna.

Kamala Mankekar was a journalist, author and social activist. She was the founder editor of *Social Change*.

K. Radhakrishna Murty was UGC Emeritus Fellow, Department of Sociology, Andhra University, Visakhapatnam.

Anita Pal is a Research Scholar at IIPS, Mumbai.

Manoranjan Pal, Professor, Economic Research Unit, Indian Statistical Institute, Kolkata

Indira Jai Prakash was a Professor of Psychology at the Bangalore University.

Imrana Qadeer is a former Professor at the Centre of Social Medicine and Community Health, School of Social Sciences, Jawaharlal Nehru University, New Delhi, and was until recently Distinguished Professor at the Council for Social Development, New Delhi.

Prabha Ramalingaswami was Associate Professor, Centre of Social Medicine and Community Health, School of Social Sciences, Jawaharlal Nehru University, New Delhi.

Kamala Gopal Rao was Professor and Head of the Department of Social Sciences, National Institute of Health Administration and Education, New Delhi.

Saumya Rastogi, School of Health Systems Studies, TATA Institute of Social Sciences, Mumbai

Sheela Saravanan, Research Associate, Department of Anthropology, South Asia Institute, Heidelberg University, Germany

K. B. Saxena is a former Union Health Secretary, Government of India, and is currently Distinguished Professor at the Council for Social Development, New Delhi.

A. K. Sharma, Professor, Department of Humanities & Social Sciences, Indian Institute of Technology Kanpur

Anjali Shenoi, Research Co-ordinator, SAMA – Resource Group for Women and Health, New Delhi

Suparna Som, Sociological Research Unit, Indian Statistical Institute, Kolkata

Sukanya Srinivasan, Research Scholar, Department of Econometrics, University of Madras

Shubhangi Vaidya, School of Inter-disciplinary and Trans-Disciplinary Studies, IGNOU, New Delhi

Index

Page|AP4|91